COLORADO Collage

From the creators of the best-selling
Colorado Cache and Crème de Colorado cookbooks,
a wonderfully fresh collection of recipes and menus.

Junior League
of Denver

CORPORATE SPONSORS

COMSAT Entertainment Group
Paragon Ranch
Safeway

Table of Contents

Front Cover Photo: Garlic Shrimp, Tropical Fruit, and Baby Lettuce Salad, page 104

Back Cover Photo's: Aprés Ski with Friends Menu, page 44
Streamside Feast Menu, page 194
Grand Finale Menu, page 340

Additional copies may be obtained by writing:

C&C Publications
Junior League of Denver, Inc.
6300 East Yale Avenue
Denver, Colorado 80222

Please enclose $24.95, plus $3.00 postage and handling. Colorado residents add $0.79 for sales tax.

The Junior League of Denver, Incorporated (founded 1918) is an organization of women committed to promoting voluntarism and to improving the community through the effective action and leadership of trained volunteers. Its purpose is exclusively educational and charitable.

- The Junior League of Denver, Incorporated envisions a community that is safe, healthy, and nurturing for all kinds of families.
- The Junior League of Denver, Incorporated reaches out to women of all races, religions, and national origins who demonstrate an interest in and commitment to voluntarism.

The proceeds generated from the sale of *Colorado Collage* will be returned to the community through the projects of the Junior League of Denver, Incorporated.

First Edition, First Printing:
90,000 copies, September 1995

Library of Congress Catalog
Card Number: 95-77515

ISBN 0-9603946-4-8

Forward

You are holding a culinary work of art. A collage of over 500 recipes chosen for their inspiring use of ingredients and for their fresh approach to good taste. Selected from more than 2,500 recipes, the ones that you will find inside have been triple-tested for perfection. They include unexpected, yet easy-to-find ingredients, a healthful approach to extraordinary flavor, and mouth-watering photography to help your imagination go wild. Quick and easy recipes have been highlighted, advance steps are thoughtfully noted, and helpful hints plus personal insights have been added throughout the book. Twelve complete menus await to inspire you to entertain with confidence.

You are also holding a wonderful gift to our community. While this cookbook was designed to fulfill your desire for delicious cuisine, the Junior League of Denver also created it to fill the hearts of those in need. The proceeds from *Colorado Collage* will be used to help make our community a place that is safer, healthier, and more nurturing for families. Profits from sales will be used to help children in crisis, promote safer environments, and support educational initiatives for children and adults alike.

So create, eat, and be merry. This book of good food is equally good for the spirit.

Cookbook Committees

Steering Committee

Editors	Cathy Carlos Hollis Judi Lattin Richardson
Administrative Assistants:	
Cookbook	Wendy Woerner Kent
Testing	Carolyn Callan Peterson
Marketing Co-Chairs	Lee Clayton Mary Keppler
Production Coordinator	Lynn Mueller Parham
Recipe Testing Coordinator	Catherine Cockerham Hilker
Treasurer	Karen B. Fisher
Sustaining Advisors:	
Cookbook	Jodi Waggoner
Testing	Judy Pardue Polidori

Cookbook Committees

Section Heads

Appetizers	Leeann Iacino
Soups & Sandwiches	Sarah Condit Rawley
Salads	Karen Zain Henry
Brunch	Corinne Lamb Ablin
Breads	Sara Busche Cobb
Pasta & Pizza	Cindy Hansen Alexander
Fish & Seafood	Cami Cooper
Meats	Kimberlee Piper Powelson
Poultry	Stephanie Ismert
Grains, Rice & Legumes	Mary Lou Hibben
Vegetables	Jean Dawson Burkhart
Desserts	Amy Jo Smith
Registered Dietician	Susan M.H. Gills, M.S., R.D.

Marketing

Assistant Chair	Stacey Davis Schuham
Membership Sales	Leslie Melzer
Public Relations	Jennifer Hosking
	Lou Ann May
	Suzanne Jardine Robinson
Sales Account Coordinator	Marty Bicknell
Sales Database Coordinator	Sarah Arnold Jacobs
Special Events	Linda Bowen Scott
	Trish Sillars-Craver

Production

Computer Coordinator	Jill Saar Sokol
Computer Input	Barbara McClearn Baumann
Production Assistants	Alexis Nash
	Marguerite Lashell Sadler
	Katie Lucht Van Schaack

Professional Credits

SPECIAL ACKNOWLEDGMENT		John Fielder *Colorado is naturally blessed with some of the most beautiful scenery in the world. Creating images of our spectacular state over the past two decades is a labor of love for nationally acclaimed photographer John Fielder, a man who puts his film where his heart is. A pre-eminent landscape photographer, he has long used his stunning images of wildlands to capture and help preserve their unique natural qualities. The Junior League of Denver would like to gratefully acknowledge and thank John for his tremendous contribution to our organization and to the preservation of our beautiful state.*
CONCEPT/DESIGN		Carter Design, Inc. *Jim Carter, Reena Carter, Heidi Domagala*
COVER DESIGN		Hamilton Creative *Lori Hamilton*
PHOTOGRAPHY	Landscape	John Fielder
	Food	Jan Oswald Photography *Jan Oswald*
		Photography Assistant *Faye Ganley*
	Food Styling	Jacqueline Buckner Food Styling *Jacqueline Buckner*

Introduction

"The recipes and menus in Colorado Collage bring together fresh and flavorful ingredients, which both complete and compliment each other."

What could be better than a collage of the best Colorado has to offer. Take a dash of blue sky, add a dollop of the majestic Rocky Mountains, throw in a day spent skiing our pristine powder slopes, and you have the perfect prelude to an evening with good friends around a table laden with fresh and delicious food.

Colorado Collage is a wonderful collection of more than 500 recipes and photographs celebrating the ingredients that make up this delightfully diverse state. It's a book that recalls the free-spirited nature, rugged individualism, and appetite for adventure that created the Old West. It's a book that has searched out the delicacies that are all around us, from fresh rainbow trout to fruits grown in the orchards of our Western Slope. It's a book that acknowledges that time is more precious than ever, a healthy lifestyle is increasingly important, and incredible taste is in high demand.

In creating a collage, the artist's task is to combine new and unexpected elements in fresh and interesting ways. And so it is with cooking. The recipes and menus in *Colorado Collage* bring together fresh and flavorful ingredients, which both complete and compliment each other. These dishes achieve a wonderful result which transcends the individual components of the recipe. However, cooking with an artist's eye goes well beyond the flavor and texture of a dish. The artistic cook also considers color, aroma, and the balance of the entire menu. Thus, we have included in our newest cookbook, a series of delightful menu suggestions. After all, it is one thing to fall in love with "Chicken en Papillote" as a main dish, but what should your first course be. What is the perfect accompaniment, and what would be the most satisfying ending? You will find out, by the way, it is "Kiwi Sorbet"!

So, with the same fierce determination that it took to settle this beautiful state, we set out to triple-test over 2,500 recipes. We searched for those that would be handed down over generations and traded among the closest of friends. We singled out those that were not only a delight to the taste buds, but were also a joy to prepare. We worked especially hard to find recipes that reflect the healthful attitudes and lifestyles for which Coloradans are known.

We offer to you, in this fresh approach to good taste, a variety of recipes that are both nutritious and tantalizing. You'll find more main dish salads, more creative ways to use beans, pasta, and rice, and more ideas to help you integrate grains, fruits, and vegetables into your diet. You'll also discover an array of interesting ethnic dishes, rich with intense seasonings, where meat is often used as an accent. We even worked diligently to make changes, wherever possible, that reduced fat without sacrificing flavor.

Don't worry though, we haven't forgotten that the West was won with a bit of bravado and a desire to live on the wild side. You'll enjoy chocolate extravaganzas, desserts that will make you melt, and a main dish or two that are down right naughty.

Within our collage of feasts for the palate, you'll also uncover a feast for the eyes. The extraordinary landscape photography of John Fielder showcases beauty from the four corners of our state. His breathtaking images reflect the changing seasons which inspire the ever-changing bounty at our tables. We hope they will also inspire fond memories for long-time residents as well as visitors who have only sampled the grandeur of Colorado.

So savor the landscapes, reflect on the beauty of the place, and experiment with the tastes, spices, and extraordinary culinary combinations that await you. Most of all, have fun with this collection. After all, Colorado food is relaxed and vibrant, just like Colorado cooks. The emphasis here is on an abundance of sharing, plenty of laughter, and that wonderful feeling that comes from enjoying good food with people you love.

Enjoy.

The Philosophy Behind the Food

Lest you think for a moment that this is a cookbook filled with canned green beans swimming in cream of mushroom soup, allow us to explain the thinking and the creative cooking behind *Colorado Collage*. Our philosophy, from the onset of this collection, was to assemble a group of recipes and menus that would celebrate the new food pyramid, reward people for trying to eat more wisely, and stimulate both taste buds and dinner conversations.

We would like to share with you some of the nutritional insights which influenced our thinking. Let's start with the new food pyramid. It allows for flexibility and creativity and can, with a bit of ingenuity, be palatable to even the hard-core sweet tooth. For healthy adults, it recommends 6-11 daily servings of grains, rice, or pasta, 2-4 servings of fruit, and 3-5 servings of vegetables. It also suggests 2-3 servings of meat, poultry, fish, beans, eggs, or nuts, and 2-3 servings of milk, yogurt, or cheese. And last, but certainly not forgotten, small amounts of oil, fats, and sweets.

Our goal has been to discover new ways to incorporate these choices into everything from weekday meals to spectacular entertaining. We have worked hard to make taste and nutrition inseparable. We believe that all foods can fit into a healthful diet, as long as low-fat choices are the norm, and high-fat selections are the exception. Why nibble away at bland leafy greens when "Lobster and Wild Rice Salad" is an option?

We have been inspired by the traditional Mediterranean diet where olive oil replaces butter. Fiber-rich foods such as whole grains and legumes can take center plate rather than standing by as a side dish. We've been pleasantly surprised at the role that fresh herbs and seasonings can play in reducing sodium. (Who needs excess salt when you have ginger root and orange zest.)

Above all, we believe that the key to good health is to be physically active and well informed about the value of a nutritious diet. So here's to a smarter, leaner, more wholesome approach to great cuisine. We want you to eat what your heart desires, but be good to your heart as well. We hope that you enjoy good cooking, an active lifestyle, and good health for a long, long time to come.

The champagne colored slopes of the Great Sand Dunes in Southern Colorado are breathtaking. They are the perfect place to reflect on the wonder of this land. And they are an inspiration for this delectable collection of appetizers created to tempt your palate.

A Champagne Celebration

appetizers

Classic Pâté Mousse 28

Indonesian Satay 271

Mango Grilled Shrimp 41

Marinated Goat Cheese 35

Smoked Salmon Dill Bites 30

wine

Blanc de Noir

Clockwise from top left:
Mango Grilled Shrimp
Marinated Goat Cheese
Smoked Salmon Dill Bites

Appetizers

These appetizers will get you off to a festive start for any occasion. Representing the spicy variety of many cultures, each one of them will make you look and feel like a professional chef.

Clockwise from top:
Chipotle Shrimp Wontons
Glazed Chicken Wings
Marinated Tortellini

Spicy Black Bean and Corn Salsa

4-6 cups

16 ounces cooked black beans
16 ounces fresh or frozen corn kernels
½ cup chopped fresh cilantro
¼ cup chopped green onion
¼ cup chopped red onion
⅓ cup fresh lime juice
3 tablespoons vegetable oil
1 tablespoon ground cumin
salt and freshly ground black pepper
½ cup chopped ripe tomatoes, drained

A delightfully colorful change to traditional salsa. *Photo, page 24.*

In large bowl, combine beans, corn, cilantro, green onion, red onion, lime juice, oil, and cumin. Season with salt and pepper to taste. Cover and chill at least 2 hours or up to overnight. Just before serving, stir in tomatoes. Serve with blue and white corn chips.

Seafood Salsa

4-5 cups

3 green onions, diced
¼ cup diced red onion
½ teaspoon minced garlic
2 jalapeño peppers, cored, seeded, and diced
3 tomatoes, cored, diced, and drained
½ cup finely chopped fresh cilantro
1 teaspoon dried oregano
¼ teaspoon ground cumin
1 tablespoon fresh lime juice
¼ pound small shrimp, cooked and peeled
¼ pound bay scallops, cooked
1 avocado, peeled, seeded, and diced
1 cup fresh or frozen corn kernels
salt

Garnish:
lime wedges
fresh cilantro leaves

In food processor, combine green onions, red onion, garlic, jalapeños, tomatoes, cilantro, oregano, cumin, and lime juice. Pulse about 4 times and set aside.

In large glass bowl, combine shrimp, scallops, avocado, and corn. Add reserved onion mixture and toss to blend. Season with salt to taste. Cover and chill 1-2 hours. Garnish with lime wedges and cilantro. Serve with tortilla chips or drain and place over fresh endive for a first course.

Island Salsa

4 cups

- 2 large ripe tomatoes, chopped
- 1 ripe mango, peeled, seeded, and chopped
- 2 kiwi fruits, peeled and chopped
- ½ cup chopped red bell pepper
- ½ cup chopped yellow bell pepper
- ½ cup chopped green bell pepper
- ¼ cup chopped red onion
- 1 tomatillo, husks removed and diced
- 1 jalapeño pepper, cored, seeded, and diced
- 2 tablespoons fresh lime juice
- ¼ cup chopped fresh cilantro
- ½ teaspoon ground cumin
- freshly ground black pepper

In large bowl, combine tomatoes, mango, kiwi, bell peppers, onion, tomatillo, jalapeño, lime juice, cilantro, cumin, and pepper to taste. Mix well and chill up to 8 hours. Serve with tortilla chips or as an accompaniment to fish or chicken.

A delicious collage of fresh fruits and vegetables.

Pistachio Pesto

3 cups

- ¾ cup shelled pistachios (about ¼ pound)
- 3 tablespoons fresh lemon juice
- 2 tablespoons minced garlic
- 2 teaspoons freshly ground black pepper
- 1 cup pitted black olives
- 1 cup pitted green olives
- 1 large bunch fresh cilantro, washed and stemmed
- ½ cup olive oil

Garnish:

thinly sliced red bell pepper

chopped shelled pistachios

In food processor, combine pistachios, lemon juice, garlic, pepper, black olives, and green olives. Process until smooth, about 1 minute. Scrape down sides of bowl and add cilantro. Process 30 seconds. Add enough of the olive oil to form a paste. Transfer to serving bowl and garnish with bell peppers and pistachios. Serve with toasted baguette slices.

Spicy Macadamia Nut Pesto

2 cups

- 1 cup loosely packed, fresh basil leaves
- ¾ cup olive oil
- 4 ounces macadamia nuts
- ½ cup loosely packed, fresh parsley leaves
- 4 small garlic cloves, peeled
- ½ teaspoon coarse salt
- 1 teaspoon crushed red pepper

Garnish:

fresh basil leaves

finely chopped macadamia nuts

thinly sliced red bell pepper

This is a wonderful new twist on pesto.

In food processor or blender, combine basil, olive oil, nuts, parsley, garlic, coarse salt, and crushed red pepper. Process until mixture forms a paste. Transfer to serving bowl. Garnish with basil leaves, macadamia nuts, and bell peppers. Serve with water crackers or toasted baguette slices.

Southwestern Layered Dip

8-10 servings

- 15 ounces cooked black beans
- 4½ cups plus 2 tablespoons cold water, divided
- 2 teaspoons minced garlic
- 1 small yellow onion, peeled and chopped
- 1½ teaspoons cumin seed
- 1 teaspoon dried marjoram
- 1 bay leaf
- 1¾ teaspoons salt, divided
- 4 6-inch corn tortillas
- pinch cayenne
- 3 large ripe tomatoes, cored and diced
- 4 green onions, finely chopped
- ½ avocado, peeled, seeded, and diced
- ¼ cup chopped fresh cilantro
- 2 tablespoons fresh lime juice
- 2 teaspoons finely grated lime zest
- 2 teaspoons vinegar
- ¼ teaspoon freshly ground pepper
- 1 large red bell pepper, roasted (page 381), peeled, and diced
- 1 large yellow bell pepper, roasted (page 381), peeled, and diced
- 2 small jalapeño peppers, cored, seeded, and chopped
- 2 ounces goat cheese, crumbled

Garnish:

finely grated lime zest

fresh cilantro sprig

Don't let the number of ingredients scare you. This dip is really quite easy and the result is deliciously rewarding.

In large saucepan, combine beans, 4½ cups of the cold water, garlic, onion, cumin, marjoram, and bay leaf. Heat to boiling. Reduce heat to low and simmer 40 minutes. Stir in 1 teaspoon of the salt and continue cooking until very soft, about 15 minutes. Remove from heat and drain, reserving liquid. Remove bay leaf and transfer half of the bean mixture and ⅓ cup of the reserved liquid to food processor. Puree until smooth and stir back into remaining bean mixture. (May be chilled overnight.)

Preheat oven to 350 degrees. Cut tortillas into quarters. Combine remaining 2 tablespoons cold water, ½ teaspoon of the salt, and cayenne. Brush lightly on both sides of tortilla quarters and place on baking sheets. Bake 12 minutes or until crisp and set aside to cool. (After cooling, chips may be stored in an airtight container up to overnight.)

In medium bowl, combine tomatoes, green onions, avocado, cilantro, lime juice, lime zest, vinegar, remaining ¼ teaspoon salt, and pepper. In deep 1½-quart bowl, layer half of the bean mixture, half of the roasted red and yellow bell peppers, half of the jalapeños, half of the tomato mixture, and half of the goat cheese. Repeat layers and garnish with lime zest and cilantro sprig. Serve with warmed reserved tortilla wedges. May also be served with warmed purchased tortilla chips.

Cowboy Crisps

10-12 servings

- 1¾ cups flour
- ½ cup yellow cornmeal
- ½ teaspoon baking soda
- ½ teaspoon sugar
- ½ teaspoon salt
- ½ cup (1 stick) butter
- 8 ounces extra-sharp cheddar cheese, shredded
- 2 tablespoons white vinegar
- ⅔ cup water
- coarsely ground black pepper

If using with a topping or dip, roll slightly thicker.

In large bowl, combine flour, cornmeal, baking soda, sugar, and salt. With pastry blender or 2 knives, cut in butter until mixture resembles coarse crumbs. With fork, stir in cheese, vinegar, and water just until mixture forms a soft dough. Divide into 4 equal pieces, wrap in plastic wrap and chill 1 hour. (May be chilled in freezer about 30 minutes.)

Preheat oven to 375 degrees. Grease large baking sheet. On lightly floured surface, with floured rolling pin, roll 1 piece of the dough into a paper-thin 10-inch circle (edges may be ragged). Cut into 8 wedges and place on prepared baking sheet. Sprinkle wedges with coarsely ground black pepper, firmly pressing pepper into dough.

Bake about 10 minutes or until browned and crisp. Remove from oven and transfer crisps to racks and cool. Repeat with remaining dough. Store at room temperature, in covered container.

Focaccia Bread With Cambozola Cheese

8-10 servings

- 2 yellow bell peppers, cored, seeded, and cut into thin strips
- 2 green bell peppers, cored, seeded, and cut into thin strips
- 2 red bell peppers, cored, seeded, and cut into thin strips
- ¼ cup olive oil
- 6 whole garlic cloves, roasted (page 381), peeled, and pureed
- 2 loaves Focaccia bread (page 163) or purchased focaccia bread
- ½ pound Cambozola cheese

Cambozola is a mild blue cheese–the perfect topping for this bread.

Preheat oven to 325 degrees. In large skillet, cook pepper strips in olive oil until tender but still firm, about 10 minutes. Spread roasted garlic on focaccia and place in oven about 10 minutes. Cut bread into serving size wedges, spread with cheese, and top with reserved peppers.

At left:
Spicy Black Bean and Corn Salsa, 20
Cowboy Crisps, 25

Prosciutto Wagon Wheels

10-12 servings

- 1 17¼-ounce box (2 sheets) frozen puff pastry, thawed
- ⅔ cup Dijon mustard, divided
- ¾ pound prosciutto, very thinly sliced, divided
- 2 cups shredded provolone, divided

Preheat oven to 425 degrees. Grease large baking sheet. Working with 1 sheet of the puff pastry, keeping remaining sheet wrapped and cold, roll out on lightly floured surface to 14-inch square. Brush with thin layer of mustard. Cover with half of the prosciutto slices, slightly overlapping and leaving ½-inch border around edges.

Sprinkle with 1 cup of the cheese. Roll pastry tightly, from long side. Pinch seams to seal and tuck ends under. Repeat with remaining pastry sheet. Cut into ½-inch pieces and place, cut side up, 1-inch apart on prepared baking sheet. Bake 10-15 minutes or until golden brown.

An incredibly easy favorite.

Mushroom Palmiers

4-5 dozen

- 1 pound fresh mushrooms
- 1½ medium onions, peeled and quartered
- 5 tablespoons butter
- 2 tablespoons flour
- 1 teaspoon fresh lemon juice
- 1½ teaspoons dried thyme or 2 tablespoons finely chopped fresh thyme
- ½ teaspoon Tabasco
- salt and freshly ground black pepper
- 1½ 17¼-ounce boxes (3 sheets) frozen puff pastry, thawed
- 2 eggs
- 4 teaspoons water

A wonderful appetizer to keep in the freezer for unexpected guests.

In food processor, finely chop mushrooms. Transfer to plate and set aside. Add onion to food processor and finely chop. In large skillet, melt butter over medium heat. Add mushrooms and onion and cook until juice evaporates, stirring occasionally, about 8 minutes. Add flour, lemon juice, thyme, and Tabasco. Season with salt and pepper to taste. Reduce heat to low and cook about 2 minutes. Set aside to cool.

Preheat oven to 400 degrees. Place 1 unfolded pastry sheet on flat surface. Spread evenly with ⅓ of the mushroom mixture. Roll up from both long edges into center, pressing 2 rolls together. Repeat with remaining 2 pastry sheets. Wrap tightly in plastic wrap and freeze 1 hour. (May be prepared to this point and frozen. Let thaw partially before proceeding.)

Slice into ¼-inch thick slices, using serrated knife. Place, cut side down, on ungreased baking sheet, 1-inch apart. In small bowl, combine eggs and water and whisk to blend. Brush over tops of Palmiers and bake 18-20 minutes.

Toasted Walnuts

2 cups

- ¼ teaspoon salt
- ¼ teaspoon Greek seasoning
- ⅛ teaspoon cayenne
- 2 cups raw whole unsalted walnuts
- 2 teaspoons walnut oil

A great treat to make ahead. Remember to keep walnut oil in the refrigerator after opening.

Preheat oven to 300 degrees. In small bowl, combine salt, Greek seasoning, and cayenne and set aside. Drop walnuts into rapidly boiling water and boil 1 minute. Drain and place in clean towel. Rub gently to remove paper-thin skins.

Spread walnuts, in single layer, on baking sheet. Bake 5 minutes. Remove from oven, toss with walnut oil, and sprinkle with reserved salt mixture. Return to oven and continue baking 8-10 minutes, stirring occasionally. Check frequently and remove from oven if walnuts begin to burn. Set aside and cool to room temperature. Store in refrigerator.

Classic Pâté Mousse

8-10 servings

- 1 10½-ounce can beef consommé with gelatin added
- ½ pound chicken or duck livers, tough bits of fiber removed and coarsely chopped
- 3 tablespoons butter, divided
- ¼ cup chopped shallots
- 1 cup whipping cream, divided
- ¼ teaspoon unflavored gelatin
- 1 tablespoon brandy
- ½ teaspoon salt
- ⅛ teaspoon freshly ground black pepper
- ⅛ teaspoon dried marjoram
- ⅛ teaspoon ground ginger
- ⅛ teaspoon ground cinnamon
- 1 teaspoon fresh lemon juice

An elegantly seasoned pâté.

Pour ¼-inch layer of the consomme into 2-cup mold. Reserve remaining consommé for another use. Chill until firmly congealed. Rinse and drain chopped livers thoroughly. In medium skillet, melt 1 tablespoon of the butter over medium heat. Add livers and shallots. Cook until lightly browned and livers are no longer pink, about 10 minutes.

In small saucepan, combine ¼ cup of the whipping cream and gelatin over low heat. Heat until gelatin is completely dissolved, 2-3 minutes. Do not stir. Remove from heat.

In food processor, cream remaining 2 tablespoons butter. Add liver mixture, gelatin mixture, brandy, salt, pepper, marjoram, ginger, cinnamon, remaining ¾ cup cream, and lemon juice. Process until thoroughly blended. Strain, pressing lightly to exude all liquid. Discard solids. Pour liquid pâté mixture gently into mold over congealed consommé. Chill overnight. Unmold by inverting mold onto serving plate. Serve with toast points, baguette slices, or melba toasts.

Smoked Trout Pâté

4-6 servings

- 8 ounces boned smoked trout, skinned
- 4 ounces cream cheese, softened
- 3 ounces goat cheese
- ¼ cup (½ stick) butter, softened
- 1 tablespoon chopped green onion
- 1 tablespoon prepared horseradish
- 1 tablespoon fresh lemon juice
- ⅛ teaspoon Tabasco
- 1 tablespoon rinsed, drained capers
- 2 tablespoons chopped fresh parsley

In food processor, combine trout, cream cheese, goat cheese, and butter. Pulse until slightly blended. Add green onion, horseradish, lemon juice, Tabasco, capers, and parsley. Process until well blended. Chill several hours and serve with water crackers or baguette slices.

Crostini With Tomatoes

12 pieces

- 12 ¼-inch thick slices French baguette
- ¾ cup diced ripe tomato
- ¼ cup drained and diced oil-packed sun-dried tomatoes
- 2 tablespoons chopped fresh basil
- 1 3½-ounce log plain goat cheese, such as Montrachet
- freshly ground black pepper

Preheat oven to 350 degrees. Place bread slices on baking sheet and bake about 5 minutes to lightly toast on 1 side. In medium bowl, combine tomato, sun-dried tomatoes, and basil. Place thin slice of goat cheese on each baguette slice. Top with tomato mixture and season generously with black pepper. Place on baking sheet and bake 3-5 minutes. Serve hot.

Olive Crostini

16 pieces

- 16 ¼-inch thick slices French baguette
- 1½ cups pitted black olives
- 6 tablespoons olive oil, divided
- 1 pound assorted fresh mushrooms, cleaned and sliced
- 2 large garlic cloves, peeled
- salt and freshly ground black pepper
- 8 thin shavings fresh Parmesan cheese
- 2 Italian plum tomatoes, cut crosswise into eight ¼-inch slices
- 8 fresh basil leaves

Use a vegetable peeler or cheese plane to cut very thin shavings from a block of Parmesan cheese.

Preheat oven to 350 degrees. Place bread slices on baking sheet and bake about 5 minutes to lightly toast on 1 side. In food processor, combine olives and 3 tablespoons of the olive oil. Pulse until finely diced. In large skillet, heat remaining 3 tablespoons olive oil over medium-high heat. Add mushrooms and garlic and cook 5 minutes. Season with salt and pepper to taste. Remove from heat.

Remove garlic from mushroom mixture and rub over surface of toasted bread. Spread olive mixture on all 16 bread slices. Cover 8 of the slices with reserved mushroom mixture. Cover remaining 8 slices with Parmesan and tomato slice. Season all 16 pieces generously with pepper. Bake 3-4 minutes or until hot. Remove from oven and place basil leaves over tomatoes. Serve hot.

Marinated Salmon Carpaccio

10-12 servings

½ cup fresh lemon juice
¼ cup plus 1 tablespoon extra virgin olive oil, divided
½ cup finely chopped red onion
salt and freshly ground black pepper
1 pound salmon fillets, skinned and any remaining bones removed
½ cup very thinly sliced fennel bulb
4 green onions, very thinly sliced
1 large tomato, peeled and diced
1 tablespoon drained capers

An exceptional choice for a light first course.

In small bowl, combine lemon juice, 1 tablespoon of the olive oil, onion, and pepper to taste. Cut salmon fillets into large bite size pieces. Gently pound pieces between 2 sheets of oiled parchment paper to about ¼-inch thickness. Cut into 1-2-inch squares. Place squares in large glass baking dish and cover with lemon juice mixture. Chill 4 hours or up to overnight.

In medium bowl, combine fennel, green onions, tomato, and remaining ¼ cup olive oil. Season with salt and pepper to taste. Just before serving, remove salmon squares from lemon juice mixture and arrange on individual serving plates or platter. Top with fennel mixture, dividing equally among servings. Top with capers and season again with pepper. Serve with toast points or baguette slices.

Smoked Salmon Dill Bites

10-12 servings

12 ¼-inch thick slices French baguette, cut diagonally from loaf
2-3 tablespoons extra virgin olive oil
1½ tablespoons honey-flavored mustard
1 tablespoon Dijon mustard
1 tablespoon finely chopped red onion
1 tablespoon drained capers
2 teaspoons snipped fresh dill weed
4 ounces goat cheese
3 ounces smoked salmon, thinly sliced

Garnish:
fresh dill sprigs
thinly sliced red onion

Very colorful and sophisticated. Perfect for appetizers or brunch. Photo, page 16.

Preheat oven to 350 degrees. Arrange bread slices on baking sheet. Brush lightly with olive oil. Bake until slightly brown and crisp, about 10 minutes. Remove from oven. (May be prepared to this point up to 6 hours in advance. Cool, cover, and let stand at room temperature.)

In small bowl, combine honey mustard, Dijon mustard, onion, capers, and dill. Spread toasts with goat cheese, then reserved mustard mixture. Top with salmon slices and garnish with dill sprig and red onion.

Kahlúa Pecan Brie

8-10 servings

- 3 tablespoons packed brown sugar
- ¼ cup Kahlúa or strong, freshly brewed coffee, cooled
- ¾ cup pecan halves, toasted (page 381)
- 1 16-ounce round Brie cheese

In medium skillet, combine brown sugar and Kahlúa. Heat, stirring constantly, until blended. Add pecans, simmer until hot, but not runny. Remove from heat.

Place Brie on microwave-safe serving plate and spoon warm pecan mixture on top. Microwave on high 1-2 minutes, or until cheese softens. Watch carefully, cheese will melt quickly. Serve with crackers and fresh fruit.

Provolone Terrine

8-10 servings

- cheesecloth
- 1 8-ounce package cream cheese, softened
- ¼ cup (½ stick) unsalted butter
- ½ teaspoon minced garlic
- ⅛ teaspoon freshly ground black pepper
- ¼ cup shelled pistachio nuts
- 1 pound provolone cheese, thinly sliced
- ¾ cup Basic Basil Pesto, (page 193), or purchased basil pesto, divided
- ½ cup drained and coarsely chopped oil-packed sun-dried tomatoes

Garnish:

- fresh basil leaves
- shelled pistachio nuts

Plan ahead–this extraordinary first course presentation needs to chill overnight.

Line one 8x4-inch loaf pan with damp cheesecloth, allowing at least 1-inch extending above edge of pan. In food processor, combine cream cheese, butter, garlic, and pepper. Process until smooth and stir in pistachios by hand. Set aside.

Stack provolone slices and cut in half. Divide 1 stack of halves into thirds. Set aside. Using large stack of provolone, cover bottom and 2½-inches up sides of prepared pan. Spread half of the pesto smoothly over provolone. Cover with 1 of the small stacks of provolone, overlapping slices. Sprinkle with half of the sun-dried tomatoes. Spread reserved cream cheese mixture smoothly over tomatoes and top with remaining half of the sun-dried tomatoes. Top with another small stack of provolone. Spread remaining half of the pesto over provolone and cover with last stack of provolone. Fold cheesecloth over terrine and press down firmly. Chill overnight or up to 5 days.

Just before serving, fold back cheesecloth and invert terrine onto serving platter. Remove cheesecloth and garnish with basil and pistachios. Slice into 1-inch slices and serve on individual plates.

Columbine Blue Dip

6-8 servings

- ½ pound blue cheese
- ⅓ cup chopped red onion
- ⅓ cup olive oil
- 1 tablespoon fresh lemon juice
- 1 tablespoon red wine vinegar
- ½ teaspoon crushed garlic
- 1 teaspoon dry mustard
- ¼ teaspoon freshly ground black pepper
- ⅓ cup chopped fresh parsley

Crumble cheese in 9-inch pie pan. In food processor, combine onion, olive oil, lemon juice, vinegar, garlic, mustard, and pepper. Pulse to blend. Pour over cheese and sprinkle with parsley. Let stand, at room temperature, 2 hours. Serve with toasted bread triangles.

Fireside Garlic With Rosemary

10-12 servings

- 6 large whole heads garlic
- 3 tablespoons butter, cut into 6 slices
- ¼ cup olive oil
- 1½ cups chicken broth, divided
- ½ cup dry white wine
- 2 teaspoons chopped fresh rosemary
- 2 fresh rosemary sprigs
- 8 ounces Roquefort cheese, crumbled (optional)
- French baguette slices

Garnish:

- 2 fresh rosemary sprigs

Be sure to save your leftover garlic– it's delicious in mashed potatoes.

Preheat oven to 375 degrees. Cut ½-inch off top end (opposite root end) of each garlic head, exposing cloves. Remove any loose papery outer skin. Place garlic, cut side up, in non-metal baking pan. Top with butter and olive oil. Add 1 cup of the chicken broth and wine to pan. Sprinkle chopped rosemary over garlic and place rosemary sprigs in broth mixture. (May be prepared 8 hours in advance, cover and chill.)

Bake uncovered, about 1 hour, basting every 15 minutes with pan juices. Add remaining chicken broth, if necessary. Garlic cloves should be very tender when pierced with fork. Sprinkle with Roquefort, if desired, and continue baking until cheese is almost melted, about 10 minutes. Discard cooked rosemary sprigs and garnish with fresh rosemary sprigs. Serve by dipping bread into cooking juices spreading with garlic and melted cheese.

Basil and Currant Spread

6-8 servings

- ⅓ cup olive oil
- 3 tablespoons chopped fresh basil
- 3 teaspoons minced garlic
- 2 8-ounce packages cream cheese, softened
- 3 tablespoons chopped fresh parsley
- ⅔ cup coarsely chopped walnuts
- ⅔ cup currants

Garnish:

walnut halves
whole basil leaves
currants

This is no ordinary raisin–a currant is a dried zante grape.

In small bowl, combine olive oil, basil, and garlic. In large bowl, cream softened cream cheese and add oil mixture. Blend well. Stir in parsley, walnuts, and currants. Chill. Best if prepared several hours in advance so that flavors may blend. Garnish with walnut halves, basil, and currants. Serve with water crackers.

Chile Cheesecake

10-12 servings

- 1 cup tortilla chips, crushed
- 3 tablespoons butter, melted
- 2 8-ounce packages cream cheese, softened
- 2 eggs
- 1 4-ounce can diced green chiles
- 1 fresh jalapeño pepper, cored, seeded, and diced
- 4 ounces colby cheese, shredded
- 4 ounces Monterey Jack cheese, shredded
- ¼ cup sour cream

chopped tomatoes
chopped green onions
diced black olives

It's simple and beautiful. This is always a crowd pleaser.

Preheat oven to 325 degrees. In medium bowl, combine tortilla chips and butter. Press into bottom of 9-inch springform pan. Bake 15 minutes, remove from oven, leaving oven on.

In large bowl, blend cream cheese and eggs. Add green chiles, jalapeño, colby, and Monterey Jack. Pour over crust and bake 30 minutes. Do not overcook. Remove from oven and cool in pan 5 minutes. Run knife around inside edge and remove sides from pan. Spread sour cream over top and decorate with tomatoes, green onions, and olives. Serve with tortilla chips.

Flatirons Fondue

4 main dish servings
6-8 appetizer servings

1 large garlic clove
6 ounces Emmental cheese, shredded (about 2 cups)
6 ounces Gruyère cheese, shredded (about 2 cups)
6 ounces Appenzeller or Gruyère cheese, shredded (about 2 cups)
1½ tablespoons flour
1½ cups dry white wine
1 tablespoon kirsch (clear cherry brandy)
1 teaspoon fresh lemon juice
generous pinch cayenne
pinch ground nutmeg
1 French bread loaf, cut into 1-inch cubes
assorted vegetables for dipping, such as boiled new potatoes, carrot slices, broccoli, and mushrooms

Variations

Southwestern Fondue:

2 seeded and minced chipotle peppers
jícama for dipping

Italian Fondue:

omit kirsch and substitute 1 tablespoon grappa
⅓ ounce dried wild mushrooms, such as porcini or shiitake, soaked in warm water 20 minutes, drained, and finely chopped

Seafood Fondue:

reduce kirsch to 1 teaspoon
2 teaspoons finely chopped fresh dill weed
cooked shrimp and scallops for dipping

A warm and inviting dish for aprés ski or a cold night in the city. Share it with your favorite friends. Photo, page 44.

Peel garlic clove, cut in half, and rub inside of fondue pot with cut sides. Discard garlic. Place shredded cheeses in large bowl and sprinkle with flour. Toss to coat and set aside.

Pour wine into fondue pot and heat to simmering over medium heat. Add reserved cheese mixture, 1 handful at a time, stirring constantly. Allow each addition to melt before adding more. (If using a variation, check for changes to original ingredients.) Stir in kirsch, lemon juice, cayenne, and nutmeg. Add ingredients for variation, if desired. Set fondue pot over lighted candle or canned fuel. Dip bread cubes and/or other suggested items into cheese mixture using fondue forks or skewers.

Sun-Dried Tomato and Basil Stuffed Brie

4-6 servings

- ½ cup chopped fresh basil
- 10 oil-packed sun-dried tomatoes, drained and oil reserved
- 2 garlic cloves, peeled
- ¼ teaspoon freshly ground black pepper
- 1 teaspoon fresh lemon juice
- 1 wedge Brie cheese (about ½ pound), thoroughly chilled

Garnish:

fresh basil leaves

A stunning compliment to any cocktail buffet.

In food processor, combine basil, sun-dried tomatoes, garlic, pepper, and lemon juice. Process until paste forms. Add oil from sun-dried tomatoes or olive oil if texture is very dry (should be spreadable but not too thin).

Remove Brie from refrigerator and cut in half, horizontally (Brie must be thoroughly chilled to make this possible). Spread bottom half with reserved sun-dried tomato mixture and top with remaining half, pressing together firmly. Bring to room temperature before serving. Serve with water crackers. (May be prepared 1 day in advance. Wrap in plastic wrap and chill.)

Marinated Goat Cheese

10-12 servings

- ½ pound log mild goat cheese
- 1 tablespoon fennel seeds, crushed
- 1½ teaspoons crushed red pepper
- 8 sprigs fresh rosemary
- 1 cup olive oil
- 1 thin piece fresh lemon peel, cut from lemon with vegetable peeler

Garnish:

fresh lemon slices

fresh rosemary sprigs

This takes three days to marinate but only minutes to disappear. Photo, page 16.

Place cheese in small dish with cover. Combine fennel seeds, crushed red pepper, rosemary, olive oil, and lemon peel and pour over cheese. Cover and marinate in refrigerator, at least 3 days or up to 3 weeks. Place cheese on serving dish and drizzle with marinade, discarding rosemary and lemon peel. Garnish with fresh lemon slices and rosemary sprigs. Serve with water crackers.

Cocktail Beef Wellingtons

40 pieces

Béarnaise Sauce:

3 egg yolks
3 tablespoons fresh lemon juice
pinch salt
½ cup (1 stick) butter, melted and heated to boiling
1 teaspoon dried tarragon

Wellington Marinade:

2 tablespoons red wine vinegar
6 tablespoons olive oil
1 teaspoon Dijon mustard
1 teaspoon fresh lemon juice
⅛ teaspoon sugar
½ teaspoon salt
⅛ teaspoon black pepper
dash cayenne

Beef Wellingtons:

16 ounces beef tenderloin, cut into bite-sized pieces
½ cup (1 stick) butter, divided
¼ cup chopped shallots
3 cups chopped fresh mushrooms
salt and freshly ground black pepper
20 sheets phyllo pastry, thawed, if frozen

An elegant hors d'oeuvre to start a memorable evening.

In blender, combine egg yolks, lemon juice, and salt. With blender running, add ½ cup hot butter, in steady stream, and continue blending until thickened. Pour into small bowl and whisk in tarragon.

In small bowl, combine vinegar, olive oil, mustard, lemon juice, sugar, salt, pepper, and cayenne. Whisk to blend. Pour over tenderloin and chill about 4 hours.

In medium skillet, melt 2 tablespoons of the butter over medium heat. Add shallots and mushrooms and cook 5 minutes. Season with salt and pepper to taste. Remove from heat and cool to room temperature.

Preheat oven to 375 degrees. Melt remaining 6 tablespoons butter. Cut phyllo sheets lengthwise, into four 3-inch strips. Cover with plastic wrap and damp towel to prevent drying. Working with 2 stacked strips at a time, brush top strip with butter and place 1 piece of drained marinated beef and a generous teaspoon of mushroom mixture ½-inch from one end. Fold over diagonally to enclose filling and continue folding to form triangle-shaped packet. (May be prepared up to 2 weeks in advance. Wrap tightly and freeze.) Place, seam side down, on baking sheet. Brush lightly with butter. Bake 10 minutes until golden brown. Serve with Béarnaise Sauce.

Aegean Olives

6-8 servings

- 2 teaspoons extra-virgin olive oil
- 2 teaspoons crushed garlic
- ¾ cup dry white wine
- 1 cup kalamata olives
- 1 cup black oil-cured olives
- 2 fresh rosemary sprigs

Garnish:

fresh rosemary sprig

Preheat oven to 400 degrees. In small baking pan, combine olive oil, garlic, wine, olives, and rosemary. Bake until olives are plump, 20-30 minutes. Serve hot or at room temperature. Place in serving bowl and divide the 2 types of olives with the rosemary sprig for garnish.

Marinated Tortellini

6-8 servings

- ¼ cup white wine vinegar
- ¾ cup olive oil
- 2 teaspoons Dijon mustard
- 2 teaspoons fresh lemon juice
- ¼ teaspoon sugar
- 1 teaspoon salt
- ¼ teaspoon Greek seasoning
- ¼ teaspoon freshly ground black pepper
- dash cayenne
- 1 14-ounce can water-packed artichoke hearts, drained and halved
- 1 cup small fresh mushrooms
- 1 cup large pitted ripe olives
- 1 cup bite size pieces red bell pepper
- 1 9-ounce package fresh cheese tortellini, cooked al dente and drained
- 1 tablespoon rinsed, drained capers
- ½ pound shrimp, cooked, peeled, and deveined (optional)

Wonderful chilled, this is the perfect picnic appetizer. Photo, page 18.

In small bowl, combine vinegar, olive oil, mustard, lemon juice, sugar, salt, Greek seasoning, pepper, and cayenne. Whisk until well blended. In medium bowl, combine artichoke hearts, mushrooms, olives, bell pepper, tortellini, capers, and shrimp, if desired. Add reserved marinade and toss to coat. Marinate in refrigerator 3 hours. Serve in lettuce lined bowl with wooden picks.

Roasted Chicken Quesadillas

6-8 servings

Easy Guacamole:

- 2 ripe avocados, peeled, pitted, and mashed
- 2 tablespoons fresh lime or lemon juice
- ¼ teaspoon garlic salt
- ⅛ teaspoon cayenne

Quesadillas:

- 2 tablespoons unsalted butter
- 1 cup sliced fresh mushrooms
- 1 cup peeled and thinly sliced red onion
- 12 flour tortillas, divided
- 1 roasted chicken, shredded
- 1 cup crumbled blue cheese
- 1 bunch fresh cilantro, trimmed and chopped
- 2 tablespoons oil, divided
- ½ cup purchased salsa
- ½ cup sour cream

A truly creative combination of ingredients. Have fun with it!

In medium bowl, combine avocados, lime juice, garlic salt, and cayenne. Cover and set aside. In medium skillet, melt butter over medium heat. Add mushrooms and onion and cook until tender, about 5 minutes. Preheat oven to 200 degrees.

Place 1 tortilla on flat surface. Cover with chicken and mushroom mixture. Sprinkle with blue cheese and cover with another tortilla. Repeat with remaining tortillas to make 6 quesadillas.

In large skillet, heat 1 tablespoon of the oil over medium heat. Add 1 quesadilla and cook 3 minutes per side. Transfer to oven-safe serving platter and place in warm oven. Cook remaining quesadillas, adding extra oil, if necessary. Cut into wedges and serve with reserved guacamole, salsa, and sour cream.

Sausage Wontons

8-10 servings

- ¾ pound Italian sausage, casings removed
- ½ cup purchased medium salsa
- ½ cup shredded Monterey Jack cheese
- 1 cup shredded sharp cheddar cheese
- 2 ounces diced green chiles
- olive oil
- 24 wonton skins

Garnish:

- sour cream
- finely chopped green onions

In large skillet, brown sausage over medium-high heat, breaking up with fork. Remove with slotted spoon and place on paper towels, squeezing to remove as much grease as possible. Discard grease from skillet. Return sausage to skillet, add salsa, cheeses, and green chiles and simmer until mixture thickens, about 5 minutes. Remove from heat and cool to room temperature.

Preheat oven to 350 degrees. Brush mini-muffin cups with olive oil. Press 1 wonton wrapper into each muffin cup. Fill each wrapper with 1 generous tablespoon of cooled sausage mixture. (May be prepared 4 hours in advance. Cover and chill.)

Bake until edges begin to brown, about 10 minutes. Transfer from muffin cups to baking sheet. Bake until bottoms are crisp, about 10 minutes longer. Transfer to serving platter. Garnish with dollop of sour cream and sprinkle with green onions. Serve hot.

Glazed Chicken Wings

10 servings

- 1 cup plus 2 tablespoons hoisin sauce
- ¾ cup plum sauce
- ½ cup soy sauce
- ⅓ cup cider vinegar
- ¼ cup dry sherry
- ¼ cup honey
- 2 tablespoons minced garlic
- 4 pounds chicken wings, tips removed

This oriental sauce is delightful with chicken, fish, or ribs. *Photo, page 18.*

In large bowl, combine hoisin sauce, plum sauce, soy sauce, vinegar, sherry, honey, and garlic. Add chicken wings and marinate, in the refrigerator, 24 hours.

Preheat oven to 375 degrees. Line baking pan with foil. Grease baking rack and place on foil lined pan. Drain chicken wings, reserving marinade. Arrange wings on rack, and bake 30 minutes. Remove from oven.

Preheat broiler. Turn wings and baste with reserved marinade. Broil 30 minutes, turning and basting every 5 minutes, until golden brown. Serve hot or at room temperature.

Asian Spring Rolls

6-8 servings

2 teaspoons cornstarch
2 tablespoons water
2 tablespoons sesame oil
1 tablespoon vegetable oil
1 tablespoon peeled, minced fresh ginger root
1 teaspoon minced garlic
2 cups fresh bean sprouts
12 ounces raw shrimp, peeled and chopped
1 8-ounce can water chestnuts, minced
¼ pound ham or cooked pork, minced
½ cup minced green onions
1 medium carrot, peeled and shredded
4 teaspoons soy sauce
15 phyllo pastry sheets, thawed if frozen
½ cup (1 stick) butter, melted
sesame seeds
hoisin sauce
Chile Soy Sauce, (page 42)

Garnish:

decoratively cut carrots
decoratively cut green onions

Make smaller versions of these spring rolls for delicious bite size appetizers.

Preheat oven to 375 degrees. In small bowl, combine cornstarch and water. Stir and set aside. In large skillet or wok, heat sesame oil and vegetable oil over medium-high heat. Add ginger and garlic and stir-fry 30 seconds. Add bean sprouts, shrimp, water chestnuts, ham, green onions, and carrot and stir-fry 2 minutes. Add soy sauce and reserved cornstarch mixture, stirring until slightly thickened. Remove from heat and set aside to cool.

Cut phyllo sheets in half crosswise. Place 1 piece on flat surface, keeping remaining phyllo covered with plastic wrap and damp towel until ready to use. Lightly brush with melted butter. Place about 1½ tablespoons filling at 1 end. Fold over 3 times to enclose filling. Fold ends in and continue rolling to form a roll. Place seam down on baking sheet. Repeat process with remaining phyllo and filling. Chill until ready to bake. Brush with melted butter. Sprinkle with sesame seeds. Bake 10-15 minutes, until golden brown. Place on individual serving plates and garnish with carrots and green onions. Serve with hoisin sauce or Chile Soy Sauce, if desired.

Chipotle Shrimp Wontons

30 pieces

- olive oil
- 1 16-ounce package wonton skins
- ½ pound shrimp, cooked, peeled, and coarsely chopped
- 1 yellow bell pepper, roasted (page 381), peeled, and chopped
- 1 red bell pepper, roasted (page 381), peeled, and chopped
- ½ cup chopped fresh cilantro
- 1 chipotle pepper in adobo sauce, drained and finely chopped
- 8 ounces fontina cheese, shredded

Skins and filling may be prepared in advance and assembled just before baking. Photo, page 18.

Preheat oven to 350 degrees. Brush mini-muffin cups with olive oil. Press 1 wonton skin into each cup. Bake about 10 minutes until tops are golden brown. Remove from oven and cool slightly.

In large bowl, combine shrimp, roasted bell peppers, cilantro, chipotle pepper, and cheese. Remove cooled skins from muffin pan and place on baking sheet. Fill each skin with reserved shrimp mixture and bake 7-10 minutes or until cheese is melted.

Mango Grilled Shrimp

6-8 servings

- ⅓ cup purchased mango-ginger chutney
- ⅓ cup fresh lime juice
- 1 tablespoon peeled, minced fresh ginger root
- 1 tablespoon minced garlic
- 1 teaspoon olive oil
- 1 pound large shrimp, peeled and deveined

Garnish:

- lime wedges
- thinly sliced mango strips
- fresh mint leaves

A truly exotic first course that is prepared quickly on the grill. Photo, page 16.

In small bowl, combine chutney, lime juice, ginger, garlic, and olive oil. Place shrimp in shallow, glass dish and cover with chutney mixture. Chill 1 hour.

Preheat grill to medium. Soak 6-8 wooden skewers in water 15 minutes. Thread shrimp onto skewers, reserving marinade. Grill 3-5 minutes per side, brushing with reserved marinade when turning. Remove from grill and transfer to serving platter.

Pour remaining marinade into saucepan and boil 2-3 minutes. Remove from heat and place in serving bowl. Serve shrimp with heated marinade as dipping sauce or place shrimp on bed of lettuce, top with heated marinade, and garnish with lime wedge, mango, and mint.

Shrimp Dumplings

10-12 servings

Chile Soy Sauce:

- 1 cup soy sauce
- 1½ tablespoons hot chile oil
- 2 fresh serrano peppers, cored, seeded, and minced

Dumplings:

- 1 tablespoon butter
- 1 pound shrimp, peeled and chopped
- 1 teaspoon cornstarch
- 1 tablespoon water
- 2 tablespoons peeled, grated fresh ginger root
- 2 tablespoons chopped fresh cilantro
- ½ pound fresh spinach, cooked, well drained, and chopped
- 1 egg, lightly beaten
- 1 teaspoon sesame oil
- ¼ teaspoon cayenne
- ½ teaspoon salt
- 1 16-ounce package round wonton skins, (square skins may be substituted if round are unavailable)
- 2 egg whites, lightly beaten

These unbelievable dumplings are packed full of flavor, perfect for beginning a special dinner.

In small bowl, combine soy sauce, chile oil, and serrano peppers and set aside. In medium skillet, melt butter over medium heat. Add shrimp and cook until pink, about 5 minutes. Remove from heat and cool to room temperature.

In large bowl, combine cornstarch and water. Add cooled shrimp, ginger, cilantro, spinach, egg, sesame oil, cayenne, and salt. Stir until well blended.

Place several wonton skins on flat surface, keeping remaining skins covered to prevent drying. Lightly moisten edges of each skin with egg white. Place small mound of filling in center of each skin. Fold over to form half-moon shape and press firmly to seal. Crimp edges along the round edge to form decorative border. Place on lightly floured baking sheet. Repeat with remaining skins and filling mixture.

Preheat oven to 200 degrees. Heat large saucepan of water to boiling over high heat. Gently drop about 15 of the dumplings into boiling water. Allow water to return to gentle boil. Reduce heat to medium and simmer until dumplings float and are tender, 3-5 minutes. Remove to plate with slotted spoon and place in oven to keep warm. Repeat with remaining dumplings. Place on individual serving plates and serve with Chile Soy Sauce.

Crabmeat Empanadas

8-10 servings

- 1 8-ounce jar apple jelly
- 1 8-ounce can crushed pineapple, drained
- 1 medium jalapeño pepper, cored, seeded, and finely chopped
- 1 pound crabmeat
- ¾ cup finely chopped red onion
- 3 tablespoons chopped fresh cilantro
- 2 8-ounce packages cream cheese, softened
- 1 tablespoon dry mustard
- 2 tablespoons ground cumin
- salt and freshly ground black pepper
- garlic powder
- 1 16-ounce package wonton skins

Make these ahead and freeze before baking.

In medium bowl, combine jelly, pineapple, and jalapeño pepper. Stir until well blended and set aside. In large bowl, combine crabmeat, onion, cilantro, cream cheese, mustard, and cumin. Blend thoroughly. Season with salt, pepper, and garlic powder to taste.

Preheat oven to 350 degrees. Grease large baking sheet. Place about 1½ tablespoons crab mixture in center of each wonton skin. Using pastry brush, brush edges of skins with water. Fold in half, pressing edges to seal. Place on prepared baking sheet. Bake until golden brown, about 15 minutes. Serve immediately with reserved jelly mixture.

Chatauqua Crab Cakes

4-6 servings

- 3 tablespoons butter, divided
- ½ cup finely diced red onion
- 1 celery rib, finely diced
- 1 carrot, peeled and shredded
- 2 tablespoons flour
- ¼ cup milk
- ½ teaspoon curry powder
- ¼ teaspoon nutmeg
- ¼ teaspoon Tabasco
- 1 egg
- 1 pound crabmeat
- 1 teaspoon salt
- 3 ounces cream cheese, softened
- 2 tablespoons fresh lemon juice

A wonderful first course.

In medium skillet, melt 2 tablespoons of the butter over medium heat. Add onion, celery, and carrot and cook 3 minutes. Sprinkle with flour and cook 1 minute. Add milk, curry powder, nutmeg, and Tabasco and stir to blend. Remove from heat and transfer to food processor. Add egg, crabmeat, and salt. Pulse 3-4 times, until just combined. Form into 8 cakes. Cover and chill 1 hour. In large skillet, melt remaining 1 tablespoon butter. Cook cakes, 5 minutes per side, until golden brown. Combine cream cheese and lemon juice and place a dollop on each cake.

Coloradans say, "after you schuss, you eat". And nothing warms the spirit more than good friends, lively tales of the day's adventure, and savory cheese fondue. Finish the evening with Baked Pears With Rum and Cream and you won't even notice your aching muscles.

Aprés Ski With Friends

appetizer

Flatirons Fondue 34

soup

Baked Tortellini Soup 63

salad

Greens With Brown Sugar Vinaigrette 106

dessert

Baked Pears With Rum and Cream 364

wines

Sauvignon Blanc

Bardolino

Clockwise from top left:
Flatirons Fondue
Baked Tortellini Soup

Soups & Sandwiches

In this eclectic array of soups and sandwiches, you'll find both easy and sophisticated recipes. Some are whole meals, while others are light enough to serve as a first course.

Clockwise from top:
Working Barn Stew
Colorado Grilled Cheese

Delicious Apple Soup

8-10 servings

- 10 medium Red Delicious apples, cored and quartered
- 2¼ cups water
- 1¼ cups apple cider
- ¾ cup sugar
- 2 whole cinnamon sticks
- 2 cups half and half
- 1¼ cups fresh orange juice
- 2 tablespoons fresh lemon juice
- 2 medium Red Delicious apples, peeled, cored and diced
- 6 tablespoons Grand Marnier

In large, heavy saucepan, combine quartered apples, water, apple cider, sugar, and cinnamon sticks over medium-high heat. Heat to boiling. Cover, reduce heat, and simmer until apples fall apart, about 45 minutes. Remove from heat and cool to room temperature.

Scrape pulp from peels and return pulp to cooking liquid, discarding peels. Cover with plastic wrap and chill 8 hours or up to overnight. Discard cinnamon sticks. Strain, reserving liquid, and place pulp in blender. Puree pulp and return to reserved liquid. Stir in half and half, orange juice, lemon juice, and 2 diced apples. Stir in Grand Marnier. Cover with plastic wrap and chill 3-4 hours.

Cold Strawberry Rhubarb Soup

4-6 servings

- 1½ cups fresh strawberries, stemmed
- 1 pound fresh rhubarb, cut into ½-inch pieces
- 1½ cups fresh orange juice
- ½ cup sugar
- ¼ cup crème de strawberry or orange-flavored liqueur

Garnish:

sour cream

fresh mint leaves

4-6 fresh strawberries with stems, thinly sliced and opened to resemble fans

A cool and elegant first course for a summer luncheon. *Photo, page 70.*

In heavy saucepan, combine strawberries, rhubarb, and orange juice. Simmer about 15 minutes or until rhubarb is soft. Remove from heat, add sugar, and stir until dissolved. Cool to room temperature. Add liqueur. Puree in blender and chill 3-4 hours. Ladle into chilled bowls and garnish with dollop of sour cream, fresh mint, and a strawberry fan.

Frosted Honeydew Soup

4 servings

2	ripe honeydew melons, peeled, seeded, and coarsely chopped
¼	cup fresh lime juice
½	cup sweet vermouth
2	tablespoons diced crystallized ginger
	extra-fine granulated sugar
⅓	cup whipping cream
⅛	teaspoon freshly grated nutmeg
	Garnish:
	fresh mint leaves

A refreshing summer soup with a hint of ginger.

Puree honeydew in blender or food processor. Transfer to large bowl and stir in lime juice, vermouth, and crystallized ginger. Sweeten soup with sugar to taste. Stir in whipping cream and nutmeg. Chill 3-4 hours. Serve in chilled bowls and garnish with mint leaves.

Chilled Red Pepper Soup

4 servings

4	red bell peppers, roasted (page 381), peeled, and chopped
10	Italian plum tomatoes, peeled and quartered
½	teaspoon freshly ground black pepper
½	teaspoon ground ginger
3	cups chicken broth
¼-½	cup fresh lemon juice
¼	cup plain yogurt
¼	cup milk
½	teaspoon sugar
	Garnish:
	large croutons

In large saucepan, combine roasted peppers, tomatoes, pepper, ginger, chicken broth, and lemon juice to taste. Cover and simmer 40 minutes. Remove from heat and set aside to cool.

Transfer to blender and puree in small batches. Return to saucepan. Add yogurt, milk, and sugar and stir to blend. Chill 3-4 hours. Serve in chilled bowls and float a large crouton on top for garnish.

Chilled Asparagus Soup

4 servings

- ¼ cup (½ stick) unsalted butter
- 2 cups chopped yellow onion
- 4 cups chicken broth
- 1 pound fresh asparagus
- ⅓ cup buttermilk
- salt and freshly ground black pepper

A culinary rite of Spring. This soup is delicious chilled or hot.

In large saucepan, melt butter over medium heat. Add onion and cook 25 minutes, stirring frequently. Add chicken broth and heat to boiling. Trim tips from asparagus and reserve. Cut 1-inch from woody ends and discard. Cut remaining spears into ½-inch pieces and drop into boiling broth mixture. Cover, reduce heat, and simmer about 45 minutes.

Remove from heat, cool, and puree in batches. Return to saucepan, add reserved tips, and simmer until tender, about 5 minutes. Remove from heat and chill. Just before serving, add buttermilk and season with salt and pepper to taste. Serve in chilled bowls.

Chilled Minted Pea Soup

4-6 servings

- 1 pound petite frozen green peas
- 2 cups chicken broth
- 2 small green onions, coarsely chopped
- 2 tablespoons fresh lime juice
- ½ teaspoon freshly grated nutmeg
- 14 fresh mint leaves
- ½ cup sour cream

Garnish:
sour cream
fresh mint leaves

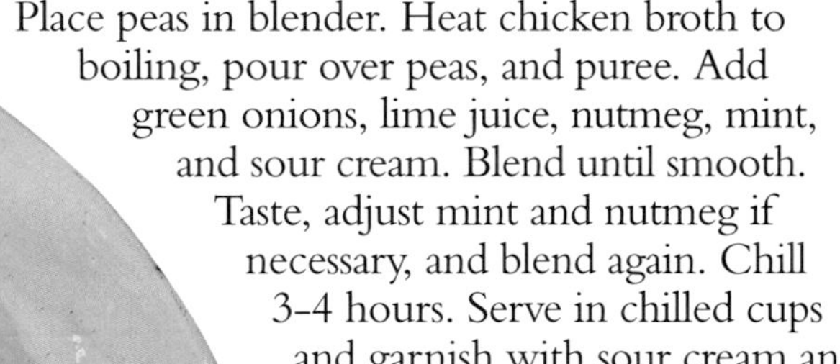

Place peas in blender. Heat chicken broth to boiling, pour over peas, and puree. Add green onions, lime juice, nutmeg, mint, and sour cream. Blend until smooth. Taste, adjust mint and nutmeg if necessary, and blend again. Chill 3-4 hours. Serve in chilled cups and garnish with sour cream and

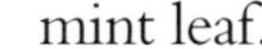

mint leaf.

Lima Bean Curry Soup

4 servings

1	10-ounce package frozen lima beans
1	cup water
2	tablespoons butter
⅓	cup sliced green onions, including tops
1-2	teaspoons curry powder
½	teaspoon dried tarragon
4	sprigs fresh parsley
1½	cups chicken broth
½	cup whipping cream
	salt and freshly ground black pepper

A wonderful creamy first course soup.

In medium saucepan, combine lima beans, water, butter, green onions, and curry powder. Heat to boiling, stirring with fork to separate beans. Reduce heat, cover, and simmer until beans are soft, 15-20 minutes, stirring occasionally. Remove from heat and cool to room temperature.

Transfer to food processor or blender and puree. Add tarragon, parsley, chicken broth, and cream. Season with salt and pepper to taste. Blend until smooth. To serve hot, return to saucepan and heat thoroughly over low heat. To serve cold, chill 3-4 hours.

Roasted Eggplant Soup

4 servings

1½	pounds eggplant, peeled and cut into 1-inch pieces
3	tablespoons olive oil, divided
½	teaspoon salt
¼	teaspoon freshly ground black pepper
¾	cup chopped onion
1	teaspoon chopped garlic
2	small tomatoes, diced
½	teaspoon dried thyme
¼	teaspoon dried sage
3	cups chicken broth
1	cup water
1½	teaspoons liquid smoke
	Garnish:
	snipped fresh chives

This soup has a distinctive smokey flavor. Perfect on a cool evening.

Preheat oven to 450 degrees. In small roasting pan, toss eggplant with 1½ tablespoons of the olive oil, salt, and pepper. Roast 15 minutes. In medium saucepan, heat remaining 1½ tablespoons olive oil over medium heat. Add onion, garlic, and tomatoes and cook until onion is soft, about 5 minutes.

Stir in roasted eggplant, thyme, and sage and cook 5 minutes. Add chicken broth and water. Reduce heat, cover, and simmer 10 minutes. Stir in liquid smoke. Transfer half of the mixture to blender and puree. Return to saucepan. Heat thoroughly, stirring frequently. Ladle soup into warmed bowls and garnish with chives.

Vegetarian Chipotle Chili

4-6 servings

- 1 tablespoon olive oil
- 1½ cups chopped carrot
- 1 cup chopped red bell pepper
- 1 cup chopped green bell pepper
- 1 cup chopped onion
- 2 teaspoons minced garlic
- 1 tablespoon chili powder
- 2 teaspoons ground cumin
- 1 28-ounce can Italian-style plum tomatoes with juice, chopped
- 1 15-ounce can red kidney beans, rinsed and drained
- 1 15-ounce can cannelini beans, rinsed and drained
- 1 15-ounce can black beans, rinsed and drained
- 1-2 tablespoons chopped canned chipotle chiles in adobo sauce
- salt and freshly ground pepper

Serve with warm flour tortillas for an easy family meal.

In large, heavy saucepan, heat olive oil over medium heat. Add carrot, bell peppers, onion, and garlic. Cook until light golden brown, about 10 minutes. Add chili powder and cumin and cook, stirring frequently, 2 minutes. Add tomatoes, kidney beans, cannelini beans, black beans, and chipotle peppers. Heat to boiling. Reduce heat and simmer until vegetables are tender, stirring occasionally, about 30 minutes. Add water if mixture is very thick. Season with salt and pepper to taste. Ladle into warmed bowls.

Mexican Bean Soup

4-6 servings

- 4 strips bacon, diced
- ¾ cup chopped onion
- ¾ cup chopped celery
- 1 4-ounce can chopped green chiles
- ½ teaspoon minced garlic
- 1 16-ounce can vegetarian-style refried beans
- ¼ teaspoon freshly ground black pepper
- ¼ teaspoon chili powder
- 2 cups chicken broth
- hot red pepper sauce

Garnish:

- shredded cheddar cheese
- crushed tortilla chips

A delicious soup in thirty minutes.

In heavy saucepan, cook bacon until crisp. Drain all but 1 tablespoon drippings. Add onion, celery, chiles, and garlic and cook 10 minutes. Add beans, pepper, chili powder, and chicken broth. Season with hot red pepper sauce to taste. Stir until well blended and simmer 10 minutes or until thoroughly heated. Serve in warmed bowls and garnish with cheese and chips.

Roasted Carrot Soup

6 servings

- 2 tablespoons olive oil
- 1½ pounds carrots, peeled and cut into ½-inch slices
- 2 large onions, peeled and coarsely chopped
- 2 teaspoons chopped garlic
- ½ teaspoon dried thyme
- ¼ teaspoon dried marjoram
- ¼ teaspoon salt
- 6-8 cups chicken broth, divided

Garnish:

snipped fresh chives or minced green onion tops

Preheat oven to 375 degrees. Heat olive oil in oven-proof stockpot over medium-high heat. Add carrots and onion and cook until onion is soft, about 10 minutes. Place stockpot in oven and bake until vegetables begin to brown, stirring occasionally, 45-60 minutes.

Remove from oven, add garlic, thyme, marjoram, salt, and 6 cups of the chicken broth. Cover and simmer on stovetop until carrots are very tender, about 30 minutes. Transfer to blender and puree until smooth, adding more chicken broth if soup is very thick. Ladle soup into warmed bowls and garnish with chives or green onions.

Hearty Mushroom Soup

4 servings

- 1 tablespoon butter
- 1 tablespoon olive oil
- 1 medium onion, peeled and grated
- 1 clove garlic, peeled and halved
- 1 pound fresh mushrooms, stemmed and thinly sliced
- 3 tablespoons tomato paste
- 3 cups chicken broth
- 2 tablespoons dry sherry
- ¼ teaspoon salt
- ⅛ teaspoon freshly ground black pepper
- 4 egg yolks
- 2 tablespoons finely chopped fresh parsley
- 3 tablespoons freshly grated Parmesan cheese

Serve as a luncheon entree with a chilled salad.

In large saucepan, heat butter and olive oil over medium heat. Add onion and garlic and cook until golden brown, 10-15 minutes. Discard garlic. Stir in mushrooms and cook 5 minutes. Add tomato paste and chicken broth. Stir until well blended. Add sherry, salt, and pepper. Simmer 10 minutes.

In small bowl, beat egg yolks, parsley, and cheese. Whisk 1 cup of the chicken broth mixture into egg mixture. Pour back into simmering soup. Mix thoroughly and serve immediately in warmed bowls.

Taj Mahal Soup

4-6 servings

- 2 tablespoons vegetable oil
- 1 medium onion, peeled and minced
- 1 1½-inch piece fresh ginger root, peeled and minced
- 1½ teaspoons minced garlic
- 1 teaspoon ground cumin
- 1 teaspoon ground turmeric
- ½ teaspoon ground coriander
- ½ teaspoon cayenne
- 1 cup dried lentils, rinsed and drained
- ¾ pound yellow squash or zucchini, thinly sliced
- 1 10-ounce package frozen spinach, partially thawed
- 4 cups chicken broth
- 1 16-ounce can whole tomatoes
- 1½ cups shredded cooked chicken (optional)

Garnish:

plain yogurt

A hearty and delicious curried lentil soup. The impressive flavor lives up to its name.

In large, heavy saucepan, heat oil over medium heat. Add onion, ginger, and garlic and cook until soft, 3-5 minutes. Add cumin, turmeric, coriander, and cayenne and stir to blend. Add lentils, squash, spinach, chicken broth, and tomatoes and heat to boiling. Reduce heat and simmer 50 minutes. Add chicken, if desired, and heat thoroughly. Ladle into warmed bowls and garnish with dollop of yogurt.

South of the Border Soup

4-6 servings

- ½ cup chopped onion
- 1 tablespoon olive oil
- 2 cups chicken or vegetable broth
- 2 cups diced unpeeled zucchini
- 1½ cups fresh or frozen corn kernels
- 1 4-ounce can chopped green chiles
- salt and freshly ground black pepper
- 1 cup milk
- 2 ounces jalapeño pepper Monterey Jack cheese, cut into ¼-inch cubes

Garnish:

minced fresh parsley

A quick and easy soup with a kick.

In large saucepan, cook onion in olive oil until tender, about 3 minutes. Stir in chicken broth, zucchini, corn, and chiles. Season with salt and pepper to taste. Heat to boiling. Reduce heat, cover, and simmer until zucchini is tender, about 5 minutes. Stir in milk. Heat thoroughly. Do not boil. Remove from heat and stir in cheese. Ladle into serving bowls and garnish with minced parsley.

Garlic Vichyssoise

6-8 servings

- 4 cups chicken broth
- 4 large cloves garlic, peeled
- 3 large potatoes, peeled and diced
- 4 medium green onions, white part only, minced
- ¼ teaspoon salt
- ⅛ teaspoon ground white pepper
- 1½ cups whipping cream

Garnish:

- 2 green onions, minced
- 6 strips bacon, crisply cooked and crumbled

Easy and elegant. The garnish gives it just the right touch of extra flavor.

In large, heavy saucepan, combine chicken broth, garlic, potatoes, green onions, salt, and white pepper. Cover and simmer over medium heat until potatoes are tender, about 30 minutes. Transfer to blender, puree in batches, and return to saucepan. Return to medium heat and stir in cream. Cook, stirring frequently, until thoroughly heated. Do not boil. Ladle into warmed bowls and garnish with green onions and bacon.

Cream of Peanut Soup

10-12 servings

- ¼ cup (½ stick) unsalted butter
- 1 cup chopped onion
- 2 celery ribs, chopped
- 3 tablespoons flour
- 8 cups chicken broth, divided
- 1½ cups smooth peanut butter
- 1¾ cups half and half

Garnish:

chopped, salted peanuts

Don't let the unusual ingredients stop you. This is unbelievably good hot or cold.

In large, heavy saucepan, melt butter over medium heat. Add onion and celery and cook until soft, but not brown, about 5 minutes. Stir in flour and cook, stirring constantly, 3 minutes. Add 2 cups of the chicken broth and stir until lumps dissolve. Stir in remaining 6 cups chicken broth and heat to boiling.

Remove from heat. Puree in blender, in batches, until smooth. Return to saucepan and stir in peanut butter and half and half. Cook over low heat until thoroughly heated. Do not boil. Garnish with chopped peanuts. May also be served cold.

Spiked Tomato Soup

4 servings

2 cups tomato juice
2 cups vegetable juice, such as V-8
5 tablespoons vodka
1 tablespoon sugar
2 teaspoons Worcestershire
1 teaspoon salt
½ teaspoon freshly ground black pepper
3 drops hot red pepper sauce

Garnish:
fresh celery ribs with leaves

In medium saucepan, combine tomato juice, vegetable juice, vodka, sugar, Worcestershire, salt, pepper, and hot red pepper sauce. Heat to boiling, stirring occasionally. Ladle into soup mugs and garnish with celery.

Exotic Chicken Soup

4-6 servings

4 cups chicken broth
1 cup diced celery
½ cup shredded coconut
1 teaspoon curry powder
1 teaspoon minced garlic
½ teaspoon ground white pepper
⅛ teaspoon cayenne
3 small tomatoes, cored, seeded, and diced
2 cups diced cooked chicken breast, at room temperature
2 firm bananas, diced

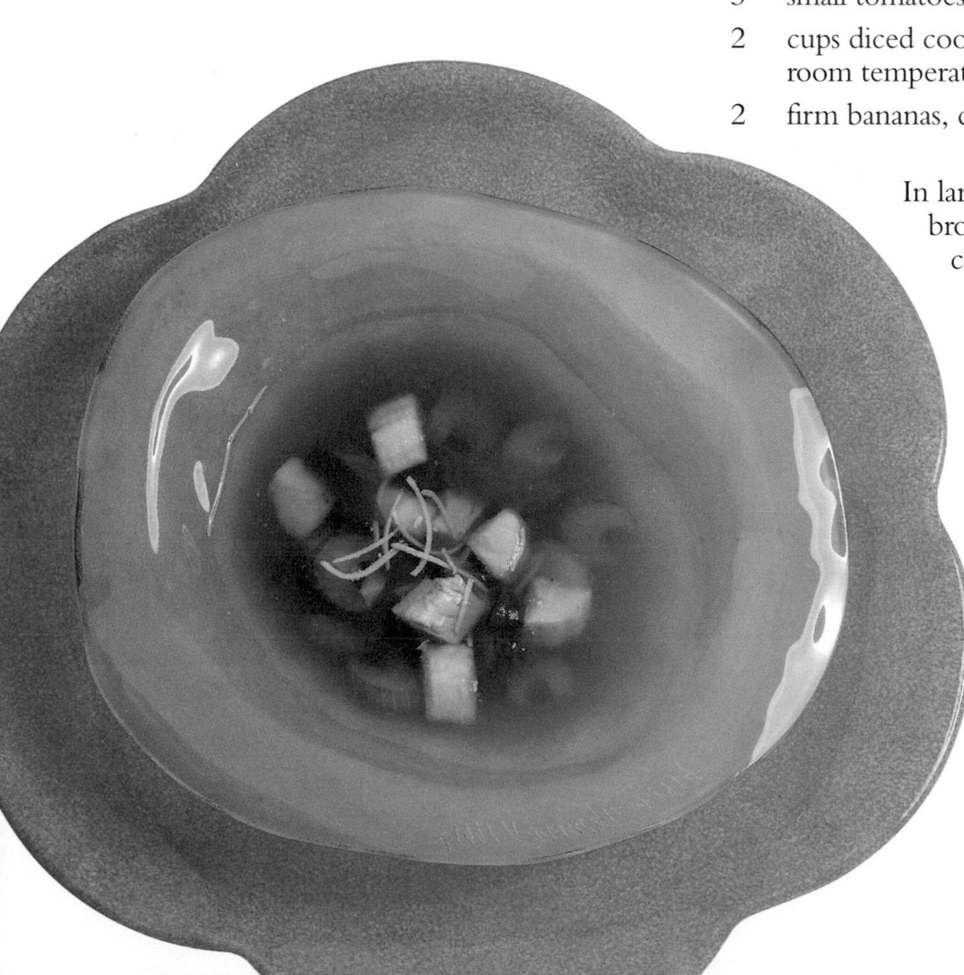

In large saucepan, heat chicken broth to boiling. Add celery, coconut, curry powder, garlic, white pepper, and cayenne and simmer 10 minutes. Add tomatoes and continue cooking 6 minutes. Add chicken and bananas, and heat thoroughly. Ladle into warmed bowls.

Tomato and Dill Soup

8 servings

2 tablespoons butter
2 cups diced onion
1 teaspoon minced garlic
2 28-ounce cans whole peeled tomatoes, drained, seeded, and coarsely chopped, divided
3 tablespoons flour
2 tablespoons tomato paste
6 cups chicken broth, divided
1 cup half and half
⅛ teaspoon ground white pepper
3 tablespoons finely chopped fresh dill

Garnish:
sour cream
fresh dill sprigs

In large saucepan, melt butter over medium heat. Add onion and garlic and cook until translucent and golden, 10-20 minutes. Add about two-thirds of the chopped tomatoes and cook over high heat, 3 minutes, stirring constantly. Remove from heat and stir in flour. Add tomato paste and gradually whisk in 2 cups of the chicken broth to avoid lumping. Heat to boiling, stirring constantly. Reduce heat and simmer 10 minutes.

Remove from heat, transfer to blender, and puree. Return to saucepan and stir in remaining 4 cups chicken broth, half and half, white pepper, and dill. Add remaining third of the tomatoes and heat thoroughly, but do not boil. Serve in warmed bowls. Garnish with dollop of sour cream and dill.

Basil Tomato Soup

8 servings

5 strips bacon, diced
1 rib celery, chopped
½ cup chopped yellow onion
1 small carrot, peeled and diced
1 red bell pepper, cored, seeded, and diced
1 green bell pepper, cored, seeded, and diced
6 fresh basil leaves, chopped, divided
1 teaspoon minced garlic
1 28-ounce can whole tomatoes
1 tablespoon chicken base or 2 cubes chicken bouillon
1 cup half and half
3 jumbo pitted ripe olives, sliced

Robust with tomato flavor, this is a rich first course soup.

Cook bacon in stockpot. Drain all but 1-2 tablespoons drippings. Add celery, onion, and carrot and cook 2 minutes. Add bell peppers, half of the basil, and garlic. Cook 2 minutes. Add tomatoes and simmer over medium heat, 5 minutes. Add chicken base and stir to dissolve. Transfer to blender and puree in batches. Return to stockpot. Add half and half, olives, and remaining basil. Simmer over medium heat, 45 minutes.

Pinto Bean Soup With Salsa

6-8 servings

Cilantro-Jalapeño Salsa:

1¼ pounds tomatoes, peeled, seeded, and cut into ¼-inch pieces
½ cup finely diced yellow onion
1-2 whole jalapeño peppers, cored, seeded, and finely diced
¾ cup loosely packed, chopped fresh cilantro
1 tablespoon fresh lime juice
salt and freshly ground black pepper

Soup:

1½ cups dried pinto beans, rinsed, sorted, soaked overnight in water, and drained
2 tablespoons unsalted butter
2 cups diced onion
6-8 cups chicken broth, divided
salt and freshly ground black pepper
2 cups milk

Garnish:

sour cream
crushed tortilla chips

This is the perfect accompaniment to Southwestern Caesar Salad, page 80.

In large bowl, combine tomatoes, onion, jalapeños, cilantro, lime juice, and salt and pepper to taste. Let stand at room temperature several hours or chill up to 2 days. Bring to room temperature before serving.

Fill large stockpot with water. Add beans and heat to boiling. Reduce heat and simmer until beans begin to soften, about 40 minutes. Remove from heat and drain beans in colander.

Melt butter in same stockpot over medium heat. Add onion and cook until golden brown, stirring occasionally, about 10 minutes. Add 6 cups of the chicken broth and drained beans. Season with salt and pepper to taste. Simmer until beans are very soft, about 1 hour and 15 minutes, adding remaining chicken broth if necessary to keep beans covered.

Remove from heat and puree in blender, in batches. Strain puree back into stockpot, pressing beans to release all liquid. Discard bean pulp. (May be prepared to this point 2 days in advance; cover and chill.)

Heat to simmering. Add milk and heat to boiling, stirring frequently. Thin with chicken broth if desired and adjust seasonings, if necessary. Serve in warmed bowls. Garnish with sour cream, chips, and Cilantro-Jalapeño Salsa. Pass remaining Cilantro-Jalapeño Salsa separately.

Polenta Herb Vegetable Soup

10 servings

Polenta:

- 1 cup water
- ¾ cup yellow cornmeal
- 2 cups milk
- 1 ¼-inch thick slice prosciutto, diced
- 3 tablespoons minced fresh parsley
- 1 tablespoon butter
- 1 teaspoon minced garlic
- ½ teaspoon salt
- freshly ground black pepper

Soup:

- ¼ cup (½ stick) butter
- 2 cups finely chopped white onion
- 3 large leeks, white part only, thinly sliced and thoroughly rinsed
- 2½ teaspoons minced garlic
- 8 cups chicken broth
- 2 small turnips, peeled, halved lengthwise, and thinly sliced
- 1 carrot, peeled, halved lengthwise, and thinly sliced
- ½ pound fresh spinach, stemmed, rinsed, rolled, and cut into thin strips
- 1 medium cucumber, peeled, halved lengthwise, seeded, and thinly sliced
- 1 medium zucchini, halved lengthwise and thinly sliced
- ½ cup minced fresh parsley
- ½ cup minced fresh chervil, or 3 tablespoons minced fresh tarragon or mint
- 1 teaspoon dried marjoram

Garnish:

- freshly shredded Emmental cheese

An unusual soup from the South of France. Serve with crusty French bread.

Butter 8x8-inch metal pan. In heavy saucepan, heat water to boiling. Combine cornmeal and milk and add to boiling water. Cook over medium heat, stirring constantly, until thick enough for a spoon to stand up in mixture, about 10 minutes. Stir in prosciutto, 3 tablespoons parsley, 1 tablespoon butter, 1 teaspoon garlic, and salt. Season with pepper to taste. Spread evenly in prepared pan. Let stand until completely set, about 1 hour. Cut into ½-inch cubes and set aside.

In large stockpot, melt ¼ cup butter over low heat. Add onion, leeks, and 2½ teaspoons garlic and cook until onion is translucent, about 20 minutes. Add chicken broth and heat to boiling. Reduce heat to medium, add turnips and carrot and cook until very soft, about 30 minutes. Stir in spinach, cucumber, zucchini, ½ cup parsley, chervil, and marjoram. Season with salt and pepper to taste. Cook 5-10 minutes, all vegetables should be tender. Place several polenta cubes in warmed bowls, top with soup and garnish with cheese.

Wild Rice Soup

10-12 servings

- ¼ cup (½ stick) butter
- 1 cup small fresh mushrooms, sliced
- 1 cup diced white onion
- 1 cup sliced celery
- ⅓ cup flour
- 6 cups chicken broth
- 2 whole chicken breasts (about 1 pound), cooked, skinned, and shredded
- 2 cups cooked wild rice
- 1 cup half and half
- 2 tablespoons dry white wine

For a delicious soup en croûte, place soup in oven-proof crocks, top with puff pastry, and bake.

In large saucepan, melt butter over medium heat. Add mushrooms and cook until tender, about 5 minutes. Add onion and celery and cook until tender, about 10 minutes. Reduce heat to low and stir in flour. Cook, stirring frequently, until golden, about 5 minutes. Gradually add chicken broth, stirring constantly, until slightly thickened and lumps dissolve. Add cooked chicken and cooked wild rice. Stir in half and half and wine. Heat thoroughly but do not boil. Serve in warmed bowls.

Chicken and Vegetable Soup With Pesto

6-8 servings

- 1 tablespoon butter
- 1 cup diced red onion
- 1 leek, white part only, cut into ¼-inch slices and thoroughly rinsed
- 1 carrot, peeled and cut into ½-inch slices
- 1 rib celery, cut into ¼-inch slices
- 1 teaspoon minced garlic
- 4 Italian plum tomatoes, seeded and chopped
- 4 cabbage leaves, coarsely chopped
- 6 ounces fresh green beans, trimmed and cut into 1-inch pieces
- 8 cups chicken broth
- 10 large spinach leaves, torn into bite size pieces
- 2 whole chicken breasts (about 1 pound), cooked, skinned, and cut into 1-inch pieces
- 3 tablespoons purchased basil pesto

Garnish:

freshly grated Parmesan cheese

In large, heavy stockpot, melt butter over medium heat. Add onion, leek, carrot, celery, garlic, tomatoes, cabbage, and green beans. Cook 5 minutes. Add chicken broth and heat to boiling. Reduce heat and simmer, uncovered, 25 minutes. Add spinach and chicken and simmer 5 minutes. Remove from heat and add pesto. Serve in warmed bowls, and garnish with Parmesan.

Basil Lemon Chicken Soup

8-10 servings

2 tablespoons vegetable oil
1 teaspoon chopped garlic
2 cups chopped onion
2 cups chopped celery
2 bay leaves
2 tablespoons dried basil
½ cup fresh lemon juice
2 tablespoons Worcestershire
8 cups chicken broth
½ cup diced red bell pepper
1 cup thinly sliced mushrooms
2 cups diced uncooked chicken
3 tablespoons butter
3 tablespoons flour
2 cups half and half
salt and freshly ground black pepper

For a lighter soup, omit butter, flour, and half and half.

In large stockpot, heat oil over medium heat. Add garlic and onion and cook until golden, stirring frequently, 10-15 minutes. Add celery, bay leaves, basil, lemon juice, Worcestershire, and chicken broth. Heat to boiling, reduce heat, cover, and simmer 45 minutes, stirring occasionally. Add bell pepper, mushrooms, and chicken. Cover and simmer 30 minutes.

In small saucepan, melt butter over medium-low heat. Add flour and cook, stirring constantly, 3-4 minutes. Add about ¾ cup of the hot soup mixture, whisking constantly to prevent lumps. Return to soup mixture and stir until well blended. Stir in half and half and season with salt and pepper to taste. Heat thoroughly, but do not boil.

Chicken Leek Noodle Soup

12 servings

- 10 cups chicken broth
- 1 cup dry white wine
- 4 boneless, skinless chicken breast halves (about 1 pound)
- ¼ cup (½ stick) unsalted butter
- 4 medium leeks, white part only, chopped and thoroughly rinsed
- 2 medium carrots, peeled and finely chopped
- 3 ribs celery, finely chopped
- 2 teaspoons salt
- 1 teaspoon freshly ground black pepper
- 8 medium mushrooms, thinly sliced
- 2 cups cooked, drained thin egg noodles
- 4 ounces fresh green beans, trimmed and sliced diagonally
- 3 tablespoons chopped fresh Italian parsley

An updated old-fashioned favorite.

In large saucepan, heat chicken broth and wine to boiling. Reduce heat, add chicken and simmer, uncovered, 15 minutes. Remove chicken with slotted spoon, reserving cooking liquid. Set aside to cool.

In large, heavy saucepan, melt butter over medium-low heat. Add leeks, carrots, celery, salt, and pepper. Simmer gently 5 minutes. Add reserved chicken broth mixture and mushrooms. Simmer uncovered, 10 minutes. Add noodles and green beans and simmer 5 minutes. Remove from heat. Shred cooled chicken and stir into soup. Add parsley and heat thoroughly.

Baked Tortellini Soup

8-10 servings

- 1½ pounds Italian sausage links
- 1 cup chopped onion
- 1 teaspoon minced garlic
- ¼ teaspoon freshly ground black pepper
- 2 tablespoons olive oil
- 4 cups beef broth
- 2 cups water
- 1½ teaspoons Italian seasoning
- 1½ cups peeled and thinly sliced carrots
- 1 16-ounce can whole peeled tomatoes
- 1 15-ounce can kidney beans, drained and rinsed
- 1 6-ounce can pitted, sliced ripe olives, drained or oil-cured olives
- 2 cups diced zucchini
- 16 ounces tri-color cheese tortellini, cooked al dente and drained

Garnish:

freshly grated Parmesan cheese

This hearty soup may also be prepared entirely on the stovetop. Photo, page 44.

Preheat oven to 400 degrees. In roasting pan, combine sausage, onion, garlic, and pepper. Add olive oil and toss to coat. Roast, uncovered, stirring occasionally, 20-30 minutes, until sausage is browned. Remove from oven. Reduce oven temperature to 325 degrees.

Drain grease from sausage and cut into ¼-inch slices. Return to roasting pan. Add beef broth, water, Italian seasoning, and carrots. Cover and return to oven. Bake 30 minutes, until sausage is tender. Remove from oven. Stir in tomatoes with juice, beans, olives, and zucchini. Bake 15-20 minutes. Add tortellini and bake 5 minutes longer. Ladle into warmed bowls and garnish with Parmesan.

Sausage and Sauerkraut Stew

8 servings

- 4½ cups water
- 4 medium red potatoes, peeled and diced
- ½ teaspoon salt
- ½ pound smoked sausage, sliced ¼-inch thick
- 16 ounces purchased sauerkraut
- 1 medium onion, peeled and diced
- ½ teaspoon minced garlic
- 1 tablespoon chopped fresh dill weed
- ¼ teaspoon caraway seeds
- 1 cup sour cream

In stockpot, combine water, potatoes, and salt. Heat to boiling. Cook until potatoes are tender, about 15 minutes. Add sausage, sauerkraut with juice, onion, garlic, dill, and caraway. Simmer until onion is soft, about 10 minutes. Just before serving, remove 1 cup soup to small bowl. Stir in sour cream and return to soup. Heat thoroughly. Do not boil. Serve immediately.

Layered Chili

6 servings

- 1 pound ground chuck
- 1 cup finely chopped onion
- 1 teaspoon minced garlic
- 1 cup purchased barbecue sauce
- 1 cup water
- 1 tablespoon chili powder
- ½ ounce unsweetened chocolate, chopped
- ½ teaspoon ground cumin
- ½ teaspoon turmeric
- ½ teaspoon ground allspice
- ½ teaspoon ground cinnamon
- ¼ teaspoon ground cloves
- ¼ teaspoon ground coriander
- ¼ teaspoon ground cardamom
- 1 teaspoon salt
- tomato juice
- 9 ounces spaghetti, cooked, drained, and buttered
- 1 15-ounce can kidney beans, rinsed and warmed
- 1 cup coarsely chopped onions
- 8 ounces cheddar cheese, shredded
- oyster crackers

Flavor is enhanced significantly when chilled overnight.

In large stockpot, combine beef, finely chopped onion, and garlic over medium heat. Cook until beef is browned and drain. Add barbecue sauce and water and heat to boiling. Add chili powder, chocolate, cumin, turmeric, allspice, cinnamon, cloves, coriander, cardamom, and salt. Cover and simmer over very low heat 30 minutes, stirring occasionally. Add tomato juice if mixture becomes dry. Remove from heat and chill overnight to allow flavors to blend.

Reheat chili over low heat. On individual servings plates, place warm spaghetti, top with hot chili, warm beans, onions, and cheese. Serve with oyster crackers on the side.

Working Barn Stew

6 servings

- 2 tablespoons olive oil
- 4 boneless, skinless chicken breast halves, (about 1 pound), cut into 1-inch pieces
- 1 cup chopped onion
- ½ medium green bell pepper, chopped
- ½ medium yellow bell pepper, chopped
- 1 teaspoon chopped garlic
- 2 14½-ounce cans stewed tomatoes
- 1 15-ounce can pinto beans, drained and rinsed
- ¾ cup purchased, medium picante sauce
- 1 tablespoon chili powder
- 1 tablespoon ground cumin
- ½ cup shredded cheddar cheese
- 6 tablespoons sour cream

A filling, zesty family stew. *Photo, page 46.*

In large stockpot, heat olive oil over medium heat. Add chicken, onion, bell peppers, and garlic and cook until chicken is no longer pink. Add tomatoes, beans, picante sauce, chili powder, and cumin. Reduce heat to low and simmer 25 minutes or up to 2 hours. Place in individual serving bowls and top with cheese and sour cream.

Pork and Green Chile Stew

4-6 servings

- 3 tablespoons oil
- 2 pounds boneless pork, cut into 1-inch cubes
- 1 cup chopped onion
- ½ teaspoon minced garlic
- ¼ cup flour
- 2 cups peeled chopped tomatoes
- 2 7-ounce cans chopped green chiles, drained
- 1 fresh jalapeño pepper, cored, seeded, and minced
- 1 teaspoon salt
- ½ teaspoon freshly ground black pepper
- ½ teaspoon sugar
- 1 cup chicken broth
- flour tortillas, warmed

A southwestern staple.

In large saucepan, heat oil over medium heat. Add pork and cook until lightly browned. Stir in onion and garlic. Add flour and cook, stirring constantly, 1-2 minutes. Add tomatoes, green chiles, jalapeño, salt, pepper, and sugar. Stir until well blended. Add chicken broth. Cover, reduce heat, and simmer about 2½ hours or until pork is tender. Serve in warmed bowls with flour tortillas.

Hot and Sour Hunan Soup

6 servings

- 8 ounces pork tenderloin
- 2 tablespoons vegetable oil
- 2 tablespoons hot black bean sauce
- 2 tablespoons thinly sliced green onions
- 4 dried Shiitake mushrooms, soaked in warm water 30 minutes, drained, dried, and thinly sliced
- 1 6-ounce can sliced bamboo shoots
- 1 pound bok choy, shredded
- 1 tablespoon soy sauce
- ½ teaspoon salt
- 8 cups chicken broth
- 6 ounces dried Chinese egg noodles, broken, soaked in warm water 3 minutes, and drained
- 3 tablespoons red wine vinegar
- 1 tablespoon chili oil
- 1 teaspoon sesame oil

You'll find black bean sauce in the Asian section of many supermarkets.

Place pork in skillet filled with 1-inch of water. Cover and simmer 20 minutes. Drain, cool slightly, and shred meat. In large, heavy saucepan, heat oil over medium heat. Add bean sauce and green onions and cook about 1 minute. Add mushrooms, reserved pork, bamboo shoots, bok choy, soy sauce, salt, and chicken broth. Heat to boiling. Reduce heat and simmer 5 minutes. Add noodles and simmer 5 minutes. Stir in vinegar, chili oil, and sesame oil. Serve immediately in warmed bowls.

Chinese Pork and Cucumber Soup

4 servings

- 5 cups chicken broth
- 1 cup water
- 2 1-inch pieces fresh ginger root, peeled and thinly sliced
- 1 cup loosely packed, fresh cilantro leaves, stems reserved
- 2 teaspoons sesame oil
- ¼ teaspoon salt
- ½ pound pork tenderloin, cut into very thin 1-inch strips
- 1 small cucumber, peeled and very thinly sliced

A delicate first course soup.

In large saucepan, combine chicken broth, water, ginger, and cilantro stems. Heat to boiling. Reduce heat, cover, and simmer 20 minutes. In medium skillet filled with ¾-inch of water, heat sesame oil and salt to boiling. Add pork, reduce heat, and stir until pork is opaque and thoroughly cooked. Remove with slotted spoon to plate, discarding liquid.

Strain chicken broth mixture and return to saucepan. Heat to boiling. Add pork mixture and cucumber. Heat thoroughly, about 1 minute. Remove from heat and add cilantro leaves. Ladle soup into warmed bowls.

Oyster Spinach Soup

6 servings

1 10-ounce box frozen chopped spinach, thawed and squeezed dry
½ cup coarsely chopped onion
½ cup chopped celery with leaves
¼ cup chopped green onions
¼ cup chopped fresh parsley
½ cup coarsely chopped iceberg lettuce
¼ cup (½ stick) butter
2 tablespoons anchovy paste
½ teaspoon Greek seasoning
½ teaspoon freshly ground black pepper
2 tablespoons fresh lemon juice
3 tablespoons flour
2 cups chicken broth
2 teaspoons Worcestershire
¼ teaspoon soy sauce
dash cayenne
1 pint small oysters, ½ cup liquid reserved
2 cups half and half
2 tablespoons freshly grated Parmesan cheese
2 tablespoons Sambuca or other anise flavored liquor

Garnish:

3 tablespoons toasted bread crumbs

This soup would please even the most discriminating Rockefeller.

In food processor, puree spinach, onion, celery, green onions, parsley, and lettuce. In large stockpot, melt butter over low heat. Add spinach mixture and cook 10 minutes, stirring frequently. Add anchovy paste, Greek seasoning, pepper, and lemon juice. Whisk in flour and cook 3 minutes. Gradually add chicken broth, Worcestershire, soy sauce, and cayenne. Heat to boiling over medium-high heat. Reduce heat to low and simmer 5 minutes. (May be prepared to this point up to 24 hours in advance. Heat soup thoroughly over medium heat before proceeding.)

Just before serving, add oysters with liquid, reduce heat to low, and simmer about 2 minutes. Add half and half, Parmesan, and Sambuca and simmer until thoroughly heated. Do not boil. Garnish with toasted bread crumbs.

Seafood Soup Provençal

8 servings

Classic Aioli:

- 2 teaspoons minced garlic
- ½ teaspoon paprika
- 1 egg
- 2 tablespoons fresh lemon juice
- salt and freshly ground black pepper
- ¾ cup olive oil

Soup:

- ¼ cup olive oil
- ¾ cup finely chopped celery
- 2 cups finely chopped onion
- 2 cups finely chopped leeks, rinsed thoroughly
- 1 cup finely chopped red or green bell pepper
- ½ cup finely diced fennel bulb
- ½ teaspoon salt
- ¼ teaspoon freshly ground black pepper
- ¼ teaspoon cayenne
- ½ cup dry white wine
- 3 cups canned tomato puree
- 4 cups fish broth or clam juice
- 1 pound firm white fish, cut into 1-inch pieces
- ½ pound shrimp, peeled and deveined
- 12 mussels in shells, scrubbed
- 1 pound bay scallops, rinsed and dried
- 1 tablespoon Sambuca
- 8 ½-inch slices French baguette, toasted

This is a true main dish soup, and a seafood lover's dream. For an easier, lighter version, serve without Classic Aioli.

In blender or small food processor, combine garlic, paprika, egg, lemon juice, and salt and pepper to taste. With blender running, add ¾ cup of the olive oil, 1 drop at a time, until mixture begins to emulsify. As mixture thickens, oil may be added in slow steady stream. Transfer to small bowl and chill up to 2 days.

In large stockpot, heat remaining ¼ cup olive oil over medium heat. Add celery, onion, leeks, bell pepper, and fennel. Cook until soft, about 5 minutes. Add salt, pepper, cayenne, wine, and tomato puree and cook 5 minutes. Stir in fish broth and simmer 20 minutes.

Add fish and cook 2 minutes. Stir in shrimp and mussels. When mussel shells open, stir in scallops and Sambuca and cook 2 minutes. Remove from heat. Place baguette slices in warmed individual serving bowls and cover with soup. Pass aioli separately.

Asian Sole Soup

4-6 servings

- 1 pound sole, or other delicate white fish
- 4 cups chicken broth
- 1 teaspoon peeled, grated fresh ginger root
- 4 fresh mushrooms, thinly sliced
- 1 head iceberg lettuce, cored and thinly sliced
- 4 teaspoons soy sauce

Garnish:

sesame oil

Simply fantastic!

Place fish in freezer 10 minutes. Remove and slice thinly against grain. In large saucepan, heat chicken broth and ginger to boiling. Add mushrooms and lettuce and return to boiling. Add soy sauce and fish and immediately remove from heat. Ladle into warmed bowls and garnish with a few drops of sesame oil. Serve immediately.

Broiled Sicilian Sandwich

4 servings

- ½ teaspoon olive oil
- ¼ cup thinly sliced onion
- ½ small zucchini, halved lengthwise and thinly sliced (about ½ cup)
- ½ teaspoon minced garlic
- ½ cup seeded, coarsely chopped tomato
- ¼ cup red bell peppers, roasted (page 381), peeled, and coarsely chopped
- ¼ teaspoon dried thyme
- ⅛ teaspoon freshly ground black pepper
- ¾ cup shredded provolone cheese (about 3 ounces), divided
- 4 1-inch thick slices Italian bread
- 2 tablespoons freshly grated Parmesan cheese

Deliciously different.

In medium skillet, heat olive oil over medium-low heat. Add onion, zucchini, and garlic and cook 5 minutes or until vegetables are tender. Add tomato, roasted bell peppers, thyme, and pepper. Cook 1-2 minutes. Sprinkle 2 tablespoons of the provolone on each bread slice. Top with ¼ cup of the onion mixture. Combine remaining provolone and Parmesan and sprinkle evenly over top. Preheat broiler and broil sandwiches, 3 inches from heat, until cheese melts. Serve immediately.

Smoked Turkey Sandwich With Apricot Mayonnaise

8 servings

Apricot Mayonnaise:

- 1½ cups mayonnaise
- ¼ cup apricot jam
- 1½ teaspoons curry powder

Sandwich:

- 4 whole pita bread rounds or 8 slices French baguette
- 1 pound sliced smoked turkey
- 2 bunches watercress, washed and trimmed
- 4 Italian plum tomatoes, sliced
- 1 avocado, peeled, seeded, and sliced
- 1 cup chopped walnuts, toasted (page 381)
- ⅓ cup currants or raisins

Photo, page 314.

In small bowl, combine mayonnaise, jam, and curry powder. Whisk until well blended. Cover and chill up to 2 days. If using pita bread, preheat oven to 350 degrees. Warm pita about 5 minutes. Cut rounds in half crosswise, forming pockets. Spread inside of pita or baguette with Apricot Mayonnaise. Stuff or top with turkey, watercress, tomatoes, avocado, walnuts, and currants.

Chicken Sandwich With Ancho Chile Mayonnaise

6 servings

- 3 dried ancho chiles, soaked in hot water overnight, drained, stemmed, and seeded
- ¼ cup coarsely chopped onion
- 1 large garlic clove, peeled and halved
- 1 tablespoon white wine vinegar
- ¾ cup olive oil
- 2 tablespoons fresh lime juice
- salt
- ⅓ cup prepared mayonnaise
- 3 whole chicken breasts, poached, skinned, and shredded
- 6 French sourdough rolls
- butter
- fresh cilantro sprigs

Ancho chiles are dried poblano chiles–they add just the right kick to this mayonnaise.

In food processor, combine chiles, onion, garlic, and vinegar. Process until smooth, occasionally scraping down sides of bowl. With machine running, add olive oil gradually through feed tube. Add lime juice and season with salt to taste. (May be prepared up to 2 weeks in advance. Cover and chill.)

In large bowl, combine reserved ancho mixture, mayonnaise, and chicken. Slice rolls lengthwise and hollow out each half. Butter hollowed rolls and toast lightly. Fill with reserved chicken mixture. Serve open-faced topped with cilantro.

At left: Cold Strawberry Rhubarb Soup, 48

Chicken Tandoori Sandwich

6 servings

6 boneless, skinless chicken breast halves (about 1½ pounds)
2 tablespoons fresh lemon juice
1 cup plain yogurt
2 tablespoons peeled, chopped fresh ginger root
1 teaspoon crushed garlic
½ teaspoon ground cumin
1 teaspoon finely chopped fresh cilantro
¼ teaspoon cayenne
¼ teaspoon turmeric

Mint Mayonnaise:

1 cup loosely packed, fresh mint leaves
1 cup loosely packed, fresh cilantro leaves
1 jalapeño pepper, cored, seeded, and minced
3 tablespoons chopped onion
2 teaspoons cider vinegar
½ cup prepared mayonnaise

Sandwich:

4 whole pita bread rounds
6 leaves red or green leaf lettuce
1 cup peeled, thinly sliced cucumber

A refreshing and unusual sandwich.

Sprinkle chicken breasts with lemon juice. Combine yogurt, ginger, garlic, cumin, 1 teaspoon cilantro, cayenne, and turmeric. Pour over chicken and turn to coat. Cover and marinate in refrigerate, 3-8 hours.

In food processor, combine mint, 1 cup cilantro, jalapeño, and onion. Process until very finely chopped. Add vinegar and mayonnaise and process until just blended. Preheat grill to medium-high or preheat broiler. Grill or broil chicken until thoroughly cooked, about 5 minutes per side. Discard marinade.

Preheat oven to 350 degrees. Warm pita rounds about 5 minutes. Cut rounds in half crosswise, forming pockets. Spread inside with Mint Mayonnaise. Line with lettuce leaves and cucumber slices. Slice grilled chicken breasts diagonally and place in pita. Top with additional Mint Mayonnaise, if desired.

Grilled Eggplant Sandwich

4 servings

- 1 large eggplant, sliced lengthwise into ¼-inch thick slices
- ¼ cup olive oil
- salt and freshly ground black pepper
- 4 baguette rolls, sliced lengthwise
- ¼ cup Basic Basil Pesto (page 193) or purchased basil pesto
- 1 ripe tomato, sliced
- 8 ounces fresh mozzarella cheese, sliced

Preheat grill to high. Brush both sides of eggplant slices with olive oil and season with salt and pepper to taste. Grill until tender but not mushy, about 5 minutes. Spread rolls lightly with pesto and top with eggplant, tomato slices, and cheese.

Tailgate Picnic Sandwich

12 servings

- ½ cup olive oil
- ¼ cup balsamic vinegar
- 1 teaspoon minced garlic
- 6 large red bell peppers, roasted (page 381), peeled, and cut into ¾-inch strips
- 2 1½-pound sourdough bread rounds
- coarse grain Dijon mustard
- 4 ounces hard salami, thinly sliced, divided
- ¼ pound fresh spinach, washed and stemmed, divided
- 6 ounces sliced provolone cheese, divided
- 12 thin slices red onion, separated into rings, divided
- 4 ounces thinly sliced cooked turkey breast, divided
- 4 ounces thinly sliced ham, divided

Take this along on your next hike.

In bowl, combine olive oil, vinegar, and garlic. Add roasted peppers and turn to coat evenly. Let stand at room temperature 3 hours. (May be prepared up to 2 days in advance. Cover tightly and chill.)

Cut tops off bread rounds and reserve. Hollow loaves, leaving ½-inch thick shell, discarding insides. Working with 1 loaf, spread inside and top with mustard. Layer half of the salami, half of the spinach, half of the marinated peppers, half of the cheese, half of the onion rings, half of the turkey, and half of the ham. Replace bread top. Wrap in plastic wrap and then in foil. Repeat with remaining loaf and ingredients. Chill overnight. Cut each loaf into 6 wedges to serve.

Bistro Sandwich

8 servings

- 1 tablespoon butter
- 1 tablespoon olive oil plus additional for brushing bread
- ¾ cup minced onion
- 1 teaspoon minced garlic
- 2 35-ounce cans whole peeled Italian plum tomatoes, drained and chopped
- 1 tablespoon chopped fresh basil
- ½ teaspoon salt
- ½ teaspoon freshly ground black pepper
- 2 bay leaves
- pinch sugar
- ½ tablespoon fresh thyme
- 1 tablespoon Herbes de Provence
- 2 tablespoons minced fresh parsley
- 1 pound loaf French bread
- 1 pound mozzarella cheese, sliced
- 3-4 ripe tomatoes, sliced
- 8 ounces provolone cheese, sliced
- 16 sun-dried tomatoes, soaked in boiling water 2 minutes and drained
- 16 niçoise olives, pitted
- ½ cup freshly grated Parmesan cheese

In large, heavy skillet, heat butter and olive oil over medium heat. Add onion and cook 5 minutes. Add garlic and cook 2 minutes, stirring frequently. Add chopped tomatoes, basil, salt, pepper, bay leaves, sugar, thyme, and Herbes de Provence. Increase heat to medium-high. Cook 25 minutes, stirring frequently, until most of the liquid has evaporated and sauce has thickened. Discard bay leaves. Taste and adjust seasonings, if necessary. Remove from heat and cool to room temperature. Stir in parsley.

Preheat oven to 400 degrees. Cut bread in half lengthwise. Hollow out, leaving about ½-inch shell, discarding insides. Brush inside of shell lightly with olive oil and toast in oven until golden brown.

Spread each toasted shell with half of the reserved tomato sauce. Layer mozzarella, sliced tomatoes, and provolone over sauce. Arrange sun-dried tomatoes and olives on top and drizzle with olive oil. Sprinkle with Parmesan. Place on baking sheet and bake until cheese bubbles. Let stand 5 minutes before slicing with serrated knife.

Artichoke and Pesto Hero

6-8 servings

- 1 cup Basic Basil Pesto (page 193) or purchased basil pesto
- 2 teaspoons Dijon mustard
- 1 pound loaf crusty French bread
- 1 14-ounce can water-packed artichoke hearts, drained and thinly sliced
- 4 ounces provolone cheese, thinly sliced
- 1 medium tomato, thinly sliced
- 2 cups (about 4 ounces) fresh spinach, stemmed

Quick and easy.

In small bowl, combine pesto and mustard. Stir until well blended. Cut bread in half lengthwise. Hollow out halves, leaving a 1-inch shell, discarding insides. Spread pesto mixture over each half. On bottom half, layer artichoke hearts, provolone, tomato, and spinach leaves. Cover with the top, cut crosswise into 6-8 pieces, and secure with wooden picks.

Colorado Grilled Cheese

4 servings

- 2 tablespoons butter, softened
- ½ teaspoon minced garlic
- ¼ teaspoon crushed red pepper
- 1 egg, lightly beaten
- ¼ cup milk
- 1 cup freshly grated Parmesan cheese
- 8 slices sourdough French bread
- 12 ounces thinly sliced turkey breast
- 1 avocado, peeled, seeded, and thinly sliced
- 1 tomato, thinly sliced
- 2 tablespoons chopped fresh cilantro
- 4 slices red onion, separated into rings
- 4 1-ounce slices Monterey Jack cheese

Photo, page 46.

In small bowl, combine butter, garlic, and crushed red pepper. Stir to blend and set aside. In separate bowl, whisk egg and milk and set aside. Spread Parmesan cheese evenly on large plate and set aside.

In large skillet, melt half of the butter mixture. Working quickly, dip 1 of the bread slices in egg mixture, coating 1 side only. Dip coated side into Parmesan. Place in skillet, cheese side down. Repeat with 3 of the remaining bread slices. Arrange turkey, avocado, and tomato on top of bread slices. Sprinkle with cilantro and top with onion rings and Monterey Jack.

Dip remaining 4 bread slices in egg mixture, coating 1 side. Dip coated side into Parmesan and place on top of sandwich, cheese side out. Increase heat to medium and cook until golden brown. Add remaining butter, turn sandwiches, and cook until golden brown.

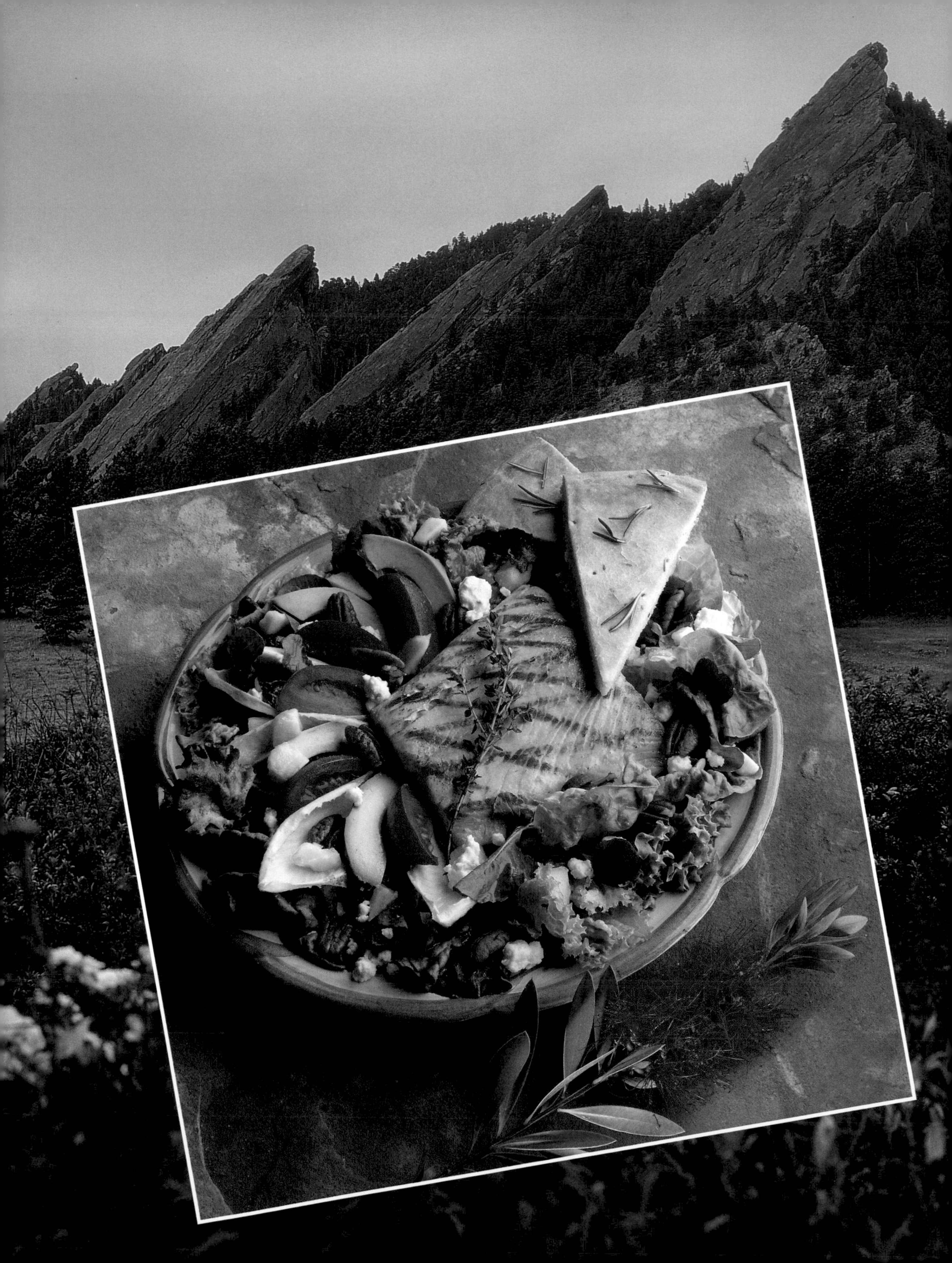

A sunset over the Boulder Flatirons—it's the kind of view that makes you relish living in Colorado, or entertain the thought of moving here. A hearty salmon salad, warm focaccia, and a bottle of Riesling are just the fare to linger over as the western sky turns orange.

Sunset Dinner Al Fresco

soup

Cold Minted Pea Soup *50*

salad

Grilled Salmon, Greens, and Balsamic Vinaigrette *105*

bread

Focaccia *163*

dessert

Lemon Snow Balls *357*

wine

Riesling

At left:
Grilled Salmon, Greens, and
Balsamic Vinaigrette
Focaccia

Salads

Salads are taking center stage as fabulous main courses these days, and this chapter is chock full of them, plus some new twists on old favorites.

At left:
Beet & Grapefruit Salad

Southwestern Caesar Salad

4-6 main dish servings
8–10 side dish servings

Chili Croutons:

⅓ cup unsalted butter, melted
1 teaspoon chili powder
¼ teaspoon cumin
¼ teaspoon salt
½ loaf French bread, cut into ½-inch cubes

Southwestern Caesar Dressing:

3 teaspoons minced garlic
2 shallots, peeled
4 anchovy fillets
2 fresh jalapeño peppers, cored and seeded
2 cups loosely packed, chopped cilantro
½ cup red wine vinegar
½ cup freshly grated Romano cheese
1 egg yolk
½ teaspoon freshly ground black pepper
1 teaspoon lemon juice
salt
1 cup olive oil

Salad:

1 teaspoon olive oil
2 cups (about 3 ears) fresh corn kernels or frozen corn kernels, thawed
3 romaine lettuce hearts or 2 large heads romaine lettuce, torn into bite size pieces and chilled
2 red bell peppers, roasted (page 381), peeled, seeded, and cut into thin strips
½ cup drained, chopped oil-packed sun-dried tomatoes
¼ cup freshly grated Romano cheese

Great buffet salad. Add grilled chicken breast strips for a main course salad.

Preheat oven to 350 degrees. In large bowl, combine melted butter, chili powder, cumin, and salt and stir to blend. Add bread cubes and toss to coat. Spread in single layer on baking pan. Bake 8-10 minutes, until crisp and golden brown, stirring occasionally. Remove from oven and set aside to cool.

In blender or food processor, combine garlic, shallots, anchovies, jalapeños, cilantro, vinegar, Romano, egg yolk, pepper, lemon juice, and salt to taste. Blend until smooth. With blender running, slowly add 1 cup olive oil and blend until smooth. Cover and chill.

In skillet, heat 1 teaspoon olive oil over medium heat. Add corn and cook 4 minutes. Remove with slotted spoon and set aside. In large bowl, combine lettuce and half of the dressing. Toss to coat. Add cooled croutons and toss. Arrange roasted bell pepper strips in spoke pattern around edge of bowl and sprinkle with reserved corn, sun-dried tomatoes, and Romano. Pass remaining dressing.

Beet and Grapefruit Salad

4-6 servings

- 4 fresh beets
- 8 teaspoons extra virgin olive oil, divided
- 2 tablespoons balsamic vinegar
- ½ bunch (about 1 cup) watercress, coarse stems removed
- ½ head Bibb lettuce, shredded
- 1-2 grapefruits, peeled, pith removed, and sectioned
- 2 ounces blue cheese, chilled and cut into thin triangular slices
- salt and freshly ground black pepper

A fascinating array of ingredients. Photo, page 78.

Cook beets in boiling water until tender, but not mushy, about 20 minutes. Remove from heat, drain, and cool. Peel and grate coarsely. In small bowl, combine grated beets, 4 teaspoons of the olive oil, and vinegar. Set aside.

In medium bowl, combine watercress and lettuce. Divide among individual serving plates. Spoon mound of beet mixture on 1 side of plate. Alternate grapefruit sections and blue cheese triangles in fan pattern around beets. Drizzle with remaining 4 teaspoons olive oil. Season with salt and pepper to taste.

Red Leaf Lettuce With Buttermilk Dressing

4-6 servings

- ½ teaspoon minced garlic
- ¼ teaspoon salt
- ½ cup buttermilk
- ¼ cup mayonnaise
- ½ teaspoon dry mustard
- ¼ teaspoon dried tarragon
- salt and freshly ground black pepper
- 1 large head red leaf lettuce, torn into bite size pieces
- 1 bunch arugula, coarse stems removed
- ½ small red onion, peeled and very thinly sliced

You may substitute watercress for arugula.

In small bowl combine garlic and salt to form a paste. Add buttermilk, mayonnaise, mustard, tarragon, and season with salt and pepper to taste. Whisk until smooth and set aside. In large bowl combine lettuce, arugula, red onion and half of the dressing. Toss to coat and pass remaining dressing.

Classic Greek Salad

6-8 servings

- ½ cup olive oil
- 5 tablespoons fresh lemon juice
- 2 teaspoons dried oregano leaves
- salt and freshly ground black pepper
- 8 cups torn romaine lettuce leaves
- 1 cup thinly sliced red onion
- 1½ cups (about 6 ounces) crumbled feta cheese
- 2 small zucchini, thinly sliced
- 16 cherry tomatoes, halved
- 16 kalamata olives

In small bowl, combine olive oil, lemon juice, and oregano. Season with salt and pepper to taste. (May be prepared up to 1 day in advance.) In large bowl combine lettuce, red onion, feta, zucchini, tomatoes, and olives. Toss with dressing and serve immediately.

Rocky Mountain Salad

6 servings

- ⅓ cup chopped onion
- 3 tablespoons cider vinegar
- 2 teaspoons spicy brown mustard
- ½ teaspoon sugar
- ½ teaspoon salt
- ¼ teaspoon freshly ground black pepper
- ¾ cup olive oil
- 2 heads romaine lettuce, torn into bite size pieces
- 1 14-ounce can water-packed artichoke hearts, drained and quartered
- 1 large avocado, peeled, seeded, and cut into bite size pieces
- ½ pound bacon, crisply cooked and crumbled
- 4 ounces freshly grated Parmesan cheese

This hearty salad is a great alternative to Caesar.

In food processor or blender, combine onion and vinegar. Process to puree onion and transfer to medium bowl. Whisk in mustard, sugar, salt, and pepper. Gradually add olive oil, whisking constantly. Whisk to thicken and set aside.

In large bowl, combine lettuce, artichoke hearts, avocado, bacon, and cheese. Add enough dressing to coat. Serve immediately.

Greens With Anise Vinaigrette and Crostini

4-6 servings

Anise Seed Vinaigrette:

1 shallot, peeled and quartered
2 garlic cloves, peeled and halved
1 teaspoon green peppercorns, packed in water or vinegar
½ teaspoon anise seed
2 tablespoons white wine vinegar
½ teaspoon salt
¼ teaspoon pepper
⅓ cup olive oil

Goat Cheese Crostini:

3 ounces soft mild goat cheese, at room temperature
1 tablespoon snipped fresh chives
salt and freshly ground black pepper
4-6 ¾-inch slices French or Italian bread
1 tablespoon freshly grated Parmesan cheese

Salad:

8 cups mixed baby greens

Garnish with yellow bell peppers for a colorful flair.

In blender or food processor, chop shallot, garlic, peppercorns, and anise seed. Add vinegar, salt, and pepper and blend well. With blender running, add olive oil in slow, steady stream and blend until emulsified or thickened. (May be prepared up to 1 week in advance. Cover and chill.) In small bowl combine goat cheese and chives and season with salt and pepper to taste. Stir until well blended. (May be prepared up to 2 days in advance. Cover and chill.)

Preheat oven to 350 degrees. Toast bread slices on baking sheet in middle of oven until golden, about 10 minutes. (May be prepared up to 2 days in advance. Cool and store in airtight container.)

Preheat broiler. Spread goat cheese mixture on toasts and sprinkle with Parmesan. Broil, 2 inches from the heat, until cheese is lightly browned, about 2 minutes. In large bowl, toss greens with vinaigrette. Make sure all leaves are well coated. Divide among individual serving plates and serve with Goat Cheese Crostini.

Citrus Salad With Pomegranate Seeds

6-8 servings

2 tablespoons fresh lemon juice
1 teaspoon Dijon mustard
7 tablespoons olive oil
1 fresh jalapeño pepper, cored, seeded, and minced
2 teaspoons chopped fresh rosemary or 1 teaspoon dried, crumbled
salt and freshly ground black pepper
4 navel oranges
2 pink grapefruit
1 medium head red leaf lettuce, leaves left whole
3 avocados, peeled, seeded, and sliced
¼ cup pine nuts, toasted (page 381)
¼ cup pomegranate seeds
1 small red onion, peeled, thinly sliced, and rings separated

A beautiful arranged salad. Dried cranberries may be substituted for pomegranate seeds.

In small bowl, combine lemon juice and mustard. Whisk in olive oil, jalapeño, and rosemary. Season with salt and pepper to taste. Cover and let stand at room temperature. Peel and remove pith from oranges and grapefruit. Slice oranges into rounds. Cut grapefruit in half lengthwise and slice crosswise into half rounds.

Line serving platter with lettuce leaves. Arrange orange slices in center, overlapping slightly. Arrange grapefruit slices around oranges. Arrange avocado slices around grapefruit. Sprinkle with pine nuts and pomegranate seeds and top with sliced red onion. Drizzle with reserved dressing.

Salad of Oranges and Onions

6-8 servings

6 large oranges, peeled, pith removed, and sliced crosswise
3 tablespoons red wine vinegar
6 tablespoons olive oil
1 teaspoon dried oregano
1 head Bibb lettuce, leaves left whole
1 medium red onion, peeled and very thinly sliced
1 cup oil-cured black olives
¼ cup snipped fresh chives
freshly ground black pepper

This unusual combination of ingredients is very refreshing.

Place oranges in shallow dish and sprinkle with vinegar, olive oil, and oregano. Toss gently, cover, and chill 30 minutes. Line individual serving plates with lettuce leaves. Arrange oranges on lettuce leaves. Top with sliced onion and olives. Drizzle remaining dressing over each salad. Sprinkle with chives and season with pepper to taste.

Fiesta Salad

8 servings

Avocado Dressing:

1 ripe avocado, peeled, seeded, and chopped
⅓ cup fresh orange juice
¼ cup fresh lime juice
1 tablespoon honey
½ teaspoon salt
⅛ teaspoon cayenne

Salad:

3 ripe avocados, peeled, seeded, and thinly sliced
2 tablespoons fresh lime juice
1 small head red leaf lettuce, leaves left whole
1 small jicama, peeled and coarsely shredded
3 seedless oranges, peeled and thinly sliced
¼ cup pitted whole ripe olives

The citrus flavor of this salad makes a good complement to spicy Mexican dishes.

In food processor or blender, combine chopped avocado, orange juice, ¼ cup lime juice, honey, salt, and cayenne. Process until smooth and set aside. Dip avocado slices in 2 tablespoons lime juice to prevent discoloration. Line serving platter with lettuce leaves. Mound shredded jícama in middle. Arrange avocado and orange slices around jícama, slightly overlapping, and top with olives. Drizzle half of the Avocado Dressing over salad and pass remaining dressing.

Greens With Pears, Asiago, and Cashews

4 servings

5 tablespoons olive oil
2 tablespoons balsamic vinegar
1 teaspoon honey
1 teaspoon Dijon mustard
1 tablespoon finely chopped green onions
salt and freshly ground black pepper
4 cups bitter greens including Belgian endive, radicchio, and green leaf lettuce
2 ripe pears, cored and thinly sliced
2 ounces Asiago cheese, shaved with vegetable peeler
2 ounces (½ cup) unsalted cashews, toasted (page 381)

In jar or cruet, combine olive oil, vinegar, honey, mustard, green onions, and salt and pepper to taste. Shake well and set aside. In large bowl, combine greens and about two-thirds of the dressing. Divide among individual serving plates. Arrange pear slices over greens in spiral pattern. Drizzle with additional dressing. Top with shaved Asiago slices and toasted cashews.

Autumn Salad

6 servings

2 tablespoons butter
3 ounces walnut halves
¼ cup seasoned rice vinegar
1 teaspoon honey
1 tablespoon Dijon mustard
1 medium head green leaf lettuce, torn into bite size pieces
1 medium head red leaf lettuce, torn into bite size pieces
1 red bell pepper, cored, seeded, and cut into strips
¾ cup peeled, julienned jícama
½ pound fresh purple figs, ends trimmed and quartered

Fresh figs are available in late summer and early fall. Figs should be firm.

In small skillet, melt butter over low heat. Add walnuts and toast gently, watching closely to prevent burning. Remove with slotted spoon and drain on paper towels. Cool to room temperature. In small bowl, combine vinegar, honey, and mustard. Whisk to blend and set aside. In large bowl, combine lettuce, bell pepper, jícama, and figs. Add dressing, toss to coat, and sprinkle with reserved walnuts.

Spinach and Kiwi Salad

6 servings

3 tablespoons safflower oil
2 tablespoons honey
¼ cup fresh lemon juice
1 medium clove garlic, peeled and quartered
½ teaspoon salt
¼ teaspoon freshly ground black pepper
3 cups torn spinach leaves
1 cup torn mustard greens
2 cups torn red leaf lettuce
2 small, ripe kiwi fruit, peeled and sliced
1 cup thinly sliced red onion

Vary this salad by adding goat cheese and dried cherries or cranberries.

Combine safflower oil, honey, lemon juice, garlic, salt, and pepper. Whisk until well blended and set aside. In large bowl combine spinach, mustard greens, and leaf lettuce. Remove garlic from dressing, pour over greens and toss. Garnish with kiwi and red onion.

Pears With Avocado and Lime

6 servings

1 tablespoon powdered sugar
2 tablespoons hot water
2 teaspoons finely grated lime zest
¼ cup fresh lime juice
3 firm ripe pears
3 ripe avocados
1 head red leaf lettuce, leaves left whole
¼ cup chopped fresh cilantro

Experiment with a variety of pears for a tantalizing first course.

Dissolve powdered sugar in hot water. Stir in lime zest and lime juice and set aside. Peel and slice pears and avocados, brushing each slice with lime juice mixture to prevent discoloration. Arrange lettuce leaves on individual serving plates. Alternate slices of pear and avocado over lettuce. Top with additional lime juice mixture and sprinkle with cilantro.

Strawberry Cucumber Salad

4 servings

2 tablespoons chopped fresh mint
1 teaspoon powdered sugar
2 tablespoons raspberry vinegar
4 tablespoons olive oil
½ English cucumber, thinly sliced
8 ounces ripe strawberries
freshly ground black pepper

In small bowl, combine mint and powdered sugar. Using wooden spoon, pound mint to draw out flavoring oils. Add vinegar and olive oil and whisk to blend. Add cucumber and marinate up to 2 hours. Just before serving, slice strawberries. Arrange on individual serving plates and season with pepper to taste. Add cucumber slices and spoon remaining dressing over each salad.

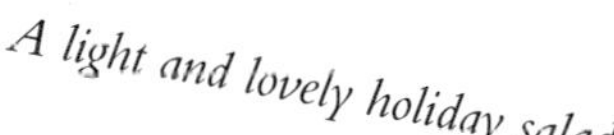

A light and lovely holiday salad.

Strawberry Salad With Cinnamon Vinaigrette

6-8 servings

- ⅓ cup olive oil
- ⅓ cup raspberry or currant vinegar
- 3 tablespoons sugar
- ½ teaspoon Tabasco
- ½ teaspoon salt
- ¼ teaspoon freshly ground black pepper
- ½ teaspoon ground cinnamon
- 2 heads romaine lettuce, torn into bite size pieces
- 1 11-ounce can mandarin oranges, drained
- 1 pint strawberries, stemmed and quartered
- 1 small red onion, peeled and thinly sliced
- ½ cup coarsely chopped pecans, toasted (page 381)
- 1 avocado, peeled, seeded, and sliced

In jar or cruet, combine olive oil, vinegar, sugar, Tabasco, salt, pepper, and cinnamon. Shake well and chill at least 2 hours. In large bowl, combine lettuce, oranges, strawberries, red onion, pecans, and avocado. Add half of the chilled dressing and toss to coat. Pass remaining dressing.

Cucina Bean Salad

4-6 main dish servings
8-10 side dish servings

- 1 15-ounce can Great Northern beans, rinsed and drained
- 1 15-ounce can black beans, rinsed and drained
- 1¼ cups peeled, chopped tomatoes
- ¾ cup diced red bell pepper
- ¾ cup diced yellow bell pepper
- ¾ cup thinly sliced green onions
- ½ cup purchased medium salsa
- ¼ cup red wine vinegar
- 2 tablespoons chopped fresh cilantro
- ¼ teaspoon salt
- ⅛ teaspoon freshly ground black pepper
- 1 large head romaine lettuce, finely shredded

Great vegetarian salad or accompaniment to grilled meats and fish.

In large bowl, combine Great Northern beans, black beans, and tomatoes, stirring gently. Add bell peppers and green onions. Stir gently to combine.

In small bowl, combine salsa, vinegar, cilantro, salt, and pepper. Whisk to blend. Pour over bean mixture and toss gently. (May be prepared to this point up to 2 days in advance.) Line large shallow bowl with shredded lettuce and top with bean mixture.

Tempting Tomato Salad

4-6 servings

1	pound ripe tomatoes, sliced or 1 pound cherry tomatoes, quartered
1	small red onion, peeled and sliced
3	tablespoons olive oil
3	tablespoons sherry vinegar or balsamic vinegar
½	teaspoon salt
1	teaspoon freshly ground black pepper
4	ounces blue cheese, crumbled
	Garlic Croutons:
½	cup olive oil
1	teaspoon minced garlic
½	teaspoon salt
1	loaf French bread, sliced 1-inch thick

A hearty side salad for your favorite grilled meats.

About thirty minutes before serving, combine tomatoes and red onion in large bowl. In small bowl, combine 3 tablespoons olive oil, vinegar, ½ teaspoon salt, and pepper. Whisk to blend, pour over tomato mixture, and toss gently.

Preheat grill to medium or preheat broiler. In small bowl, combine ½ cup olive oil, garlic, and salt. Brush on 1 side of bread slices. Grill, brushed side down, or broil, brushed side up, until lightly browned, 2–4 minutes. Turn and cook until lightly browned. Break or cut into pieces. Just before serving, add blue cheese and Garlic Croutons to tomato mixture and toss.

Green Beans, Feta, and Pecans

4-6 servings

1½	pounds fresh green beans, trimmed and cut into 1-inch pieces
⅔	cup olive oil
1	teaspoon dried dill weed
⅓	cup white wine vinegar
½	teaspoon minced garlic
¼	teaspoon salt
¼	teaspoon freshly ground black pepper
1	cup coarsely chopped pecans, toasted (page 381)
½	cup diced red onion
1	cup crumbled feta cheese

Cook green beans in large saucepan of boiling water, about 4 minutes. Drain, immerse in cold water, drain, and pat dry. In small bowl, combine olive oil, dill, vinegar, garlic, salt, and pepper. Whisk to blend. Place beans in shallow serving bowl. Sprinkle with pecans, red onion, and feta. Just before serving, top with dressing and toss.

Blue Cheese Potato Salad

6 servings

- 2½ pounds unpeeled red potatoes
- ¼ cup dry white wine or dry champagne
- salt and freshly ground black pepper
- ½ cup mayonnaise
- ½ cup sour cream
- 1½ tablespoons Dijon mustard
- 1½ tablespoons cider vinegar
- 4 ounces blue cheese, crumbled
- 3 green onions, finely chopped
- 1 cup coarsely chopped celery

A flavorful new twist to all-American potato salad.

Boil potatoes until just tender when pierced with fork. Do not overcook. Drain and cool to room temperature. Cut into bite size pieces and place in large bowl. Add wine and season with salt and pepper to taste. Let stand until wine is absorbed. In small bowl, combine mayonnaise, sour cream, mustard, vinegar, blue cheese, green onions, and celery. Add to potatoes and stir well. Let stand at room temperature 30 minutes before serving.

Roasted Red Pepper Salad

6 servings

- 4 large red bell peppers or 2 red and 2 yellow bell peppers, roasted (page 381), peeled, seeded, and cut into thin strips
- 2 tablespoons fresh basil leaves, rolled and thinly sliced
- 2 tablespoons balsamic vinegar
- ¼ cup olive oil
- salt and freshly ground black pepper

Balsamic vinegar is a must for this dish.

In large bowl combine roasted peppers and sliced basil leaves. Place vinegar in small bowl and whisk in olive oil. Season with salt and pepper to taste. Pour over roasted pepper mixture. Let marinate in refrigerator 3-6 hours. Serve cold or at room temperature.

Farfalle, Brie, and Tomatoes

12-16 servings

- 4 large ripe tomatoes, seeded and diced
- 1 pound Brie cheese, rind removed and cut into 1-inch cubes
- 1 cup loosely packed, chopped fresh basil leaves
- 1 teaspoon minced garlic
- ⅔ cup extra virgin olive oil
- 1 teaspoon salt
- ½ teaspoon freshly ground black pepper
- 1 pound bow tie pasta, cooked al dente, rinsed in cold water, and drained

Prepare in the morning for an afternoon picnic.

In large bowl, combine tomatoes, Brie, basil, garlic, olive oil, salt, and pepper. Cover and let stand, at room temperature, up to 4 hours. Add cooked pasta and toss. Serve immediately or at room temperature.

Spicy Thai Shrimp and Pasta

4-6 main dish servings
8 side dish servings

- ¾ cup rice vinegar
- 2 tablespoons purchased chili sesame oil
- 2 tablespoons soy sauce
- 2 tablespoons peeled, grated fresh ginger root
- 1 tablespoon Dijon mustard
- salt and freshly ground black pepper
- 12 ounces angel hair pasta, cooked al dente, rinsed in cold water, and drained
- 1 pound medium to large shrimp, cooked, peeled, and deveined
- 2 6-ounce jars marinated artichoke hearts, drained and halved
- 1 cup chopped green onions
- ¼ cup chopped fresh cilantro
- ¼ cup chopped fresh mint
- 1 yellow bell pepper, cored, seeded, and julienned

To make your own chili sesame oil, combine sesame oil with ¼ teaspoon crushed red pepper.

In blender or food processor, combine vinegar, chili sesame oil, soy sauce, ginger, and mustard. Process until well blended. Season with salt and pepper to taste. Cover and chill. In large bowl, combine pasta, shrimp, artichoke hearts, green onions, cilantro, and mint. Toss with enough dressing to coat. Arrange bell peppers on top in decorative pattern. Pass remaining dressing.

Penne With Grilled Tomato Vinaigrette

4-6 main dish servings
8 side dish servings

Grilled Tomato Vinaigrette:

2 medium tomatoes, peeled, halved, and seeded
2 teaspoons minced garlic
⅓ cup red wine vinegar
2 tablespoons lemon juice
1 teaspoon salt
1 teaspoon freshly ground black pepper
½ cup vegetable oil

Salad:

8 ounces penne pasta, cooked al dente, rinsed in cold water, and drained
5 tablespoons finely chopped green onions
1 medium red bell pepper, cored, seeded, and chopped
18 fresh snow peas, trimmed and halved
½ cup halved black olives or oil-cured olives
1 14-ounce can water-packed artichoke hearts, drained and chopped
¼ cup chopped red onion
1 boneless, skinless chicken breast half (about 4 ounces), grilled and sliced (optional)

This vinaigrette is wonderful on any green salad.

Preheat grill to medium-high. Grill tomato halves until soft and slightly charred. Remove from grill and chill. (Tomatoes may also be cooked in a very hot cast iron skillet.) In food processor or blender, combine tomatoes, garlic, vinegar, lemon juice, salt, and pepper. Process until smooth. With processor running, slowly add oil and process until well blended. Set aside.

In large bowl, combine pasta, green onions, bell pepper, snow peas, olives, artichoke hearts, red onion, and chicken, if desired. Add half of the dressing and toss to coat. Add additional dressing if needed.

Roasted Duck, Green Beans, and Cranberries

6 servings

- 4-6 duck breasts, thawed if frozen
- ½ cup olive oil
- ½ cup raspberry vinegar
- ½ teaspoon salt
- 1 tablespoon sour cream
- freshly ground black pepper
- 2 cups orange juice
- ½ cup sugar
- ½ pound (about 2 cups) fresh cranberries
- 1½ pounds fresh green beans, trimmed
- 1 cup pecan halves, toasted (page 381)
- 5 oranges, peeled, sliced, and halved
- 3 green onions, sliced diagonally into ¾-inch pieces

You may substitute chicken or turkey, but the duck version is out of this world.

Roast, grill, or broil duck breasts to desired degree of doneness. Slice into thin strips and set aside. In jar or cruet, combine olive oil, vinegar, salt, sour cream, and pepper to taste. Shake well and set aside.

In large saucepan, combine orange juice, sugar, and cranberries over medium heat. Heat to boiling, skimming any foam that forms. When berries begin to burst, remove from heat and cool thoroughly. Drain and reserve berries.

In large saucepan, blanch green beans, about 4 minutes, in boiling salted water. Drain, immerse in cold water, and drain. Divide duck strips and green beans equally among individual serving plates, in spoke pattern. Combine cranberries, pecans, and oranges. Mound equally in center of plates. Drizzle with dressing to taste and sprinkle with green onions. Serve immediately.

Chicken, Wild Rice, and Tarragon

4-6 servings

- 1¾ cups chicken broth
- ½ cup uncooked wild rice
- 2 cups cubed cooked chicken or turkey
- ¾ cup diced celery
- ¾ cup diced crisp red apple
- 1 green onion, thinly sliced
- 2 tablespoons minced fresh tarragon or 2 teaspoons dried tarragon, crumbled
- 2½ tablespoons olive oil
- 1½ tablespoons tarragon vinegar
- 1 teaspoon Dijon mustard
- ¼ teaspoon sugar
- salt and freshly ground black pepper

Garnish:

thinly sliced red apple

Leftover turkey works well in this recipe.

In small saucepan, combine chicken broth and wild rice. Heat to boiling. Cover, reduce heat to medium-low, and simmer until rice is tender and liquid is absorbed, about 50 minutes. Transfer to medium bowl. Cover and chill. Combine chilled wild rice, chicken, celery, apple, green onion, and tarragon. In small bowl, whisk olive oil, vinegar, mustard, and sugar. Pour over wild rice mixture and toss well. Season with salt and pepper to taste and chill. (May be prepared 1 day in advance.) Garnish with thinly sliced red apples.

Mediterranean Potato Salad With Chicken

6 servings

- 1 clove garlic, peeled
- 1 anchovy fillet, rinsed and patted dry
- ½ teaspoon salt
- 1 tablespoon chopped fresh parsley
- ⅓ cup plain yogurt
- ¼ cup mayonnaise
- 12 pitted green olives, finely chopped
- 1 teaspoon drained capers
- 1 tablespoon balsamic vinegar
- 2 teaspoons Dijon mustard
- ½ teaspoon freshly ground black pepper
- 1 pound small red potatoes, boiled and sliced
- 2 cups coarsely chopped cooked chicken
- ½ cup niçoise or kalamata olives
- 1½ cups halved cherry tomatoes

Using large flat knife blade, mash garlic, anchovy, and salt to form a paste. Transfer to small bowl and whisk in parsley, yogurt, mayonnaise, green olives, capers, vinegar, mustard, and pepper. In large bowl, combine potatoes, chicken, and dressing and toss gently. Let stand 20 minutes. Just before serving, top with niçoise olives and tomatoes.

Chicken on Greens With Chile Buttermilk Dressing

4 servings

Chile Buttermilk Dressing:

- 2 green onions, finely chopped
- ⅔ cup buttermilk
- ¼ cup drained chopped green chiles
- ¼ teaspoon salt

Salad:

- ¼ cup yellow cornmeal
- ¼ cup flour
- 1 teaspoon ground cumin
- ¾ teaspoon salt
- ¾ teaspoon freshly ground black pepper
- 1 egg
- ¼ cup milk
- 4 boneless, skinless chicken breast halves (about 1 pound), pounded to ½-inch thickness
- 3 tablespoons vegetable oil
- 6 cups torn mixed salad greens
- 1 large red bell pepper, cored, seeded, and thinly sliced

Serve with fresh fruit and tortilla chips to make an easy weekday dinner.

In small bowl combine green onions, buttermilk, green chiles, and salt. Chill. On waxed paper, combine cornmeal, flour, cumin, salt, and pepper. In shallow dish, beat egg and milk. Coat chicken in cornmeal mixture, then dip in egg mixture, allowing excess to drip off. Coat again in cornmeal mixture and set aside.

In large skillet, heat oil over medium-high heat. Add chicken and cook 6–8 minutes or until lightly browned and cooked thoroughly, turning once. Remove and place on paper towels to drain. (May be prepared to this point up to 1 hour in advance. Cover chicken and keep warm.)

Divide mixed greens and sliced red pepper among individual serving plates. Cut chicken crosswise into strips and place on top of greens. Serve with Chile Buttermilk Dressing.

Bistro Chicken Salad

6-8 servings

- 1 cup chicken broth
- 5 whole cloves
- 1½ pounds boneless, skinless chicken breasts
- ½ pound fresh green beans, trimmed and cut diagonally into 1-inch pieces
- 4 small red new potatoes, cut into ¼-inch slices
- 2 tablespoons olive oil
- 1½ teaspoons salt
- 1 teaspoon freshly ground black pepper
- 4 teaspoons fresh lemon juice
- 2 teaspoons Dijon mustard
- ½ teaspoon dried oregano leaves, crumbled
- 1 pint cherry tomatoes, halved
- ½ cup pitted and chopped Greek olives
- 1 large head romaine lettuce, torn into bite size pieces

For an elegant version of this salad, use Haricot Verts (thin French beans), trimmed and boiled 3 minutes. Serve with a Sauvignon Blanc

In medium saucepan, heat chicken broth and cloves to boiling. Add chicken, reduce heat to low, and simmer 10-15 minutes. Remove from heat, drain, and set aside to cool. Cut into bite site pieces.

Place 2 inches water in saucepan, add green beans and heat to boiling. Reduce heat to low and simmer 7 minutes. Remove with slotted spoon to colander, reserving water, and rinse with cold water. In same saucepan, heat potatoes to boiling and cook 2-3 minutes. Remove to colander and rinse with cold water.

In medium bowl, combine olive oil, salt, pepper, lemon juice, mustard, and oregano. Whisk to blend and set aside. Combine reserved chicken, green beans, potatoes, cherry tomatoes, olives, and lettuce. Toss with dressing to coat.

Grilled Pork and Mango Salad

6 servings

Ginger Jalapeño Vinaigrette:

- ¾ cup extra virgin olive oil
- ¼ cup rice wine vinegar
- 1 tablespoon soy sauce
- 1 1-inch piece ginger root, peeled and minced
- 2 jalapeño peppers, cored, seeded, and thinly sliced
- salt and freshly ground black pepper

Salad:

- 1 1½-pound whole pork tenderloin
- ¼ cup olive oil
- salt and freshly ground black pepper
- 6 cups mixed greens, torn into bite size pieces
- 10 radishes, thinly sliced
- 1 English cucumber, thinly sliced
- 1 cup snow peas
- 1 small red onion, thinly sliced
- 2 mangos, peeled and sliced, or chopped
- ½ cup unsalted peanuts, toasted (page 381) and chopped

Papaya or plums may be substituted for mangos.

In small jar or cruet, combine ¾ cup olive oil, vinegar, soy sauce, ginger, and jalapeños and shake well. Season with salt and pepper to taste and chill.

Preheat grill to medium-high. Brush pork tenderloin with ¼ cup olive oil. Season with salt and pepper to taste. Sear 2 minutes per side. Reduce temperature to medium, and grill 10 minutes per side, turning once. Remove to platter, let stand 10 minutes, and slice thinly.

In large bowl, combine greens, radishes, cucumber, snow peas, and red onion. Whisk dressing vigorously and lightly coat greens with half of the vinaigrette. Divide among individual serving plates, distributing jalapeños and ginger evenly. Arrange pork slices and mango on top and sprinkle with peanuts. Pass remaining vinaigrette.

Greens With Prosciutto and Warm Balsamic Vinaigrette

6-8 servings

- 3 cups mixed greens (including romaine, red leaf, and curly endive), torn into bite size pieces
- 1 small head radicchio, torn into bite size pieces
- 1 cup lightly packed, fresh basil leaves
- 1 cup lightly packed, fresh flat Italian parsley leaves
- ½ cup (2 ounces) pine nuts, toasted, (page 381) divided
- 4 green onions, thinly sliced diagonally, divided
- 3 ounces Parmigiano-Reggiano cheese, grated, divided
- 3 ounces thinly sliced Prosciutto, cut into bite size squares, divided

Warm Balsamic Vinaigrette:

- ⅔ cup extra virgin olive oil
- 8 large garlic cloves, cut into ¼-inch pieces
- ¼ cup balsamic vinegar
- 3 tablespoons red wine vinegar
- 1 tablespoon packed dark brown sugar
- ¼ teaspoon salt
- ⅛ teaspoon freshly ground black pepper

Fresh, high quality ingredients make this Northern Italian salad sensational.

In large bowl, combine greens, radicchio, basil, and parsley. Add all but 3 tablespoons of the pine nuts, most of the green onions, half of the cheese, and half of the prosciutto. Toss to blend and arrange on large platter.

In medium skillet, heat olive oil over very low heat. Add garlic and cook 8 minutes or until barely browned. Remove with slotted spoon and discard, reserving oil in skillet. Add balsamic and red wine vinegar. Increase heat to medium and cook about 5 minutes. Carefully add brown sugar, mixture will splatter. Cook 1 minute. Taste for sweet-tart balance. Stir in additional brown sugar or balsamic vinegar, if desired. If dressing tastes too sharp, simmer several minutes longer. Season with salt and pepper and remove from heat.

Scatter remaining pine nuts, green onions, cheese, and prosciutto over salad. Reheat vinaigrette, if necessary, whisking vigorously to blend, and spoon half over salad. Serve immediately and pass remaining vinaigrette.

Grilled Sirloin Salad

4 servings

½ cup soy sauce
6 tablespoons sugar
1 tablespoon peeled, finely grated ginger root
1 tablespoon minced garlic
1 pound New York steak, at least 1 inch thick
8 cups mixed greens including escarole, radicchio, Boston, and red leaf lettuce
¼ English cucumber, julienned
1 cup thinly sliced red onion

Jalapeño Dressing:

¼ cup soy sauce
2 tablespoons fresh lemon juice
2 teaspoons minced jalapeño pepper
2 tablespoons peanut oil
2 tablespoons olive oil

Garnish:

1 teaspoon black sesame seeds
12 fresh cilantro sprigs

In shallow dish, combine ½ cup soy sauce, sugar, ginger, and garlic. Stir to dissolve sugar. Add steak, turn to coat, cover, and marinate in refrigerator, 2 hours. Turn occasionally.

Preheat grill to high. In large bowl, combine greens, cucumber, and red onion. In small bowl, combine ¼ cup soy sauce, lemon juice, and jalapeño. Gradually whisk in peanut oil and olive oil. Grill steak about 3 minutes per side for rare or to desired degree of doneness. Remove from grill and slice thinly across grain.

Toss greens with dressing and divide among individual salad plates. Arrange one quarter of the steak on each plate of greens. Sprinkle with sesame seeds and garnish with cilantro sprigs.

Lobster and Wild Rice Salad

4 luncheon servings
8 first course servings

1	cup raw wild rice, rinsed, soaked in water 30 minutes, and drained
4	cups water
½	teaspoon salt
2	small whole lobsters or 3 lobster tails
1	cup plain yogurt
4	tablespoons honey
¼	cup fresh lime juice
1	large mango, peeled, seeded, and diced
2	green onions, sliced
¼	cup olive oil
¼	cup fresh lemon juice
	salt and freshly ground black pepper
6	cups mixed greens (mild greens, arugula, and radicchio), torn into bite size pieces
¼	cup coarsely chopped macadamia nuts

A unique special occasion entree which goes well with Brut Champagne.

In large saucepan, combine drained wild rice, 4 cups water, and ½ teaspoon salt. Heat to boiling. Cover, reduce heat, and simmer until tender and slightly curled, 30-40 minutes. Transfer to colander and drain.

If using live lobsters, heat 2 or more gallons salted water to boiling. Drop lobsters into rapidly boiling water and cook 8-12 minutes, depending on size. Lobsters are done when tail is curled under body and feels firm. Remove from pan, immerse in ice water to cool, and drain.

If using lobster tails, slit tail lengthwise and remove meat from the shell. Place on top of shell. Preheat broiler and broil until tail meat is firm, 12-15 minutes. Do not overcook.

In small bowl, combine yogurt, honey, and lime juice. Whisk until honey dissolves. Taste and add more honey or lime, if desired. Carefully remove meat from lobsters, keeping pieces as intact as possible. Slice tail meat and set aside.

In large bowl, combine cooked wild rice, mango, green onions, olive oil, and lemon juice. Season with salt and pepper to taste. (May be prepared to this point up to 24 hours in advance. Wrap lobster in plastic wrap and chill. Cover rice mixture and chill. Taste and adjust seasonings before proceeding.)

In large bowl, combine greens with about half of the yogurt dressing. Toss to coat and arrange on individual serving plates. Top with mound of wild rice mixture and lobster meat. Drizzle additional dressing on top, if desired, or serve dressing on side. Garnish with chopped macadamia nuts.

Beautiful tossed or arranged, this salad can be made with any firm fish such as swordfish or tuna. Season 1 pound boneless fillets or medallions and sauté, bake, or broil. Chill and arrange on greens.

Clockwise from top: Lobster and Wild Rice Salad, 101 Elegant Niçoise, 102

Elegant Niçoise

6-8 servings

Red Wine Vinaigrette:

½ tablespoon Dijon mustard
¼ cup red wine vinegar
1 teaspoon sugar
½ teaspoon salt
½ teaspoon freshly ground black pepper
1 tablespoon minced fresh parsley
½ cup olive oil

Salad:

6 small tuna steaks
1 pound small new potatoes
2 pounds fresh green beans, trimmed
8 Italian plum tomatoes, quartered
1 small red onion, peeled and thinly sliced
½ cup niçoise olives or oil-cured olives
¼ cup chopped fresh parsley
½ teaspoon salt
1 teaspoon freshly ground black pepper
1 head green leaf or romaine lettuce, leaves left whole
6 hard boiled eggs, peeled and quartered
1 2-ounce can anchovy fillets, drained

Compliment this elegant main dish salad with French bread and a Pinot Blanc. Photo, page 100.

In small bowl, combine mustard, vinegar, sugar, ½ teaspoon salt, ½ teaspoon pepper, and 1 tablespoon parsley. Whisk in oil. Place half in shallow dish, reserving rest for later. Add tuna steaks and marinate, in refrigerator, 2-4 hours. Boil potatoes in salted water, 10-15 minutes. Skins should pierce with tip of sharp knife. Drain, quarter, and transfer to large bowl.

Cook green beans in boiling salted water 5-7 minutes, until just tender. Add to potatoes and toss to combine. Add tomatoes, red onion, olives, ¼ cup parsley, ½ teaspoon salt, and 1 teaspoon pepper. Pour ½ cup of the vinaigrette over potato mixture and mix gently.

Preheat grill to medium-high or preheat broiler. Remove tuna steaks from marinade and grill or broil tuna, about 10 minutes per inch of thickness, turning once. (May be prepared to this point up to 8 hours in advance. Cover and chill all ingredients.)

Line serving platter with lettuce leaves and top with potato mixture. Overlap cooked tuna steaks on top of potato mixture. Place hard boiled eggs around edge of platter. Arrange anchovy fillets in lattice pattern on top of tuna and drizzle with remaining vinaigrette.

Grilled Scallops With Shiitake Mushroom Dressing

4 servings

Shiitake Mushroom Dressing:

- ½ cup balsamic vinegar
- ½ cup extra virgin olive oil
- ¼ cup Dijon mustard
- salt and freshly ground black pepper
- ¼ pound fresh shiitake mushrooms, thinly sliced

Salad:

- 1 pound sea scallops
- 12 ounces mixed greens, including arugula, radicchio, dandelion greens, romaine, and endive
- 1 red bell pepper, cored, seeded, and thinly sliced
- 1 3½-ounce log goat cheese, such as Montrachet style, crumbled
- ¼ cup pine nuts, toasted (page 381)

Garnish

fresh nasturtiums

A very dramatic main dish presentation.

Preheat grill to medium-high. In small saucepan, combine vinegar, olive oil, mustard, and salt and pepper to taste. Whisk to blend. Add mushrooms and simmer gently until mushrooms are tender, about 10 minutes. Remove from heat and cover with foil to keep warm. Place scallops on skewers, brush lightly with warm dressing and grill until just opaque, 4-6 minutes, turning once. Remove, cool slightly, and remove from skewers.

Line large platter with greens. Arrange bell pepper slices around edge. Sprinkle with goat cheese. Arrange warm scallops in center and drizzle with dressing. Sprinkle with pine nuts and garnish with nasturtiums. Serve immediately.

Garlic Shrimp, Tropical Fruit, and Baby Lettuce

4-6 main dish servings

- ⅓ cup champagne vinegar
- 1½ cups extra virgin olive oil, divided
- salt and freshly ground black pepper
- 1½ pounds large shrimp, peeled and deveined
- 1-2 tablespoons crushed garlic
- 1½ teaspoons coarse salt
- 6 cups assorted baby lettuces
- 1 very ripe papaya, peeled, seeded, and cubed
- 1 very ripe mango, peeled, seeded and cubed
- 1 kiwi, peeled and cubed

Garnish

fresh pansies or other edible flowers

A beautiful summer salad, especially nice with a Rhine Riesling. This salad is featured on our cover.

In small bowl, combine vinegar and ¾ cup olive oil. Season with salt and pepper to taste and set aside. Place shrimp in glass dish. Add remaining ¾ cup olive oil and garlic, and marinate at room temperature, about 45 minutes. Remove from marinade and thread on skewers.

Preheat grill to medium. Sprinkle shrimp with coarse salt. Grill 3-5 minutes, until pink and opaque. Remove to platter, cool slightly, and remove shrimp from skewers. In large bowl, combine lettuce, grilled shrimp, papaya, mango, and kiwi. Add half of the dressing and toss to coat. Garnish with pansies and pass remaining dressing.

Shrimp With Capers

6-8 servings

- 1½ pounds medium to large shrimp, cooked, peeled, and deveined
- ⅔ cup finely chopped fresh parsley
- 3 tablespoons chopped green onions
- 1 tomato, peeled and chopped
- 2 tablespoons drained capers
- 1 teaspoon dried basil
- ½ teaspoon salt
- ½ teaspoon sugar
- 1 cup mayonnaise
- freshly ground black pepper

Garnish:

fresh parsley sprigs

In large bowl, combine shrimp, parsley, green onions, tomato, capers, basil, salt, sugar, mayonnaise, and pepper to taste. Stir gently to blend. Taste and add additional salt and pepper, if desired. Chill at least 3 hours or up to 24 hours. Garnish with sprigs of parsley. Serve on lettuce lined plates, or in an avocado half or hollowed tomato.

Grilled Salmon, Greens, and Balsamic Vinaigrette

4 main dish servings

Balsamic Vinaigrette:

- ⅔ cup olive oil
- ½ cup balsamic vinegar
- 2 tablespoons Dijon mustard
- ½ teaspoon dried thyme
- salt and freshly ground black pepper

Salad:

- 4-6 cups mixed greens including Bibb, leaf, arugula, and endive, torn into bite size pieces
- 4 ounces feta cheese, crumbled
- ¾ cup pecan halves, toasted (page 381)
- 1½ cups ripe papaya or mango, peeled, seeded, and cut into bite size pieces
- 3 small Italian plum tomatoes, quartered
- 1 avocado, peeled, seeded, and thinly sliced
- 1 8-ounce salmon fillet

A show stopper that's easy to prepare. Photo, page 76.

Preheat grill to medium-high. In small bowl, combine olive oil, vinegar, mustard, thyme, and salt and pepper to taste. Whisk to blend and set aside. In large shallow bowl, combine greens, feta, pecans, papaya or mango, and half of the Balsamic Vinaigrette. Toss to combine. Alternate quartered tomatoes and sliced avocado around edge of bowl in spoke pattern and set aside.

Grill salmon, skin side down, until just opaque, about 10 minutes per inch of thickness. Remove to platter, remove skin, and place in center of salad. Spoon additional vinaigrette over salmon and pass remaining vinaigrette. Serve immediately.

Fresh Citrus Dressing

1½ cups

- ⅔ cup olive oil
- 3 tablespoons fresh lime juice
- ⅓ cup freshly grated Parmesan cheese
- 2 tablespoons finely chopped green onions
- 1 teaspoon salt
- ½ teaspoon minced garlic
- ¼ teaspoon freshly ground black pepper
- ½ teaspoon Worcestershire
- dash Tabasco

In jar or cruet, combine olive oil, lime juice, Parmesan, green onions, salt, garlic, pepper, Worcestershire, and Tabasco. Shake well and chill. Shake well before serving.

Brown Sugar Vinaigrette

1 cup

- ⅔ cup safflower oil
- ⅓ cup red wine vinegar
- 1 tablespoon packed brown sugar
- 1 teaspoon Dijon mustard
- ½ teaspoon minced garlic
- salt and freshly ground black pepper

A versatile vinaigrette.

In jar or cruet, combine safflower oil, vinegar, brown sugar, mustard, garlic, and salt and pepper to taste. Shake well and chill. Shake well before serving.

Curry Vinaigrette

1½ cups

- ¾ cup olive oil
- ⅓ cup red wine vinegar
- 1 tablespoon water
- 2 tablespoons balsamic vinegar
- 1 tablespoon soy sauce
- ½ teaspoon minced garlic
- 1 teaspoon curry powder
- 2 tablespoons chopped fresh chives
- ¼ teaspoon salt
- ½ teaspoon freshly ground black pepper

Excellent with mixed greens or spinach.

In jar or cruet, combine olive oil, red wine vinegar, water, balsamic vinegar, soy sauce, garlic, curry powder, chives, salt, and pepper. Shake well and chill up to 2 weeks. Shake well before serving.

Ginger Fruit Dressing

1 cup

- 4 ounces cream cheese, softened
- ½ cup sour cream
- 3 tablespoons milk
- 1 tablespoon sugar
- 1 teaspoon freshly grated lemon zest
- 2 tablespoons coarsely chopped crystallized ginger

This wonderful ginger flavor intensifies with time.

With electric mixer, combine cream cheese, sour cream, milk, sugar, lemon zest, and crystallized ginger. Blend thoroughly. Chill up to 3 days. Serve with cantaloupe, honeydew, strawberries, papaya, and raspberries.

Lime Mint Dressing

1 cup

- ¼ cup fresh lime juice
- 2 tablespoons sour cream
- 2 teaspoons sugar
- ½ cup fresh mint leaves
- ¼ cup vegetable oil
- salt

In blender or food processor, combine lime juice, sour cream, sugar, and mint. Pulse to blend. With blender running, add oil slowly and blend until thickened. Season with salt to taste. Transfer to bowl and chill. Serve with sliced nectarines, peaches, and cantaloupe.

Pineapple Fruit Dressing

2 cups

- ½ cup whipping cream
- ½ cup sugar
- ¼ teaspoon salt
- 2 tablespoons cornstarch
- 1 egg, well beaten
- 1 cup pineapple juice
- 1 tablespoon fresh lemon juice
- 2 tablespoons butter

Garnish:

fresh mint leaves

This is also delicious as a light summer dessert.

Whip cream to soft peaks and set aside. Sift sugar, salt, and cornstarch into saucepan. Add beaten egg, pineapple juice, and lemon juice and stir well. Cook over low to medium heat until thick, stirring constantly. If sauce begins to separate, whisk vigorously. Remove from heat and add butter. Let cool to room temperature and fold in whipped cream. Chill. (May be prepared 1 day in advance.) Serve with an assortment of fruits including peaches, strawberries, mixed berries, grapes, and melon. Garnish with mint leaves.

Nestled on our beautiful Western Slope is one of Colorado's most incredible secrets. Rolling orchards burst with some of the most fabulous fruit in the country. The bounty from this land is the perfect complement to a Sunday brunch in your own blooming garden.

Brunch in Bloom

brunch

Clockwise from top left:
Classic Colorado Quiche
Raspberry Poached Pears
Cream Cheese Crepes
With Apricot Sauce

Brunch

No bacon and eggs here! The brunch chapter is full of surprises, from make-ahead stratas to elegant buffet dishes and wonderful new waffle variations.

Clockwise from top left:
Cinnamon Twists
Strawberries With Lemon Cream
Lemon Waffles With Blackberries

Blueberry Stuffed French Toast

8-10 servings

- 12 slices French bread, cut into 1-inch cubes
- 2 8-ounce packages cream cheese, chilled and cut into 1-inch cubes
- 1 cup fresh blueberries, rinsed and drained
- 12 large eggs
- ⅓ cup maple syrup
- 2 cups milk

Blueberry Syrup:

- 1 cup sugar
- 2 tablespoons cornstarch
- 1 cup water
- 1 cup fresh blueberries, rinsed and drained
- 1 tablespoon unsalted butter

Grease 13x9-inch baking pan. Place half of the bread cubes evenly in prepared pan. Scatter cream cheese cubes over bread and sprinkle with 1 cup blueberries. Arrange remaining bread cubes over blueberries. In large bowl combine eggs, syrup, and milk and whisk to blend. Pour evenly over reserved bread mixture. Cover with foil and chill overnight.

Preheat oven to 350 degrees. Bake, covered with foil, in middle of oven 30 minutes. Remove foil and continue baking 30 minutes, or until puffed and golden brown.

In small saucepan combine sugar, cornstarch, and water over medium-high heat. Cook, stirring occasionally, 5 minutes or until thickened. Stir in 1 cup blueberries and simmer, stirring occasionally, 10 minutes, or until most berries burst. Add butter and stir until melted. (May be prepared up to 1 day in advance. Chill and reheat gently.) Transfer to serving bowl. Place French Toast on individual serving plates and top with Blueberry Syrup.

Honey Brunch Mimosas

6 servings

- 1 6-ounce can frozen lemonade concentrate
- ¼ cup Grand Marnier or other orange-flavored liqueur
- ¼ cup honey, warmed
- 1 bottle (750 milliliters) dry champagne, chilled

Garnish:

fresh strawberries

A delightful eye-opener!

In large pitcher, combine lemonade concentrate and Grand Marnier. Add warmed honey and stir until dissolved. Just before serving, stir in champagne. Pour into individual champagne glasses and garnish with strawberries, if desired.

Apple Breakfast Tart

6-8 servings

Crust:

- 1¼ cups flour
- ⅓ cup sugar
- ¼ teaspoon nutmeg
- ½ teaspoon baking powder
- ½ teaspoon salt
- ½ cup (1 stick) unsalted butter, chilled
- 1 egg
- 1 tablespoon milk

Filling:

- 1 8-ounce package cream cheese, softened
- ¼ cup sugar
- 2 egg yolks
- ½ teaspoon pure vanilla extract

Topping:

- 2 large McIntosh apples, peeled, cored, and thinly sliced
- ⅓ cup sugar
- ½ teaspoon cornstarch
- ½ teaspoon ground cinnamon

Equally wonderful for breakfast or dessert.

Preheat oven to 350 degrees. Grease 10-inch tart pan or pie pan. In large bowl or food processor, combine flour, ⅓ cup sugar, nutmeg, baking powder, and salt. Cut butter into flour mixture until crumbly. In small bowl, beat egg and milk and add to flour mixture. Blend until dough forms a ball. Pat dough into prepared pan.

With electric mixer or in food processor, blend cream cheese and ¼ cup sugar. With mixer running, add egg yolks and vanilla and blend until smooth. Spread evenly over crust. Layer apples over cream cheese mixture, in circular pattern, slightly overlapping slices. In small bowl, combine remaining ⅓ cup sugar, cornstarch, and cinnamon and sprinkle over apples.

Bake 30 minutes, reduce oven temperature to 300 degrees and continue baking 10 minutes or until golden brown.

Peach Bellinis

4-6 servings

- 4 very ripe medium peaches, peeled and sliced
- 1 bottle (750 milliliters) dry champagne or sparkling wine, chilled

In food processor or blender, puree peaches until smooth liquid is formed. Pour into large pitcher. Add champagne slowly, stirring to blend. Serve immediately.

Apple Apricot Soufflés

4 servings

- 4 teaspoons butter plus additional for coating soufflé dishes
- ¼ cup sugar plus additional for coating soufflé dishes
- 2 large Granny Smith apples or other tart apples, peeled, cored, and thinly sliced
- 1 tablespoon apricot preserves
- 2 teaspoons water
- pinch ground cinnamon
- 2 egg yolks
- 2 tablespoons flour
- ½ cup milk, scalded
- 2 tablespoons dark rum
- 2 teaspoons pure vanilla extract
- 4 egg whites, at room temperature
- pinch salt
- powdered sugar

Easy to make and impressive to serve.

Generously butter four 1-cup soufflé dishes and coat with sugar. In small heavy saucepan, combine apples, apricot preserves, water, and cinnamon. Cover and cook over medium-low heat, mashing with fork occasionally, until thickened and smooth, 20-25 minutes. Remove from heat and set aside to cool.

Preheat oven to 425 degrees. In medium saucepan, combine ¼ cup sugar, egg yolks, and flour and whisk to blend. Stir in hot milk. Heat to boiling, stirring constantly. Reduce heat and simmer gently 2 minutes, stirring constantly. Remove from heat and stir in rum, 4 teaspoons butter, and vanilla. Fold in cooled apple mixture. Taste, and add more sugar, if desired.

In medium bowl, beat egg whites and salt until stiff, but not dry. Fold a quarter of the egg white mixture into apple mixture, then gently fold in remaining whites. Divide evenly between prepared soufflé dishes. Bake until puffed and browned, 10-15 minutes. Immediately sift powdered sugar lightly over top. Serve immediately.

Mountain Granola

12 cups

- 8 cups oatmeal
- ½ cup vegetable oil
- ½ cup packed brown sugar
- 1 cup honey
- 1 teaspoon pure vanilla extract
- ¼ teaspoon salt
- 1½ cups shelled, unsalted sunflower seeds, toasted (page 381)
- ⅔ cup sesame seeds, toasted (page 381)
- 1 cup sliced unsalted almonds, toasted

Great with fruit and yogurt.

Preheat oven to 350 degrees. Place oatmeal in large bowl. In medium saucepan, heat oil, brown sugar, and honey over medium heat, until thin, about 5 minutes. Remove from heat. Add vanilla and salt. Pour over oatmeal, add sunflower seeds, sesame seeds, and almonds and toss to combine. Spread evenly on 2 baking sheets and bake 15 minutes, stirring every 5 minutes.

Cinnamon Twists

18-24 rolls

- 1½ cups milk, divided
- 1 cup (2 sticks) unsalted butter, divided
- 1 ¼-ounce package dry yeast
- ½ cup plus 1 tablespoon sugar, divided
- 3 eggs
- 4-4½ cups flour
- 1 teaspoon salt
- ½ cup brown sugar
- 1 tablespoon ground cinnamon
- 2 cups powdered sugar

Photo, page 110.

In medium saucepan, heat 1 cup of the milk just to boiling, stirring constantly. Add ½ cup butter and stir until melted. Remove from heat and let cool to 105 degrees. In small bowl, combine yeast and 1 tablespoon of the sugar. Whisk milk mixture into yeast mixture, stirring until yeast dissolves.

In large bowl, beat eggs and remaining ½ cup sugar with electric or hand mixer. Add yeast mixture and beat until well blended. Add 4 cups of the flour and salt. If mixture is sticky, continue to add flour, 1 tablespoon at a time, until dough is smooth and forms a ball. Cover bowl with plastic wrap and set aside to rise until doubled in bulk, about 2 hours.

Preheat oven to 400 degrees. Grease 13x9x2-inch glass baking pan. Knead dough on lightly floured surface until no longer sticky. Do not knead excessively or dough will be tough. Roll dough into 18x24-inch rectangle, about ¼-inch thick.

Melt remaining ½ cup butter. In small bowl, combine melted butter, brown sugar, and cinnamon and spread over dough. Cut dough into 1-inch strips. Fold each strip in half, end to end, and twist several times. Place in prepared pan. Set aside to rise until doubled in bulk, about 45 minutes. Bake 20 minutes or until rolls are light brown on bottom. Remove from oven and cover with foil to keep warm. In medium bowl, combine powdered sugar and remaining ½ cup milk. Beat or whisk until smooth and pour over warm rolls.

Strawberries With Lemon Cream

20-30 pieces

- 1 8-ounce package cream cheese, softened
- ⅓ cup powdered sugar
- 2 teaspoons finely grated lemon zest
- 1½ tablespoons fresh lemon juice
- 2 pints large, and well-shaped, fresh strawberries

Photo, page 110.

In food processor, combine cream cheese, powdered sugar, lemon zest, and lemon juice. Process until smooth and chill 1 hour.

Cut stems from strawberries leaving a flat surface. Rinse and pat dry. Place on tray, cut side down. Cut a "V-shaped" pocket in the pointed end of each berry, cutting about two thirds of the way through to the bottom. Remove the "V-shaped" slice. Press sides apart slightly. Spoon chilled cream cheese mixture into pastry bag, fitted with star tip with ¼-inch opening. Pipe filling into center of each berry. It should fill in pocket and come out top. Chill up to 3 hours.

Apple Streusel Coffee Cake

10-12 servings

Streusel Filling and Topping:

- 1 cup whole walnuts or pecans
- ⅓ cup packed light brown sugar
- 2 tablespoons sugar
- 1½ teaspoons ground cinnamon
- ½ cup unbleached flour
- ¼ cup (½ stick) unsalted butter, softened
- ½ teaspoon pure vanilla extract

Coffee Cake:

- 4 egg yolks
- ¾ cup sour cream, divided
- 1½ teaspoons pure vanilla extract
- 2 cups unbleached flour
- 1 cup sugar
- ½ teaspoon baking powder
- ½ teaspoon baking soda
- ¼ teaspoon salt
- ¾ cup (1½ sticks) unsalted butter, softened
- 1 Granny Smith apple, peeled, cored, and sliced ¼-inch thick, tossed with 2 teaspoons lemon juice

You may substitute fresh or frozen peaches for apples.

In food processor, combine nuts, brown sugar, 2 tablespoons sugar, and cinnamon. Process until nuts are coarsely chopped. Remove ¾ cup and reserve for filling. Add ½ cup flour, ¼ cup butter, and ½ teaspoon vanilla to remaining nut mixture. Combine until crumbly. Set aside for topping.

Preheat oven to 350 degrees. Grease 9-inch springform pan and line bottom with waxed or parchment paper. Grease and flour paper.

In small bowl, combine egg yolks, ¼ cup of the sour cream, and 1½ teaspoons vanilla and set aside. In large bowl, combine 2 cups flour, 1 cup sugar, baking powder, baking soda, and salt. Stir until blended. Add ¾ cup butter and remaining ½ cup sour cream. Using an electric mixer, beat 2 minutes at medium-high speed. Add egg yolk mixture, one third at a time, beating 20 seconds after each addition. Pour two thirds of the batter into prepared pan.

Smooth surface with spatula and sprinkle with reserved ¾ cup filling. Place apple slices over filling. Drop remaining batter over apples and spread evenly with spatula. Sprinkle with reserved topping mixture. Bake 55-65 minutes or until center springs back when pressed lightly. If cake appears too brown after 45 minutes, cover loosely with buttered foil. Remove from oven and cool in pan on rack. Gently remove sides of pan. If desired, remove cake from pan bottom by sliding large spatula carefully under cake and paper, loosening entire bottom of cake. Carefully slide onto serving plate.

Cinnamon Bread Custard With Fresh Berries

6-8 servings

8 slices purchased cinnamon-raisin bread
½ cup (1 stick) butter, melted
4 eggs
2 egg yolks
¾ cup sugar
3 cups milk
1 cup whipping cream
1 tablespoon pure vanilla extract
1 cup hot water
powdered sugar
1 cup fresh blueberries or blackberries
1 cup fresh raspberries
1 cup fresh strawberries, sliced

Brush both sides of bread slices with melted butter. Line 13x9x2-inch baking pan with buttered bread slices. In large bowl, beat eggs and egg yolks. Whisk in sugar, milk, cream, and vanilla. Strain and pour over bread slices. Chill 2 hours or up to overnight.

Preheat oven to 350 degrees. Place baking pan on large baking sheet with sides. Pour hot water into baking sheet to provide steam for custard as it bakes. Bake 25-30 minutes, until top is lightly browned. Cool slightly, cut into squares and top with powdered sugar and fresh berries.

Baked Papaya Delight

8 servings

1½ cups cottage cheese
12 ounces cream cheese, softened and cut into small pieces
2 tablespoons purchased mango chutney
1 teaspoon curry powder
½ cup chopped water chestnuts
2 tablespoons golden raisins
4 ripe papayas, peeled, halved, and seeded
¼ cup sugar
½ teaspoon cinnamon
¼ cup (½ stick) butter, melted

Preheat oven to 450 degrees. In food processor, combine cottage cheese, cream cheese, chutney, and curry powder and blend until smooth. Stir in water chestnuts and raisins. Fill papaya halves with cottage cheese mixture. Combine sugar and cinnamon and sprinkle over cheese mixture. Drizzle with melted butter. Bake until thoroughly heated, about 15 minutes. Serve immediately

Peak to Peak Pancake With Fresh Berries

4 servings

- 2½ tablespoons unsalted butter
- 1¼ cups milk
- ¾ cup flour
- 3 eggs
- ⅓ cup sugar
- ¼ teaspoon salt
- ¼ teaspoon pure vanilla extract
- powdered sugar
- fresh berries, such as raspberries, strawberries, or blueberries
- maple syrup, heated

Preheat oven to 400 degrees. Place butter in 9-inch glass pie pan and melt in oven. In blender or food processor, combine milk, flour, eggs, sugar, salt, and vanilla and process until smooth. Remove pie pan from oven and increase oven temperature to 425 degrees. Pour batter into pie pan and return to oven. Bake 20 minutes. Reduce oven temperature to 325 degrees and bake 8-10 minutes. Invert on serving platter. Sprinkle with powdered sugar and serve with fresh berries and warm maple syrup on the side.

An easy oven-baked pancake.

Lemon Waffles With Blackberries

8 waffles

- 2½ cups fresh or frozen blackberries
- ¼ cup plus 2 tablespoons sugar, divided
- 2 cups flour
- 1½ teaspoons baking powder
- ½ teaspoon baking soda
- 1 cup lemon-flavored yogurt
- ¾ cup milk
- 2 large eggs, at room temperature
- 5 tablespoons unsalted butter, melted
- 2 teaspoons finely grated lemon zest

Garnish:
powdered sugar

Photo, page 110.

Place blackberries in medium glass bowl. Sprinkle with 2 tablespoons of the sugar and stir to combine. Using wooden spoon, mash berries to bring out juices. Let stand at room temperature 30 minutes or up to 2 hours.

Preheat waffle iron. Preheat oven to 200 degrees. In medium bowl, combine flour, remaining ¼ cup sugar, baking powder, and baking soda. In separate bowl, combine yogurt, milk, eggs, butter, and lemon zest and whisk to blend. Pour into flour mixture, stirring to form smooth batter.

Lightly grease waffle iron. Bake waffles according to manufacturer's directions. Transfer to oven, placing directly on rack so they will stay crisp. Repeat with remaining batter. Transfer waffles to individual serving plates and top with blackberry mixture. Dust with powdered sugar, if desired.

Raspberry Poached Pears

16 servings

- 2 10-ounce packages frozen sweetened raspberries, thawed
- ½ cup crème de cassis
- 8 firm ripe pears, peeled and left whole, or halved and cored
- ¼ cup finely chopped pistachio nuts

A colorful addition to any brunch buffet. *Photo, page 108.*

In food processor or blender, puree raspberries until smooth. Strain through fine sieve to remove seeds. Add creme de cassis. Place pears in large saucepan and add raspberry mixture. Cover and simmer gently until tender, 8-10 minutes. Remove pears from pan with slotted spoon, cool, and chill.

Transfer cooking liquid to small saucepan and boil, stirring constantly, until reduced to thick syrup, 10-12 minutes. Remove from heat and set aside to cool. Spoon thin layer of cooled syrup on large serving platter. Top with pears and drizzle with additional syrup. Sprinkle with pistachios.

Banana Oatmeal Waffles

8 waffles

- 1 cup old fashioned oats
- 1 cup flour
- 1 tablespoon double acting baking powder
- ½ teaspoon baking soda
- ½ teaspoon ground cinnamon
- pinch freshly grated nutmeg
- 3 tablespoons packed brown sugar
- 1½ cups buttermilk
- 2 large eggs
- 2 medium ripe bananas, peeled and diced
- ¼ cup (½ stick) unsalted butter, melted

Garnish:

- sliced bananas
- warmed maple syrup

This batter works well for pancakes, too. Substitute fresh chopped peaches when in season.

Preheat waffle iron. Preheat oven to 200 degrees. In large bowl, combine oats, flour, baking powder, baking soda, cinnamon, nutmeg, and brown sugar. In separate bowl, combine buttermilk and eggs and whisk until well blended. Pour over oat mixture and stir until just combined. Stir in bananas and melted butter.

Lightly grease waffle iron. Bake waffles according to manufacturer's directions. Transfer to oven, placing directly on rack so they will stay crisp. Repeat with remaining batter. Transfer waffles to individual serving plates and top with bananas and warm maple syrup. (May be prepared in advance and frozen in plastic bags with sheets of waxed paper separating each waffle. Place frozen waffles directly on rack in preheated 350 degree oven and bake about 10 minutes, or heat waffles in toaster.)

Orange Glazed Bananas

6 servings

- 6 firm bananas, peeled and halved lengthwise
- ¾ cup fresh orange juice
- ¼ cup Grand Marnier or other orange-flavored liqueur
- 3 tablespoons unsalted butter
- ⅓ cup chopped walnuts
- ⅓ cup packed brown sugar
- sour cream

Preheat oven to 400 degrees. Arrange bananas in shallow baking dish. Combine orange juice and Grand Marnier and pour over bananas. Dot with butter. Bake 5 minutes, basting occasionally. Remove from oven and preheat broiler. Sprinkle bananas with walnuts and brown sugar and broil until sugar is melted and nuts are glazed and toasted, about 5 minutes. Serve warm with sour cream.

Gingerbread Waffles With Pear Syrup

8 waffles

Ginger Cream:

1 cup whipping cream
2 teaspoons sugar
2 tablespoons finely chopped crystallized ginger

Pear Syrup:

¼ cup maple syrup
1 firm ripe pear, peeled, cored, and sliced
2 tablespoons currants or raisins
1 teaspoon finely chopped crystallized ginger

Waffles:

2 cups flour
1½ teaspoons baking powder
1 teaspoon ground cinnamon
1 teaspoon ground ginger
¼ teaspoon ground cloves
¼ teaspoon salt
2 eggs, separated
¼ cup (½ stick) unsalted butter
½ cup packed dark brown sugar
½ cup light molasses
1 cup milk

A surprisingly sophisticated twist on waffles.

With electric or hand mixer, whip cream and 2 teaspoons sugar to soft peaks. Fold in 2 tablespoons crystallized ginger. Place in serving bowl. (May be prepared 1 day in advance. Cover and chill until ready to serve.)

In small saucepan, combine maple syrup, pears, currants, and 1 teaspoon crystallized ginger over low heat. Heat 10 minutes, remove from heat, and place in serving bowl.

Preheat waffle iron. Preheat oven to 200 degrees. In medium bowl, combine flour, baking powder, cinnamon, ground ginger, cloves, and salt. Set aside. In medium bowl, beat 2 egg whites with clean beaters until stiff but not dry. Set aside. In large bowl, with electric or hand mixer, beat butter and brown sugar until fluffy. Beat in molasses, 2 egg yolks, and milk. Stir in reserved flour mixture and fold in beaten egg whites.

Bake waffles according to manufacturer's directions. Transfer to oven, placing directly on rack so they will stay crisp. Place waffles on individual serving plates and top with warm Pear Syrup and a dollop of Ginger Cream.

Snow Peas With Minted Cheese

40 pieces

- 1 8-ounce package cream cheese
- ¼ cup chopped fresh parsley
- ¼ cup chopped fresh mint
- ½ teaspoon minced garlic
- 40 snow peas, blanched in boiling water 30 seconds, immersed in ice water, and drained

Cool, crunchy, and refreshing.

In food processor, combine cream cheese, parsley, mint, and garlic. Process until well blended. Open curved sides of snow peas with sharp knife. Spoon cream cheese mixture into pastry bag fitted with star tip with ¼-inch opening. Pipe filling into each pea pod. Arrange on platter, cover with plastic wrap, and chill until serving time.

Sausage Mushroom Rolls

8 servings

- 12 ounces sage-flavored bulk sausage
- ¼ cup minced onion
- ½ pound fresh mushrooms, chopped
- 1 teaspoon minced garlic
- 1 teaspoon dried sage
- ½ teaspoon dried thyme
- pinch salt
- 1 8-ounce package cream cheese, softened and cut into cubes
- 6 sheets phyllo pastry, thawed if frozen
- ½ cup (1 stick) butter, melted
- ⅔ cup fine dry bread crumbs

Perfect with scrambled eggs and fresh fruit.

In large skillet, brown sausage. Drain sausage thoroughly and add onion, mushrooms, garlic, sage, thyme, and salt. Cook until mushrooms are soft. Transfer to bowl and add cream cheese. Stir until cheese is melted. (May be prepared to this point up to 1 day in advance. Cover and chill.)

Preheat oven to 375 degrees. Place 1 phyllo sheet on flat surface, with long edge nearest you. Keep remaining sheets covered with plastic wrap and damp towel to prevent drying. Brush phyllo sheet with melted butter and sprinkle lightly with bread crumbs. Top with another phyllo sheet, brush with melted butter and sprinkle lightly with bread crumbs. Repeat with 4 remaining sheets.

Place sausage mixture along long edge. Roll tightly, jelly roll style. Fold ends under and place, seam side down, on baking pan. Brush top with butter. Cut eight ⅛-inch deep scores in top with sharp knife. Bake until golden brown, about 30 minutes. Slice and serve.

Cream Cheese Crêpes With Apricot Sauce

4-8 servings

- 1 8-ounce package cream cheese, softened
- ¼ cup (½ stick) plus 2 tablespoons butter, softened, divided
- ¼ cup sugar
- 1 teaspoon pure vanilla extract
- 1 teaspoon almond extract
- 3 teaspoons finely grated orange zest, divided
- 8 purchased crêpes
- ⅔ cup apricot jam
- ⅓ cup fresh orange juice
- 1 tablespoon fresh lemon juice
- 1 teaspoon Grand Marnier or other orange-flavored liqueur
- 6 tablespoons sliced almonds, toasted (page 381)

Photo page, 108.

Preheat oven to 350 degrees. Butter large baking pan. In food processor, combine cream cheese, ¼ cup of the butter, sugar, vanilla, almond extract, and 2 teaspoons of the orange zest. Process until fluffy. Spread 1 tablespoon or more, if desired, of the cream cheese mixture over each crêpe. Fold in sides and roll. Place, seam side down, in prepared pan. Bake 8-10 minutes.

In small saucepan, combine jam, remaining 2 tablespoons butter, orange juice, lemon juice, Grand Marnier, and remaining 1 teaspoon orange zest. Heat, stirring frequently, until smooth and slightly thickened. Spoon over warm crêpes and sprinkle with almonds.

Pepper Prosciutto Baked Eggs

6 servings

- 3 medium yellow or red bell peppers, halved lengthwise
- 3 ounces thinly sliced prosciutto, divided
- 6 eggs
- salt and freshly ground pepper
- 2 tablespoons Parmesan cheese
- 1 tablespoon chopped fresh herbs, such as basil, tarragon, or rosemary

A colorful and refreshingly different egg dish.

Preheat oven to 400 degrees. Remove seeds and scrape insides of pepper halves, being careful not to break through skin. Place peppers, cut side up, on baking sheet and bake 15 minutes. Remove from oven. Line pepper halves with prosciutto and carefully break 1 egg into each half. Return to oven and bake 15 minutes.

Remove from oven. Sprinkle each egg with salt and pepper to taste and 1 teaspoon Parmesan. Bake an additional 1-2 minutes, just until cheese begins to melt. Watch carefully, egg yolks will cook very quickly. Remove from oven, top with herbs, and serve immediately.

Spring Asparagus Tart

6-8 servings

2	cups flour
1¼	teaspoons salt, divided
½	cup (1 stick) unsalted butter, chilled and cut into small pieces
¼	cup shortening
¼-½	cup cold water
1	pound asparagus, trimmed, reserving 6 spears for top, and cut into ½-inch pieces
4	eggs
15	ounces ricotta cheese
1	teaspoon freshly ground black pepper
½	teaspoon ground nutmeg
3	green onions, chopped, including tops
½	pound bacon, crisply cooked and crumbled

An attractive entree, just right for luncheons.

In food processor, combine flour, ¼ teaspoon of the salt, butter, and shortening. Process until mixture resembles coarse crumbs. With processor running, add enough of the water to form dough that just holds together. Remove from bowl and flatten into disk. Wrap in plastic wrap and chill 30 minutes.

Preheat oven to 400 degrees. Place large baking sheet in oven. Roll out dough on floured surface to 14-inch circle. Place in 10-inch quiche dish with 1-inch sides. Pierce bottom and side of crust with fork to prevent shrinkage. Place on preheated baking sheet and bake 10-12 minutes, or until lightly browned. Remove from oven and cool.

Reduce oven temperature to 375 degrees. To large pan of boiling water, add asparagus pieces and cook 3 minutes. Drain, dry, and set aside. In large bowl, combine eggs, ricotta, remaining 1 teaspoon salt, pepper, and nutmeg. Whisk to blend and carefully stir in green onions, crumbled bacon, and cooked asparagus. Spoon into cooled crust and arrange reserved asparagus spears on top. Bake until firm, about 35 minutes. Serve warm or at room temperature.

Clockwise from top:
Spring Asparagus Tart, 125
Smoked Salmon
Cheesecake, 130

Classic Colorado Quiche

6-8 servings

Pastry:

1¼ cups flour
¼ teaspoon salt
½ cup (1 stick) unsalted butter, well chilled and cut into small pieces
2 tablespoons or more very cold water

Filling:

1 cup sliced fresh mushrooms
1 tablespoon butter
1 cup grated cheddar cheese
1 10-ounce package frozen chopped spinach, thawed and squeezed dry
3 eggs
1½ cups whipping cream
2 teaspoons Worcestershire
½ teaspoon sugar
¼ teaspoon crushed garlic
½ teaspoon onion salt
⅛ teaspoon freshly ground black pepper
6 strips bacon, crisply cooked and crumbled, divided
⅓ cup freshly grated Parmesan cheese

Photo, page 108.

In food processor, combine flour and salt. Add ½ cup butter and process until mixture resembles coarse meal. Gradually add water and process just until dough holds together. Press dough into flat disk, and wrap tightly in plastic wrap. Chill at least 30 minutes.

Preheat oven to 350 degrees. Roll out pastry dough and place in 10-inch pie pan. Press into bottom and sides. Trim edges and prick all over crust with fork. Line with foil and cover bottom with pie weights or dried beans. Bake 5 minutes, remove from oven, remove weights and foil, and cool.

In small skillet, cook mushrooms in 1 tablespoon butter, over medium heat, until soft. Remove from heat and set aside. Sprinkle cheddar evenly over bottom of cooled crust. In large bowl, combine spinach, eggs, cream, Worcestershire, sugar, garlic, onion salt, pepper, cooked mushrooms, and half of the crumbled bacon. Pour into crust, using fork to gently distribute mushrooms and spinach evenly. Sprinkle with Parmesan.

Bake 20 minutes, sprinkle remaining bacon over top and continue baking 25-40 minutes, until knife inserted into center comes out clean. If browning too quickly, tent with foil. Remove from oven and let stand 5-10 minutes.

Artichoke Soufflés

6 servings

- butter to coat soufflé dishes
- 1 14-ounce can water-packed artichoke hearts, drained
- ¼ cup olive oil
- 1 tablespoon white wine vinegar
- 1 teaspoon dried tarragon
- ½ teaspoon crushed garlic
- salt and freshly ground black pepper
- 5 eggs, separated
- 6 tablespoons sour cream
- 1½ cups freshly grated Parmesan cheese
- 1 tablespoon brandy
- ¼ teaspoon ground nutmeg
- ¼ teaspoon cayenne
- 1 cup fresh white bread crumbs
- ¼ teaspoon cream of tartar

An elegant dish to serve with ham.

Preheat oven to 350 degrees. Butter six 1-cup ramekins or soufflé dishes. In blender or food processor, combine artichoke hearts, olive oil, vinegar, tarragon, garlic, and salt and pepper to taste. Puree and divide equally among prepared ramekins, smoothing to form an even layer.

In large bowl, combine 5 egg yolks, sour cream, Parmesan, brandy, nutmeg, cayenne, and bread crumbs. In medium bowl, beat 5 egg whites and cream of tartar until stiff. Gently fold into egg yolk mixture. Pour evenly over artichoke mixture. Bake 25-30 minutes, until puffed and lightly browned.

Eggs Mornay

4 servings

- 5 tablespoons butter, softened, divided
- 4 slices French bread
- 1 heaping tablespoon flour
- 2 cups cold milk
- salt and freshly ground black pepper
- ¼ cup grated Gruyère or Swiss cheese
- 1 egg yolk
- 4 eggs, poached to desired doneness

Garnish:

- 1 slice cooked ham, diced
- 1 hard boiled egg, yolk and white minced separately

Brush 3 tablespoons of the butter over both sides of bread. In large skillet, brown bread slices about 2 minutes per side. Remove to plate and cover with foil to keep warm. In medium saucepan, melt remaining 2 tablespoons butter over medium heat. Stir in flour and milk and heat to boiling, stirring constantly, to thicken. Season with salt and pepper to taste. Simmer 2 minutes. Remove from heat and stir in cheese and egg yolk. Cover with foil to keep warm. Place 1 poached egg on 1 toasted bread slice. Cover with warm sauce and garnish with ham and minced egg yolk and white. Serve with fresh fruit.

Shredded Potato Pancakes With Lox

8 servings

2	pounds russet potatoes, divided
½	cup vegetable oil, divided
	salt and freshly ground black pepper
1	pound thinly sliced lox
	sour cream
	Garnish:
	chopped green onion

Preheat oven to 200 degrees. Peel half of the potatoes and coarsely shred. (A food processor works well for shredding potatoes.) Press between several paper towels to remove excess moisture. In large, heavy skillet, heat ¼ cup of the oil over medium-high heat until hot, but not smoking.

In large bowl, toss grated potatoes with salt and pepper to taste, and form into 4 patties. Place in hot oil and cook, pressing down with spatula, 5 minutes per side, or until golden brown and thoroughly cooked. Transfer to paper towel lined platter and keep warm in oven. Repeat process with remaining potatoes and oil. Top with smoked lox and sour cream. Garnish with green onions.

A quick and easy treat.

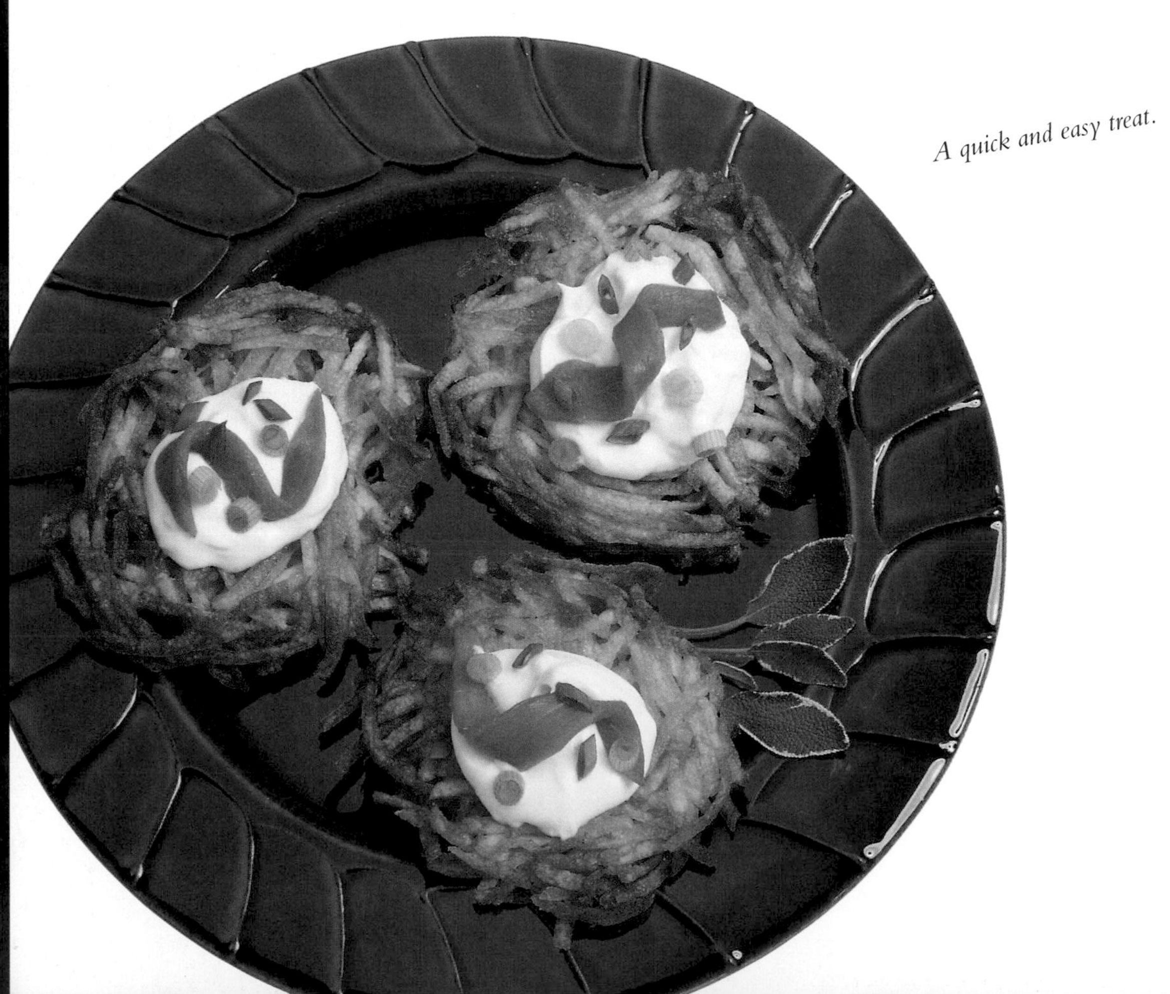

Elegant Breakfast Strata

10-12 servings

- 1 cup milk
- ½ cup dry white wine
- 1 loaf day-old French bread, cut into ½-inch slices
- 2 cups loosely packed, chopped fresh cilantro
- 3 tablespoons olive oil
- ½ pound Bruder Basil cheese or smoked Gouda cheese, thinly sliced, divided
- 3 ripe tomatoes, thinly sliced, divided
- ½ cup Basic Basil Pesto, (page 193), or purchased basil pesto, divided
- 4 eggs
- salt and freshly ground black pepper
- ½ cup whipping cream

Bruder Basil cheese may be found at specialty cheese shops.

Lightly grease 12-inch au gratin dish or 10-inch deep-dish pie pan. In shallow bowl, combine milk and wine. Dip bread, 1 or 2 slices at a time, in milk mixture. Gently squeeze as much liquid as possible from bread, taking care not to tear. Place bread slices in prepared dish.

Cover bread with cilantro and drizzle with olive oil. Layer half of the cheese and half of the tomato slices over the bread. Top with half of the pesto. Repeat layers of cheese, tomato, and pesto. In medium bowl, beat eggs and season with salt and pepper to taste. Pour evenly over layered mixture. Carefully pour cream over top and cover with plastic wrap. Chill overnight.

About 3 hours before serving, remove strata from refrigerator and bring to room temperature. Preheat oven to 350 degrees. Place pan on baking sheet and bake, uncovered, until puffy and browned, about 1 hour.

Cranberry Surprise

6-8 servings

- 2 eggs
- 1½ cups sugar
- ½ cup (1 stick) butter, melted
- 1 cup sifted flour
- ½ cup chopped pecans
- 2 cups whole fresh cranberries or frozen cranberries, thawed

Frozen cranberries are available at many large supermarkets.

Preheat oven to 325 degrees. Grease 10-inch pie pan. In a medium bowl, combine eggs, sugar, butter, flour, pecans, and cranberries. Pour into prepared pan. Bake 50-60 minutes. Serve warm.

Curried Spicy Potatoes

4 servings

- 1½ pounds (about 4 medium) white potatoes
- 3 tablespoons water
- 4 teaspoons curry powder
- salt and freshly ground black pepper
- 2 tablespoons butter
- ½ cup chopped shallots
- ⅓ cup green onions, chopped, including tops

Easy and flavorful. Serve with ham or sausage.

Cook whole potatoes in boiling salted water until just tender, about 30 minutes. Cool slightly, peel, and cut into 1-inch cubes. Place in medium bowl. Add water and curry powder and toss to coat. Season with salt and pepper to taste.

In large heavy skillet, heat butter over medium-high heat. Add shallots, green onions, and reserved potatoes. Cook until potatoes are crusty and golden brown on all sides, stirring occasionally, about 15 minutes.

Smoked Salmon Cheesecake

12 servings

- 4½ tablespoons butter, divided
- ½ cup dry bread crumbs
- ¾ cup grated Gruyère cheese, divided
- 1 teaspoon minced fresh dill weed or ½ teaspoon dried dill weed
- 1 medium onion, peeled and minced
- 28 ounces cream cheese, softened
- 4 eggs
- ⅓ cup half and half
- ½ teaspoon salt
- ½ pound smoked salmon, coarsely chopped, divided

This combination of salmon and Gruyère is fabulous! *Photo, page 124.*

Preheat oven to 325 degrees. Butter 8 or 9-inch springform pan, using about 1½ tablespoons of the butter. Use springform pan with tight seal to avoid leakage. In small bowl, combine bread crumbs, ¼ cup of the Gruyère, and dill. Toss to blend and sprinkle in prepared pan, turning and tapping to coat evenly. Chill while preparing filling.

In medium, heavy skillet with lid, melt remaining 3 tablespoons butter over low heat. Add onion, cover, and cook until soft, stirring occasionally, about 10 minutes. In food processor, blend cream cheese until smooth. Add eggs, remaining ½ cup Gruyère, half and half, and salt. Process until smooth. Gently stir in cooked onion and all but 2 tablespoons of the salmon by hand. Pour into prepared pan. Top with remaining 2 tablespoons salmon.

Set springform pan in large roasting pan and fill roasting pan with enough water to come halfway up sides of springform pan. Bake 1 hour and 20 minutes. Turn off oven and cool cheesecake in oven, with door ajar, 1 hour. Transfer pan to rack and cool to room temperature before removing sides of pan. Store in refrigerator and bring to room temperature before serving. Best 24-36 hours after baking.

Genoa Torte

8-10 servings

- 1½ pounds frozen bread dough, thawed
- ½ pound sliced Genoa salami, divided
- 1 pound small whole mushrooms, cleaned and stems removed
- 1 6-ounce can whole black olives, drained and dried
- ½ pound sliced provolone cheese, divided
- ½ pound thinly sliced ham, divided
- 2 10-ounce packages frozen chopped spinach, thawed and squeezed very dry
- 3 4-ounce jars pimentos, drained and dried
- 1 14-ounce can water-packed artichoke hearts, drained, quartered, and dried
- 1 egg yolk
- 1 tablespoon water

Preheat oven to 350 degrees. Roll a quarter of the thawed bread dough into 10-inch circle and set aside. Roll out remaining dough and line 10-inch springform pan. Leave 1-inch of extra dough hanging over sides of pan.

Please be sure that all ingredients are very dry before beginning assembly. If all ingredients are not well drained, cooking time will be increased and torte may be soggy. Layer half of the salami evenly over bottom of crust. Top with mushrooms, olives, half of the provolone, half of the ham, spinach, pimentos, and remaining half of the salami. Layered ingredients will be close to top of pan. Fold excess dough over filling and continue layering with remaining half of the ham, artichoke hearts, and remaining half of the provolone.

In small bowl, combine egg yolk and water and whisk to blend. Brush outside edge of reserved dough with egg yolk mixture. Place, brushed side down, over layered mixture and press edges to seal. Brush top with egg yolk mixture. Prick dough with fork several times and let rise slightly, about 20 minutes.

Bake 45 minutes or until golden brown. Remove from oven and cool in pan, about 2 hours. Remove sides of pan and serve at room temperature. Store in refrigerator.

Smoked Salmon Lasagna

12-16 servings

- ½ cup (1 stick) unsalted butter
- ⅓ cup flour
- 4 cups milk
- 1 teaspoon salt
- ½ teaspoon ground white pepper
- ¼ cup freshly grated Parmesan cheese
- ¼ cup grated Gruyère cheese
- 2 tablespoons dry sherry
- ½ cup grated cheddar cheese
- 1 cup grated mozzarella cheese
- 1 cup grated provolone cheese
- 1½ cups grated Romano or Parmesan cheese
- 1 pound plain or spinach lasagna noodles, cooked al dente and drained
- 3 large tomatoes, peeled, seeded, minced, and drained
- ½ pound mushrooms, thinly sliced
- 1 pound smoked salmon, chopped

An elegant buffet dish for a special occasion.

In medium saucepan, melt butter over low heat. Add flour and cook, stirring constantly, 3 minutes. Whisk in milk and heat to boiling. Boil over medium-high heat, whisking constantly, 10 minutes or until thickened. Remove from heat and stir in salt, white pepper, Parmesan, Gruyère, and sherry. Set aside. In large bowl, combine cheddar, mozzarella, provolone, and Romano.

Preheat oven to 350 degrees. Grease 13x9x2-inch baking pan. Spread one quarter of the cheese mixture in prepared pan. Layer one third of the cooked noodles, one third of the sauce mixture, half of the tomatoes, half of the mushrooms, half of the salmon and another quarter of the cheese mixture. Repeat layers beginning with noodles. Top with remaining noodles, remaining sauce mixture, and remaining cheese mixture. (May be prepared up to 1 day in advance. Cover and chill. May be prepared up to 2 weeks in advance and frozen. Thaw before baking.) Bake 45-60 minutes or until golden brown on top and thoroughly heated. Let stand 15 minutes before serving.

Pêche Royale

6 servings

- 6 teaspoons peach liqueur, French if available, divided
- 1 bottle (750 milliliters) dry champagne, chilled

A sophisticated brunch drink or apéritif.

Place 1 teaspoon of the peach liqueur in each of 6 champagne flutes and fill with champagne.

Lemon Cheese Strudel

10-12 servings

- 1¼ cups sugar, divided
- 1½ tablespoons cinnamon
- 1 cup (2 sticks) butter, softened, divided
- 1 8-ounce package cream cheese, softened
- 1½ tablespoons finely grated lemon zest
- ⅓ cup sour cream
- 3 egg yolks
- 16 sheets phyllo pastry, thawed, if frozen

In small bowl, combine ¾ cup of the sugar and cinnamon. In large bowl, beat ¼ cup of the butter and ½ cup sugar until smooth. Add cream cheese and lemon zest and beat until fluffy. Blend in sour cream and egg yolks.

Preheat oven to 350 degrees. Melt remaining ¾ cup butter. Brush 2 baking sheets with melted butter. Place 1 phyllo sheet on flat surface. Keep remaining sheets covered with plastic wrap and damp towel to prevent drying. Brush phyllo sheet with melted butter and sprinkle with 2 teaspoons of the sugar mixture. Top with second phyllo sheet and repeat process with half of the phyllo sheets.

Spoon half of the cream cheese mixture down long edge of phyllo stack, leaving a 1-inch border. Roll up, jelly roll style. Fold ends under and place, seam side down, on prepared baking sheet. Brush top with butter. Cut several ⅛-inch deep scores in top with sharp knife to vent. Repeat process for second strudel. Bake until golden brown and crisp, about 30 minutes. Cool and slice.

Coffee Punch

8 servings

- 2 ice cube trays
- 6 8-ounce cups freshly brewed coffee, cooled to room temperature, divided
- 1 cup whipping cream
- ¼ cup powdered sugar
- 1¾ teaspoons pure vanilla extract, divided
- 1 pint premium vanilla ice cream
- 1½ cups milk
- ⅓ cup sugar
- ¾ teaspoon ground nutmeg

Garnish:

ground nutmeg

A refreshing and unusual addition to brunch on a hot summer day.

Fill 2 ice cube trays with 3 cups of the cooled coffee and freeze until solid, about 2 hours. Just before serving, whip cream until slightly thickened, add powdered sugar and ¼ teaspoon of the vanilla. Using small scoop or tablespoon, scoop ice cream into large serving pitcher or punch bowl.

In medium bowl, combine remaining 3 cups coffee, milk, sugar, remaining 1½ teaspoons vanilla, and nutmeg. Pour over ice cream and stir gently. Remove ice cubes from trays and place in ice cream mixture or in glasses. Carefully pour coffee mixture into tall glasses, filling to 1-inch below top. Top with reserved whipped cream mixture and garnish with nutmeg, if desired.

Ahhh, now we know precisely where the words "amber waves of grain" were inspired. The beauty of our plains and their incredible harvest have inspired homemade breads and autumn feasts for generations of Coloradans.

Bountiful Harvest

salad

Autumn Salad 86

main dish

Burgundy Beef Pie 237

bread

Sourdough Onion Twist 153

dessert

Frozen Pumpkin Praline Torte 352

wine

Cabernet Franc

Clockwise from top:
Sourdough Onion Twist
Burgundy Beef Pie

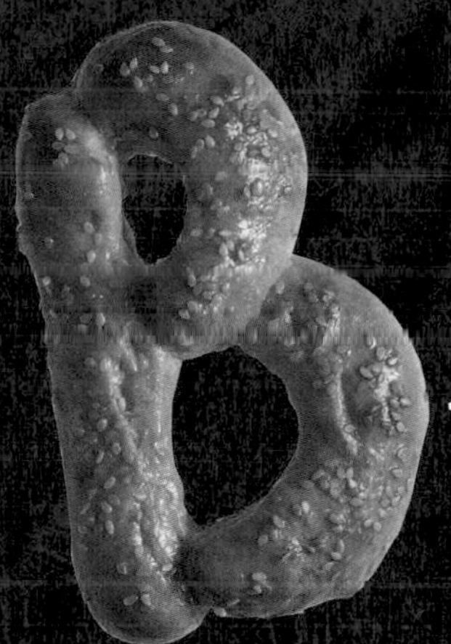

Breads

Nothing enhances a meal like homemade bread! We've included easy to make yeast breads with unique flavors and specialty breads to add authenticity to ethnic fare. We've also added tea and scones for an afternoon repose.

Clockwise from top:
Chef's Cheddar Onion Loaf
Pistachio Breakfast Ring

Cinnamon Swirl Bread

2 loaves

2	¼-ounce packages dry yeast
1½	cups warm milk (105-115 degrees)
½	cup (1 stick) unsalted butter, softened
7-8	cups unbleached flour
½	cup plus 7 tablespoons sugar, divided
1	teaspoon salt
4	eggs, divided
¼	cup ground cinnamon

In large bowl, dissolve yeast in milk. Add butter, 7 cups of the flour, 7 tablespoons of the sugar, salt, and 3 of the eggs. Stir until well blended. Turn dough out onto lightly floured surface and knead 8-10 minutes, adding additional flour as needed, until dough is smooth and elastic. Dough should be stiff and should not stick to kneading surface. Place dough in oiled bowl, turning to coat entire surface. Cover with plastic wrap and towel and let rise until doubled in bulk, about 40 minutes.

Grease two 9x5-inch loaf pans. Punch dough down and divide into 2 equal pieces. Let rest 5 minutes. Roll each piece into a 12x9-inch rectangle, about ½-inch thick. Brush dough with water. Combine cinnamon and remaining ½ cup sugar. Sprinkle generously over dough. Roll each rectangle, jelly roll style, to form two 9-inch loaves. Pinch ends together to seal. Place in prepared pans. Cover as before and let rise until doubled in bulk, about 1 hour.

Preheat oven to 375 degrees. In small bowl, beat remaining egg and brush over tops of loaves. Bake 25-30 minutes or until loaves sound hollow when tapped on top. Remove from oven and cool in pans 10 minutes. Remove from pans and cool on rack.

Pistachio Breakfast Ring

12-16 servings

- 1 ¼-ounce package dry yeast
- ½ cup plus 1 tablespoon sugar, divided
- ¼ cup warm water (105-115 degrees)
- 1 cup warm milk (105-115 degrees)
- ¼ cup (½ stick) unsalted butter
- 2 teaspoons salt
- 3-4 cups unbleached flour
- ¼ cup (½ stick) unsalted butter, melted
- 1 cup pistachio nuts, shelled and coarsely chopped
- 1 egg, lightly beaten

A combination of sweet and hearty flavors make this a delightful breakfast bread. *Photo, page 136.*

In large bowl, combine yeast, 1 tablespoon of the sugar, and water. Set aside 5 minutes until slightly bubbly. Add milk, butter, salt, and remaining ½ cup sugar. Add 3 cups of the flour, 1 cup at a time, beating well after each addition. Turn dough out onto lightly floured surface and knead 8-10 minutes, or until dough is smooth and elastic. Add additional flour, as needed to prevent sticking. Place dough in oiled bowl, turning to coat entire surface. Cover with plastic wrap and towel and let rise until doubled in bulk, about 1½ hours.

Grease large baking sheet. Punch dough down and turn out onto floured surface. Let rest 5 minutes. Using floured rolling pin, roll into 12x18-inch rectangle. Brush top with melted butter and sprinkle with pistachios. Beginning with long side of rectangle, roll up to form 18-inch long loaf. Join ends of loaf together and pinch to form ring. Carefully place ring on prepared baking sheet. Using sharp knife, make diagonal cuts in dough two-thirds of the way through, at ¾-inch intervals. Cover as before and let rise until doubled in bulk, about 1 hour. Preheat oven to 350 degrees. Brush entire surface with beaten egg. Bake 30-35 minutes or until golden brown. Remove from oven and cool on baking sheet 10 minutes. Remove and cool on rack.

German Christmas Bread

16-20 servings

- ½ cup chopped golden raisins
- ½ cup chopped dried peaches
- ½ cup chopped dried cherries
- 1 cup chopped almonds
- ¼ cup Amaretto liqueur
- 2 ¼-ounce packages dry yeast
- ½ cup plus 2 teaspoons sugar, divided
- ½ cup warm water (105-115 degrees)
- 1 cup scalded milk, cooled to lukewarm (100-110 degrees)
- ½ cup (1 stick) unsalted butter, softened
- 2 eggs
- 1½ teaspoons salt
- 1½ teaspoons ground nutmeg
- 2 teaspoons finely grated lemon zest
- 6 cups unbleached flour, divided
- ¼ cup (½ stick) unsalted butter, melted
- ½ teaspoon ground cinnamon
- ¼ cup sugar

Glaze:

- 1 cup powdered sugar
- ¼ teaspoon almond extract
- 1½ tablespoons water

This bread is also known as "Stollen" and is far too good to save for the holidays.

In small bowl, combine raisins, peaches, cherries, almonds, and Amaretto. In large bowl, sprinkle yeast and 2 teaspoons of the sugar over water. Stir to dissolve. Add milk, remaining ½ cup sugar, and butter. Stir until well blended. Beat in eggs, salt, nutmeg, lemon zest, and 3 cups of the flour. Add half of the reserved fruit mixture and 2 cups of the flour. Mix until well blended, dough will be stiff.

Turn dough out onto lightly floured surface and knead 8-10 minutes, or until dough is smooth and elastic. Add additional flour as needed to prevent sticking. Place dough in oiled bowl, turning to coat entire surface. Cover with plastic wrap and towel and let rise until doubled in bulk, about 1 hour.

Grease large baking sheet. Punch dough down and divide in half. Let rest 5 minutes. Using floured rolling pin, roll 1 piece into a 12x8-inch rectangle. Brush dough lightly with melted butter. Combine cinnamon and sugar and sprinkle half over dough. Place half of the remaining fruit mixture down center of dough. Fold both sides of dough over filling to form a 12x4-inch loaf and pinch edges together to seal.

Place dough, seam-side down, on prepared baking sheet. Repeat with remaining dough. Cover as before and let rise until doubled in bulk, about 1 hour. Preheat oven to 375 degrees. Brush tops with remaining melted butter and bake 20 minutes, or until golden brown.

Combine powdered sugar, almond extract, and water. Whisk until smooth. Remove bread from oven. Cool on baking sheet 10 minutes. Spread glaze over tops of warm loaves, remove and cool on rack.

Cranberry Maple Muffins

12 muffins

- 1 cup sugar
- 2 eggs
- ½ cup (1 stick) unsalted butter
- ½ cup buttermilk
- 2 teaspoons pure maple extract
- 1½ cups unbleached flour
- ½ cup chopped walnuts
- 2 teaspoons baking powder
- ½ teaspoon salt
- 1½ cups fresh or frozen cranberries, halved

Preheat oven to 375 degrees. Line 12 muffin cups with paper liners. In large bowl, combine sugar, eggs, butter, buttermilk, and maple extract. Stir in flour, walnuts, baking powder, salt, and cranberries. Spoon batter into prepared muffin cups. Bake 30 minutes, or until tops are golden brown and wooden pick inserted in center of muffin comes out clean.

Pumpkin Harvest Muffins

24 muffins

- 2 tablespoons unsalted butter, softened
- 3 cups plus 2 tablespoons unbleached flour, divided
- 3½ teaspoons ground cinnamon, divided
- 2 cups sugar, divided
- ½ cup wheat germ
- ¾ teaspoon salt
- 2 teaspoons baking soda
- ¼ teaspoon ground nutmeg
- 1 teaspoon ground cloves
- ¼ teaspoon ground allspice
- 1 16-ounce can solid pack pumpkin
- ¾ cup vegetable oil
- 4 eggs, lightly beaten
- 2 cups unpeeled grated Granny Smith apples
- 1 cup raisins

A delicious and nutritious way to start the morning.

Preheat oven to 400 degrees. Line 24 muffin cups with paper liners. In small bowl, combine butter, 2 tablespoons of the flour, 2 teaspoons of the cinnamon, and ½ cup of the sugar. Mix until well blended and crumbs form. Set aside.

In large bowl, combine remaining 3 cups flour, wheat germ, remaining 1½ cups sugar, salt, baking soda, remaining 1½ teaspoons cinnamon, nutmeg, cloves, and allspice. In separate bowl, combine pumpkin, oil, and eggs. Whisk to blend, add to wheat germ mixture, and stir until well blended. Stir in apples and raisins. Spoon batter into prepared muffin cups. Sprinkle reserved butter mixture on each muffin. Bake 20-25 minutes, or until tops are golden brown and wooden pick inserted in center comes out clean.

Very Berry Muffins

12 muffins

- 3 cups unbleached flour
- 1½ cups sugar
- 1 teaspoon baking powder
- ½ teaspoon salt
- 4½ teaspoons ground cinnamon
- 1¼ cups milk
- 2 eggs
- 1 cup (2 sticks) unsalted butter, melted
- 1 cup fresh or frozen blueberries
- ½ cup diced fresh or frozen strawberries
- ½ cup fresh or frozen raspberries

Preheat oven to 375 degrees. Place paper liners in 12 muffin cups. In large bowl, combine flour, sugar, baking powder, salt, and cinnamon. Make a well in center of mixture. Pour milk, eggs, and melted butter into well and stir until well blended. Fold in blueberries, strawberries, and raspberries. If using frozen berries, do not allow berries to thaw before adding to batter. Spoon batter into prepared muffin cups, filling each, three quarters full. Bake 20 minutes, or until golden brown and wooden pick inserted in center of muffin comes out clean.

Kids love these.

Spiced Pear Muffins

18 muffins

- 2 pounds firm ripe pears, peeled, cored, and diced
- 1 cup sugar
- ½ cup vegetable oil
- 2 eggs, lightly beaten
- 2 teaspoons pure vanilla extract
- 2 cups unbleached flour
- 2 teaspoons baking soda
- 2 teaspoons ground cinnamon
- 1 teaspoon ground nutmeg
- 1 teaspoon salt
- 1 cup raisins or dried cherries
- 1 cup chopped pecans

Preheat oven to 325 degrees. Place paper liners in 18 muffin cups. In small bowl, combine pears and sugar. Set aside. In large bowl, combine oil, eggs, and vanilla. Stir in reserved pear mixture. Add flour, baking soda, cinnamon, nutmeg, and salt. Stir to combine, but do not overmix. Fold in raisins and pecans. Spoon batter into prepared muffin cups. Bake 30 minutes, or until golden brown and wooden pick inserted in the center comes out clean.

Chocolate Chip Espresso Muffins

6 large muffins or 12 regular muffins

- 6 tablespoons (¾ stick) unsalted butter, softened
- ⅔ cup sugar
- 1 egg
- 1 teaspoon pure vanilla extract
- 2 tablespoons powdered instant espresso
- 2 tablespoons boiling water
- 1¾ cups unbleached flour
- 1½ teaspoons baking powder
- ½ teaspoon salt
- ¼ cup milk
- ¾ cup semisweet chocolate chips

A wonderful quick-start to your morning.

Preheat oven to 375 degrees. Grease 12 regular muffin cups or 6 large muffin cups. In large bowl, combine butter and sugar. Beat with electric mixer until fluffy. Beat in egg and vanilla until well blended.

In small bowl, combine instant espresso and boiling water. In separate bowl, combine flour, baking powder, and salt. Add gradually to butter mixture. Add espresso mixture and milk to butter mixture and blend. Fold in chocolate chips. Spoon batter into prepared muffin cups. Bake 20 minutes for regular muffins or 25-30 minutes for large muffins, or until wooden pick inserted in center comes out clean. Tops should be golden brown.

Cream Cheese Crescents

8 servings

½ cup sour cream
¼ cup sugar
½ teaspoon salt
¼ cup (½ stick) unsalted butter
1 ¼-ounce package dry yeast
¼ cup warm water (105-115 degrees)
1 egg, lightly beaten
2 cups unbleached flour

Cream Cheese Filling:

8 ounces cream cheese, softened
6 tablespoons sugar
1 egg
½ teaspoon pure vanilla extract
½ teaspoon almond extract

Glaze:

½ cup powdered sugar
1 tablespoon milk
½ teaspoon pure vanilla extract

In medium saucepan, heat sour cream over low heat. Add ¼ cup sugar, salt, and butter. Stir until butter melts. Remove from heat and cool to room temperature. In large bowl, sprinkle yeast over water. Set aside 5 minutes until slightly bubbly. Add sour cream mixture, egg, and flour to yeast mixture, and stir until well blended. Place dough in airtight container and refrigerate 8-12 hours.

In medium bowl, combine cream cheese, 6 tablespoons sugar, egg, vanilla, and almond extract and blend thoroughly. Grease large baking sheet. Remove dough from refrigerator and divide into 2 equal pieces. Let rest 5 minutes. Place 1 piece on well floured surface. Using floured rolling pin, roll out into a 12x8-inch rectangle. Spread with half of the filling mixture. Roll, jelly roll style, to form 12-inch loaf. Bring ends of loaf around to form a crescent. Place crescent on prepared baking sheet. Cut diagonal slits, about a third of the way through dough, at 2-inch intervals. Repeat with remaining piece of dough. Cover with towel and let rise until doubled in bulk, about 1 hour.

Preheat oven to 350 degrees. Combine powdered sugar, milk, and vanilla. Stir until smooth and set aside. Bake crescents 12-15 minutes or until golden brown. Remove from oven and spread with glaze while still warm. Cool on baking sheet 10 minutes. Remove and cool on racks.

Scottish Oat Scones

8 scones

- 1½ cups unbleached flour
- 1 cup quick cooking oats
- ½ cup packed light brown sugar
- 1 teaspoon baking powder
- ½ teaspoon salt
- 5 tablespoons unsalted butter, chilled and cut into ½-inch pieces
- ½ cup golden raisins
- ⅔ cup buttermilk
- 1 egg
- powdered sugar

Preheat oven to 400 degrees. Grease 8-inch round baking pan. In large bowl, combine flour, oats, brown sugar, baking powder, and salt. Cut butter into flour mixture using pastry blender. Dough will be lumpy. Fold in raisins.

In small bowl, combine buttermilk and egg and beat until well blended. Add to flour mixture and stir until well blended. With floured hands, pat dough into prepared pan. Using sharp, floured knife, deeply score top of dough forming 8 wedges.

Bake 20-22 minutes or until golden brown, scones should spring back when pressed lightly on top. Remove from oven and cool in baking pan for 10 minutes. Remove from pan and cool on rack. Dust with powdered sugar. Serve warm.

Citrus Scones

8-12 scones

- 2 cups unbleached flour
- ⅓ cup plus 1 tablespoon sugar, divided
- 2 teaspoons baking powder
- ½ teaspoon baking soda
- ¼ teaspoon salt
- 3 tablespoons unsalted butter, chilled and cut into ½-inch pieces
- 1 cup lemon yogurt
- ¼ cup orange juice
- 2 teaspoons finely grated orange zest

This is the perfect afternoon tea scone.

Preheat oven to 400 degrees. Grease 9-inch round baking pan. In large bowl, combine flour, ⅓ cup of the sugar, baking powder, baking soda, and salt. Cut butter into flour mixture using pastry blender. Dough will be lumpy. Add yogurt, orange juice, and orange zest. Stir to combine.

With floured hands, pat dough into prepared pan. Using sharp, floured knife, deeply score top of dough, making 8-12 wedges. Sprinkle with remaining 1 tablespoon sugar. Bake 20-22 minutes or until golden brown on top. Remove from oven and cool in baking pan for 10 minutes. Remove from pan and cool on rack. Serve warm

Contemplating Tea

Tea's Rich Heritage

The romance, aura, and soothing medicinal qualities of a cup of tea have been known for centuries. In China it is generally believed that drinking tea contributes to longevity. In the late 16th century, Dutch traders brought the first tea to Europe, and China green teas dominated the market until the 1800's when black teas from Sri Lanka, India, and other countries first began to make their impact on the market. Tea became India's major plantation industry in the 19th century. The ritual and ceremony of tea drinking is still strong for the Chinese and Japanese, as well as the English, where "Afternoon tea" has become a cherished tradition.

How to Make a Perfect Cup of Tea

The key to making a good cup of tea is to make sure the water is at, or close to boiling point when it hits the tea leaves. Start with fresh cold water. Warm the tea pot before beginning the steeping process by pouring some boiling water in the pot, swirling it around and discarding. The best tea is made with loose leaf tea, in a pot, using a strainer over the cup when pouring the steeped tea. Tea should be brewed for a full 4 minutes before drinking. If using milk, 2% milk is preferred to whole milk. Use 1 teaspoon loose tea per cup, for teas which have a small leaf and make strong tea such as English Breakfast, Nilgiri, Ceylon, and Kenya. Most other teas use ½ teaspoon per cup.

Types of Teas

China Teas: These teas are generally large leaf delicate teas which should not be made too strong, and do not require milk. One to two teaspoons per pot brings the best flavor. Some of the best known China teas are:

Oolong—with neither the astringency of green tea or strength of black tea.
Lapsang Souchong—a clean tasting classic tea known for its distinct, smooth, smoky flavor.
Jasmine Scented Orange Pekoe—often drunk with Chinese meals. Brew lightly.
Gunpowder Green—so named because it looks like old-fashioned rolled gunpowder. Makes a light straw colored tea.
Best Keemun—a black tea which was originally made as English Breakfast Tea in the 1820's. Serve with milk or a slice of lemon, lightly brewed.

Darjeeling: This is the "champagne" of teas. These are the most sought after teas in the world, found only in a limited area of the Himalayan foothills, with the fragrance of a field of blackcurrent bushes. They have large well formed leaves called Orange Pekoes—Orange because of the copper color of the leaf before it its dried, and Pekoe from the Chinese word meaning "tea leaf." Brew for 4-5 minutes, and milk may be added.

Assam: These are full bodied, with more astringency than Ceylons. Drink with milk.

Ceylon: These are grown in the hills of Sri Lanka. Ceylon teas have a clean, strong flavor and a rich taste that is a perfect match with milk.

Blended and Scented Teas: Long established blends are some of the most famous teas of all.

English Breakfast—Indian and Ceylon teas are blended to produce an excellent tea to be drunk all day, and with milk.
Earl Grey—named for the earl, blended with Darjeeling, Black China Keemun, and Bergamot. This is a great afternoon tea, to be drunk with milk or without.

Herbal Teas or Tisanes: Herbal teas are not really teas, but tisanes—tealike drinks made by steeping various herbs, flowers, spices, and fruits in boiling water. These drinks are caffeine free, tasty, and interesting alternatives. Blackcurrent, peppermint, camomile, mango, and peach are just a few of the many scented teas available. They are served without milk.

At left:
English Breakfast Scones, 148
Strawberry Variation
Peach Apricot Variation

English Breakfast Scones

16 scones

- 3 cups unbleached flour
- ½ cup sugar
- 1 tablespoon baking powder
- ½ teaspoon salt
- ¾ cup (1½ sticks) unsalted butter, chilled and cut into ½-inch pieces
- 4 ounces cream cheese, chilled
- 1 egg
- ½ cup plus 2 tablespoons buttermilk

Variations

Strawberry Scones:

- 1 9-ounce jar strawberry fruit spread
- ⅔ cup frozen strawberries, chopped into ½-inch pieces

Peach Apricot Scones:

- 1 9-ounce jar apricot fruit spread
- ⅔ cup dried peaches, chopped into ½-inch pieces

Blueberry Scones:

- ½ cup frozen blueberries

Onion Herb Scones:

- 1 tablespoon dried basil
- 1 tablespoon dried thyme
- 1 tablespoon dried oregano
- 1 small onion, peeled and finely chopped

For extra tender scones, drop dough directly onto baking sheet instead of rolling out. *Photo, page 146.*

Preheat oven to 400 degrees. Grease large baking sheet. In large bowl, combine flour, sugar, baking powder, and salt. Add butter and cream cheese and mix just to combine. Dough will be lumpy. Add egg and buttermilk and mix 2-3 minutes until dough forms a ball. Add 1 of the variations listed and stir just to combine.

Turn dough out onto lightly floured surface. Using floured rolling pin, gently roll out to ½-inch thickness. Do not handle or roll dough any more than necessary to prevent toughness. Cut scones into 2-inch squares. Place on prepared baking sheet.

Bake 10 minutes. Reduce oven temperature to 375 degrees and continue baking 15 minutes or until golden brown. Remove from oven and cool on baking sheet 10 minutes. Remove and cool on rack. Serve warm.

Southwestern Cheddar Scones

6 scones

- 1½ cups unbleached flour
- ¾ cup yellow cornmeal
- 1¼ teaspoons baking powder
- 1 teaspoon sugar
- ½ teaspoon salt
- ⅛ teaspoon cayenne
- 3 tablespoons unsalted butter, chilled
- ¾ cup plus 2 tablespoons shredded cheddar cheese, divided
- 1 egg, separated
- ¼ cup milk
- ¼ cup cream style corn
- ½ cup chopped green chiles

This hearty scone is great with chili or soup.

Preheat oven to 425 degrees. Grease large baking sheet. In large bowl, combine flour, cornmeal, baking powder, sugar, salt, and cayenne. Whisk to blend. Add butter and blend until mixture resembles coarse meal. Stir in ¾ cup of the cheddar cheese.

In small bowl, combine egg yolk and milk, whisk to blend and add to reserved flour mixture. Add corn and chiles. Stir just until soft dough forms. Turn dough out onto lightly floured surface and knead gently 8-10 times. Pat into 6-inch round shape and cut into 6 equal pie-shaped pieces. Arrange on prepared baking sheet and brush tops with egg white. Sprinkle remaining cheddar cheese over each scone. Bake 15-17 minutes. Serve warm.

Tropical Fruit Bread

2 loaves

- ⅔ cup unsalted butter, softened
- 2 cups sugar
- 4 eggs
- 1 ripe papaya (about 1 pound), peeled, seeded, and diced
- ¾ cup pineapple juice
- 3⅓ cups unbleached flour
- 2 teaspoons baking soda
- 1½ teaspoons salt
- ½ teaspoon baking powder
- 1 teaspoon ground cinnamon
- 1 teaspoon ground cloves
- ⅔ cup chopped macadamia nuts

Preheat oven to 350 degrees. Grease two 9x5-inch loaf pans. In large bowl, cream butter and sugar until fluffy. Stir in eggs, papaya, and pineapple juice. Add flour, baking soda, salt, baking powder, cinnamon, cloves, and nuts and stir until well blended. Pour into prepared pans. Bake 70 minutes, or until golden brown and wooden pick inserted into center comes out clean.

Tart Cherry Oat Soda Bread

1 loaf

- 2 cups whole wheat flour
- 1½ cups unbleached flour
- ½ cup plus 1 tablespoon quick cooking oats, divided
- 1 teaspoon salt
- 1 teaspoon baking powder
- 1 teaspoon baking soda
- ¾ cup dried tart or sour cherries, soaked in 1 cup boiling water to plump, drained, liquid reserved
- 1 tablespoon caraway seeds (optional)
- 1 cup plain yogurt
- ¾ cup plus 1 tablespoon milk, divided
- 2 tablespoons honey

Preheat oven to 375 degrees. Grease baking sheet. In large bowl, combine whole wheat flour, unbleached flour, ½ cup of the oats, salt, baking powder, baking soda, cherries, and caraway seeds, if desired.

In small bowl, combine yogurt, ¾ cup of the milk, and honey. Stir until well blended. Add to reserved flour mixture and blend to form a soft dough. If dough is too dry, add reserved cherry liquid, 1 teaspoon at a time. Turn dough out onto lightly floured surface and knead gently 8-10 times or about 30 seconds.

Form into round loaf and place on prepared baking sheet. Brush loaf with remaining 1 tablespoon milk, and sprinkle remaining 1 tablespoon oats on top. Bake 35-40 minutes or until golden brown. Remove from oven, and cool on baking sheet 10 minutes. Remove and cool on rack.

Try this bread toasted.

Western Slope Peach Bread

1 loaf

- ½ cup (1 stick) unsalted butter, softened
- 1 cup sugar
- 1 egg
- ½ teaspoon almond extract
- 2 cups unbleached flour
- 1 teaspoon baking soda
- ½ teaspoon salt
- 1 teaspoon ground cinnamon
- ½ teaspoon ground nutmeg
- 1 cup coarsely chopped fresh or frozen peaches
- ½ cup apple or peach juice
- ½ cup chopped almonds (optional)

Preheat oven to 350 degrees. Grease 9x5-inch loaf pan. Line bottom of pan with waxed or parchment paper. In large bowl, cream butter and sugar until fluffy. Beat in egg and almond extract. In large bowl, combine flour, baking soda, salt, cinnamon, and nutmeg. Stir until well blended. Alternately add flour mixture, peaches, and apple juice to butter mixture, stirring until well blended. Stir in almonds, if desired. Pour into prepared pan.

Bake 55-65 minutes until golden brown. Remove from oven and cool in pan 10 minutes. Remove from pan and cool on rack.

Quick and Easy Dinner Rolls

24 rolls

- 5-6 cups unbleached flour, divided
- ½ cup sugar
- 1½ teaspoons salt
- 2 ¼-ounce packages dry yeast
- 1 cup milk
- ⅔ cup water
- ¼ cup (½ stick) unsalted butter, softened
- 2 eggs

You may substitute 1½ cups whole wheat flour for 1½ cups of the white flour in this low-fat recipe.

In large bowl, combine 2 cups of flour, sugar, salt, and yeast. In medium saucepan, combine milk, water, and butter, and heat until warm (butter need not melt). Gradually add milk mixture to flour mixture and beat with electric mixer, 2 minutes, at medium speed. Add eggs and ¾ cup of the flour. Beat 2 minutes at high speed. Stir in remaining flour, as needed, until dough is stiff.

Turn dough out onto lightly floured surface and knead until smooth and elastic, about 8 minutes. Place dough in oiled bowl, turning to coat entire surface. Cover with plastic wrap and towel, and let rise 20 minutes. Punch down. Grease 13x9x2-inch baking pan. Shape dough into 1 long loaf and place on cutting board. Using sharp knife, cut dough into 24 pieces. Roll each piece into a ball, place in prepared pan, and cover as before. Refrigerate 4-12 hours.

Preheat oven to 375 degrees. Remove rolls from refrigerator and let stand 20 minutes. Bake 15-20 minutes, or until golden brown. Remove from oven and cool in baking pan 10 minutes. Remove from pan and serve warm.

Traditional Sourdough Starter

2⅔ cups

- 2 cups unbleached flour
- 3 tablespoons sugar
- 1 ¼-ounce package dry yeast
- ½ teaspoon salt
- 2 cups warm water (105-115 degrees)

In large bowl, combine flour, sugar, yeast, salt, and water. Mix until well blended. Cover with cloth and set in warm place 2-3 days, stirring several times each day. Place starter in plastic container and cover with plastic wrap. Poke 3 air vents in top of plastic wrap and store in refrigerator.

Remove amount of starter needed for recipe. Replenish starter with equal parts of water and flour, every 7-10 days. After replenishing, leave starter out at room temperature overnight. Return to refrigerator and use as needed. If clear liquid forms on top, stir to combine.

Matchless Sourdough Oatmeal Bread

3 loaves

- 2 cups steel cut (not rolled) oatmeal
- 2 cups boiling water
- ¾ cup packed light brown sugar, divided
- 1½ cups Traditional Sourdough Starter (recipe above)
- 5½ cups unbleached flour, divided
- 3½ cups whole wheat flour
- 1 ¼-ounce package dry yeast
- 1 cup warm milk (105-115 degrees)
- ½ cup (1 stick) unsalted butter, melted
- 2 teaspoons salt

This hearty recipe requires overnight proofing to strengthen the sourdough flavor.

In large bowl, combine oatmeal, water, and ¼ cup of the brown sugar. Cool to lukewarm. Add sourdough starter and 2 cups of the unbleached flour. Beat until smooth. Cover with plastic wrap and towel and set aside 8-12 hours.

In large bowl, combine whole wheat flour with remaining 3½ cups unbleached flour. In small bowl, sprinkle yeast over milk. Stir to dissolve yeast and set aside 5 minutes until slightly bubbly. Uncover oatmeal mixture and stir. Add yeast mixture, melted butter, salt, and remaining ½ cup brown sugar. Blend thoroughly. Add whole wheat flour mixture, 2 cups at a time, until a soft, workable dough forms.

Turn dough out onto lightly floured surface and knead 8-10 minutes or until smooth and elastic. Place dough in oiled bowl, turning to coat entire surface. Cover with plastic wrap and towel and let rise until doubled in bulk, 1-2 hours.

Grease three 9x5-inch loaf pans. Punch dough down and divide into 3 pieces. Let rest 5 minutes. Shape each piece into a loaf and place into prepared pans. Cover loaves loosely with plastic wrap and let rise until doubled in bulk, about 1 hour.

Preheat oven to 350 degrees. For a crispy crust, place 1 cup water in an ovenproof bowl and place in oven while baking bread. Bake 50-60 minutes or until loaves sound hollow when tapped on top. Remove from oven and cool in pans 10 minutes. Remove from pans and cool on rack.

Sourdough Onion Twist

1 loaf

1	¼-ounce package dry yeast
¾	cup warm water (105-115 degrees), divided
1	cup Traditional Sourdough Starter, (page 152)
½	cup plus 2 teaspoons unsalted butter, melted, divided
¼	cup sugar
1½	teaspoons salt
1	egg, lightly beaten
½	cup scalded milk, cooled to lukewarm (100-110 degrees)
4-5	cups unbleached flour
	Filling:
1	tablespoon unsalted butter
½	cup diced onion
2	tablespoons unsalted butter, melted
1½	tablespoons freshly grated Parmesan cheese
1	tablespoon sesame seeds
¼	teaspoon garlic powder
1	teaspoon paprika

Photo, page 134.

In small bowl, sprinkle yeast over ¼ cup of the water. Set aside 5 minutes until slightly bubbly. In large bowl, combine sourdough starter, remaining ½ cup water, ½ cup of the melted butter, sugar, salt, egg, milk, and reserved yeast mixture. Add 2 cups of the flour and stir until well blended. Add 2 more cups of the flour and stir until well blended. Add additional flour ¼ cup at a time, as needed, to form medium-stiff dough.

Turn dough out onto lightly floured surface and knead 5 minutes or until dough is smooth and elastic. Place dough in oiled bowl, turning to coat entire surface. Cover with plastic wrap and towel and let rise until doubled in bulk, about 1 hour.

In medium skillet, heat 1 tablespoon butter over medium heat. Add onion and saute until translucent, about 10 minutes. Transfer to medium bowl. Add 2 tablespoons melted butter, Parmesan, sesame seeds, garlic powder, and paprika. Set aside. Grease large baking sheet. Punch down dough. Turn dough out onto well floured surface and knead gently 3 minutes. Let rest 5 minutes. Using floured rolling pin, roll dough into a 12x18-inch rectangle. Cut dough into three 4x18-inch strips.

Spread reserved onion filling evenly over each strip, leaving 1 long edge of each strip uncovered. Starting with long covered edges, roll each strip, jelly roll style, to form an 18-inch long loaf. Pinch edges and ends to seal. Place loaves, side-by-side, on prepared baking sheet. Pinch 1 end of loaves together to seal. Braid loaves and pinch ends together to seal. Cover as before and let rise until doubled in bulk, about 1-2 hours.

Preheat oven to 350 degrees. Bake 30 minutes or until golden brown. Remove from oven. Brush with remaining 2 teaspoons melted butter, and cool on baking sheet 10 minutes. Remove and cool on rack.

Columbine Sour Cream Bread

2 loaves

- 1 ¼-ounce package dry yeast
- 3 tablespoons sugar
- ¼ cup warm water (105-115 degrees)
- 2 cups sour cream, at room temperature
- 1 teaspoon salt
- ¼ teaspoon baking soda
- 4½-5 cups unbleached flour, divided

Sour cream softens the texture of this bread. Great toasted.

In small bowl, sprinkle yeast and sugar over water. Set aside 5 minutes until slightly bubbly. In large bowl, combine sour cream, salt, and baking soda. Stir in reserved yeast mixture. Add 4 cups of the flour, 1 cup at a time, stirring to form a sticky dough. Turn dough out onto floured surface. Using 2 rubber spatulas, fold dough over several times, adding additional flour to prevent sticking. Knead 8-10 minutes. Place dough in oiled bowl, turning to coat entire surface. Cover with plastic wrap and towel and let rise until doubled in bulk, about 1 hour.

Grease two 9x5-inch loaf pans. Punch dough down and turn out onto lightly floured surface. Knead 1 minute and divide dough in half. Shape each piece into a loaf and place in prepared pans. Cover as before and let rise until doubled in bulk, about 45 minutes. Preheat oven to 375 degrees. Bake 30-35 minutes or until loaves sound hollow when tapped on top. Remove from oven and cool in pans 10 minutes. Remove from pans and cool on rack.

Crystal River Rye Bread

2 loaves

- 2 tablespoons caraway seeds
- 1 cup hot water (120-130 degrees)
- 1 ¼-ounce package dry yeast
- 1 cup warm buttermilk (105-115 degrees)
- 1 tablespoon salt
- 2 tablespoons unsalted butter, softened
- ½ cup honey
- 3 cups rye flour
- 1 cup whole wheat flour
- 1½ cups unbleached flour, divided
- 2 tablespoons cornmeal

Three flours add variety to this healthful loaf.

In large bowl, combine caraway seeds and hot water. Let stand 10 minutes to soften seeds. When water has cooled slightly, sprinkle in yeast. Add buttermilk, salt, butter, honey, rye flour, whole wheat flour, and 1 cup of the unbleached flour. Stir until well blended. If dough is sticky, add additional flour, ¼ cup at a time, until dough is no longer sticky. Turn dough out onto lightly floured surface and knead 8-10 minutes, or until dough is smooth and elastic.

Place dough in oiled bowl, turning to coat entire surface. Cover with plastic wrap and towel and let rise until doubled in bulk, 2-3 hours. Grease large baking sheet and sprinkle with cornmeal. Punch dough down and divide in half. Shape each piece into a loaf and place on prepared baking sheet. Cover with towel and let rise until doubled in bulk, about 1 hour. Preheat oven to 375 degrees. Bake 30-40 minutes or until loaves sound hollow when tapped on bottom. Remove from oven and cool on baking sheet 10 minutes. Remove and cool on rack.

Corn Shortbread

48 rounds

- ½ cup (1 stick) unsalted butter, softened
- ½ cup sugar
- 1 cup yellow cornmeal
- 2 eggs, at room temperature
- 1 teaspoon salt
- 1½ cups unbleached flour, divided

Preheat oven to 375 degrees. Grease large baking sheet. In large bowl, cream butter and sugar 2 minutes. Add cornmeal, eggs, and salt and blend until smooth. Add 1¼ cups of the flour and stir until well blended. Dough should be moist, but not sticky.

Turn dough out onto a lightly floured surface and roll to ¼-inch thickness, adding additional flour if dough sticks to rolling pin or surface. Using 2-inch round or any shape cookie cutter, cut about 48 rounds from dough. Place rounds on baking sheet, not allowing edges to touch. Bake 20-22 minutes or until rounds are lightly browned. Serve warm or at room temperature.

Challah

2 loaves

- 2 ¼-ounce packages dry yeast
- ½ cup honey
- 1¾ cups warm water (105-115 degrees)
- 8-8½ cups unbleached flour, divided
- 4 teaspoons salt
- 1 cup vegetable oil
- 3 eggs

Topping:
(optional)

- 1 egg
- 1 teaspoon water
- 2-3 tablespoons sesame seeds or poppy seeds

This traditional Jewish yeast bread has a light and airy texture.

In large mixing bowl, combine yeast, honey and water. Set aside 5 minutes until slightly bubbly. Add 2 cups of the flour and salt. Mix well. Blend in oil, eggs, and 6 cups of the flour, stirring to form soft dough. Turn dough out onto lightly floured surface and knead 8-10 minutes, or until dough is smooth and elastic. Add additional flour as needed to prevent sticking. Place dough in oiled bowl, turning to coat the entire surface. Cover with plastic wrap and towel and let rise until doubled, 2-3 hours.

Grease 2 large baking sheets. Punch dough down and divide in half. Divide each half into 3 parts. Shape each into a 16-inch long loaf, totalling 6 pieces. Place 3 of the pieces, side by side, on 1 of the prepared baking sheets. Pinch 1 end of loaves together and braid. Pinch ends together to seal. Repeat with remaining dough on remaining baking sheet. Cover as before and let rise until doubled in bulk, about 1 hour.

Preheat oven to 325 degrees. If topping is desired, beat egg and water lightly. Brush over braids and sprinkle with sesame seeds. Bake 40-45 minutes or until loaves sound hollow when tapped on bottom. Remove from oven. Cool on baking sheets 10 minutes. Remove and cool on rack.

Front Range Multi-Grain Bread

2 loaves

4 tablespoons sugar, divided
1½ cups warm water (105-115 degrees)
2 ¼-ounce packages dry yeast
4 cups unbleached flour, divided
1 cup very warm milk (115-125 degrees)
3 tablespoons unsalted butter, softened
1 tablespoon salt
1 cup regular oats
⅓ cup wheat germ
2 cups whole wheat flour
⅓ cup sunflower seeds

This all-purpose bread is terrific for sandwiches.

In large bowl, dissolve 2 tablespoons of the sugar in water. Sprinkle in yeast and set aside 5 minutes until slightly bubbly. Gradually add 1½ cups of the unbleached flour and beat until smooth. Cover with plastic wrap and set aside in warm place 1 hour.

In large bowl, combine warm milk, butter, salt, and remaining 2 tablespoons sugar. Stir until butter has melted. Cool to lukewarm. Stir in reserved yeast mixture, oats, wheat germ, and whole wheat flour. Stir to combine. Add 2 cups of the unbleached flour and stir to form a soft dough, adding additional flour, ¼ cup at a time, if needed.

Turn dough out onto lightly floured surface and knead in sunflower seeds. Add more flour, if needed to prevent sticking. Knead 8-10 minutes, or until dough is smooth and elastic. Place dough in oiled bowl, turning to coat entire surface. Cover with plastic wrap and towel and let rise until doubled in bulk, about 30 minutes.

Grease two 9x5-inch loaf pans. Punch dough down and knead on lightly floured surface 1 minute. Let rest 5 minutes. Divide dough in half. Form dough into 2 loaves and place in prepared pans. Cover as before and let rise until doubled in bulk, about 30 minutes.

Preheat oven to 375 degrees. Bake 45-50 minutes or until loaves sound hollow when tapped on top. Remove from oven and cool in pans 10 minutes. Remove from pans and cool on rack.

Honey Oat Bread

2 loaves

- ½ cup honey
- 1½ cups very warm water (115-125 degrees)
- 2 ¼-ounce packages dry yeast
- 2 cups quick cooking oats, divided
- 5-6 cups unbleached flour, divided
- 2 teaspoons salt
- ½ cup (1 stick) unsalted butter, softened
- 3 eggs, divided
- 1 tablespoon water

This is a slightly sweet bread with a fine texture.

In large bowl, combine honey and 1½ cups of the water. Set aside 10 minutes. Add yeast to honey mixture and set aside 5 minutes until slightly bubbly. Add 1½ cups of the oats, 5 cups of the flour, salt, butter, and 2 of the eggs. Stir until well blended. Add additional flour, ¼ cup at a time, until a stiff dough is formed. Turn dough out onto lightly floured surface and knead 8-10 minutes, or until dough is smooth and elastic. Place dough in oiled bowl, turning to coat entire surface. Cover with plastic wrap and towel and let rise until doubled in bulk, about 1 hour.

Grease two 9x5-inch loaf pans. Punch dough down and divide in half. Shape each piece into a loaf. Beat remaining egg with 1 tablespoon water. Sprinkle remaining ½ cup oats on work surface. Brush egg mixture over top of loaves and roll in oats to cover top. Place in prepared pans. Cover as before and let rise until doubled in bulk, about 1 hour. Preheat oven to 375 degrees. Bake 25-35 minutes or until loaves sound hollow when tapped on top. Remove from oven and cool in pans 10 minutes. Remove from pans and cool on rack.

Brew Pub Bread

2 loaves

- 2 cups dark beer
- 1 cup oatmeal
- 2 teaspoons salt
- ½ cup molasses
- ¼ cup (½ stick) unsalted butter, softened
- 1 ¼-ounce package dry yeast
- ⅓ cup warm water (105-115 degrees)
- 5-6 cups unbleached flour

A subtle beer flavor makes this a nice accompaniment to hearty soups and sandwiches.

In small saucepan, heat beer to boiling. In large bowl, combine oatmeal, salt, molasses, butter, and hot beer. Set aside and cool to lukewarm. Dissolve yeast in water. Add to oatmeal mixture and stir to blend. Stir in flour, 2 cups at a time, stirring well after each addition. Turn dough out onto lightly floured surface and knead 8-10 minutes, or until smooth and elastic. Place in oiled bowl, turning to coat entire surface. Cover with plastic wrap and towel and let rise until doubled in bulk, about 1 hour. Punch dough down, and divide in half. Shape each piece into a loaf and place in ungreased 9x5-inch loaf pans. Cover as before and let rise until doubled in bulk, about 45 minutes.

Preheat oven to 375 degrees. Bake 30-45 minutes, or until loaves sound hollow when tapped on top and sides pull away from pans. Remove from oven and cool in pans 10 minutes. Remove from pans and cool on rack.

Hearty Health Bread

3 loaves

- 2 ¼-ounce packages dry yeast
- 1 cup whole wheat flour
- 6-6½ cups unbleached flour, divided
- 1 cup oatmeal
- 1 cup whole bran cereal
- 1 cup raisins
- 1½ cups cottage cheese
- 2 tablespoons unsalted butter, softened
- 2 teaspoons salt
- ½ cup molasses
- ⅔ cup packed light brown sugar
- ½ cup sunflower seeds
- 2½ cups boiling water

Whole wheat flour and bran cereal add fiber to this single-rise bread.

Grease three 9x5-inch loaf pans. In small bowl, combine yeast, whole wheat flour, and 2 cups of the unbleached flour. In large bowl, combine oatmeal, bran cereal, raisins, cottage cheese, butter, salt, molasses, brown sugar, and sunflower seeds. Add boiling water and stir until butter melts. Add flour mixture and stir until well blended. Add 3 additional cups of the unbleached flour and stir until well blended.

Turn dough out onto lightly floured surface and knead 8-10 minutes, or until dough is smooth and elastic. Add additional flour as needed to prevent sticking. Divide dough into 3 equal pieces. Form each piece into a small loaf and place in prepared pans. Cover with plastic wrap and towel and let rise until doubled in bulk, about 1 hour. Preheat oven to 375 degrees. Bake 30-40 minutes or until loaves sound hollow when tapped on top. Remove from oven and cool in pans 10 minutes. Remove from pans and cool on rack.

Roundup Bubble Bread

1 loaf

- 2 pounds frozen dinner roll dough, thawed
- ⅓ cup unsalted butter, melted and cooled to room temperature
- ¼ teaspoon dried basil, crumbled
- 2 tablespoons chopped fresh parsley
- 2 tablespoons chopped green onions
- 2 teaspoons minced garlic
- 1 tablespoon freshly grated Parmesan cheese

An easy, savory version of monkey bread.

Grease 12-cup bundt pan. Arrange dinner roll dough in prepared pan. In small bowl, combine melted butter, basil, parsley, green onions, and garlic. Pour over dough. Cover with plastic wrap and towel and let rise until doubled in bulk, about 1 hour.

Preheat oven to 375 degrees. Sprinkle cheese over bread. Bake 30-35 minutes or until golden brown. Remove from oven and cool in pan 10 minutes. Turn out onto serving plate. Pull apart to serve, do not cut. Serve warm.

Armenian Cracker Bread

4 10x14-inch pieces

- 1 cup warm water (105-115 degrees)
- 1 ¼-ounce package dry yeast
- 1 teaspoon sugar
- ¼ cup (½ stick) unsalted butter, melted and cooled to lukewarm
- 1½ teaspoons salt
- 1 cup whole wheat flour
- 1½-2 cups unbleached flour, divided
- ¼ cup milk

Topping Variations

Seeded:

- 1 tablespoon coarse salt
- 1 tablespoon sesame seeds or poppy seeds

Parmesan Oregano:

- ½ cup freshly grated Parmesan cheese
- ½ teaspoon dried oregano

Cinnamon Sugar:

- 1 teaspoon ground cinnamon
- ¼ cup sugar
- ¼ teaspoon ground nutmeg

These easy and unusual homemade crackers keep for weeks in a sealed container.

Pour water into large bowl. Sprinkle yeast and sugar over water. Stir with fork to dissolve yeast. Let stand 5 minutes until mixture is slightly bubbly. Add melted butter, salt, whole wheat flour, and 1 cup of the unbleached flour and beat until smooth. Add enough of the remaining ½-1 cup unbleached flour to form a stiff dough. Turn dough out onto lightly floured surface and knead 8-10 minutes, or until dough is smooth and elastic. Add additional flour as needed to prevent sticking. Place dough in oiled bowl, turning to coat entire surface. Cover with plastic wrap and towel and let rise until doubled in bulk, about 1 hour.

Preheat oven to 350 degrees. Punch down dough and divide into 4 equal pieces. Using floured rolling pin, roll 1 piece into a 10x14-inch rectangle. Transfer to baking sheet and brush with milk. Select Topping Variation and sprinkle over dough. Repeat with remaining pieces of dough.

Bake 20 minutes or until golden brown. Remove from oven and cool on baking sheet 10 minutes. Remove and cool on rack. Serve bread whole, breaking off individual pieces.

Bonanza Bacon Bread

2 loaves

- 1 pound thick-cut bacon, cut into ½-inch pieces
- ½ cup minced green onions
- 1 teaspoon minced garlic
- 1½ ¼-ounce packages dry yeast
- 1 teaspoon sugar
- 1½ cups warm water, divided
- 4 eggs, at room temperature, divided
- 1 egg yolk, at room temperature
- 5-5½ cups unbleached flour
- 1 teaspoon salt
- 1 teaspoon freshly ground black pepper
- 6 tablespoons (¾ stick) unsalted butter, softened
- 1 tablespoon milk

Try this bread with hot cereal in the morning.

In large skillet, cook bacon over low heat until crisp. Remove and drain on paper towels, reserving drippings. Drain all but 2 tablespoons of the drippings from skillet. Add green onions and cook, stirring frequently, until lightly browned. Stir in garlic, remove from heat, and cool to room temperature.

In large bowl, combine yeast, sugar, and ½ cup of the water. Let stand 5 minutes until bubbly. Add 3 of the eggs and egg yolk and stir gently until smooth. Stir in remaining 1 cup water, 1½ cups of the flour, reserved green onion mixture, salt, and pepper. Add remaining 3½-4 cups flour, 1 cup at a time, alternately adding butter, 1 tablespoon at a time, until mixture forms a soft dough.

Turn dough out onto lightly floured surface and knead in reserved cooked bacon, ½ cup at a time. Continue kneading about 6 minutes until the dough is smooth and elastic. Place dough in oiled bowl, turning to coat the entire surface. Cover with plastic wrap and towel, and let rise until doubled in bulk, about 1 hour. Punch dough down, turn out onto lightly floured surface and knead until smooth. Divide dough in half. Cover with towel and let rest 10 minutes.

Preheat oven to 375 degrees. Line baking sheet with waxed or parchment paper. Form each half of the dough into an 8x5-inch oval and place on prepared baking sheet. Cover with towel and let rise until doubled in bulk, about 1 hour. In small bowl, combine remaining egg and milk. Whisk to blend and brush over tops of loaves. Using a serrated knife, make several cuts ⅛-inch deep in each loaf.

Bake 40 minutes, or until golden brown and loaves sound hollow when tapped on bottom. Remove from oven, and cool on baking sheet 10 minutes. Remove and cool on rack.

Chef's Cheddar Onion Loaf

2 loaves

- 2 ¼-ounce packages dry yeast
- 1 cup warm water (105-115 degrees)
- 1 cup warm milk (105-115 degrees)
- 1 tablespoon sugar
- 1 teaspoon salt
- 3 tablespoons olive oil
- 5-6 cups unbleached flour, divided
- 1 cup finely chopped onion
- 2½ cups shredded sharp cheddar cheese

For additional color, add 3 tablespoons chopped green onions to cheddar mixture. Photo, page 136.

In large bowl, dissolve yeast in water and milk. Set aside 10 minutes until slightly bubbly. Add sugar, salt, olive oil, and 5 cups of the flour. Stir until well blended. If dough is sticky, add additional flour, ¼ cup at a time. Turn dough out onto lightly floured surface and knead 8-10 minutes, or until dough is smooth and elastic. Place dough in oiled bowl, turning to coat entire surface. Cover with plastic wrap and towel and let rise until doubled in bulk, about 1 hour.

Grease two 9x5-inch loaf pans. Punch dough down and divide into 6 equal pieces. Shape each piece into an 8-inch loaf, by rolling with hands. Combine onion and cheese and spread on flat surface. Roll 3 of the dough pieces in onion mixture until well covered. Twist onion coated loaves together to form 1 loaf. Twisting will disperse onion and cheese. Repeat process with remaining 3 parts. Place in prepared pans and sprinkle any remaining onion mixture on top. Cover as before and let rise until doubled in bulk, about 1 hour. Preheat oven to 350 degrees. Bake 30-40 minutes or until loaves sound hollow when tapped on top. Remove from oven and cool in pans 10 minutes. Remove from pans and cool on rack.

New Delhi Flat Bread

8 5-inch loaves

- 2¼ cups unbleached flour
- ½ cup plain yogurt
- 1 egg, slightly beaten
- 1 teaspoon sugar
- ¼ teaspoon salt
- ¼ teaspoon baking soda
- 1½ teaspoons baking powder
- ½ cup milk
- olive oil
- poppy seeds or sesame seeds

Here's a great way to make your own pita bread.

In large bowl, combine flour, yogurt, egg, sugar, salt, baking soda, and baking powder. Add milk, and stir to form soft dough. Turn dough out onto lightly floured surface and knead 8-10 minutes, or until dough is smooth and elastic. Place dough in oiled bowl, turning to coat entire surface. Cover with plastic wrap and towel and let rest in warm place, 3 hours.

Divide dough into 8 equal pieces. On lightly floured surface, flatten each piece into a 1-inch thick disk. Using floured rolling pin, roll each piece into a 5-inch circle, about ¼-inch thick. Preheat oven to 450 degrees. Place 2 baking sheets in oven, 5 minutes. Brush bread with olive oil and sprinkle with poppy seeds. Place dough on hot sheets. Bake 7-9 minutes or until golden brown. Remove from oven and cool on baking sheets 5 minutes. Remove and cool on rack.

Sweet and Salty Flat Bread

1 loaf

- 1½ teaspoons cornmeal
- 1½ cups unbleached flour
- 1½ cups whole wheat flour
- 1 ¼-ounce package dry yeast
- 1 tablespoon sugar
- 1 teaspoon salt
- 1¼ cups warm water (105-115 degrees)
- ¼ cup plus 1 tablespoon olive oil, divided
- ¼ cup ripe olives, halved and pitted
- ¼ cup green olives, halved and pitted
- 3 tablespoons chopped fresh rosemary or 3 teaspoons dried rosemary
- 2 teaspoons sugar
- 1 teaspoon coarse salt
- ½ teaspoon freshly ground black pepper

For thin bread, use 14-inch pan. For thicker bread, use 12-inch pan.

Grease round pizza pan and sprinkle with 1½ teaspoons cornmeal. In large bowl, combine unbleached flour, whole wheat flour, yeast, sugar, and salt. Add water and ¼ cup of the olive oil and stir until the dough is well blended and sticky. Place dough on prepared pan. Gently press into pan with floured fingers. Cover with plastic wrap and towel. Let rise until doubled in bulk, about 1 hour.

Preheat oven to 350 degrees. Brush top of dough with remaining 1 tablespoon olive oil and sprinkle olives over top. Combine rosemary, sugar, coarse salt, and pepper and sprinkle over olives. Bake 30-40 minutes, or until golden brown and loaf sounds hollow when tapped on bottom. Remove from oven. Cool on pan 10 minutes. Remove and cool on rack.

Focaccia

1 loaf

1¾ cups unbleached flour
1 ¼-ounce package dry yeast
1 teaspoon sugar
¾ teaspoon salt
¾ cup hot water (120-130 degrees)
2½ tablespoons olive oil

Topping Variations

Gorgonzola Pine Nut:

2 tablespoons olive oil
½ cup crumbled Gorgonzola cheese
2 tablespoons pine nuts

Feta Pesto Tomato:

1½ tablespoons olive oil
½ cup pesto
½ cup crumbled feta cheese
6 sun-dried tomatoes, diced

Garlic Rosemary:

3 tablespoons olive oil
1 teaspoon minced garlic
2 tablespoons fresh or 1 tablespoon dried rosemary

Photo, page 76.

In large bowl, combine flour, yeast, sugar, and salt. In small bowl, combine water and olive oil. Slowly add to flour mixture, stirring to form sticky dough. Turn dough out onto lightly floured surface, kneading in additional flour as needed, until dough is smooth and elastic. Place dough in oiled bowl, turning to coat entire surface. Cover with plastic wrap and towel and let rise until doubled in bulk, about 40 minutes.

Preheat oven to 375 degrees. Grease 13-inch round baking sheet. Punch dough down and let rest 5 minutes. Turn dough out onto lightly floured surface. Using floured rolling pin, roll dough into a 12-inch round. Place on prepared baking sheet. Build up edges of dough slightly to form crust. Cover as before and let rise 15-30 minutes. Poke indentations over surface of dough with fingers. Select Topping Variation. Drizzle with olive oil and top with remaining ingredients.

Bake 30 minutes or until lightly browned on top and sides. Remove from oven and cool on baking sheet 5 minutes. Cut into wedges and serve warm.

Italian Country Flat Bread

1 loaf

- 2½–3 cups unbleached flour, divided
- 1 ¼-ounce package dry yeast
- 2 teaspoons salt, divided
- 1¼ cups hot water (120–130 degrees)
- ¼ pound prosciutto or ham, diced
- ¼ cup freshly grated Romano cheese
- 1 cup freshly grated Parmesan cheese
- 2 eggs, at room temperature
- ¼ cup olive oil
- ½ teaspoon freshly ground black pepper

This may be prepared and kneaded in a heavy-duty electric mixer equipped with a dough hook.

In large bowl, combine 2 cups of the flour, yeast, and 1 teaspoon of the salt. Slowly pour water over flour mixture, stirring to blend. Add more flour, ¼ cup at a time, to form soft dough. Turn dough out onto lightly floured surface and knead 8–10 minutes, or until smooth and elastic. Place dough in oiled bowl, turning to coat entire surface. Cover with plastic wrap and towel and let rise until doubled in bulk, about 45 minutes.

Grease 12–14-inch round baking sheet. In medium bowl, combine prosciutto, Romano, Parmesan, eggs, olive oil, remaining 1 teaspoon salt, and pepper. Stir until well blended. Punch dough down. Turn out onto lightly floured surface. Sprinkle prosciutto mixture over dough, and knead into dough. If dough is too sticky, sprinkle more of the flour on surface and continue to knead in flour and prosciutto mixture. Knead 8–10 minutes and let rest 5 minutes. With floured hands, press dough onto prepared baking sheet. Cover as before and let rise until doubled in bulk, about 1 hour.

Preheat oven to 425 degrees. Bake 15–18 minutes or until loaf sounds hollow when tapped on top. Remove from oven, and cool on baking sheet 10 minutes. Remove and cool on rack.

Stuffed Spinach Feta Bread

1 loaf

- 2 ¼-ounce packages dry yeast
- 1¼ cups warm water
- 1½ cups whole wheat flour
- 1½ cups unbleached flour
- 3 tablespoons snipped fresh dill
- 1½ teaspoons coarse salt
- 1½ teaspoons sugar
- ¼ cup olive oil
- 15 ounces frozen chopped spinach, thawed and squeezed dry
- 1¼ cups crumbled feta cheese
- 1¼ cups grated mozzarella cheese
- ¾ cup ricotta cheese
- 2½ teaspoons minced garlic
- 1 teaspoon freshly ground black pepper
- 4 oil-packed sun-dried tomatoes, drained and chopped into ½-inch pieces
- 1 egg, well beaten

In large bowl, sprinkle yeast over water and stir. Set aside 5 minutes until slightly bubbly. Add whole wheat flour, unbleached flour, dill, coarse salt, sugar, and olive oil and mix until well blended. Dough should be soft, but not sticky. If dough is sticky, add more flour, ¼ cup at a time, until dough is no longer sticky. Turn dough out onto lightly floured surface and knead 8-10 minutes, or until smooth and elastic. Place dough in oiled bowl, turning to coat entire surface. Cover with plastic wrap and towel and let rise until doubled in bulk, about 40 minutes.

In medium bowl, combine spinach, feta, mozzarella, ricotta, garlic, pepper, and sun-dried tomatoes. Grease medium baking sheet. Punch dough down. Turn dough out onto lightly floured surface and knead 30 seconds. Allow dough to rest 5 minutes. Using floured rolling pin, roll dough out to form 12x8-inch rectangle. Spread spinach mixture over dough, leaving a ½-inch border. Roll up dough to form 12-inch long loaf. Place on prepared baking sheet. Brush beaten egg over top. Cover as before and let rise until doubled in bulk, about 40 minutes.

Preheat oven to 425 degrees. Bake 20-25 minutes or until loaf sounds hollow when tapped on top. Remove from oven and cool on baking sheet 10 minutes. Remove and cool on rack. Serve warm.

Even in the heart of the city, you are still enveloped by the majesty of the mountains. And, whether you're enjoying a night at the symphony or just dining by city lights, you can create an elegant urban dinner with bold flavors and bright colors.

Dinner With a View

soup

Garlic Vichyssoise *55*

salad

Greens With Anise Vinaigrette and Crostini *83*

main dish

Scallops and Fettuccine *170*

bread

Italian Country Flat Bread *164*

dessert

Tiramisu *359*

wine

Blanc de Noir

Clockwise from top:
Italian Country Flat Bread
Scallops and Fettuccine

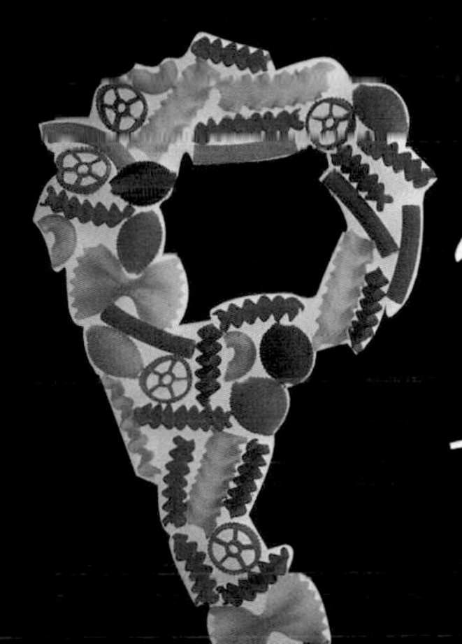

asta & Pizza

Pastas have come of age! They're versatile and easy to prepare. Full of unexpected combinations and fresh ingredients, you'll love this selection, whether you're taking them to a pot-luck or a dinner party.

Clockwise from top:
Phyllo Pizza With Rosemary
Green Mountain Pizza

Scallops and Fettuccine

4 main dish servings

- 3 tablespoons butter
- 2 tablespoons olive oil
- 2 red bell peppers, cored, seeded, and cut into thin strips
- 1 teaspoon minced garlic
- 1 tablespoon finely grated lemon zest
- ½ teaspoon crushed red pepper
- ½ cup chicken broth
- ¼ cup dry white wine
- 2 tablespoons fresh lemon juice
- 1 pound sea scallops
- ¾ cup chopped fresh parsley
- 12 ounces fettuccine, cooked al dente and drained

Garnish:

freshly grated Parmesan cheese

Here's a fresh and healthful change from a cream sauce. Photo, page 166.

In large skillet, melt butter over medium heat. Add olive oil, bell peppers, garlic, lemon zest, and crushed red pepper. Cook 2 minutes. Stir in chicken broth, wine, and lemon juice and cook until reduced by half. Add scallops and cook 2 minutes or until opaque and thoroughly cooked. Sprinkle with parsley. Toss with hot fettuccine, garnish with Parmesan, and serve immediately.

Evergreen Pasta With Scallops

6-8 main dish servings

- 1 pound asparagus, trimmed and cut into 1½-inch pieces
- ½ pound small green beans, trimmed and cut into 1½-inch pieces
- 1 10-ounce package frozen peas, thawed
- salt and freshly ground black pepper
- 1½ tablespoons butter
- 2 pounds bay scallops
- ¾ cup Basic Basil Pesto (page 193) or purchased basil pesto
- ¾ cup whipping cream
- 3 tablespoons fresh lemon juice
- 12-16 ounces fettuccine, cooked al dente and drained

A rule of thumb for matching sauces with types of pasta is to use wide pasta, such as fettuccine, with butter and cream based sauces.

To large pot of boiling water, add asparagus and green beans and cook until crisp tender, about 5 minutes. Drain, add peas, and season with salt and pepper to taste. Transfer to bowl and set aside.

In large, heavy skillet, melt butter over medium heat. Add scallops and season with salt and pepper to taste. Cook until just cooked through, about 2 minutes. Remove from heat and add reserved asparagus mixture, pesto, cream, lemon juice, and cooked pasta. Cook, over low heat, stirring constantly, until pasta is coated with sauce and thoroughly heated. Serve immediately or at room temperature.

Greek Shrimp Fettuccine

4-6 main dish servings

- 4 tablespoons olive oil, divided
- 1 pound medium shrimp, peeled and deveined
- ¼ teaspoon crushed red pepper
- ½ teaspoon minced garlic
- ⅓ cup dry white wine
- 4 cups tomatoes, seeded and coarsely chopped
- ⅓ cup chopped fresh basil
- 1 teaspoon dried oregano
- salt and freshly ground black pepper
- 6 ounces feta cheese, crumbled
- 12 ounces fettuccine, cooked al dente and drained

As a general rule, serve 3-4 ounces of pasta per main course serving, or 2 ounces for a first course serving.

Preheat oven to 400 degrees. In large skillet, heat 3 tablespoons of the olive oil over medium-high heat. Add shrimp and cook until just pink, about 2 minutes. Stir in crushed red pepper and transfer to large baking pan.

In large skillet, heat remaining 1 tablespoon olive oil over medium heat. Add garlic and cook 30 seconds. Add wine and simmer 1 minute. Stir in tomatoes, basil, oregano, and salt and pepper to taste. Simmer, uncovered, 10 minutes. Remove from heat.

Sprinkle feta cheese over shrimp mixture and cover with tomato mixture. Cover and bake 10-15 minutes. Remove from oven, add fettuccine, and toss well. Serve immediately.

Picante Shrimp Pasta

6 main dish servings

- ½ cup olive oil
- 1½ pounds medium shrimp, peeled and deveined
- 1 green bell pepper, cored, seeded, and cut into 2-inch strips
- 1 yellow bell pepper, cored, seeded, and cut into 2-inch strips
- 1 cup sliced fresh mushrooms
- 2 teaspoons minced garlic
- 1 tablespoon chopped fresh cilantro
- 2 medium tomatoes, chopped
- 2 cups purchased picante sauce
- 12 ounces rigatoni, cooked al dente and drained
- ½ cup freshly grated Parmesan cheese

The spicier the picante sauce, the more kick this pasta will have.

In large skillet, heat olive oil over medium heat. Add shrimp, bell peppers, mushrooms, garlic, and cilantro. Cook, stirring frequently until shrimp are pink, about 3 minutes. Stir in tomatoes and picante sauce. Simmer 3 minutes. Pour over hot pasta and toss. Sprinkle with Parmesan and serve immediately.

Mandarin Shrimp Pasta

4 main dish servings

- 1 pound medium shrimp, shelled and deveined
- 1 cup Italian salad dressing, purchased or homemade, divided
- 2 tablespoons chunky peanut butter
- 1 tablespoon soy sauce
- 1 tablespoon honey
- 1 1-inch piece fresh ginger root, peeled and grated
- ½ teaspoon crushed red pepper
- 1 tablespoon vegetable oil
- 1 tablespoon sesame oil
- 1 medium carrot, peeled and shredded
- 6 green onions, chopped, including tops
- 12 ounces angel hair pasta, cooked al dente and drained
- 3 tablespoons chopped fresh cilantro
- 1 10-ounce can mandarin oranges, drained
- ⅓ cup almonds, toasted (page 381)

Popular folklore suggests that Marco Polo discovered pasta on his travels to China and brought the idea home to Italy.

Marinate shrimp in ⅓ cup of the salad dressing in refrigerator, 1 hour. In small bowl, combine peanut butter, soy sauce, honey, ginger, crushed red pepper, and remaining ⅔ cup salad dressing. Whisk to blend.

In large skillet, combine vegetable oil and sesame oil over high heat. Heat until very hot but not smoking. Add carrot, cook 1 minute, stirring frequently. Add shrimp, discarding marinade, and green onions. Cook, stirring constantly, until shrimp are opaque, about 3 minutes. Remove from heat.

In large bowl, combine cooked pasta, peanut butter mixture, shrimp mixture, and cilantro. Toss to blend, top with mandarin oranges, and sprinkle with toasted almonds. Serve hot or cold. For a variation, substitute 2 boneless, skinless chicken breasts, cut into 1-inch pieces, for shrimp, and add one 8-ounce can sliced water chestnuts, drained.

Linguine With White River Clam Sauce

4-6 main dish servings

- 2 tablespoons olive oil
- 1 tablespoon minced garlic
- 2 6½-ounce cans chopped clams, drained, juice reserved
- ½ cup chopped fresh parsley
- ¼ cup dry white wine
- 2 teaspoons chopped fresh basil or 1 teaspoon dried basil, crumbled
- 12 ounces linguine, cooked al dente and drained

A light and easy version of traditional white clam sauce.

In medium skillet, heat olive oil over medium-high heat. Add garlic and cook 1 minute. Add reserved clam juice and parsley and simmer 3 minutes. Add clams, wine, and basil. Simmer 5 minutes. Toss with hot linguine. Serve hot.

Red Clam Sauce Linguine

4 main dish servings

- 1 tablespoon olive oil
- 2 teaspoons minced garlic
- 1 6-ounce can tomato paste
- ¾ cup water
- 2 teaspoons Worcestershire
- 1 teaspoon sugar
- 1 tablespoon chopped fresh basil
- 1 tablespoon chopped fresh oregano
- 1 tablespoon chopped fresh rosemary
- ⅛ teaspoon freshly ground black pepper
- 1 10-ounce can whole baby clams, drained, juice reserved
- 12 ounces linguine, cooked al dente and drained

Garnish:

fresh basil leaves

When substituting dried herbs, use one-third of the amount of fresh herbs.

In medium saucepan with lid, heat olive oil over medium heat. Add garlic and cook until golden. Remove from heat, add tomato paste, water, Worcestershire, sugar, basil, oregano, rosemary, and pepper. Cover, reduce heat to low, and simmer 15 minutes. Add clams and enough of the reserved clam juice to thin sauce as desired. Toss with linguine, garnish with basil leaves, and serve hot.

Summit Smoked Salmon Fettuccine

4 main dish servings

- 1 cup whipping cream
- ¾ cup purchased clam juice
- 1 teaspoon flour
- 9 ounces fettuccine, cooked al dente and drained
- 6 ounces smoked salmon, thinly sliced and cut into bite size pieces
- 5 green onions, chopped, including tops
- ½ pound snow peas, halved, at room temperature
- 1 tablespoon snipped fresh dill weed or 1 teaspoon dried dill weed
- 1½ tablespoons drained capers

This is an elegant dish and only takes minutes to prepare.

In large heavy skillet, combine cream, clam juice, and flour over medium heat. Heat to boiling and cook, stirring frequently, until sauce thickens, about 3 minutes. Add cooked pasta, salmon, green onions, snow peas, dill weed, and capers. Toss to coat, serve immediately.

Seafood Ziti

6-8 main dish servings

- 3 tablespoons olive oil
- 1 teaspoon minced garlic
- 1½ ounces (about 16) sun-dried tomatoes, thinly sliced
- 2 cups sliced fresh mushrooms
- ¼ pound shucked fresh clams
- ½ pound bay scallops
- ½ pound shrimp, peeled and deveined
- 2 cups half and half
- ¾ cup freshly grated Parmesan cheese
- 16 ounces ziti, cooked al dente and drained

Garnish:

large fresh parsley sprig

thinly sliced sun-dried tomatoes

This luscious dish is suitable for any dinner party. Accompany with a Chardonnay.

In large heavy skillet, heat olive oil over medium-high heat. Add garlic and cook 1 minute. Add sun-dried tomatoes, mushrooms, clams, scallops, and shrimp. Cook until shrimp are opaque, about 4 minutes. Add half and half and cook until reduced and thickened enough to coat a spoon, about 10 minutes. Add Parmesan and stir until smooth. Toss with hot ziti, garnish with parsley and sun-dried tomatoes, and serve immediately.

Penne With Shrimp, Sausage, and Cream

4 main dish servings

- ½ pound mild or hot Italian sausage, bulk style or casings removed
- 1½ teaspoons minced garlic
- 1 tablespoon minced shallots
- 1 teaspoon dried thyme
- 1 16-ounce can chopped tomatoes, juice reserved
- ½ teaspoon Chinese chili paste, such as Sambal Oelek
- ⅓ cup whipping cream
- 8-12 large shrimp, peeled, deveined, and halved lengthwise
- 8 ounces penne, cooked al dente and drained
- ¼ cup freshly grated Parmesan cheese

Garnish:

fresh thyme sprig

Serve spicy sauces over short tubular pastas such as penne or ziti.

In large skillet, brown sausage over medium heat. Drain all but 1 tablespoon drippings. Place sausage on paper towel and set aside. In same skillet, cook garlic, shallots, and thyme, 1 minute. Add tomatoes with juice, chili paste, cream, and reserved sausage and simmer 10 minutes. Add shrimp, cook over low heat, stirring occasionally until shrimp are pink, about 5 minutes. Add pasta and toss gently. Pour into large bowl, sprinkle with Parmesan, and garnish with fresh thyme sprig. Serve immediately.

Sausage Rigatoni

6 main dish servings

- 1 pound bulk Italian sausage
- 8 ounces rigatoni, cooked al dente and drained
- 4 cups tomato sauce, divided
- ½ pound provolone cheese, sliced
- ¾ cup sour cream
- 2 teaspoons dried basil
- 2 teaspoons dried oregano
- 2 teaspoons garlic powder
- ½ teaspoon freshly ground black pepper
- ½ pound mozzarella cheese, sliced
- ½ pound freshly grated Parmesan cheese

Try making this the evening before, then bake after a day of cross-country skiing.

Preheat oven to 350 degrees. Butter 13x9x2-inch baking pan. In large skillet, brown sausage, drain, and discard drippings. Place rigatoni in prepared pan. Top with 2 cups of the tomato sauce, provolone, sour cream, and sausage. Sprinkle with basil, oregano, garlic powder, and pepper. Top with mozzarella and remaining 2 cups tomato sauce. Sprinkle with Parmesan and bake about 30 minutes or until thoroughly heated.

Bow-Tie Primavera

6 main dish servings

- 12 ounces bow-tie pasta, cooked al dente and drained
- ⅓ cup olive oil
- ½ cup finely chopped red onion
- 2 tablespoons salt
- ¾ pound fresh snow peas
- ½ pound sugar snap peas
- ¼ pound prosciutto, sliced and cut into ¼-inch strips
- 2 ripe Italian plum tomatoes, quartered
- 2 medium red or yellow bell peppers, cored, stemmed, and cut into thin strips
- ¼ cup chopped fresh basil
- ¼ cup chopped fresh chives
- salt and freshly ground black pepper
- ¼ cup raspberry vinegar
- ¼ cup freshly grated Parmesan cheese
- 3 tablespoons coarsely grated orange zest

This beautiful spring luncheon dish is flavorful and low-fat. Photo, page 182.

In large bowl, toss pasta with olive oil and chopped red onion. Set aside and bring to room temperature. To large saucepan of boiling water, add salt, snow peas, and sugar snap peas and boil 1 minute. Drain, immerse in ice water, and let stand 10 minutes. Drain, pat dry, and add to pasta mixture. Add prosciutto, tomatoes, bell peppers, basil, and chives. Season with salt and pepper to taste. Sprinkle with raspberry vinegar and Parmesan and toss. Sprinkle with orange zest and serve at room temperature.

Southwestern Chicken Spaghetti

4 main dish servings

- 1 teaspoon olive oil
- 2 boneless, skinless chicken breast halves (about 8 ounces), cut into thin strips
- 1½ cups Mountain Marinara Sauce (page 193) or purchased marinara
- 1 cup cooked or canned black beans, rinsed and drained
- ½ cup fresh or frozen corn kernels
- ¼ cup diced fresh Anaheim chile pepper or canned green chiles
- 2 tablespoons chopped fresh cilantro
- ½ teaspoon ground cumin
- ⅛ teaspoon crushed red pepper
- 12 ounces spaghetti, cooked al dente and drained

Garnish this healthful spicy southwestern dish with sprigs of fresh cilantro.

In medium skillet, heat olive oil over medium-high heat. Add chicken and cook until no longer pink, about 5 minutes. Stir in marinara sauce, black beans, corn, chiles, cilantro, cumin, and crushed red pepper. Heat to boiling, reduce heat to medium-low, and simmer 5 minutes. Spoon sauce over spaghetti and serve immediately.

Telluride Tortellini With Chicken

4-6 main dish servings

- 2 tablespoons butter
- ½ teaspoon minced garlic
- 5 anchovy fillets, drained and diced
- 3-4 cups Mountain Marinara Sauce, (page 193) or purchased marinara sauce
- ¼ cup white wine
- 2 boneless, skinless chicken breast halves (about 8 ounces), cooked and cubed
- 1 14-ounce can water-packed artichoke hearts, drained and quartered
- 6 green onions, sliced, including tops
- ½ cup halved oil-cured black olives or canned ripe olives
- 1 tablespoon drained capers
- ½ cup freshly grated Parmesan cheese plus additional for passing
- 9 ounces spinach tortellini, cooked al dente and drained
- 9 ounces plain tortellini, cooked al dente and drained

Great meal with a green salad and crusty French bread.

In large saucepan, melt butter over medium heat. Add garlic and anchovies and cook 3 minutes. Add marinara and wine and simmer 5 minutes. Add cooked chicken, artichoke hearts, green onions, olives, capers, and ½ cup Parmesan. Heat to boiling, reduce heat, and simmer 5 minutes. Pour over warm tortellini. Pass additional Parmesan.

Smoked Chicken and Wild Mushroom Pasta

6 main dish servings

- 1 tablespoon olive oil
- 1 teaspoon minced garlic
- ¼ cup finely chopped shallots
- 3 ounces fresh shiitake mushrooms, sliced
- 3 ounces portobello, porcini, cremini, or button mushrooms, sliced
- 8 ounces skinless, smoked chicken, cut into 4x½-inch strips
- 3 ounces oil-packed sun-dried tomatoes, drained and thinly sliced
- ¼ cup coarsely chopped fresh oregano
- 1 cup chicken broth
- salt and freshly ground black pepper
- 9 ounces fusilli pasta, cooked al dente and drained
- 6 ounces provolone cheese, shredded

Prepare this healthful casserole ahead of time to enjoy with friends after a day in the mountains. Serve with a Semillon.

Preheat oven to 400 degrees. In large skillet, heat olive oil over medium heat. Add garlic and shallots and cook until lightly browned, about 2 minutes. Add mushrooms, chicken, sun-dried tomatoes, and oregano. Cook 1 minute, stirring constantly. Add chicken broth and simmer 4-5 minutes until sauce is slightly reduced. Season with salt and pepper to taste.

Add pasta, toss to coat, and transfer to 2-quart baking dish. Top with provolone and bake 5-10 minutes, or until cheese is melted. (May be prepared up to 24 hours in advance. Increase chicken broth to 1½ cups and increase baking time to 20-30 minutes. Tent with foil if cheese begins to brown.)

Pistachio Pasta With Turkey

4-6 main dish servings

- ¾ cup Basic Basil Pesto (page 193) or purchased basil pesto, at room temperature
- 1 cup shelled pistachio nuts
- ½ cup coarsely chopped fresh basil
- ½ pound smoked turkey breast, cut into thin strips, at room temperature
- 12 ounces fettuccine, cooked al dente and drained

Garnish:

whole fresh basil leaves

In large bowl, combine pesto, pistachios, basil, and turkey. Add hot fettuccine and toss to coat. Garnish with basil leaves.

Cherry Creek Orzo

4-6 side dish servings

- 6 cups water
- ¼ teaspoon crumbled saffron threads
- 1 cup uncooked orzo
- 2 teaspoons freshly grated orange zest
- 2 tablespoons fresh orange juice
- salt
- 3 tablespoons olive oil
- ⅔ cup dried sweet cherries or cranberries
- 3 tablespoons slivered almonds, toasted (page 381)
- 3 green onions, sliced diagonally, including tops

Orzo is a rice shaped pasta and a good source of complex carbohydrates.

In medium saucepan, heat water and saffron to boiling over high heat. Add orzo and boil 8 minutes or until orzo is al dente. Drain and set aside. In medium bowl, combine orange zest, orange juice, and salt to taste. Add olive oil in slow, steady stream, whisking constantly, until dressing is blended and slightly thickened. Add orzo, cherries, toasted almonds, and green onions. Toss and serve at room temperature.

Vegetable Pesto Pasta

4-6 main dish servings
6-8 side dish servings

- 1 pound fresh green beans, cut into 1-inch pieces
- 2 medium new potatoes, cut into ½-inch cubes
- 1 tablespoon olive oil
- 1 teaspoon minced garlic
- 1 14½-ounce can stewed tomatoes
- ½ cup Basic Basil Pesto (page 193) or purchased basil pesto
- 12 ounces penne pasta, cooked al dente and drained
- freshly grated Parmesan cheese

This is a great vegetarian main dish or a wonderful accompaniment to grilled lamb.

Steam green beans and potatoes until just tender, about 12 minutes. In large skillet, heat olive oil over medium-high heat. Add garlic and tomatoes and cook until liquid is reduced slightly. Add pesto and heat thoroughly. Remove from heat.

In large bowl, combine pasta, green bean mixture, and pesto mixture. Toss to coat and sprinkle with Parmesan to taste. Serve hot or at room temperature.

Caramelized Onion Pasta

4 main dish servings
6 side dish servings

- 1 tablespoon butter
- 1 tablespoon olive oil
- 3 medium onions, peeled and thinly sliced
- 8 ounces wide egg noodles, cooked al dente and drained
- 2 eggs, lightly beaten
- ⅓ cup raisins
- ½ teaspoon salt
- ½ teaspoon freshly ground black pepper

This pasta is great as a side dish for any pork entree or grilled steak.

Preheat oven to 375 degrees. Butter 10-inch pie pan. In large, heavy skillet, heat butter and olive oil over medium-high heat. Add onions and cook, stirring frequently, until golden brown, about 15 minutes. Remove from heat.

In large bowl, combine onions, noodles, eggs, raisins, salt, and pepper. Toss gently and transfer to prepared pan. (May be prepared to this point up to 24 hours in advance. Cover and chill.) Bake 20 minutes, 30 minutes if chilled, or until set and golden brown. Cut into wedges and serve.

Roasted Vegetable Penne

4-6 main dish servings
6-8 side dish servings

- 1 large red bell pepper, halved and halves cut into eighths
- 1 large yellow bell pepper, halved and halves cut into eighths
- 1 large orange bell pepper, halved and halves cut into eighths
- 1 large green bell pepper, halved and halves cut into eighths
- ¼ cup plus 2 tablespoons olive oil, divided
- ¾ pound eggplant, cut into ½-inch squares
- 1 pound zucchini, halved and sliced ½-inch thick
- salt and freshly ground black pepper
- 12 ounces penne pasta, cooked al dente and drained
- ¼ cup chopped fresh Italian parsley
- 1 tablespoon balsamic vinegar
- ½ cup freshly grated Parmesan cheese
- ⅛ teaspoon crushed red pepper

This wonderfully colorful autumn dish is low-fat and high in mono-unsaturated fat or "good cholesterol".

Preheat oven to 450 degrees. Toss peppers with about 1 tablespoon of the olive oil. Pour onto large baking sheet and roast 10-15 minutes. Toss eggplant with 2 tablespoons of the olive oil. Add to peppers and continue roasting 15-20 minutes. Stir frequently and watch carefully to avoid having top pieces burn.

Toss zucchini with 1 tablespoon of the olive oil and add to pepper mixture. Roast 5 minutes. Remove from oven and season with salt and pepper to taste. Transfer to large bowl and add cooked pasta, Italian parsley, vinegar, Parmesan, and crushed red pepper. Toss, adding remaining 2 tablespoons olive oil, if desired. Serve immediately.

Springtime Linguine

4 main dish servings

1	pound fresh asparagus, trimmed and cut diagonally into ½-inch pieces
½	cup olive oil
1½	teaspoons minced garlic
8	green onions, cut diagonally into ½-inch pieces, including tops
8	Italian plum tomatoes, quartered
¼	cup chopped fresh basil
16	ounces linguine, cooked al dente and drained
¼	cup freshly grated Parmesan cheese
	Garnish:
	fresh basil leaves

Cook asparagus in boiling salted water, 8-10 minutes. Drain and set aside. In large saucepan, heat olive oil over medium heat. Add garlic, green onions, and tomatoes and simmer about 4 minutes. Add reserved asparagus and basil and heat thoroughly. Toss with hot linguine and sprinkle with Parmesan. Garnish with basil leaves, and serve immediately or at room temperature.

Fresh and delicious.

Dynasty Citrus Pasta

6 side dish servings

- 1 tablespoon finely minced garlic
- 1 tablespoon olive oil
- 3 tablespoons soy sauce
- 2 tablespoons dry sherry
- 2 tablespoons rice vinegar
- 1 tablespoon sesame oil
- 1 tablespoon packed light brown sugar
- ½ teaspoon Chinese chili paste, such as Sambal Oelek
- ¼ teaspoon ground green peppercorns
- 1 teaspoon finely grated orange zest
- ½ cup chopped green onions
- ¼ cup sesame seeds
- 9 ounces fresh or dried Asian noodles, or angel hair pasta, cooked al dente and drained
- 1 11-ounce can mandarin oranges

In small bowl, combine garlic and olive oil. In separate small bowl, combine soy sauce, sherry, vinegar, sesame oil, brown sugar, chili paste, peppercorns, orange zest, and green onions. Set aside. Place sesame seeds in small skillet over high heat. Cook, stirring constantly, until light golden, about 2 minutes. Watch carefully, they will burn easily. Remove from heat and immediately pour into small bowl and cool. Add to soy sauce mixture.

In small skillet, heat reserved garlic mixture 30 seconds over medium heat. Add soy sauce mixture and heat thoroughly. (May be prepared to this point up to 1 day in advance. Chill and reheat gently before proceeding.) Pour over hot noodles and toss. Transfer to heated platter or individual serving plates. Top with mandarin oranges.

Sun-dried Tomato and Jalapeño Pasta

4-6 main dish servings

- 1 cup drained and thinly sliced oil-packed sun-dried tomatoes
- ½ cup kalamata olives, pitted and finely chopped
- 1 teaspoon minced garlic
- 1 fresh jalapeño pepper, cored, seeded, and finely chopped
- 1 cup chopped fresh basil
- 12 ounces rotini pasta, cooked al dente and drained
- 2-3 tablespoons olive oil

Quick and easy.

In large bowl, combine sun-dried tomatoes, olives, garlic, jalapeño, and basil. Add pasta, sprinkle with olive oil, and toss. Serve immediately or at room temperature.

Angel Hair With Tomatoes, Basil, and Croutons

4 main dish servings

- ¼ cup (½ stick) butter, melted
- 1½ teaspoons minced garlic, divided
- 4-5 cups 1-inch cubes Italian bread
- coarse salt
- 3 cups coarsely chopped ripe tomatoes
- ½ fresh serrano pepper, seeded and minced
- 12 ounces angel hair pasta, cooked al dente and drained
- ¼ cup olive oil
- 2 cups chopped fresh basil

Enjoy this dish in the summer when tomatoes are ripe on the vine.

Preheat oven to 400 degrees. Combine butter and 1 teaspoon of the garlic. Pour over bread cubes and toss. Place in single layer on large baking sheet. Bake about 10 minutes or until golden, stirring frequently. Remove from oven and season with coarse salt to taste.

In large bowl, combine tomatoes, serrano pepper, and remaining ½ teaspoon garlic. Add hot pasta and toss. Drizzle with oil and toss again. Sprinkle basil and half of the reserved croutons over pasta. Pass remaining croutons.

Wild Mushroom Linguini

4 main dish servings
6-8 side dish servings

- ¼ cup (½ stick) butter
- 3 tablespoons olive oil
- ⅓ ounce dried shiitake mushrooms, soaked in hot water 10 minutes, drained, and sliced
- 4 ounces fresh button mushrooms, sliced
- ¼ cup drained and thinly sliced oil-packed sun-dried tomatoes
- ½ cup coarsely chopped walnuts
- 1 tablespoon drained capers
- 1½ cups half and half
- ⅓ cup dry sherry
- ¾ cup freshly grated Parmesan cheese, divided
- 9 ounces linguine, cooked al dente and drained
- 2 grilled chicken breasts (optional)

Without the optional chicken, this makes a great, robust vegetarian main course.

In large skillet, melt butter over medium heat. Add olive oil and mushrooms and cook 2 minutes. Add sun-dried tomatoes, walnuts, and capers and cook 5 minutes. Add half and half and sherry and heat thoroughly. Gradually stir in ½ cup of the Parmesan. Toss linguine with sauce, sprinkle with remaining Parmesan and serve immediately. Add strips of grilled chicken breast, if desired.

Clockwise from top:
Bow-Tie Primavera, 175
Angel Hair With Tomatoes, Basil, and Croutons, 183

Fresh Herb Pasta

4 main dish servings
6-8 side dish servings

- 1½ cups whipping cream
- ¼ cup (½ stick) unsalted butter
- ½ teaspoon salt
- ⅛ teaspoon ground nutmeg
- ⅛ teaspoon cayenne
- 1 cup mixed, chopped fresh herbs, such as mint, basil, chives, parsley, or thyme
- ⅓ cup freshly grated Parmesan cheese
- 12 ounces angel hair pasta, cooked al dente and drained

Use any combination of herbs available or growing in your garden.

In heavy saucepan, combine cream, butter, salt, nutmeg, and cayenne. Heat to simmering over medium-high heat. Reduce heat and simmer until sauce is slightly thickened, about 15 minutes. Add herbs and Parmesan. Whisk to blend and simmer 5 minutes, until cheese is melted. Pour over pasta, toss to coat, and serve immediately.

Tomato Lemon Pasta

4-6 side dish servings

- 1 tablespoon butter
- 2 tablespoons chopped shallots
- ½ cup drained and thinly sliced, oil-packed sun-dried tomatoes
- 1 cup whipping cream
- 1 teaspoon chopped fresh oregano
- ¼ teaspoon crumbled saffron threads (optional)
- salt
- ground white pepper
- 1 tablespoon finely grated lemon zest
- 8 ounces rotini pasta, cooked al dente and drained

Garnish:

fresh oregano or parsley sprigs

Substitute 1 teaspoon snipped fresh dill weed for oregano and saffron for a different twist.

In large skillet, melt butter over medium heat. Add shallots and cook 2 minutes. Add sun-dried tomatoes, cream, oregano, and saffron, if desired. Simmer until sauce is reduced by one third. Season with salt and white pepper to taste. Sprinkle with lemon zest. Toss with hot pasta, garnish with oregano or parsley, and serve immediately. For a main dish, add 2 cooked boneless, skinless chicken breasts, cut into 1-inch pieces.

Alpine Asparagus Lasagna

8 main dish servings

- 4 pounds fresh asparagus
- 2 tablespoons olive oil
- salt
- ¼ cup (½ stick) butter
- ¼ cup flour
- ½ cup water
- 1½ cups chicken broth
- 2 cups shredded mozzarella cheese
- 1 tablespoon finely grated lemon zest
- 16 ounces lasagna noodles, cooked al dente and drained
- 1⅔ cups freshly grated Parmesan cheese, divided
- 1 cup whipping cream

Pencil-thin asparagus is perfect for this wonderful springtime dish. Try with Salad of Oranges and Onions, page 84.

Preheat oven to 500 degrees. Cut and discard 1-inch from bottom of asparagus stalks. Toss stalks with olive oil. Arrange in single layer, on 15x10-inch baking sheet. Roast 5-10 minutes until crisp tender. Remove from oven, sprinkle with salt to taste, and set aside to cool.

Reduce oven temperature to 400 degrees. Cut roasted asparagus into ½-inch pieces and set aside. In large saucepan, melt butter over medium heat. Add flour and cook, stirring constantly, 3 minutes. Combine water and chicken broth and add, in slow, steady stream, whisking constantly. Cook 5 minutes. Add mozzarella and lemon zest and stir until smooth.

Butter 13x9x2-inch baking pan. Place single layer of lasagna noodles in prepared pan. Pour half of the sauce mixture over noodles. Layer half of the reserved asparagus over sauce. Sprinkle with ½ cup of the Parmesan. Top with second layer of noodles, remaining sauce, remaining asparagus, ½ cup of the Parmesan, and another layer of noodles.

In small bowl, combine cream and a pinch salt. Whip to soft peaks and spoon evenly over noodles. Sprinkle remaining ⅔ cup Parmesan on top. Bake 30 minutes, or until golden brown and bubbling. Let stand 20 minutes.

Spinach Cannelloni

6-8 main-dish servings

¼	cup (½ stick) butter, divided
2	10-ounce packages frozen spinach, thawed and squeezed dry
15	ounces ricotta cheese
¼	cup freshly grated Parmesan cheese
¼	cup freshly grated Romano cheese
2	cups grated mozzarella cheese, divided
¼	teaspoon ground nutmeg
2	eggs
½	pound fresh mushrooms, chopped
1	medium onion, peeled and chopped
½	teaspoon minced garlic
1	28-ounce can crushed tomatoes
1	tablespoon red wine vinegar
1	teaspoon crushed red pepper
1	teaspoon dried basil
1	teaspoon dried oregano
1	1-pound package egg roll skins
	Garnish:
1	fresh basil sprig
2	tablespoons chopped fresh parsley

This is a spicy vegetarian entree which is pared nicely with a Chianti Riserva. Remember–spinach is a good source of zinc and iron.

In large saucepan, melt 2 tablespoons of the butter over medium-high heat. Add spinach and cook 3 minutes. Add ricotta, blend well, and cook about 3 minutes. Add Parmesan, Romano, 1 cup of the mozzarella, nutmeg, and eggs. Stir until well blended and remove from heat.

In separate large saucepan, melt remaining 2 tablespoons butter over medium-high heat. Add mushrooms and onion and cook until onions are translucent, about 10 minutes. Add garlic, tomatoes, vinegar, crushed red pepper, basil, and oregano. Simmer 15 minutes. Remove from heat.

Preheat oven to 350 degrees. Pour about two-thirds of the tomato mixture into 10x15x2-inch baking pan. Place 1 egg roll skin on flat surface. Place a generous ¼ cup of the spinach mixture along 1 edge. Roll up, beginning with filling side and seal edge with small amount of water. Place, seam side down, over tomato mixture in baking pan.

Repeat process to form about 14 cannelloni rolls. Cover with remaining one-third tomato mixture. Cover pan with foil and bake 45 minutes. Remove foil, sprinkle with remaining 1 cup mozzarella and continue baking 5 minutes or until cheese melts. Garnish with basil and parsley.

Scallop Stuffed Pasta Shells

4-6 main dish servings

- 3 tablespoons olive oil
- 1 medium onion, peeled and chopped
- 2 tablespoons finely grated orange zest
- ¼ teaspoon dried thyme
- 1 bay leaf
- 1 32-ounce can whole peeled tomatoes, chopped and juice reserved
- 2 cups freshly grated Parmesan cheese
- 2 cups ricotta cheese
- ¼ cup chopped fresh cilantro
- 1 egg
- 16 jumbo pasta shells, cooked al dente and drained
- 4 large sea scallops, each cut into 4 slices

Treat your guests to a Bardolino with this pasta.

Preheat oven to 350 degrees. In large saucepan, heat olive oil over medium heat. Add onion and cook until translucent, about 5 minutes. Add orange zest, thyme, bay leaf, and tomatoes with juice. Simmer 30 minutes.

In medium bowl, combine Parmesan, ricotta, cilantro, and egg. Pour half of the tomato mixture into 13x9x2-inch baking pan. Pat pasta shells dry and fill with about 1 tablespoon of the reserved cheese mixture. Place 1 scallop slice in cheese mixture and place, open side down, in baking pan. Repeat with remaining 15 shells. Pour remaining tomato mixture over shells. Cover with foil. (May be prepared to this point up to 8 hours in advance. Cover and chill.) Bake 45-50 minutes, 1 hour if chilled, or until scallops are opaque.

Backcountry Pizza Crust

2 12-inch crusts

- 1 ¼-ounce package dry yeast
- ¼ cup warm (105-115 degrees) water
- 3 cups flour
- 1 teaspoon salt
- 2 tablespoons olive oil
- 1 tablespoon honey
- ¾ cup cold water

In small glass bowl, dissolve yeast in warm water and let stand 10 minutes, until slightly bubbly. In large bowl, combine flour, salt, olive oil, honey, and cold water. Add yeast mixture and stir to blend. Knead by hand until smooth and glossy, about 10 minutes. Form into ball and place dough in oiled bowl, turning to coat entire surface. Cover with plastic wrap and towel and let rise until doubled in bulk, about 1 hour.

Preheat oven to 450 degrees. Divide in half and shape each piece into a 12-inch round. (May be prepared to this point up to 2 months in advance. Place dough in freezer-safe plastic bag and freeze. Thaw, at room temperature, 30 minutes before proceeding.) Crust may be prebaked 10 minutes before adding toppings, or top uncooked crust with desired toppings and bake 10-15 minutes, or until crust is golden brown.

Phyllo Pizza With Rosemary

4 main dish servings
8 appetizer servings

- 8 sheets phyllo pastry, thawed if frozen
- 6 tablespoons (¾ stick) butter, melted
- ¾ cup freshly grated Parmesan cheese, divided
- 1½ cups grated mozzarella cheese
- 1 medium red onion, peeled and very thinly sliced
- 6 Italian plum tomatoes, very thinly sliced
- 1 green bell pepper, cored, seeded, and sliced into very thin rings
- ¼ cup chopped fresh rosemary
- salt and freshly ground black pepper

Try growing a rosemary plant in a south facing window. Cut into bite size pieces for a unique appetizer pizza. *Photo, page 168.*

Preheat oven to 375 degrees. Line 15x10-inch baking sheet with 2 of the phyllo sheets. Cover remaining phyllo with plastic wrap and damp towel to prevent drying. Brush with melted butter and sprinkle with 2 tablespoons of the Parmesan. Repeat process with 6 remaining sheets, using 2 sheets each time.

Sprinkle mozzarella over top. Arrange red onion, tomatoes, and bell peppers on top. Be careful not to overload this delicate crust. Sprinkle with rosemary, and salt and pepper to taste. Bake 20-25 minutes, or until edges are golden.

Rustic Salad Pizza

4 main dish servings
8 appetizer servings

- 1 small head radicchio, thinly sliced
- ½ medium red onion, peeled and thinly sliced
- ½ medium red bell pepper, cored, seeded, and thinly sliced
- 2 medium Italian plum tomatoes, cored, seeded, and thinly sliced
- 1 medium jalapeño pepper, cored, seeded, and thinly sliced
- 3 tablespoons red wine vinegar
- 2 tablespoons olive oil
- ½ teaspoon salt
- ½ teaspoon freshly ground black pepper
- ½ teaspoon sugar
- 8 ounces Gouda cheese, thinly sliced
- 1 Backcountry Pizza Crust (page 188) or 16-ounce purchased pizza crust, such as Boboli

A lighter pizza that is different and delicious.

In large bowl, combine radicchio, red onion, bell pepper, tomatoes, jalapeño, vinegar, olive oil, salt, pepper, and sugar. Let stand, at room temperature, 30 minutes, stirring occasionally.

Preheat oven to 500 degrees. Drain radicchio mixture, discarding liquid. Arrange half of the cheese evenly over crust. Cover with radicchio mixture, spreading evenly. Top with remaining cheese. Bake 10-15 minutes or until cheese melts. Let stand 5 minutes before cutting.

Blanca Peak Cheese Pizza

4 main dish servings
8 appetizer servings

- 1 Backcountry Pizza Crust (page 188) or 16-ounce purchased pizza crust, such as Boboli
- 1 teaspoon olive oil
- ½ cup grated mozzarella cheese
- ½ cup freshly grated Parmesan cheese
- ½ cup freshly grated fontina cheese
- ½ cup crumbled blue cheese or feta cheese
- 2 Italian plum tomatoes, thinly sliced
- 1 tablespoon drained capers

This is a cheese lover's delight.

Preheat oven to 450 degrees. Brush top of crust with olive oil. In medium bowl, combine mozzarella, Parmesan, fontina, and blue cheese. Spread evenly over crust. Decoratively arrange tomatoes over cheese and sprinkle with capers. Bake 10-15 minutes, or until cheese is melted and bubbly.

Tri-Color Vegetarian Pizza

4 main dish servings
8 appetizer servings

- ⅔ cup Basic Basil Pesto (page 193) or purchased basil pesto
- 1 Backcountry Pizza Crust (page 188) or 16-ounce purchased pizza crust, such as Boboli
- ¾ cup ricotta cheese
- 2 cups shredded mozzarella cheese
- 1 tablespoon freshly grated Parmesan cheese
- 2 tablespoons milk
- 4 Italian plum tomatoes, quartered
- ½ green bell pepper, cored, seeded, and cut into thin strips
- 1 2¼-ounce can sliced black olives, drained or ¼ cup oil-cured olives, pitted

Preheat oven to 450 degrees. Spread pesto evenly over crust. In medium bowl, combine ricotta, mozzarella, Parmesan, and milk. Spread over pesto. Alternate tomatoes and peppers in spiral design over cheese layer. Top with olives. Bake 10-12 minutes or until hot and bubbly.

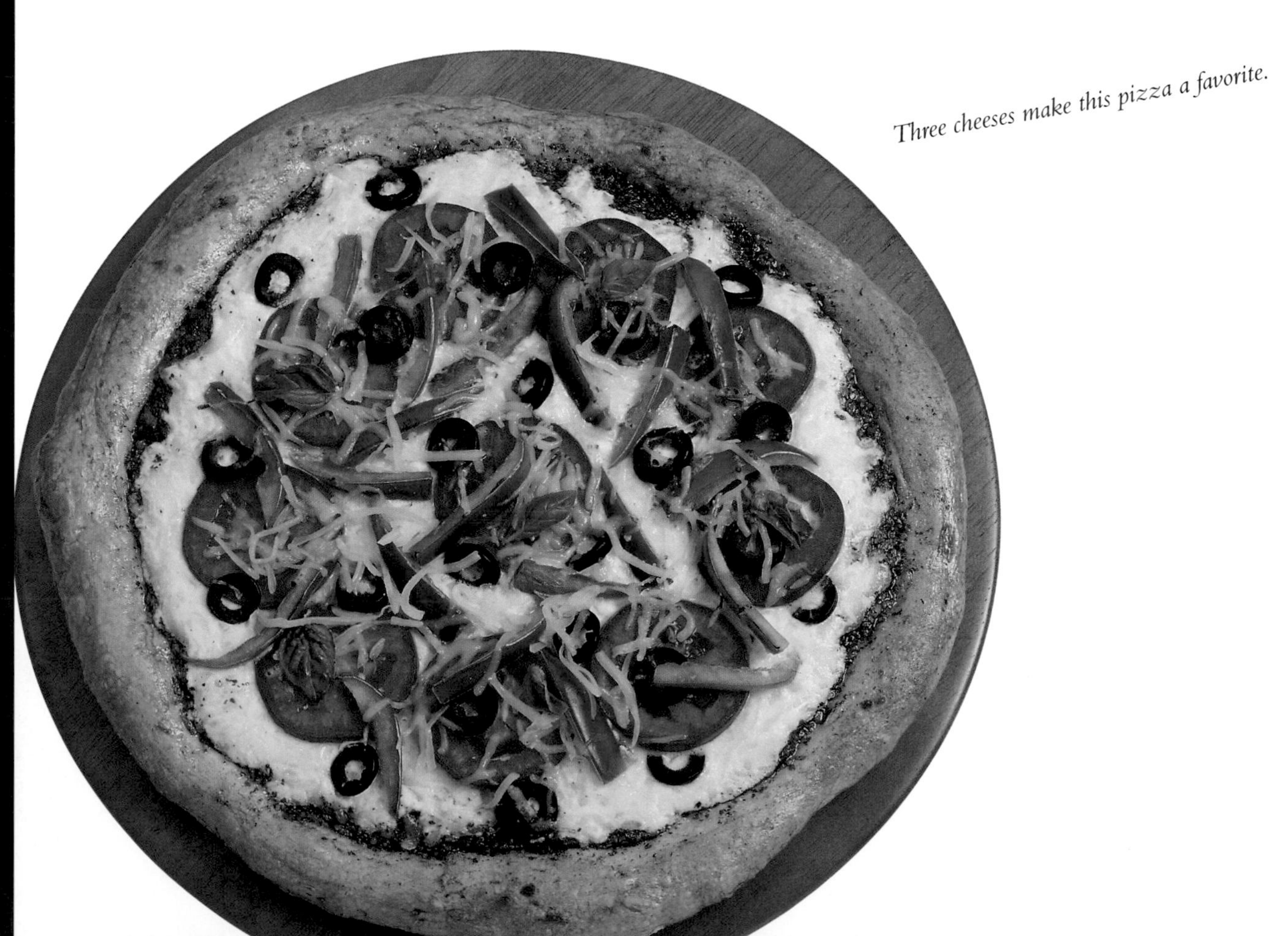

Three cheeses make this pizza a favorite.

Mediterranean Pizza

4 main dish servings
8 appetizer servings

- ½ teaspoon minced garlic
- 1 Backcountry Pizza Crust (page 188) or 16-ounce purchased pizza crust, such as Boboli
- ⅔ cup Mountain Marinara Sauce, (page 193) or purchased marinara sauce
- 12 large fresh spinach leaves
- 4 ounces feta cheese, crumbled
- 1 6½-ounce jar marinated artichoke hearts, drained and quartered
- 1 2¼-ounce can sliced black olives or ¼ cup pitted, halved kalamata olives

Preheat oven to 450 degrees. Spread minced garlic over crust with back of spoon. Spread evenly with marinara sauce. Arrange spinach leaves over sauce, sprinkle with feta, and arrange artichoke hearts and olives decoratively over top. Bake 10-15 minutes. For another bold pizza, substitute Redstone Tomato Pesto (page 193) for the marinara sauce.

Baja Shrimp Pizza

4 main dish servings
8 appetizer servings

- 8 ounces Monterey Jack cheese, grated
- 1 Backcountry Pizza Crust (page 188) or 16-ounce purchased pizza crust, such as Boboli
- 1 large red onion, peeled, thinly sliced, and caramelized (page 381) or ½ cup thinly sliced red onion
- 1 small jalapeño pepper, cored, seeded, and finely chopped
- ¾ pound shrimp, cooked, peeled, and deveined
- ½ pound fresh mushrooms, sliced
- 3 Italian plum tomatoes, quartered
- ¼ cup chopped fresh cilantro
- 2 tablespoons Italian salad dressing, homemade or purchased

Try a wheat beer with this pizza.

Preheat oven to 425 degrees. Sprinkle cheese over pizza crust and top with red onion and jalapeño. Arrange shrimp in a spiral design on top and sprinkle with mushrooms. Arrange tomatoes on top and sprinkle with cilantro and Italian dressing. Bake 10 - 15 minutes.

Green Mountain Pizza

4 main dish servings
8 appetizer servings

¾	cup alfredo sauce, purchased or homemade
1	Backcountry Pizza Crust (page 188) or 16-ounce purchased pizza crust, such as Boboli
10	large fresh spinach leaves, rinsed and dried
6	green onions, sliced diagonally, including tops
2	boneless, skinless chicken breast halves (about 8 ounces total), cooked and shredded
½	pound bacon, cut into ½-inch pieces and crisply cooked
1	cup grated mozzarella cheese
1	cup grated Swiss cheese

Photo, page 168.

Preheat oven to 450 degrees. Spread alfredo sauce evenly over pizza crust. Arrange spinach leaves over sauce. Add green onions, shredded chicken, and bacon. Sprinkle cheeses over top. Bake 15 minutes or until bubbly.

Western Barbeque Chicken Pizza

4 main dish servings
8 appetizer servings

3	boneless, skinless chicken breast halves (about 12 ounces total)
1⅓	cups purchased barbeque sauce, divided
6	ounces provolone cheese, grated
6	ounces Gouda cheese, grated
1	Backcountry Pizza Crust (page 188) or 16-ounce purchased pizza crust, such as Boboli
½	medium onion, peeled and thinly sliced
¼	cup chopped fresh cilantro

Better make 2 because this pizza will go fast!

In large resealable plastic bag, combine chicken and ⅔ cup of the barbeque sauce. Marinate, in refrigerator, 4 hours or up to overnight.

Preheat oven to 325 degrees. Place chicken and marinade in small baking dish, bake 30 minutes or until chicken is tender and no longer pink. Remove from oven. Increase oven temperature to 450 degrees.

Sprinkle cheeses evenly over crust leaving ½-inch border. Spoon remaining ⅔ cup barbeque sauce over cheese. Shred cooked chicken and arrange over sauce, top with onion. Bake 10-12 minutes. Sprinkle with cilantro and serve.

Mountain Marinara Sauce

3 cups

- 2½ teaspoons minced garlic
- ¼ cup olive oil
- 1 ounce (about 2 tablespoons) anchovy paste
- 3 tablespoons chopped fresh basil
- ½ teaspoon chopped fresh oregano
- 2 tablespoons chopped fresh parsley
- ½ teaspoon freshly ground black pepper
- 1 28-ounce can crushed Italian tomatoes

This light and healthful sauce works on pizza or pasta.

In medium saucepan, cook garlic in olive oil over medium heat. Add anchovy paste, basil, oregano, parsley, and pepper. Simmer, stirring frequently, until anchovy paste dissolves. Add tomatoes and heat to boiling. Reduce heat and simmer, uncovered, 15-20 minutes.

Basic Basil Pesto

2¼ cups

- ½ cup pine nuts
- ½ cup walnuts
- 1 teaspoon coarse salt
- ½ teaspoon ground white pepper
- 1 tablespoon minced garlic
- 3 cups loosely packed, fresh basil leaves
- 4 ounces Asiago cheese, grated
- 2 ounces Parmesan cheese, grated
- 1 cup olive oil

Try freezing pesto in ice cube trays for added convenience.

In food processor, combine pine nuts, walnuts, coarse salt, white pepper, garlic, and basil. Pulse until finely chopped. Add Asiago and Parmesan and process until smooth. With processor running, add olive oil in slow steady stream. Process until well blended. Place in jar and store in refrigerator up to 1 week, or place in tightly sealed freezer-safe container and freeze up to 3 months.

Redstone Tomato Pesto

2 cups

- ½ cup tightly packed sun-dried tomatoes, soaked in boiling water 10 minutes and drained
- ⅓ cup walnuts, toasted (page 381)
- ½ cup water
- ⅓ cup olive oil
- ½ cup freshly grated Parmesan cheese
- ¾ teaspoon fresh thyme leaves
- 2 tablespoons fresh lemon juice
- salt and freshly ground black pepper

This incredible pesto is also great on hamburgers.

In food processor, combine sun-dried tomatoes, toasted walnuts, water, olive oil, Parmesan, thyme, and lemon juice. Pulse machine several times then process until smooth. Season with salt and pepper to taste. Serve over pasta or spread on baguette slices.

High in our Rocky Mountains you'll find deep pools, cascading streams, and the most incredible trout anywhere. An angler's paradise, Colorado rivers produce remarkable, fresh fare for our tables. Dress it up with dijon, accent it with savory potatoes, and hang a "gone fishin" sign on the door.

Streamside Feast

main dish

Dijon Trout With Dill Cucumbers 199

side dish

Savory Roasted New Potatoes 333

side dish

Peas With Pine Nuts 332

dessert

Plum Almond Tartlets 365

wine

Colorado or Rhine Riesling

Clockwise from top left:
Dijon Trout With Dill Cucumbers
Savory Roasted New Potatoes
Peas With Pine Nuts

Seafood & Fish

Fish and Seafood are becoming popular alternatives to beef. The focus here is on lighter sauces, interesting flavor combinations, and recipes that taste and look sophisticated, but are easy to prepare.

At left: Cioppino

Lemon Sage Trout

8 servings

- 8 ½-pound whole boned trout, heads removed
- 1 tablespoon coarse salt
- 2 teaspoons freshly ground black pepper
- ½ cup fresh lemon juice
- ½ cup extra virgin olive oil
- ¼ cup chopped fresh sage
- 8 pieces foil, each large enough to wrap 1 trout
- 48 fresh whole sage leaves

This is an elegant buffet, first course, or appetizer dish.

Lay trout open, skin side down. Make 3 diagonal slashes in flesh on each side. Combine coarse salt and pepper and rub entire cavity and each slash. Place trout in enamel or glass baking dishes. Do not overlap.

In glass bowl, whisk lemon juice, olive oil, and chopped sage. Pour over trout, coating each and allowing mixture to penetrate slashes. Cover tightly with plastic wrap and chill 3-12 hours, turning occasionally.

Preheat oven to 400 degrees. Lightly oil foil pieces. Place trout, skin side down, in center of foil, reserving marinade. Place 1 whole sage leaf over each slash. Drizzle reserved marinade evenly over trout. Fold foil over to cover fish and fold edges together several times to seal. Place packets on baking sheets and bake 8-10 minutes. Remove from oven and set aside to cool. Place trout on serving platter and spoon about 1 tablespoon of the cooking juices over each trout. Serve at room temperature.

Lost Canyon Trout

6 servings

- ¼ cup Dijon mustard
- 1 teaspoon minced garlic
- 1 tablespoon light molasses
- 1 tablespoon honey
- 6 large boned trout, heads removed
- ¾ cup pecans, toasted (page 381)
- ¼ cup fresh white bread crumbs
- 1 teaspoon chili powder
- 3 tablespoons olive oil, divided

In small bowl, combine mustard, garlic, molasses, and honey. Open trout and place, skin side down, on baking sheet or in large baking pan. Do not overlap. Cover flesh evenly with reserved mustard mixture and let stand, at room temperature, 30 minutes.

Preheat oven to 200 degrees. In food processor, combine toasted pecans, bread crumbs, and chili powder and pulse until fine. Pour onto plate. In large skillet, heat 1 tablespoon of the olive oil over medium heat. Dredge flesh sides of trout in bread crumb mixture. Place 1 or 2 of the trout, skin side down, in skillet and cook until crisp and browned, about 4 minutes. Turn and continue cooking about 2 minutes. Transfer to platter and place in oven to keep warm. Repeat with remaining trout, adding additional olive oil when necessary. Serve immediately.

Dijon Trout With Dill Cucumbers

4 servings

- 1 English cucumber, thinly sliced
- ½ cup white wine vinegar
- 2 tablespoons water
- 1 teaspoon sugar
- ¼ teaspoon salt
- dash white pepper
- 1 tablespoon minced dill weed or 2 tablespoons minced fresh parsley
- ¼ cup (½ stick) unsalted butter, softened
- 1 tablespoon minced fresh parsley
- 2 tablespoons fresh lemon juice
- 4 large boned trout
- salt and freshly ground black pepper
- 16 teaspoons Dijon mustard, divided
- vegetable oil

Trout may be presented as a fillet or whole. *Photo, page 194.*

In shallow glass dish or resealable plastic bag, combine cucumber, vinegar, water, sugar, salt, white pepper, and dill. Cover and chill 2 hours. In small bowl, combine butter, parsley, and lemon juice. Stir until well blended and let stand, at room temperature, up to 2 hours.

Preheat broiler and oil broiler pan. Lay trout open. Lightly salt and pepper flesh. Place on broiler pan, skin side up. Spread 2 teaspoons of the mustard over skin side of each trout. Broil, 5 inches from heat, 4 minutes, brushing twice with oil. Remove from oven, turn trout, and spread 2 teaspoons of the mustard over flesh sides. Return to oven and broil 3 minutes, brushing twice with oil. Place a bed of the chilled cucumbers on serving plates. Place trout over cucumbers and dot each fish with 2 teaspoons of the reserved parsley butter.

Snapper in Black Bean Sauce

4 servings

- 1½ tablespoons Chinese fermented black beans or black bean paste
- 4 teaspoons peeled, minced fresh ginger root
- 1 teaspoon crushed garlic
- 1 tablespoon packed brown sugar
- 2 tablespoons sake or dry sherry
- 3 tablespoons soy sauce
- 2 tablespoons sesame oil
- ½ cup chicken broth
- 2 tablespoons peanut oil
- 1½ pounds snapper fillets, skinned
- salt and freshly ground black pepper

Garnish:

- 1 medium tomato, peeled, seeded, and chopped
- 4 green onions, cut into julienne strips
- 1 tablespoon chopped fresh cilantro

Rock fish, black bass, or striped bass may be substituted for snapper.

In food processor, combine beans, ginger, and garlic. Process until smooth. Add brown sugar, sake, soy sauce, sesame oil, and chicken broth. Process until well blended.

In large, heavy skillet, heat peanut oil over high heat. Season snapper with salt and pepper to taste. When oil just begins to smoke, sear snapper 15 seconds per side. Pour bean mixture around snapper. Reduce heat, cover, and simmer 5-7 minutes, or until snapper is opaque and flaky, basting 2-3 times. Transfer snapper to warmed serving plates and pour sauce on top. Garnish with tomato, green onions and cilantro.

Snapper With Orange Pecan Sauce

3-4 servings

- 2 tablespoons coarse grain Dijon mustard
- ½ cup fresh orange juice
- 1 pound snapper fillets or rock fish fillets
- salt and freshly ground black pepper
- flour for dredging
- 2 tablespoons unsalted butter

Garnish:

- 1 tablespoon finely grated orange zest
- chopped fresh parsley
- ½ cup pecans, lightly toasted (page 381)

This recipe may be doubled easily. Serve with Green Bean Sauté, page 319.

In small bowl, combine mustard and orange juice. Season snapper with salt and pepper to taste. Dredge snapper in flour, shaking to remove excess. In large skillet melt butter over medium-high heat. Add snapper and cook until browned, about 3 minutes per side. Pour reserved orange juice mixture over snapper and stir, scraping up any browned bits. Cover and cook until snapper is just cooked through, about 5 minutes. Transfer to individual serving plates and garnish with orange zest, parsley, and toasted pecans.

Sole With Ginger Sake Sauce

4 servings

1 14½-ounce can whole tomatoes, juice reserved
2 tablespoons olive oil
2 tablespoons peeled, minced fresh ginger root, divided
1½ teaspoons chopped garlic
2 tablespoons chopped shallots
2 tablespoons sake or dry sherry
½ teaspoon sugar
½ teaspoon Chinese chili sauce
4 6-ounce sole fillets
2 tablespoons soy sauce
1 tablespoon fresh lemon juice
1 tablespoon butter
Garnish:
¼ cup snipped fresh chives

Sole is very low-fat. Paired with this flavorful sauce, it makes a delectable entree.

Place tomatoes with juice in glass bowl. Break tomatoes into small pieces. In medium skillet, heat olive oil over medium heat. Add 1 tablespoon of the ginger, garlic, and shallots and cook 1 minute. Add tomatoes and juice, sake, sugar, and chili sauce and heat to boiling. Reduce heat to low and simmer 30 minutes.

Transfer to food processor or blender. Process about 1 minute. Strain to remove seeds, forcing sauce through strainer with back of spoon. (May be prepared to this point up to 1 day in advance. Cover and chill.)

Preheat oven to 550 degrees and switch to broil setting. Lightly oil baking sheet. Place sole, skin side down, on prepared baking sheet. In small bowl, combine remaining 1 tablespoon ginger, soy sauce, and lemon juice. Divide mixture among fillets and rub into sole.

Broil, 5 inches from heat, without turning, until opaque and just firm to the touch, about 2 minutes. Heat reserved sauce to low boil. Whisk in butter. Remove from heat. Transfer sole to warmed individual serving plates. Spoon heated sauce around sole and garnish with chives.

Broiled Salmon With Zesty Lime Mustard

4 servings

2 tablespoons coarse grain mustard
2 tablespoons finely grated lime zest
2 tablespoons fresh lime juice
½ teaspoon salt
¼ teaspoon freshly ground black pepper
4 6-ounce salmon fillets

Real fast food and great with a Pinot Noir.

Preheat broiler. In medium bowl, combine mustard, lime zest, lime juice, salt, and pepper. Place salmon, skin side down, on broiler pan and brush top with mustard mixture. Broil, 5 inches from heat, until center is opaque, 8-10 minutes.

Salmon With Sun-Dried Tomato Relish

4 servings

Sun-Dried Tomato Relish:

1 small English cucumber, peeled, seeded, and diced
½ small red onion, peeled and diced
½ yellow bell pepper cored, seeded, and diced
½ red bell pepper cored, seeded, and diced
½ cup drained and diced oil-packed sun-dried tomatoes, oil reserved
1 tablespoon fresh lemon juice
2 tablespoons rice wine vinegar
2 tablespoons olive oil

Fish:

¼ cup chopped fresh tarragon or 1 tablespoon dried tarragon
¼ cup chopped fresh chervil or 1 tablespoon dried chervil
¼ cup fresh lemon juice
¼ cup rice wine vinegar
⅓ cup olive oil
¼ teaspoon salt
1 English cucumber, very thinly sliced
4 6-ounce salmon fillets

A bold and bright pairing of delicious ingredients.

In glass bowl, combine diced cucumber, red onion, bell peppers, sun-dried tomatoes, 1 tablespoon reserved sun-dried tomato oil, 1 tablespoon lemon juice, 2 tablespoons vinegar, and 2 tablespoons olive oil. Let stand 30 minutes or up to overnight.

In medium bowl, combine tarragon, chervil, ¼ cup lemon juice, ¼ cup vinegar, ⅓ cup olive oil, and salt. In separate bowl, combine half of the tarragon mixture and sliced cucumbers and chill. Combine remaining half of the tarragon mixture and salmon in shallow dish and marinate, at room temperature, 30 minutes.

Preheat grill to medium-high. Cook salmon 4-5 minutes per side, discarding marinade. Place drained chilled cucumbers on individual serving plates. Place salmon over cucumbers and top with Sun-Dried Tomato Relish.

Sesame Salmon and Hunan Noodles

4 servings

- 6-8 ounces dried oriental-style noodles, such as Chuka Soba
- 4 tablespoons sesame oil, divided
- ½ cup soy sauce, divided
- 2 tablespoons rice wine vinegar
- 1 tablespoon sugar
- 1 tablespoon hot chili oil
- 1 tablespoon plus 1 teaspoon peeled, minced fresh ginger root, divided
- 2 tablespoons sliced green onions
- ⅓ cup fresh peas, thawed frozen peas, or snow peas, cut into thirds
- ⅓ cup shredded carrots
- ⅓ cup sliced fresh mushrooms
- ⅓ cup thinly sliced red bell pepper
- 3-4 tablespoons fresh lemon juice
- freshly ground black pepper
- 4 4-ounce salmon fillets
- mixed salad greens, rinsed and dried

Cook noodles according to package directions. Drain well, place in large bowl, and toss with 2 tablespoons of the sesame oil. In small bowl, combine ¼ cup of the soy sauce, vinegar, sugar, hot chili oil, and 1 teaspoon of the ginger. Stir until well blended and add to noodles. Toss to blend. Add green onions, peas, carrots, mushrooms, and bell pepper. Toss and chill 2 hours.

In shallow glass dish, combine lemon juice, remaining ¼ cup soy sauce, remaining 2 tablespoons sesame oil, remaining 1 tablespoon ginger, and pepper to taste. Add salmon and turn to coat. Cover tightly with plastic wrap and chill 2 hours. Preheat grill to medium-high. Grill salmon, discarding marinade, 4-5 minutes per side. Place salad greens on serving plates and top with noodle mixture and salmon. Serve immediately, or chill and serve cold.

Perfect for a patio dinner.

Grilled Salmon With Warm Pineapple Sauce

6 servings

- 2 tablespoons fresh lemon or lime juice
- 2 teaspoons minced garlic
- ½ teaspoon freshly ground black pepper
- 6 6-ounce salmon fillets
- 2 tablespoons butter
- 2 tablespoons minced shallots
- 2 teaspoons seeded, minced jalapeño pepper
- 3 tablespoons peeled, minced fresh ginger root
- 1¼ cups fresh orange juice
- ½ teaspoon curry powder
- 2 cups fresh chopped pineapple
- 2 tablespoons chopped fresh mint

A delicious and healthful dish with very little cholesterol.

In shallow glass dish, combine lemon juice, garlic, and pepper. Add salmon and marinate, at room temperature, 30 minutes. Preheat grill to medium-high. In medium skillet, heat butter over medium heat. Add shallots, jalapeño, and ginger and cook 2 minutes. Add orange juice and curry powder and cook until reduced by half, about 10 minutes. Add pineapple and mint, reduce heat to low, and cook until thoroughly heated. Grill salmon 4-5 minutes per side. Place salmon on individual serving plates and spoon warm pineapple sauce on top.

Salmon With Italian Tomato Caper Sauce

4 servings

- 1 pound Italian plum tomatoes, halved and seeded
- ¼ cup loosely packed, fresh arugula
- ¼ cup loosely packed, fresh basil
- ¼ cup loosely packed, fresh Italian parsley
- ½ cup olive oil plus additional for brushing
- 2 shallots, peeled
- 1½ tablespoons fresh lemon juice
- ¼ cup drained capers
- salt and freshly ground black pepper
- 4 6-ounce salmon fillets

Garnish:

lemon wedges

Arugula is a salad green with a peppery mustard flavor. Mustard greens may be substituted, or increase the amount of fresh herbs. Serve with Cabernet Sauvignon.

In food processor, combine tomatoes, arugula, basil, parsley, ½ cup of the olive oil, shallots, lemon juice, and capers. Pulse until finely diced but not pureed. Season with salt and pepper to taste. (May be prepared up to 1 day in advance. Cover and chill. Bring to room temperature before serving.)

Preheat broiler. Brush both sides of salmon with olive oil and season with salt and pepper to taste. Broil, 5 inches from heat, without turning, until just cooked through, 8-10 minutes. Place salmon on individual serving plates and spoon tomato mixture on top. Garnish with lemon wedges.

Crusted Salmon With Herbed Mayonnaise

6 servings

Herbed Mayonnaise:

- ⅓ cup minced fresh Italian parsley
- ⅓ cup minced fresh cilantro
- ¼ cup minced green onions
- 2 tablespoons red wine vinegar
- ½ teaspoon minced garlic
- ¼ teaspoon dried oregano
- ¼ teaspoon freshly ground black pepper
- ⅛ teaspoon cayenne
- 1 cup prepared mayonnaise

Fish:

- ¼ cup chopped fresh Italian parsley
- ¼ cup freshly grated Parmesan cheese
- 2 tablespoons chopped fresh thyme or 2 teaspoons dried thyme
- 1 teaspoon finely grated lemon zest
- ¼ teaspoon salt
- 2 small cloves garlic, peeled
- 1¼ cups fresh white bread crumbs
- ¼ cup butter (½ stick), melted, divided
- 2½ pounds salmon fillet, 1 piece if available

This impressive entree is great for entertaining. Much of the preparation can be done in advance.

In small bowl, combine ⅓ cup parsley, cilantro, green onions, vinegar, ½ teaspoon minced garlic, oregano, pepper, and cayenne. Stir until well blended and let stand, at room temperature, 30 minutes, or cover with plastic wrap and chill overnight.

Preheat oven to 450 degrees. Grease large, shallow baking pan. In food processor or blender, combine ¼ cup parsley, Parmesan, thyme, lemon zest, and salt. With processor running, drop 2 cloves garlic through feed tube and process until finely chopped. Transfer to large bowl and add bread crumbs. Toss to blend. (May be prepared in advance. Cover and chill overnight. Bring to room temperature before proceeding.) Add 3 tablespoons of the melted butter and toss to combine.

Pat salmon dry and place, skin side down, in prepared pan. Brush with remaining 1 tablespoon melted butter. Pack crumb mixture on salmon. Bake 20-25 minutes or until center is opaque. If using several small fillets, cook 10 minutes per inch of thickness. If crumbs brown too quickly, cover loosely with foil. Transfer to serving platter. Stir mayonnaise into chilled herb mixture and serve on the side.

Salmon and Mushrooms in Phyllo

6 servings

- 3 tablespoons pine nuts
- 3 tablespoons olive oil, divided, plus additional for brushing phyllo
- 3 tablespoons finely chopped shallots
- ½ teaspoon minced garlic
- 6 ounces mixed fresh wild mushrooms, such as shiitake, portobello, and crimini, trimmed, and coarsely chopped
- ¼ teaspoon dried thyme
- 2 tablespoons snipped fresh chives
- 1 tablespoon chopped fresh basil
- ⅛ teaspoon cayenne
- salt and freshly ground black pepper
- 2 tablespoons freshly grated Parmesan cheese
- 1 16-ounce package phyllo pastry sheets, thawed if frozen
- 1 lemon, halved
- 6 4-5-ounce salmon fillets, skinned
- Ginger Shallot Cream Sauce (page 213)

You may spray phyllo sheets with olive oil spray instead of brushing with olive oil. Puff pastry may be substituted for phyllo. This entree goes well with a Chardonnay.

Preheat oven to 400 degrees. In large skillet, combine pine nuts and 1 tablespoon of the olive oil over medium heat. Cook until nuts are lightly browned. Remove with slotted spoon and set aside. Place remaining 2 tablespoons olive oil in same skillet. Add shallots and garlic and cook until shallots are soft, about 5 minutes. Add mushrooms, thyme, chives, basil, and cayenne. Season with salt and pepper to taste. Cook until mushrooms give up their juice. Remove from heat and cool. Stir in Parmesan and set aside.

Remove phyllo from package and cover with plastic wrap and damp towel. Squeeze juice of lemon over salmon and season with salt and pepper to taste. Trim phyllo to 12x8-inch rectangles. Brush 1 sheet with olive oil and cover with another sheet, brush with olive oil. Repeat a third time. Place 2 heaping tablespoons of the mushroom mixture on the phyllo and top with 1 salmon fillet. Fold in sides and bottom and fold over top, tucking top into the bottom to form an envelope-style packet.

Place on baking sheet. Repeat with remaining ingredients to form 6 packets. (May be prepared up to 3 hours in advance. Cover and chill.) Brush tops with olive oil. Bake 25 minutes or until golden brown. Serve with Ginger Shallot Cream Sauce, if desired.

Crispy Black Pepper Salmon

4 servings

- ½ cup dry white wine
- ¼ cup white Worcestershire
- 1 cup chicken broth
- ¼ teaspoon salt
- dash white pepper
- 1 medium onion, peeled and very thinly sliced
- 4 6-ounce salmon fillets
- 2 tablespoons freshly cracked black pepper
- 2 tablespoons olive oil
- 1 bunch fresh spinach, washed, stemmed, and dried

Cold water fish such as salmon and mackerel, contain oils that are heart healthful.

In shallow baking dish, combine wine, Worcestershire, chicken broth, salt, and white pepper. Add onion and salmon. Cover and chill 30 minutes or up to 2 hours.

Spread pepper on large plate. Remove salmon, reserving marinade and onion. Press both sides of salmon into pepper to coat and set aside. In large skillet, heat olive oil over medium heat. Remove onion, reserving marinade, and add to skillet. Cook until onion is soft, about 5 minutes. Remove with slotted spoon and set aside.

Increase heat to medium-high. When olive oil begins to smoke, place salmon, flesh side down, in skillet and cook until crisp and browned, about 4 minutes per side. Return onion to skillet, keeping to one side of salmon and add reserved marinade. When salmon is just cooked through, 6-10 minutes, remove from skillet and place on warmed individual serving plates.

Add spinach to skillet and cook just until limp, keeping separate from onion. Divide spinach and onion equally among plates. Place spinach on 1 side of salmon and onion on the other. Continue cooking marinade until reduced by half and divide equally over salmon.

Tuna With Mango Avocado Salsa

6 servings

Mango Avocado Salsa:

2 fresh mangos, peeled, seeded, and chopped
⅔ cup diced red bell pepper
2 tablespoons chopped fresh cilantro
⅓ cup minced red onion
2 tablespoons white wine vinegar
1 tablespoon sugar
½ teaspoon salt
1 teaspoon freshly ground black pepper
1 tablespoon olive oil
1 avocado

Tuna:

6 6-ounce tuna or swordfish steaks
salt and freshly ground black pepper
2 tablespoons white wine vinegar
1 tablespoon sugar
1 tablespoon olive oil

This salsa is fabulous over any kind of fish.

In glass bowl, combine mangos, bell pepper, cilantro, red onion, 2 tablespoons vinegar, 1 tablespoon sugar, ½ teaspoon salt, 1 teaspoon pepper, and 1 tablespoon olive oil. Chill 30 minutes.

Season tuna with salt and pepper to taste. Combine 2 tablespoons vinegar, 1 tablespoon sugar, and 1 tablespoon olive oil. Drizzle over tuna. Let stand, at room temperature, 30 minutes. Preheat grill to medium. Grill tuna 10 minutes per inch of thickness, turning once.

Just before serving, peel, seed, and dice avocado and add to salsa mixture. Stir to blend and adjust seasonings to taste. Serve over tuna.

Mediterranean Halibut

4 servings

- 4 Italian plum tomatoes, seeded and diced
- 2 tablespoons chopped kalamata olives
- ¼ cup drained capers
- 1 teaspoon minced garlic
- 3 tablespoons olive oil, divided
- 3 tablespoons fresh lemon juice, divided
- ¼ cup dry white wine
- ½ cup crumbled feta cheese, divided
- 2 tablespoons minced shallots
- 2 tablespoons chopped fresh basil
- salt and freshly ground black pepper
- 4 6-8-ounce halibut fillets

Snapper or grouper may be substituted for halibut.

In glass bowl, combine tomatoes, olives, capers, garlic, 2 tablespoons of the olive oil, 1½ tablespoons of the lemon juice, wine, ¼ cup of the feta, shallots, basil, and salt and pepper to taste. Let stand at room temperature.

Preheat oven to 425 degrees. Brush bottom of shallow baking pan with remaining 1 tablespoon olive oil. Season both sides of halibut with salt and pepper to taste. Place in prepared baking pan. Squeeze remaining 1½ tablespoons lemon juice over halibut and top with tomato mixture. Sprinkle with remaining ¼ cup feta. Bake until just cooked through, about 15 minutes. Arrange halibut on individual serving plates and spoon pan juices on top.

Halibut With Carrot Fennel Salad

4 servings

¼ cup dark rum
¼ cup molasses
2 tablespoons olive oil
3 tablespoons orange juice
1 tablespoon peeled, minced fresh ginger root
1 tablespoon minced garlic
1 tablespoon freshly cracked black pepper
1 teaspoon minced, seeded jalapeño pepper
4 6-ounce halibut fillets

Carrot Fennel Salad:

2 cups julienned or shredded carrots
2 cups julienned or shredded fennel bulb
½ cup rice wine vinegar
¼ cup olive oil

Orange Vinaigrette:

½ cup frozen orange juice concentrate
½ cup olive oil
½ teaspoon sesame oil
2 teaspoons Dijon mustard
2 teaspoons rice wine vinegar
salt and freshly ground black pepper

Garnish:

cilantro or fresh parsley

The sweet, soft flavors of fennel tossed with the tanginess of orange combine beautifully. Despite the pepper in the marinade, this is not a spicy entree. Try an Alsacian Riesling with this dish.

In shallow dish, combine rum, molasses, 2 tablespoons olive oil, 3 tablespoons orange juice, ginger, garlic, pepper, and jalapeño. Whisk to combine. Add halibut and turn to coat. Marinate, in refrigerator, 30 minutes or up to overnight.

Thirty minutes before serving, combine carrots, fennel, ½ cup vinegar and ¼ cup olive oil. Toss to coat, cover, and chill. In small bowl, combine orange juice concentrate, ½ cup olive oil, sesame oil, mustard, and 2 teaspoons vinegar. Season with salt and pepper to taste.

Preheat grill to medium-high. Grill halibut about 4 minutes per side, basting frequently with marinade. Drain chilled Carrot Fennel Salad. Spoon Orange Vinaigrette onto individual serving plates, mound drained Carrot Fennel Salad in center and place halibut on top. Drizzle about 1 tablespoon of the Orange Vinaigrette over halibut, and garnish with cilantro or parsley.

Grilled Swordfish With Tropical Salsa

4 servings

Tropical Salsa:

1 cup fresh pineapple, diced and juice reserved
1 red bell pepper, cored, seeded, and diced
3 tablespoons minced green onions
½ cup peeled, diced jícama
1 small jalapeño pepper, cored seeded, and diced
1 tablespoon minced fresh cilantro
2 tablespoons rice wine vinegar
1 tablespoon olive oil
salt

Marinade:

¼ cup reserved fresh pineapple juice (supplement with canned if necessary)
¼ cup fresh lime juice
2 tablespoons olive oil
1 tablespoon minced fresh thyme or 1 teaspoon dried thyme
½ teaspoon minced garlic
1 teaspoon finely grated lime zest

Fish:

4 6-8-ounce swordfish steaks

In glass bowl, combine pineapple, bell pepper, green onions, jícama, jalapeño, cilantro, vinegar, 1 tablespoon olive oil, and salt to taste. Chill 3 hours or up to overnight. Allow to stand at room temperature 1 hour before serving.

Combine pineapple juice, lime juice, 2 tablespoons olive oil, thyme, garlic and lime zest. Place swordfish in shallow glass dish and pour marinade over fish, turning to coat. Marinate in refrigerator, 3 hours, turning once.

Preheat grill to medium. Grill swordfish about 5 minutes per side or 10 minutes per inch of thickness. Place on individual serving plates and spoon Tropical Salsa over top.

A healthful entree with a vibrant and flavorful salsa.

Fresh Fruit Salsa

3 cups

- 2 tablespoons fresh lime juice
- 1 pink grapefruit, sectioned and chopped
- ½ teaspoon crushed garlic
- 2 ripe nectarines, diced, or frozen peaches, thawed and diced
- 3 Italian plum tomatoes, diced
- 1 tablespoon finely diced red onion
- 1 small jalapeño pepper, cored, seeded, and minced
- 1½ tablespoons raspberry preserves
- salt and freshly ground black pepper

Seasonal fruits may be substituted.

In glass bowl, combine lime juice, grapefruit, garlic, nectarines, tomatoes, red onion, jalapeño, raspberry preserves, and salt and pepper to taste. Cover tightly with plastic wrap and let stand, at room temperature, up to 2 hours. Serve with grilled or broiled fish.

Fresh Fruit Marinade

¾ cup

- 2 tablespoons fresh lime juice
- ½ cup fresh grapefruit juice
- 1 teaspoon crushed garlic
- 1 tablespoon raspberry preserves
- salt and freshly ground black pepper

Great with swordfish, tuna, or marlin.

Combine lime juice, grapefruit juice, garlic, and raspberry preserves. Season with salt and pepper to taste. Pour over fish and let stand, at room temperature, up to 30 minutes. Cook as desired and serve with Fresh Fruit Salsa (recipe above).

Papaya Corn Salsa

4 cups

- 1 cup fresh or frozen corn, blanched in boiling water 2 minutes and well drained
- 1 ripe papaya, peeled, seeded, and diced
- ⅓ cup finely diced red onion
- 2 Italian plum tomatoes, seeded and diced
- 1½ teaspoons finely minced garlic
- 1 tablespoon finely grated lime zest
- ¼ cup fresh lime juice
- 2 tablespoons chopped fresh cilantro

This salsa is very versatile and is fabulous on chicken and turkey.

In glass bowl, combine corn, papaya, red onion, tomatoes, garlic, lime zest, and lime juice. Cover tightly with plastic wrap and chill 2 hours. (May be prepared up to 8 hours in advance, but add papaya no more than 2 hours before serving.) Just before serving, add cilantro and toss. Serve with grilled or broiled fish.

Three Citrus Marinade

2 cups

- ¼ cup fresh lime juice
- ¼ cup fresh lemon juice
- 1 cup fresh orange juice
- ½ cup olive oil
- 2 teaspoons minced garlic
- 2 teaspoons coarsely ground black pepper
- 3 bay leaves, crushed
- 2 tablespoons chopped fresh cilantro
- salt

Experiment with this delightful marinade. It's great with scallops, shrimp, or fish.

Combine lime juice, lemon juice, orange juice, olive oil, garlic, pepper, bay leaves, cilantro, and salt to taste. Let stand, at room temperature, 30 minutes. Using only small amount of marinade, allow shellfish to marinate 10-15 minutes and fish 30-60 minutes. Grill shellfish or fish, brushing frequently with reserved marinade. Drizzle with fresh marinade and serve.

Mesa Verde Mango Relish

2 cups

- 1 large ripe mango, peeled, seeded, diced
- ½ English cucumber, halved lengthwise, seeded, and finely diced
- 1 red bell pepper, cored, seeded, diced
- ½ cup finely diced red onion
- ¼ cup fresh lime juice
- ¼ cup fresh orange juice
- 2 tablespoons chopped fresh cilantro
- salt

In glass bowl, combine mango, cucumber, bell pepper, red onion, lime juice, and orange juice. Cover and chill 30 minutes or up to 4 hours. Add cilantro, toss, and season with salt to taste. Serve over grilled fish.

Ginger Shallot Cream Sauce

¾ cup

- ½ cup dry white wine
- ½ cup rice wine vinegar
- 3 tablespoons minced shallots
- 1 2-inch piece fresh ginger root, peeled and thinly sliced
- ½ cup whipping cream
- 3-5 tablespoons cold butter, cut into pieces

This sauce may be doubled easily. Increase cooking time to reduce sauce.

In heavy saucepan, combine wine, vinegar, shallots, and ginger over medium-high heat and heat to boiling. Cook until reduced by half, about 15 minutes (will be the consistency of a glaze). Stir in cream and cook until reduced by half, about 10 minutes. Strain into clean saucepan. (May be prepared to this point up to 3 hours in advance and chilled.) Return to low heat. Whisk in butter, 1 piece at a time. Serve immediately over grilled salmon or tuna.

Aussie Shellfish Curry

4 servings

- 1 cup coconut milk or whipping cream
- ¼ cup brandy
- ½ cup Sweet Chili Sauce (recipe below)
- 1 teaspoon or more curry paste or curry powder
- 1 teaspoon minced fresh parsley
- ½ pound shrimp, peeled and deveined
- ½ pound scallops
- ½ pound raw lobster meat, cut into chunks
- ½ pound firm white fish, such as halibut or sea bass, cut into bite size pieces
- 4 cups cooked white rice

This incredible recipe showcases a variety of seafood.

In large stockpot with steamer insert, place 1-2 inches water. Heat to boiling over high heat. In large skillet, combine coconut milk, brandy, Sweet Chili Sauce, curry paste, and parsley. Set aside.

When water reaches full rolling boil, add seafood to steamer basket, cover, and cook 4-5 minutes, or until opaque. Remove from heat and set lid off-center to allow seafood to stay warm without cooking further or drying out.

Place coconut milk mixture over medium-low heat. Cook, stirring constantly, until thickened. Do not boil. Test consistency by scraping bottom of skillet with wooden spoon. When sauce moves slowly to fill in space, gently stir in steamed seafood. Serve over cooked rice.

Sweet Chile Sauce

2½ cups

- 6 ounces golden raisins (1 cup firmly packed)
- 6 tablespoons chili powder
- ¾ cup sugar
- 1 cup white vinegar
- 2½ teaspoons crushed garlic
- 1½ teaspoons salt
- 1½ teaspoons peeled, grated fresh ginger root
- 1 large red bell pepper, cored, seeded, and quartered
- 1 jalapeño pepper or 2-3 fresh red chiles, cored, seeded, and chopped

Try this as a pizza sauce with shrimp or duck.

In large saucepan, combine raisins, chili powder, sugar, vinegar, garlic, salt, ginger, bell pepper, and jalapeño. Heat to boiling, reduce heat, and simmer until raisins plump, about 10 minutes. Remove from heat and set aside to cool. Transfer to food processor or blender and process until smooth. Place in tightly sealed container and store, in refrigerator, up to 3 months. Serve over grilled fish or shrimp.

Cioppino

6 servings

- ¼ cup olive oil
- 1 medium green bell pepper, cored, seeded, and chopped
- 1½ cups chopped onion
- 1 28-ounce can Italian plum tomatoes with basil, juice reserved
- 1 28-ounce can tomato puree
- 2 tablespoons tomato paste
- 2 cups dry red wine
- 1½ teaspoons dried basil
- 1½ teaspoons dried oregano
- 1½ teaspoons dried thyme
- ⅛ teaspoon salt
- 1 bay leaf
- 2 teaspoons crushed red pepper
- 1 sprig fresh parsley
- 24 hard shelled clams, scrubbed
- ¾ pound shrimp, shelled, deveined, and tails left on
- 1½ pounds halibut or other firm mild white fish, cut into 1½-inch pieces
- ¾ pound sea scallops, halved
- 6 tablespoons minced fresh parsley

Guests will savor the rich flavors of this classic Italian dish, especially when served with a light bodied Italian or Spanish red wine, such as a Rioja. It's fabulous over pasta too.
Photo, page 196

In 4-quart saucepan with lid, heat olive oil over medium-low heat. Add bell pepper and onion. Cook until soft, stirring frequently, about 5 minutes. Add tomatoes with juice, tomato puree, tomato paste, wine, basil, oregano, thyme, salt, bay leaf, crushed red pepper, and parsley sprig. Heat to boiling. Reduce heat and simmer 1½ hours, stirring and scraping bottom of pan occasionally.

Discard bay leaf and parsley sprig. Heat to full boil, stir in clams, and cover. Check clams every 5 minutes for a total of 20 minutes. With each check, remove opened clams with tongs to bowl and reserve. Discard any unopened clams after 20 minutes. Taste and season with salt, if necessary. Add shrimp, halibut, and scallops and reduce heat. Simmer 5–7 minutes or until halibut is just cooked and flakes with fork. Gently stir in cooked clams and sprinkle with minced parsley. Ladle into large serving bowls and serve with warm crusty bread.

Shrimp Fajitas With Chipotle Tomatillo Salsa

8 servings

Chipotle Tomatillo Salsa:

2 tablespoons olive oil, divided
1 pound tomatillos, husked and quartered
1 small red onion, peeled, and diced
2–3 dried or canned chipotle chile peppers, seeded and finely minced
½ cup loosely packed, chopped fresh cilantro
1 tablespoon red wine or balsamic vinegar

Fajitas:

¼ cup fresh lime juice
¼ cup vegetable oil
¼ cup tequila
1½ teaspoons minced garlic
1 teaspoon ground cumin
½ teaspoon salt
½ teaspoon sugar
½ teaspoon Tabasco
1 pound shrimp, peeled and deveined
1 large onion, peeled and thinly sliced
1 small green bell pepper cored, seeded, cut into thin strips
1 small red bell pepper cored, seeded, cut into thin strips
8 flour tortillas, warmed

Garnish:

guacamole
sour cream

In skillet, heat 1 tablespoon of the olive oil over medium-high heat. Add tomatillos and cook about 5 minutes. Remove, chop, and set aside. Add remaining 1 tablespoon olive oil to same skillet. Add red onion and reduce heat to medium. Cook until browned, about 8 minutes. Return reserved tomatillos to skillet and stir in chipotle chiles. Remove from heat and stir in cilantro and vinegar. (May be prepared up to 2 days in advance. Cover and chill.) Serve warm or at room temperature.

In large glass bowl, combine lime juice, ¼ cup oil, tequila, garlic, cumin, salt, sugar, and Tabasco. Add shrimp and onion and toss to coat. Cover and chill 2 hours.

Drain shrimp and onion, reserving 1 tablespoon marinade. In large skillet, heat reserved marinade over medium-high heat. Add bell peppers and cook 5 minutes, stirring frequently. Add shrimp and onion and cook, stirring constantly, 3 minutes or until shrimp are pink. Fill warmed tortillas with shrimp mixture and garnish with guacamole and sour cream. Serve with Chipotle Tomatillo Salsa on the side.

Shrimp Enchiladas Con Queso

4-8 servings

- 2 tablespoons olive oil, divided
- ½ cup chopped red bell pepper
- ½ cup minced onion
- 1 jalapeño pepper, cored, seeded, and minced
- 1 fresh green chile pepper, cored, seeded, and diced
- ½ teaspoon minced garlic
- ½ teaspoon dried oregano
- ½ teaspoon salt
- pinch freshly ground black pepper
- pinch cayenne
- 3 tablespoons flour
- 3 tablespoons water
- 1 cup milk
- 1 cup grated Monterey Jack cheese, divided
- ¼ cup sour cream
- 1 pound medium shrimp, peeled and deveined
- ¾ cup chopped green onions, divided
- 2 medium tomatoes, peeled, seeded, and chopped, divided
- 8 8-inch flour tortillas

Garnish:

- guacamole
- Chipotle Tomatillo Salsa (page 216) or purchased salsa

This is a great south of the border seafood recipe for entertaining.

Preheat oven to 350 degrees. Grease large baking dish. In large heavy saucepan, heat 1 tablespoon of the olive oil over medium heat. Add bell pepper, onion, jalapeño, green chile, garlic, and oregano. Cook until tender, about 5 minutes, stirring occasionally. Stir in salt, pepper, and cayenne.

In small bowl, combine flour and water, whisk to blend and add to bell pepper mixture. Add milk and stir until well blended. Reduce heat and simmer until slightly thickened, stirring constantly, about 3 minutes. Add ½ cup of the Monterey Jack and stir until melted. Remove from heat and stir in sour cream.

In large skillet, heat remaining 1 tablespoon olive oil over high heat. Add shrimp and ½ cup of the green onions. Stir until shrimp just turn pink, about 2 minutes. Stir in half of the bell pepper mixture and half of the tomatoes. Remove from heat. Spoon approximately ½ cup of the shrimp mixture onto 1 tortilla and roll tightly. Place, seam down, in prepared baking dish and repeat with remaining tortillas. (May be prepared to this point up to 2 hours in advance. Cover and chill.)

Top enchiladas with remaining half of the bell pepper mixture. Cover with foil and bake 30-40 minutes, until thoroughly heated. Top with remaining ½ cup Monterey Jack, ¼ cup green onions and remaining half of the tomatoes. Garnish with guacamole and salsa and serve immediately.

Barbequed Shrimp With Corn Cakes

4 servings

- ½ cup sour cream
- 2 tablespoons chopped fresh cilantro
- ¼ teaspoon Tabasco
- 4 tablespoons fresh lime juice, divided

Corn Cakes:

- ½ cup flour
- ¼ cup yellow cornmeal
- ½ teaspoon baking powder
- salt and freshly ground black pepper
- ¾ cup buttermilk
- 1 large egg, lightly beaten
- 1 cup fresh or frozen corn kernels
- ¼ cup diced green onions
- ¼ cup snipped fresh chives
- ¼ cup (½ stick) unsalted butter, melted, divided

Shrimp:

- 16 jumbo shrimp, shelled and deveined
- ½ cup purchased barbeque sauce, divided

Garnish:

- fresh cilantro sprigs

Ideal for summer entertaining.

Preheat oven to warm. Preheat grill to medium-high. In small bowl, combine sour cream, cilantro, Tabasco, and 2 tablespoons of the lime juice.

In large bowl, combine flour, cornmeal, baking powder, and salt and pepper to taste. Stir in buttermilk and egg. Fold in corn, green onions, chives, and 2 tablespoons of the melted butter.

In large non-stick skillet, heat small amount of the remaining melted butter over medium-high heat. Ladle batter into skillet, forming 4-inch cakes. Turn when batter begins to bubble on surface and bottoms are light brown, about 2 minutes. Continue cooking about 1 minute, until thoroughly cooked and browned. Transfer to platter and place in warm oven until ready to serve. Repeat with remaining batter, making 8 cakes.

Grill shrimp about 3 minutes. Turn and brush generously with barbeque sauce. When pink and firm, transfer to plate and brush again with barbeque sauce. Drizzle with remaining 2 tablespoons lime juice. Place 2 warm corn cakes on individual serving plate. Arrange 4 shrimp on cakes and top with sour cream mixture. Drizzle small amount of barbeque sauce over shrimp and garnish with cilantro sprigs.

Thai Coconut Shrimp

4-6 servings

- 1½ cups coconut milk
- 2 tablespoons dry sherry or sake
- 1½ teaspoons Chinese chili sauce
- 1 tablespoon sugar
- ¼ teaspoon salt
- 2 tablespoons peanut oil
- 2 tablespoons butter
- 2 pounds large shrimp, peeled and deveined
- 1 tablespoon minced garlic
- ½ tablespoon peeled, minced fresh ginger root
- ½ tablespoon minced shallots
- ⅓ cup chopped fresh basil leaves
- ⅓ cup chopped fresh mint leaves
- ⅓ cup chopped green onions
- 1½ tablespoons cornstarch
- 1½ tablespoons water
- 1½ tablespoons fresh lime juice
- cooked dried oriental-style noodles or cooked white rice
- ¼ cup chopped peanuts

Garnish:

lime wedges

An incredibly different dish.

In medium bowl, combine coconut milk, sherry, chili sauce, sugar, and salt. Set aside. Preheat wok over high heat. Add peanut oil and butter. Stir fry shrimp, garlic, ginger, and shallots until shrimp are pink, about 3 minutes. Add basil, mint, and green onions and stir-fry 15 seconds. Add reserved coconut milk mixture and heat to boiling. Combine cornstarch and water and add to shrimp mixture. Cook until thickened and stir in lime juice.

Rinse cooked noodles in hot water and drain. Serve shrimp mixture over noodles. Sprinkle with peanuts and garnish with lime wedges.

Shrimp and Asparagus in Ginger Sauce

4 servings

- 1 pound large shrimp, peeled and deveined
- 2 large green onions, minced, including tops
- 3 tablespoons soy sauce
- ¼ cup rice wine, divided
- 2 tablespoons sesame oil, divided
- 1 tablespoon peeled, chopped fresh ginger root
- ½ teaspoon minced garlic
- 2 tablespoons packed brown sugar
- ½ teaspoon hot chili oil
- 1 teaspoon finely grated orange zest
- ½ teaspoon finely grated lemon zest
- ¾ cup chicken broth, divided
- 1 teaspoon cornstarch
- 1½ pounds thin fresh asparagus, trimmed and cut into 2-inch pieces
- 2 green onions, cut into julienne strips
- 3 cups cooked white rice

Garnish:

finely grated orange zest

This combination of shrimp, asparagus, and rice is low in fat and high in flavor. Serve this with a light white wine such as an Orvieto.

In shallow dish, combine shrimp, green onions, soy sauce, 2 tablespoons of the wine, 1 tablespoon of the sesame oil, ginger, garlic, brown sugar, chili oil, orange zest, and lemon zest. Cover tightly and chill 2-3 hours, stirring occasionally.

In small bowl, combine ½ cup of the chicken broth, remaining 2 tablespoons wine, and cornstarch. In large non-stick skillet, heat remaining 1 tablespoon sesame oil over high heat. Add reserved shrimp mixture and cook until shrimp are just pink. Remove shrimp to bowl with slotted spoon, reserving liquid in skillet.

Add remaining ¼ cup broth and asparagus to same skillet and reduce heat to medium-low. Cover and cook until asparagus is just tender, about 3 minutes. Add cornstarch mixture and cooked shrimp to skillet and stir until sauce is translucent, about 2 minutes. Stir in green onions. Mound cooked rice in individual serving bowls and top with shrimp mixture. Garnish with orange zest.

At left:
Shrimp and Asparagus in Ginger Sauce, 221

Easy Spicy Shrimp

4 servings

1	teaspoon paprika
½–1	teaspoon cayenne
½–1	teaspoon freshly ground black pepper
¼	teaspoon crushed red pepper
½	teaspoon salt
½	teaspoon dried thyme leaves
½	teaspoon dried oregano leaves
2	pounds large shrimp, unpeeled but deveined
2	teaspoons Worcestershire
1	teaspoon Tabasco
2	teaspoons minced garlic
2	tablespoons butter, melted
¾	cup chicken broth
½	cup dry white wine
1-2	tablespoons olive oil
4	green onions, thinly sliced
1	loaf French bread

In large bowl, combine paprika, cayenne, pepper, crushed red pepper, salt, thyme, and oregano. Add shrimp and toss to coat. Let stand 15 minutes or up to 1 hour.

In small bowl, combine Worcestershire, Tabasco, and garlic and set aside. In separate bowl, combine melted butter, chicken broth, and wine and set aside. In large skillet, heat olive oil over high heat. Add shrimp mixture and Worcestershire mixture and cook 2 minutes. Add butter mixture and cook until shrimp are pink and firm. Remove shrimp, with slotted spoon, to deep bowl. Add green onions to skillet mixture and cook until slightly reduced, 2-3 minutes. Pour over shrimp. Serve with warm French bread.

Shrimp Creole

6-8 servings

- 3 tablespoons butter
- 1 cup chopped onion
- 1 teaspoon chopped garlic
- ¾ cup chopped celery
- ½ cup chopped green bell pepper
- 1 16-ounce can whole tomatoes
- 1 12-ounce can tomato sauce
- 2 bay leaves
- 2 teaspoons salt
- ½ teaspoon freshly ground black pepper
- 2 tablespoons sugar
- 2 tablespoons chopped fresh parsley
- 2 teaspoons Tabasco
- 3 tablespoons Worcestershire
- ½ teaspoon dried rosemary
- 2½ pounds shrimp, peeled and deveined
- 5 cups cooked white rice

A delicious lighter version of the classic dish.

In 4-quart saucepan, melt butter over high heat. Add onion and cook 3 minutes, stirring frequently. Reduce heat to medium-low and continue cooking, stirring frequently, until onion is a rich brown color but not burned. Add garlic, celery, and bell pepper. Cook, stirring occasionally, until tender, about 3 minutes.

Add tomatoes, tomato sauce, bay leaves, salt, pepper, sugar, parsley, Tabasco, Worcestershire, and rosemary. Heat to boiling. Reduce heat and simmer uncovered, 15 minutes, scraping bottom of pan frequently with wooden spoon. (May be prepared to this point up to 1 day in advance. Cover and chill. Heat to simmering before proceeding.) Add shrimp, turn off heat, cover, and let stand, stirring occasionally, 10 minutes or until shrimp are pink. Mound rice on individual serving plates and spoon shrimp and sauce around rice.

Black Pepper Shrimp

4 servings

- ⅓ cup molasses
- ⅓ cup Worcestershire
- ⅓ cup dark beer (open and let stand 1 hour)
- 2 tablespoons olive oil
- 1 pound large shrimp, shelled and deveined
- ¼ cup chicken broth, divided
- 1½ teaspoons freshly cracked black pepper
- 1 teaspoon Chinese chili paste, such as Sambal Oelek
- 1 tablespoon minced garlic
- 1 teaspoon cornstarch
- 1 teaspoon water
- 4 cups cooked white rice

This is a healthful dish for pepper lovers. Serve with Asparagus Stir-Fry, page 318.

In small bowl, combine molasses, Worcestershire, and beer. In medium skillet, heat olive oil over medium-high heat. Add shrimp and enough of the chicken broth to prevent shrimp from sticking. Cook until shrimp just turn pink. Remove with slotted spoon and set aside.

To same skillet, add pepper, chili paste, garlic, and remaining broth. Cook 30 seconds, stirring constantly. Stir in molasses mixture. Cook until reduced by half. In small bowl, combine cornstarch and water. Add to chicken broth mixture and continue cooking, stirring frequently, until thickened. Add shrimp, toss to coat, and heat thoroughly. Mound rice on individual serving plates, place shrimp around edge and spoon sauce over shrimp.

Roasted Macadamia Nut Grouper

4 servings

- 2 slices fresh bread
- ¾ cup macadamia nuts, toasted (page 381)
- 2 tablespoons finely minced shallots
- 2 tablespoons chopped fresh parsley
- 2 tablespoons fresh lime juice
- ¼ cup coarse grain Dijon mustard
- ¼ teaspoon Tabasco
- 4 4-6-ounce grouper fillets or 1 large fillet

If using 1 large fillet, baking time should be about 30 minutes.

Preheat oven to 425 degrees. Grease rack and place in baking pan. In food processor, pulse bread to fine crumbs. Remove to bowl and set aside. Place toasted macadamia nuts in processor, pulse until fine. Add to crumbs. Add shallots and parsley, toss to blend, and set aside.

In small bowl combine lime juice, mustard, and Tabasco. Coat each fillet with mustard mixture and place on prepared rack. Pack crumb mixture on top of each fillet. Bake 10 minutes per inch of thickness.

Cripple Creek Crab Cakes

4 servings

Horseradish Caper Sauce:

- ¼ cup mayonnaise
- 2-3 tablespoons prepared horseradish
- 1 tablespoon fresh lemon juice
- ¼ teaspoon Tabasco
- 1 tablespoon finely diced onion
- 1 teaspoon chopped capers
- 2 tablespoons catsup (optional)

Crab Cakes:

- 1 pound lump crab meat, shell fragments removed
- ½ red bell pepper, cored, seeded, and finely diced
- ¼ cup diced onion
- 4 green onions, chopped, including tops
- ½ teaspoon minced garlic
- 1 egg, slightly beaten
- 2 tablespoons Dijon mustard
- 1 tablespoon fresh lemon juice
- 1 teaspoon Worcestershire
- 1 teaspoon Tabasco
- 4 slices fresh bread
- 2-4 tablespoons vegetable oil

Garnish:

lemon wedges

The optional catsup makes the sauce slightly sweet.

In small bowl, combine mayonnaise, horseradish, lemon juice, ¼ teaspoon Tabasco, 1 tablespoon onion, capers, and catsup, if desired. Stir to blend, cover, and chill.

Line baking sheet with waxed paper. In large bowl, combine crab, bell pepper, ¼ cup onion, green onions, and garlic. In separate bowl combine egg, mustard, lemon juice, Worcestershire, and 1 teaspoon Tabasco. Fold into crab mixture.

Place bread slices in food processor and process to fine crumbs. Fold about ¼ cup of the bread crumbs into crab mixture to bind. With your hands, form 8 oval cakes. Dredge cakes in remaining crumbs. Place cakes on prepared baking sheet and chill 1-4 hours.

In large skillet, heat oil over medium heat. Cook crab cakes 3-4 minutes per side, turning once, until golden brown. Serve with Horseradish Caper Sauce and garnish with lemon wedges.

There are wonderful places in Colorado where you swear you can hear the cowboys whistling, "Don't Fence Me In." You get a hankering for sizzling fillets, creamy potatoes, and home-grown green beans. You'll retire to the ranchhouse, and drift off dreaming of riding the range.

Rocky Mountain Roundup

appetizer

Fireside Garlic With Rosemary 32

main dish

Fillets With Pepper Relish 230

side dish

Heavenly Potatoes 334

side dish

Cashew Green Beans 319

dessert

Chocolate Raspberry Tart 350

wine

Syrah

Clockwise from top left:
Heavenly Potatoes
Cashew Green Beans
Fillets With Pepper Relish

Meats

This outstanding collection of recipes features meats paired with the freshest of relishes and salsas, numerous grilled entrees for simple but elegant outdoor entertaining, and fabulous flavors.

At left:
Buffalo Bill Steaks

Fillets With Pepper Relish

4 servings

- ½ cup water
- 2 tablespoons sugar
- 1 tablespoon cider vinegar
- 2-4 fresh jalapeño peppers, cored, seeded, and thinly sliced
- ¼ cup thinly sliced onion
- 1 teaspoon mustard seed
- ½ cup thinly sliced red bell pepper
- ½ cup thinly sliced yellow bell pepper
- ½ cup very thinly sliced carrot
- 1 beef tenderloin (about 1½ pounds), cut into eight ½-inch slices
- salt and freshly ground black pepper

Photo, page 226.

In small saucepan, combine water, sugar, and vinegar and heat to boiling. Add jalapeños, onion, and mustard seed. Cook 3 minutes, stirring occasionally. Add bell peppers and carrots. Cook 2 minutes, stirring occasionally. Vegetables should remain crisp. Remove from heat. (May be prepared 1 day in advance. Cover and chill.)

Preheat grill to medium-high. Season beef slices with salt and pepper to taste. Grill 3 minutes per side for medium-rare or to desired degree of doneness. (Beef may be cooked in lightly oiled skillet, over high heat until brown, 1-2 minutes per side.) Arrange 2 slices on individual serving plates and surround with small spoonfuls of pepper relish.

Italian Blue Fillets

4 servings

- 2 tablespoons vegetable oil
- 4 beef tenderloin fillets (about 2 inches thick), at room temperature
- salt and freshly ground black pepper
- 2 tablespoons butter
- 1 tablespoon minced shallots
- ¼ cup chopped pistachio nuts
- ½ cup red wine
- 4 ounces Gorgonzola cheese, crumbled
- ¼ cup chicken broth

Gorgonzola, Italy's classic blue cheese, is paired with pistachios to create a simple, yet elegant entree. Serve with Merlot.

In large skillet, heat oil over high heat. Add fillets and brown 1-2 minutes per side. Season with salt and pepper to taste. Reduce heat to low and cook 8-10 minutes per side for medium-rare. Remove to platter and cover loosely with foil to keep warm. Discard drippings.

In same skillet, melt butter over medium heat. Add shallots and cook until soft and just golden brown, about 3 minutes. Add pistachios and wine. Stir, loosening any brown bits from skillet. Continue cooking, stirring occasionally, until liquid is almost evaporated, about 10 minutes. Remove from heat, add cheese, and stir until melted. Return to medium heat, add broth and cook, stirring constantly, until thick and creamy, about 2 minutes. Place beef on individual serving plates and top with sauce.

Fillets With Horseradish Dijon Crumbs

4 servings

- 1 tablespoon butter
- ⅓ cup dry bread crumbs
- 3 tablespoons drained prepared horseradish
- 2 teaspoons Dijon mustard
- 1 teaspoon chopped fresh parsley
- ½ teaspoon salt plus additional
- 1 teaspoon coarsely ground fresh black pepper plus additional
- 4 6-8-ounce beef tenderloin fillets (about 1½ inches thick)
- 3 tablespoons vegetable oil
- 1 medium onion, peeled and thinly sliced
- ½ cup dry red wine

Fabulous served with Creamy Polenta With Pepper Melange, page 297.

In medium skillet, melt butter over medium heat. Add bread crumbs, horseradish, mustard, parsley, salt, and pepper. Cook, stirring constantly, until bread crumbs are golden brown. Transfer to bowl. Wipe skillet clean.

Pat fillets dry and season with salt and pepper to taste. In same skillet, heat oil over medium-high heat until hot, but not smoking. Brown fillets, 1 minute per side. Reduce heat to medium-low and cook 5-6 minutes per side for medium-rare. Transfer to platter and cover with foil to keep warm.

Discard drippings from skillet. Add onion and cook over medium heat, stirring frequently until golden. Add wine and heat to boiling, scraping up brown bits. Boil until reduced to a glaze. Spoon over fillets and top with reserved horse radish mixture.

Peppered Steak With Bacon and Onions

4-8 servings

- 2 cloves garlic, flattened with side of knife
- 4 12-14 ounce New York strip steaks, (about 1½ inches thick)
- coarsely ground fresh black pepper (about ¼ cup)
- 12 ounces bacon, cut into 1-inch slices
- 2 large red onions, peeled and cut into 1-inch chunks (about 2 cups)
- ⅓ cup red wine vinegar

Rub garlic over all surfaces of steaks. Cover steaks with pepper, pressing into meat. In large skillet, cook bacon until just crisp. Remove from skillet and discard drippings, leaving brown bits in skillet. Add onion and vinegar and cook over medium heat until tender, about 3 minutes. Return bacon to skillet and cook until liquid evaporates, about 2 minutes.

Preheat grill to high. Grill steaks about 6 minutes per side for rare, or to desired degree of doneness. Place steaks on individual serving plates and top evenly with onion mixture.

Chilled Tenderloin With Two Sauces

8 servings

1 3-3½ pound beef tenderloin, at room temperature
salt and freshly ground black pepper
Garnish:
fresh parsley sprigs

Horseradish Cucumber Sauce:
1 cucumber, peeled, seeded, and finely diced (about ¾ cup)
¾ cup sour cream
3 tablespoons drained prepared horseradish
1 teaspoon white wine vinegar
2 teaspoons minced, stemmed fresh tarragon
salt and freshly ground black pepper
Garnish:
fresh tarragon sprigs

Curried Yogurt Sauce:
¾ cup plain yogurt, divided
2 tablespoons purchased mango chutney
1 teaspoon fresh lime juice
½ cup prepared mayonnaise
1 tablespoon curry powder
2 tablespoons minced red onion
salt and freshly ground black pepper
Garnish:
minced red onion

An elegant make-ahead entree, ideal for a patio meal accompanied by a Syrah.

Preheat oven to 500 degrees. Grease roasting pan. Season beef with salt and pepper to taste and place in prepared pan. Roast, in middle of oven, 25-30 minutes, or until meat thermometer registers 135-140 degrees for medium-rare or to desired degree of doneness. Remove from oven and cool to room temperature. Slice crosswise into ½-inch slices. Arrange slices on platter and garnish with parsley sprigs. (May be prepared up to 2 days in advance. Wrap tightly in foil and chill.)

Horseradish Cucumber Sauce:
In medium bowl, combine cucumber, sour cream, horseradish, vinegar, tarragon, and salt and pepper to taste. Cover and chill 2 hours or up to 24 hours. Transfer to serving dish and garnish with tarragon sprigs.

Curried Yogurt Sauce:
In food processor or blender, combine ½ cup of the yogurt, chutney, and lime juice. Process until smooth. Transfer to bowl and add remaining ¼ cup yogurt, mayonnaise, curry powder, red onion, and salt and pepper to taste. Whisk to blend. Cover and chill 8 hours or up to 3 days. Transfer to serving dish and garnish with minced red onion.

Stuffed Tuscany Tenderloin

10 servings

- 2 tablespoons vegetable oil
- 1 medium onion, peeled and minced
- ½ pound fresh spinach, rinsed, stemmed, and chopped
- ½ teaspoon salt
- ½ teaspoon freshly ground black pepper
- ¼ cup freshly grated Parmesan cheese
- ¼ cup finely chopped oil-packed sun-dried tomatoes
- 1 3-4 pound beef tenderloin, cut from center of tenderloin
- 1 beef bouillon cube
- ¼ cup dry sherry
- 1½ cups water

Garnish:

fresh parsley sprigs

This easy to make stuffing creates a flavorful dish to celebrate a special occasion. Serve with Risotto With Artichokes, page 299.

In large skillet, heat oil over medium heat. Add onion and cook until tender and golden, stirring occasionally. Add spinach, salt, and pepper. Cook just until spinach wilts, stirring constantly, about 1 minute. Remove from heat and stir in Parmesan and sun-dried tomatoes.

Preheat oven to 425 degrees. Make a lengthwise cut along center of tenderloin, cutting almost in half, but not all of the way through. Lay open, spread with spinach mixture, and fold to enclose filling. Tie securely with string. Place, cut-side up, on rack in roasting pan. Cover stuffing with foil to prevent drying out. Cook 35-40 minutes, or until meat thermometer registers 135-140 degrees for medium-rare or to desired degree of doneness.

Place on cutting board and cover with foil to keep warm. Remove rack from roasting pan. Skim and discard fat from drippings, add bouillon cube, sherry, and water. Heat to boiling over medium-high heat, stirring to loosen brown bits. Remove from heat. Slice tenderloin 1-inch thick and arrange on warmed platter. Garnish with parsley sprigs and serve with reserved sauce.

Elegant Roasted Tenderloin

8 servings

- 1 3-pound beef tenderloin, at room temperature
- ¼ cup (½ stick) butter, softened, divided
- ¼ cup chopped green onions
- ½ teaspoon minced garlic
- 2 tablespoons soy sauce
- 1 teaspoon Dijon mustard
- freshly ground black pepper
- ¾ cup dry sherry

This is wonderful with Green Bean Pepper Parmesan, page 321, and a Côte Rôtie.

Preheat oven to 400 degrees. Spread tenderloin with 2 tablespoons of the butter. Place on rack in shallow roasting pan and cook uncovered, 25 minutes. While tenderloin is cooking, in small skillet, cook green onions and garlic in remaining 2 tablespoons butter until tender, about 5 minutes. Add soy sauce, mustard, and pepper. Stir in sherry and heat just to boiling.

Remove beef from oven and top with green onion mixture. Continue cooking 20 minutes, basting frequently with pan drippings. Remove from oven when internal temperature reaches 135-140 degrees for medium-rare. Let stand 10 minutes and carve into 1-inch slices.

Peppered Rib Roast With Jalapeño Apricots

6-8 servings

- ⅓ cup coarsely cracked black pepper
- ½ teaspoon ground cardamom
- 1 4-pound boneless rib eye roast, trimmed
- 1 cup soy sauce
- ¾ cup red wine vinegar
- 1 tablespoon tomato paste
- 1 teaspoon paprika
- 2 teaspoons minced garlic
- 1 teaspoon chopped fresh parsley
- 1 16-ounce can apricot halves
- ½ cup green jalapeño pepper jelly
- 1 medium jalapeño pepper, thinly sliced

An outstanding variation of the classic rib roast.

In small bowl, combine pepper and cardamom. Pat firmly on all sides of roast. Place roast in shallow glass pan. In small bowl, combine soy sauce, vinegar, tomato paste, paprika, garlic, and parsley. Pour over roast, cover, and marinate overnight in refrigerator, turning occasionally.

Preheat oven to 325 degrees. Remove roast from refrigerator and discard marinade. Wrap roast tightly in foil, leaving small opening. Insert oven proof meat thermometer through opening in foil, taking care not to let thermometer touch foil. Bake 1½ hours or until meat thermometer inserted into center registers 140-160 degrees. Transfer roast to serving platter and top with remaining juices. Let stand 10 minutes before carving.

Fill apricot halves with 1 teaspoon jelly and top with jalapeño slice. Serve 2 or 3 apricot halves per person to accompany roast.

San Juan Flank Steak

4-6 servings

- 1 1½-pound flank steak
- ½ cup olive oil
- ¼ cup white vinegar
- 1½ teaspoons salt
- ¼ teaspoon Tabasco
- 2 teaspoons oregano
- 2 teaspoons chili powder
- ½-1 teaspoon minced garlic

South of the border flavor great with Savory Roasted New Potatoes, page 333.

Pierce steak all over with fork. Place in shallow dish or plastic bag. In small bowl, combine olive oil, vinegar, salt, Tabasco, oregano, chili powder, and garlic. Pour over steak and marinate in refrigerator, overnight, turning occasionally. Preheat grill to medium-high. Grill steak, reserving marinade, 4-5 minutes per side for medium-rare, basting frequently with marinade. Slice against grain.

Grilled Onion Flank Steak

6 servings

- 1 cup soy sauce
- ½ cup vegetable oil
- 1 large onion, peeled and sliced
- 1 2-pound flank steak

Simplicity made perfect with grilled onions.

In medium bowl, combine soy sauce, oil, and onion. Pour over flank steak and marinate in refrigerator, overnight, turning occasionally. Preheat grill to medium-high. Place steak on grill and place onion on top, discarding marinade. Cook 6-8 minutes. Turn steak, allowing onion to cook on grill and become crisp. Grill 5-6 minutes for medium-rare. Scrape onion off grill. Thinly slice flank steak diagonally across grain. Serve grilled onion over meat.

Beef Ratatouille Pie

6-8 servings

- 1½ pounds extra-lean ground beef
- 14 saltine crackers, crushed
- ½ cup chopped red bell pepper
- 1 cup tomato puree, divided
- ½ teaspoon Italian seasoning
- 3 teaspoons salt, divided, plus additional
- ¼ teaspoon freshly ground black pepper plus additional
- 1 medium eggplant, quartered and thinly sliced
- 2 small zucchini, thinly sliced
- 2 small yellow squash, thinly sliced
- 4 tablespoons olive oil, divided
- 1 teaspoon dried thyme, crumbled
- 1 large yellow onion, peeled, quartered, and sliced
- 1 large red onion, peeled, quartered, and sliced
- 2 small green bell peppers, cored, seeded, and sliced into thin strips
- 1 teaspoon minced garlic
- ½ pound ripe tomatoes, chopped
- 1½ teaspoons dried basil
- ½ cup minced fresh parsley leaves

Garnish:

- 3 tablespoons minced fresh parsley leaves
- freshly grated Romano cheese

This array of garden vegetables and Italian flavor creates classic comfort food.

Preheat oven to 350 degrees. In large bowl, combine beef, crushed crackers, red bell pepper, ½ cup of the tomato puree, Italian seasoning, 1 teaspoon of the salt, and ¼ teaspoon pepper. Press into bottom and sides of 10-inch deep-dish pie pan. Bake 20 minutes. Remove from oven, leaving oven on. Drain and set aside.

Sprinkle eggplant, zucchini, and yellow squash with remaining 2 teaspoons salt. Let stand 30 minutes to release moisture and pat dry. In skillet with lid, heat 2 tablespoons of the olive oil over high heat. Add eggplant, zucchini and yellow squash and cook 3 minutes. Stir in thyme. Transfer to plate.

In same skillet, heat remaining 2 tablespoons olive oil over high heat. Add onions and bell peppers and cook just until soft. Stir in garlic, tomatoes, and remaining ½ cup tomato puree. Cover, reduce heat to medium, and cook 5 minutes. Remove cover and cook until juices have evaporated. Add basil and ½ cup parsley and season with salt and pepper to taste.

Spread about one third of the tomato mixture evenly over prepared meat shell. Cover with half of the eggplant mixture. Add another third of the tomato mixture and cover with remaining eggplant mixture. Top with remaining tomato mixture. Cover with foil and bake 25 minutes. Remove foil and continue baking 20 minutes. Garnish with 3 tablespoons parsley and sprinkle with Romano.

BURGUNDY BEEF PIE

6 servings

- 1½ cups plus 2 tablespoons flour, divided
- 1½ teaspoons salt, divided
- ½ cup chilled butter, cut into small pieces
- ¼ cup very cold water
- 1 tablespoon olive oil
- 1 tablespoon plus 1 teaspoon butter
- 1 cup coarsely chopped onion
- 1 teaspoon minced garlic
- 1½ pounds boneless beef chuck, cut into 1½-inch pieces
- 1 teaspoon freshly ground black pepper
- 2 cups ½-inch sliced carrots
- 2 cups ½-inch cubed new potatoes
- ½ cup chopped fresh Italian parsley
- 1 tablespoon Dijon mustard
- 1 cup red wine
- 1 cup beef broth
- 1 tablespoon red wine vinegar
- 1 teaspoon dried thyme
- 2 tablespoons packed dark brown sugar
- 8 ounces fresh mushrooms, quartered
- ½ pound fresh green beans, trimmed and halved
- 1 egg
- 1 tablespoon water

This hearty fall or winter dish will warm the soul. *Photo, page 134.*

Combine 1½ cups of the flour and ½ teaspoon of the salt. Cut in ½ cup chilled butter pieces, using 2 knives, until mixture resembles coarse meal. Add cold water and blend. Turn out onto lightly floured surface and knead until smooth, about 4 minutes, dough will be slightly crumbly. Flatten into disk and wrap in plastic wrap. Chill 30 minutes.

In large, deep skillet, heat olive oil and 1 tablespoon of the butter over medium heat. Add onion and garlic and cook 2 minutes. Remove with slotted spoon and set aside. Add beef to same skillet, a few pieces at a time, and brown on all sides.

Combine remaining 2 tablespoons flour, remaining 1 teaspoon salt, and pepper. Sprinkle over beef and toss to coat. Add carrots, potatoes, parsley, mustard, wine, beef broth, vinegar, thyme, and brown sugar. Stir to blend. Heat to boiling over medium heat. Reduce heat, cover, and simmer 1 hour.

In small skillet, heat remaining 1 teaspoon butter over medium heat. Add mushrooms and cook until just tender, 1-2 minutes. Drain and add to beef mixture. Add reserved onion mixture and green beans and simmer an additional 15 minutes. Taste and adjust seasonings if necessary.

Preheat oven to 425 degrees. In small bowl, whisk egg and water. Pour beef mixture into ungreased 2½-quart baking dish with 2-inch sides. Roll out dough and place on top. Trim dough, leaving 1-inch overhang. Brush edge of dish with egg mixture and press dough onto dish. Crimp edges decoratively and brush top with egg mixture. Cut slit in top to vent. Place on baking sheet and bake until crust is golden, 20-25 minutes. Serve immediately.

Colorado Chili Meat Loaf

8-10 servings

- 2 tablespoons olive oil
- 1 medium onion, peeled and finely diced
- 1 red bell pepper, cored, seeded, and finely diced
- 2 teaspoons minced garlic
- 2 fresh jalapeño peppers, cored, seeded, and minced
- 2 tablespoons chili powder
- 2 teaspoons salt
- 2 teaspoons oregano
- 2 teaspoons ground cumin
- 1 28-ounce can Italian tomatoes peeled, crushed, and drained
- 1½ pounds lean ground beef
- ½ pound ground sausage
- 1 cup fine dry bread crumbs
- 2 eggs, lightly beaten
- 1 cup fresh or frozen corn kernels
- 3 green onions, thinly sliced, including tops
- 8 ounces sharp Cheddar cheese, grated

This recipes makes two loaves, cook one and freeze the other. Leftovers make wonderful cold sandwiches.

In large skillet, heat olive oil over high heat. Add onion, bell pepper, garlic, jalapeños, chili powder, salt, oregano, and cumin. Cover, reduce heat to low, and cook, stirring occasionally, until vegetables are soft, about 10 minutes. Add tomatoes and cook, covered, stirring occasionally, 10 minutes. Remove from heat and let cool to room temperature.

Preheat oven to 350 degrees. In large bowl, combine beef and sausage. Add cooled tomato mixture, bread crumbs, eggs, corn, and green onions and mix well. Press into two 9x5-inch loaf pans. (May be prepared in advance, covered, and frozen. Thaw before baking.)

Bake 50 minutes or until meat thermometer inserted into center registers 160 degrees. Pour off any pan juices. Sprinkle cheese evenly over meat loaf and return to oven until cheese melts, about 4 minutes.

Oriental Beef With Kumquats

6 servings

- 3 tablespoons soy sauce
- 2 tablespoons hoisin sauce
- 1 tablespoon packed brown sugar
- 1 teaspoon sesame oil
- ½ teaspoon ground ginger
- 1½ teaspoons crushed garlic
- 1¼ pounds flank steak, cut diagonally into thin strips
- ⅓ cup sugar
- 1 cup water
- 1½ cups fresh kumquats
- vegetable cooking spray
- 1 tablespoon peeled, chopped fresh ginger root
- 3 cups fresh bean sprouts, divided
- 2 cups red bell pepper strips, divided
- 2 cups green bell pepper strips, divided
- 1 cup thinly sliced green onions, divided
- ½ cup very thinly sliced carrots

In large, resealable plastic bag, combine soy sauce, hoisin sauce, brown sugar, sesame oil, ground ginger, and garlic. Add beef strips and marinate in refrigerator, about 4 hours.

In medium saucepan, combine sugar and water and heat to boiling. Add kumquats, reduce heat, and simmer, uncovered, about 10 minutes. Drain, cool, cut kumquats in half, and set aside.

Coat large skillet or wok with cooking spray and place over medium-high heat. Add beef with marinade, and cook 2 minutes or to desired degree of doneness. Remove to plate with slotted spoon and cover with foil to keep warm.

Add ginger root, half of the bean sprouts, half of the bell peppers, and half of the green onions. Cook 4 minutes, remove to plate with slotted spoon. Add remaining bean sprouts, bell peppers, green onions, and carrots. Cook 4 minutes, add reserved beef mixture, reserved bean sprout mixture, and half of the kumquats. Toss gently to combine. Arrange on serving platter and top with remaining kumquats.

Mount Evans Short Ribs

5-6 servings

- ½ cup flour
- 2 teaspoons salt
- ½ teaspoon freshly ground black pepper
- 4 pounds boneless, lean beef short ribs
- 2 tablespoons butter or more
- 2 medium onions, peeled and sliced
- 3 tablespoons white vinegar
- ½ teaspoon Tabasco
- ¼ cup molasses
- ¼ cup catsup
- 1 12-ounce can beer
- 6 medium carrots, peeled and quartered

This family dish may also be cooked in the oven. Cover and bake in preheated 325 degree oven, 3-3½ hours.

In large bowl, combine flour, salt, and pepper. Reserve ¼ cup for sauce. Add ribs to remaining flour mixture and coat thoroughly. In large skillet, melt butter over medium heat. Add ribs and brown on all sides, 20-25 minutes. Remove to platter and set aside.

Add onions to same skillet and cook until soft, about 3 minutes, adding additional butter if necessary. Remove from heat. In medium bowl, combine vinegar, Tabasco, molasses, catsup, beer, and reserved flour mixture. Whisk to blend. Place carrots in crock style slow cooker. Top with half of the reserved ribs, and half of the cooked onions. Repeat layers and top with reserved sauce. Cook on high 5 hours, or until meat is very tender.

Veal Chops With Basil Butter

4 servings

- 4 veal loin chops (about ¾-inch thick)
- 3 tablespoons olive oil
- 1 tablespoon fresh lemon juice
- 3 fresh basil leaves, bruised (bend leaves to release flavor)

Basil Butter:

- ¼ cup (½ stick) butter, softened
- 1 tablespoon finely chopped fresh basil
- ½ teaspoon minced garlic
- salt and freshly ground black pepper

An easy and sophisticated preparation of veal chops. Leftover Basil Butter may be used as a spread for bread.

Place veal chops in shallow dish. In small bowl, combine olive oil, lemon juice, and basil leaves. Pour over veal, cover, and marinate in refrigerator, 4-8 hours, turning occasionally. In small bowl, combine butter, basil, and garlic. Season with salt and pepper to taste. Cover and let stand at room temperature.

Preheat grill to medium-high. Grill chops, reserving marinade, about 4 minutes or until juices break through. Turn and grill about 4 minutes, basting frequently with reserved marinade. Transfer to serving platter and top with Basil Butter.

VEAL CHOPS IN CAPER CREAM

6 servings

- 2 tablespoons butter
- 2 tablespoons olive oil
- 6 veal loin chops (about ¾-inch thick)
- salt and freshly ground black pepper
- 2 tablespoons minced shallots
- ½ cup beef broth
- ¼ cup dry vermouth
- 1½ tablespoons fresh lemon juice
- ½ cup whipping cream
- 2 tablespoons rinsed and drained capers

Garnish:

- chopped fresh parsley
- thinly sliced lemons

This elegant entree is nice with a Pinot Noir. It may also be prepared with boneless, skinless chicken breasts. The veal or chicken may also be grilled.

Preheat oven to 200 degrees. In large skillet, heat butter and olive oil over medium heat. Add veal and brown, about 7 minutes. Turn and season with salt and pepper to taste. Continue cooking 7-9 minutes, until springy to touch and pink in center. Transfer to heated platter. Cover with foil and place in oven to keep warm, leaving door ajar.

Discard all but 1 tablespoon drippings. Add shallots and cook 2 minutes, stirring constantly. Add beef broth, vermouth, and lemon juice and heat to boiling. Boil until reduced slightly, scraping up brown bits. Stir in cream and capers and season with salt and pepper to taste. Remove chops from oven and pour juices from platter into broth mixture, simmer until thickened. Pour over chops and garnish with parsley and lemon slices.

Crusted Pork Roast With Dijon Cider Gravy

8-10 servings

¼ cup (½ stick) plus 1 tablespoon butter, softened, divided
1 4½-pound rolled and tied, boneless pork loin roast
2 tablespoons flour
2 tablespoons Dijon mustard
1 tablespoon dry mustard
1 tablespoon cracked black peppercorns
1 tablespoon cracked dried green peppercorns
1 tablespoon cracked white peppercorns
1 tablespoon whole mustard seed
2 teaspoons packed brown sugar
2 teaspoons dried thyme, crumbled

Dijon Cider Gravy:

1½ cups apple cider
3 tablespoons Calvados or Applejack
2 tablespoons flour
¾ cup chicken broth
1 tablespoon cider vinegar
1 teaspoon Dijon mustard
salt and freshly ground black pepper

This roast will fill your kitchen with a wonderful aroma. Serve with Elegant Carrot Puree, page 325.

Position rack to bottom third of oven and preheat to 450 degrees. In large skillet, melt 1 tablespoon of the butter over medium-high heat. Add roast and brown on all sides, about 4 minutes per side. Remove from skillet. Cool 10 minutes. Transfer to roasting pan.

In small bowl, combine remaining ¼ cup butter, flour, 2 tablespoons Dijon mustard, dry mustard, black peppercorns, green peppercorns, white peppercorns, mustard seed, brown sugar, and thyme. Spread mixture over top and sides of roast. Place in oven and cook 25 minutes. Reduce heat to 325 degrees and continue cooking about 1 hour or until meat thermometer inserted into center registers 155-160 degrees. Remove from oven and transfer to cutting board. Cover loosely with foil to keep warm.

Remove 2 tablespoons of the pan drippings, supplementing with water if necessary, and transfer to medium saucepan. Set aside. Discard any remaining drippings from roasting pan, leaving brown crusty bits in pan. Place over medium-low heat. Add cider and boil until liquid is reduced to about ¾ cup, scraping up brown bits, about 8 minutes. Stir in Calvados and boil 1 minute.

Place saucepan with reserved drippings over medium-high heat. Add 2 tablespoons flour and stir until golden brown, about 2 minutes. Whisk in cider mixture from roasting pan and broth. Simmer until thickened, stirring occasionally, about 4 minutes. Remove from heat. Whisk in vinegar and 1 teaspoon mustard. Season with salt and pepper to taste. Slice roast and serve with Dijon Cider Gravy.

Caribbean Pork Roast

6-8 servings

- 1 2-3 pound rolled and tied, boneless pork loin roast
- 1 cup packed brown sugar
- 2 tablespoons dark rum
- 1 teaspoon minced garlic
- 2 teaspoons ground ginger
- 2 whole bay leaves, crumbled
- 1 teaspoon salt
- ½ teaspoon freshly ground black pepper
- ½ teaspoon ground cloves
- ½ cup chicken broth
- ¼ cup light rum
- 1 tablespoon flour
- ¼ cup fresh lime juice

This gives you fabulous flavor with little effort. All meats should be allowed to stand 10 minutes after cooking, before being sliced.

Preheat oven to 375 degrees. Place pork in roasting pan. Cook 1½-2 hours or until meat thermometer inserted into center registers 160 degrees. Remove from oven, leaving oven on.

In small bowl, combine brown sugar, dark rum, garlic, ginger, bay leaves, salt, pepper, and cloves. Stir to form a paste. Cut string from pork, lay open, and spread with brown sugar mixture. Return to oven and cook about 6 minutes, until pork is glazed. Transfer to platter and cover with foil to keep warm.

Place roasting pan on stove-top or pour drippings into saucepan, scraping up any browned bits. Heat over medium heat. Add chicken broth and light rum and heat to boiling. Sprinkle with flour and whisk to blend. Heat to boiling, whisking constantly. Add lime juice and boil until slightly thickened, whisking constantly, about 2 minutes. Slice pork and serve with sauce.

Pork Tenderloin With Peppercorn Sauce

4-6 servings

- 3 pork tenderloins (about 2½ pounds total)
- salt and freshly ground black pepper
- ¼ cup Dijon mustard, divided
- 2 tablespoons olive oil
- 1 teaspoon butter
- 2 teaspoons dried green peppercorns, cracked
- 3 tablespoons whipping cream
- 3 tablespoons dry white wine

Wonderful served with Wild Rice With Peppers and Roasted Pecans, page 303.

Cut pork tenderloins, across the grain, into ⅓-inch thick slices. Sprinkle with pepper to taste. Spread 2 tablespoons of the mustard on 1 side of pork slices. In large skillet, heat oil over medium-high heat. Add pork and brown on both sides. Add butter and continue cooking, turning to coat, until no longer pink. Remove to platter, salt to taste, and cover loosely with foil to keep warm.

To same skillet, add green peppercorns and remaining 2 tablespoons mustard. Stir until well blended. Add cream and wine and heat to boiling. Reduce heat and simmer 1 minute. Drizzle over pork.

Tomatillo Pork Fajitas

4-6 servings

- ½ pound tomatillos, husked, rinsed, cored, and halved
- ½ medium onion, peeled and quartered
- 3 large garlic cloves, peeled, divided
- 1 medium serrano pepper, cored, halved, and seeded, divided
- ⅔ cup water
- ½ cup tightly packed, fresh cilantro leaves
- 1 tablespoon fresh lime juice
- ½ teaspoon coarse salt, divided
- 1 ¾-pound pork tenderloin, trimmed
- 1 teaspoon ground cumin
- 1 teaspoon dried oregano, crumbled
- ½ teaspoon freshly ground black pepper
- ⅓ cup finely chopped tomato
- 2 green onions, thinly sliced
- 4-6 8-inch flour tortillas

Garnish:

fresh cilantro leaves

In small saucepan, combine tomatillos, onion, 2 of the garlic cloves, half of the serrano pepper, and water. Heat to boiling over medium-high heat. Reduce heat and simmer until tomatillos are tender, about 5 minutes. Drain, reserving cooking liquid.

In food processor or blender, combine remaining 1 garlic clove, remaining half serrano pepper, cilantro, lime juice, and ¼ teaspoon of the coarse salt. Pulse to coarsely chop. Add reserved tomatillo mixture and 2 tablespoons reserved liquid and pulse to coarsely chop. Transfer to serving bowl, cover, and let stand, at room temperature, up to 1 hour.

Preheat grill to medium-high, or broiler. Cut pork into 4 diagonal slices and pound to ½-inch thickness. In small bowl, combine cumin, oregano, remaining ¼ teaspoon coarse salt, and pepper. Rub mixture on both sides of pork slices. Grill or broil, about 4 minutes per side, until browned and thoroughly cooked. Transfer to plate or cutting board and cover with foil to keep warm. Grill or broil tortillas, about 30 seconds, until lightly browned.

Slice pork, against the grain, into ½-inch strips and divide among warmed tortillas. Add tomato and green onions to reserved tomatillo mixture. Spoon over pork and roll up tortillas. Spoon additional tomatillo mixture on top and garnish with cilantro leaves.

Rocky Mountain Pork

8 servings

- ¾ cup fresh lemon juice
- ½ cup soy sauce
- 6 tablespoons honey
- 2 small shallots, peeled and halved
- 2 large garlic cloves, peeled and halved
- 2 bay leaves, crumbled
- ½ teaspoon salt
- 2 teaspoons freshly ground black pepper
- 1 teaspoon dry mustard
- ½ teaspoon ground ginger
- 1 teaspoon chopped fresh parsley
- 3 pounds pork tenderloin

A quick and easy family meal.

In food processor, combine lemon juice, soy sauce, honey, shallots, garlic, bay leaves, salt, pepper, mustard, ginger, and parsley. Puree and pour over tenderloin and turn to coat. Cover and marinate in refrigerator overnight, turning occasionally.

Preheat grill to medium-high. Grill pork, reserving marinade, turning frequently, about 20 minutes or until meat thermometer inserted into center registers 170 degrees. Remove to serving platter and cover with foil to keep warm. Place reserved marinade in saucepan and heat to boiling. Boil until slightly reduced, about 5 minutes. Slice pork and serve with heated marinade.

Pork Medallions With Apples

4 servings

- 5 tablespoons butter, divided
- 4 Golden Delicious apples, peeled, cored, and cut into ⅛-inch slices
- 1 teaspoon sugar
- 1½ pounds pork tenderloin, trimmed
- salt and freshly ground black pepper
- 2 tablespoons chopped shallots
- 1 tablespoon chopped fresh thyme
- ¼ cup Calvados or Applejack
- 1 cup whipping cream
- ¼ cup apple cider

A classic dish from Normandy. Be adventurous and serve a hard cider with dinner.

In large skillet melt 2 tablespoons of the butter over medium-high heat. Add apples and sugar and cook until golden brown, about 6 minutes. Remove from heat. Cut pork into 1-inch thick slices and pound, between plastic wrap, to ¼-inch thickness.

In separate large skillet, melt 2 tablespoons of the butter over high heat. Season pork with salt and pepper to taste and cook until just cooked through, about 2 minutes per side. Transfer to plate and cover loosely with foil to keep warm.

In same skillet, melt remaining 1 tablespoon butter over medium heat. Add shallots and thyme and cook 2 minutes. Add Applejack and boil until reduced to a glaze, scraping up any browned bits. Stir in cream and cider and boil until mixture thickens, about 3 minutes. Season with salt and pepper to taste. Reheat apples over low heat. Arrange pork slices on individual serving plates. Top with sauce and reserved cooked apple slices.

Teriyaki Pork Chops With Calypso Salsa

6 servings

- ⅔ cup soy sauce
- ⅓ cup packed brown sugar
- ⅓ cup water
- ¼ cup rice wine vinegar
- 1½ teaspoons finely chopped garlic
- 1 2-inch piece fresh ginger root, peeled and finely chopped
- 6 1½-inch thick pork chops

Calypso Salsa:

- 2 cups finely diced fresh pineapple
- 1 cup finely diced papaya
- ¾ cup finely diced red bell pepper
- ½ cup finely diced onion
- ½ teaspoon minced garlic
- 1 small fresh serrano pepper, cored, seeded, and minced
- 3 tablespoons shredded mint leaves
- salt

Garnish:

- fresh mint leaves

This marinade and salsa also work well with pork tenderloin.

In medium saucepan, combine soy sauce, brown sugar, water, vinegar, 1½ teaspoons garlic, and ginger. Heat to boiling, stirring until sugar is dissolved. Remove from heat and cool to room temperature. Place pork chops in shallow glass dish or resealable plastic bag. Add cooled soy sauce mixture and marinate in refrigerator overnight, turning occasionally.

In medium bowl, combine pineapple, papaya, bell pepper, onion, ½ teaspoon garlic, serrano pepper, mint, and salt to taste. Let stand at room temperature 1 hour. (May be prepared to this point up to 1 day in advance. Cover salsa and chill. Bring to room temperature before serving.)

Pour marinade from pork chops into saucepan. Heat to boiling and boil 5 minutes. Oil grill surface and preheat to medium-high. Grill chops 7-9 minutes per side, or until thoroughly cooked, basting with heated marinade during last 5 minutes of grilling. Transfer to serving platter and garnish with mint leaves. Serve with Calypso Salsa.

At left:
Teriyaki Pork Chops With Calypso Salsa, 247

Pork With Cherry Rhubarb Chutney

4 servings

Cherry Rhubarb Chutney:

¾ cup sugar
⅓ cup cider vinegar
1 tablespoon peeled, minced fresh ginger root
1 teaspoon ground cumin
½ teaspoon ground cinnamon
1 tablespoon minced garlic
½ teaspoon ground cloves
¼ teaspoon crushed red pepper
4 cups chopped fresh rhubarb (about 1½ pounds)
⅔ cup chopped red onion
½ cup (about 3 ounces) dried tart cherries

Pork:

2 pork tenderloins (about 1½ pounds total)
¼ teaspoon ground cloves
2 teaspoons ground cumin
salt and freshly ground black pepper
1 tablespoon olive oil

The pork may also be grilled. Serve chutney on the side.

In large saucepan, combine sugar, vinegar, ginger, 1 teaspoon cumin, cinnamon, garlic, ½ teaspoon cloves, and crushed red pepper. Simmer over low heat, stirring until sugar dissolves. Add rhubarb, red onion, and cherries. Increase heat to medium-high and cook until rhubarb is tender and mixture thickens slightly, 5-10 minutes. Cool completely. (May be prepared up to 1 day in advance. Cover and chill.) Bring to room temperature before serving.

Preheat oven to 400 degrees. Sprinkle pork with ¼ teaspoon cloves, 2 teaspoons cumin, and season with salt and pepper to taste. In large skillet, heat olive oil over high heat. Add pork and brown on all sides, about 5 minutes. Transfer to roasting pan. Brush pork with 6 tablespoons of the Cherry Rhubarb Chutney. Roast until meat thermometer inserted into center registers 155-160 degrees, brushing occasionally with 6 more tablespoons chutney, about 25 minutes. Cut pork into 1-inch slices. Serve with remaining chutney.

Winter Park Spareribs

4 servings

- 2 1-inch pieces fresh ginger root
- 2 pounds pork spareribs, cut into 1-rib pieces
- 6 tablespoons soy sauce
- 5 tablespoons sugar
- 3 green onions, trimmed and halved lengthwise
- 3 tablespoons dry sherry

A great family meal. Serve with Tossed Cherry Tomatoes, page 339.

Peel ginger and press with side of knife to release juices. In large skillet, combine ribs, soy sauce, sugar, peeled ginger, green onions, and sherry. Add enough water just to cover ribs. Heat to boiling, reduce heat, and cover. Simmer about 45 minutes, turning ribs every 10 minutes.

Remove lid and increase heat to high. Remove ginger and green onions. Boil vigorously, turning ribs to coat. Liquid will reduce and become the consistency of a glaze in about 30 minutes. Remove from heat and transfer to platter.

Roasted Picnic Pork

8-10 servings

- 2 cups diced fresh pineapple
- ¼ cup diced red onion
- ½ cup diced red bell pepper
- 1 jalapeño pepper, cored, seeded, and minced
- ½ cup stemmed, chopped fresh cilantro
- 3 tablespoons fresh lime juice
- 2 tablespoons packed dark brown sugar
- 2 tablespoons dark rum
- 1 raw pork picnic or ham, boned, trimmed, and tied (about 5 pounds)
- 1 tablespoon white vinegar or more
- 1 tablespoon freshly ground black pepper
- 1 tablespoon minced garlic
- 2 tablespoons chopped fresh oregano
- 1 bay leaf, finely crumbled
- 1 teaspoon ground cumin
- 1 tablespoon olive oil

Flavor reminiscent of a summer pig roast. Mix shredded pork with barbecue sauce for great sandwiches.

Combine pineapple, red onion, bell pepper, jalapeño, cilantro, lime juice, brown sugar, and rum. Stir until well blended, cover, and chill up to 1 week.

Preheat oven to 200 degrees. The day before serving, make shallow slits on the surface of pork with tip of sharp knife. Pour vinegar onto the palm of your hand and rub it all over pork, using more vinegar if necessary.

In small bowl, combine pepper, garlic, oregano, bay leaf, cumin, and olive oil to form a paste. Rub over pork, forcing into slits. Wrap tightly in 2-3 layers of heavy-duty foil. Place in roasting pan and bake at least 10 hours or up to 18 hours. Remove foil, pork should fall apart and shred when pulled with a fork. Serve with pineapple salsa.

Lime Pork Chops With Plum Relish

4 servings

Plum Relish:
- 1 tablespoon fresh lime juice
- ⅔ cup finely chopped sweet red plums
- ¼ cup finely chopped tomato
- 2 tablespoons finely chopped green onions
- 2 tablespoons packed brown sugar
- 4 drops Tabasco

Pork Chops:
- 2 teaspoons minced fresh thyme
- 4 1½-inch thick pork chops
- ¼ teaspoon salt
- ¼ teaspoon freshly ground black pepper
- ½ cup fresh lime juice
- vegetable cooking spray

This jewel-toned relish turns ordinary pork chops into an entree you will want to serve family or guests.

In medium bowl, combine 1 tablespoon lime juice, plums, tomato, green onions, brown sugar, and Tabasco. Cover and chill. Press thyme into both sides of pork chops and sprinkle with salt and pepper. Place in shallow dish and pour ½ cup lime juice over chops. Cover and marinate in refrigerator, 3 hours, turning once.

Preheat grill to medium-high. Carefully coat grill with cooking spray. Grill chops, reserving marinade, 7-9 minutes per side, or until thoroughly cooked. Baste occasionally with reserved marinade. Remove to individual serving plates and top each chop with ¼ cup Plum Relish.

Glazed Country Ribs

4 servings

- 2 teaspoons crushed garlic
- ¼ cup chicken broth
- ¼ cup soy sauce
- ¼ cup honey
- 3 tablespoons catsup
- 1 tablespoon dry sherry
- 2-3 pounds country-style pork ribs

Soothing homey flavor at its best.

In small bowl, combine garlic, chicken broth, soy sauce, honey, catsup, and sherry. Pour over ribs. Cover and marinate in refrigerator, overnight, turning occasionally. Proceed with your choice of the following cooking methods.

Oven method: Preheat oven to 400 degrees. Place ribs on rack in roasting pan, reserving marinade. Roast 10 minutes, remove from oven, reduce heat to 350 degrees. Brush ribs with marinade, return to oven and cook 45 minutes, turning and basting with marinade every 10 minutes.

Grill method: Place drip pan in bottom of grill. Preheat to medium-high. Place ribs on grill, reserving marinade. Grill 45-60 minutes, turning and basting with marinade every 10 minutes. Ribs are done when meat near bone is no longer pink.

Grilled Rack of Lamb

6 servings

- 1 teaspoon crushed garlic
- ¼ teaspoon salt
- 2 tablespoons Dijon mustard
- 1 tablespoon soy sauce
- 2 tablespoons fresh lemon juice
- 2 teaspoons chopped fresh rosemary
- 1 teaspoon chopped fresh thyme
- ¼ cup olive oil
- 2 frenched racks of lamb

"Frenched" is a term used to describe a rack that has been trimmed to expose the rib bones.

Combine garlic, salt, mustard, soy sauce, lemon juice, rosemary, thyme, and olive oil. Pour over lamb and marinate in refrigerator 4 hours or up to overnight. Preheat grill to medium. Wrap exposed rib bones tightly with foil to prevent burning. Grill 8-10 minutes per side for medium-rare. Transfer to platter and slice between ribs.

Rack of Lamb with Hazelnut Crust

4-6 servings

- 2-4 frenched racks of lamb (about 3 ribs per serving)
- 2 tablespoons oil
- 1 teaspoon salt
- 3 tablespoons coarse grain mustard
- ¾ cup fresh bread crumbs
- ¾ cup hazelnuts, toasted, peeled (page 381) and chopped
- 5 tablespoons chopped fresh rosemary, divided
- 4 ounces semi-soft goat cheese, crumbled
- 2 cups red wine
- 1 cup lamb stock or beef broth
- 1-2 tablespoons butter

Serve with Potato and Yam Gratin, page 333, and a Beaujolais.

Preheat oven to 425 degrees. Rub lamb with oil and salt. Place in roasting pan, fat side down. Roast 8 minutes. Turn and continue roasting 8 minutes. Remove from oven, leaving oven on.

In medium bowl, combine mustard, bread crumbs, hazelnuts, 2 tablespoons of the rosemary, and goat cheese. Spread over lamb. Return to oven and cook 10-15 minutes, until crust is golden brown. Remove from oven and cover with foil to keep warm.

In saucepan, combine wine, lamb stock, and remaining 3 tablespoons rosemary. Heat to boiling. Cook until reduced by half. Add butter and whisk until well blended. Transfer to serving bowl. Slice lamb between ribs and pass sauce.

Herb Crusted Rack of Lamb

4 servings

- 1 1¾-pound rack of lamb, trimmed
- 2 tablespoons olive oil
- salt and freshly ground black pepper
- ½ cup finely chopped fresh parsley
- 1½ teaspoons finely minced garlic
- ½ cup fresh French bread crumbs
- 1 teaspoon chopped fresh rosemary
- 1 teaspoon finely grated lemon zest
- 3 tablespoons unsalted butter, melted

Garnish:

freshly grated Parmesan cheese

Preheat oven to 400 degrees. Rub lamb with olive oil and season with salt and pepper to taste. Place, fat side down, on rack in roasting pan. Roast 20 minutes, until browned. Remove from oven and increase temperature to 500 degrees.

Combine parsley, garlic, bread crumbs, rosemary, and lemon zest. Turn rack over and pat parsley mixture evenly over meat. Drizzle with butter and return to oven for 5 minutes or until internal temperature registers 130 degrees. Remove from oven and let stand 10 minutes before carving. Garnish with Parmesan cheese.

Larkspur Lamb Kabobs

6 servings

- 2 tablespoons balsamic vinegar
- ½ teaspoon chopped fresh rosemary
- ½ teaspoon chopped fresh thyme
- 1 teaspoon minced garlic
- ¼ cup olive oil
- 1 tablespoon soy sauce
- 1 tablespoon dry sherry
- 2 pounds lamb, cut into 1½-inch cubes
- 12-16 small white pearl onions, peeled
- 2 green bell peppers, cored, seeded, and cut into 1-inch pieces
- 2 yellow bell peppers, cored, seeded, and cut into 1-inch pieces
- 12 small Italian plum tomatoes
- 8-12 ounces small mushrooms, stemmed
- 2 small zucchini, cut into 1-inch slices

Serve with Lemon Rice With Pine Nuts, page 307.

In small bowl combine vinegar, rosemary, thyme, garlic, olive oil, soy sauce, and sherry. Pour over lamb pieces and onions. Cover and marinate in refrigerator, overnight.

Remove lamb and onions, reserving marinade. Slide lamb onto skewers, alternating with onions, bell peppers, tomatoes, mushrooms, and zucchini. Preheat grill to medium-high. Grill kabobs about 10 minutes, or to desired degree of doneness, basting with reserved marinade. Serve immediately.

Rosemary Orange Lamb Chops

4 servings

- ½ cup olive oil
- ¼ cup red wine
- 1 tablespoon brown sugar
- ½ teaspoon minced garlic
- ¼ cup fresh orange juice
- 2 tablespoons chopped fresh rosemary
- 4-8 lamb chops (about 1-inch thick), trimmed

In small bowl, combine olive oil, wine, brown sugar, garlic, orange juice, and rosemary. Pour over lamb chops. Cover, and marinate in refrigerator, at least 6 hours, turning occasionally. Preheat grill to medium or preheat broiler. Grill or broil 5 minutes per side, for medium-rare. Serve with mint sauce or mint jelly.

Minted Lamb en Croûte

8 servings

- 2 cups loosely packed, fresh mint leaves
- 3 cloves garlic, peeled and halved
- ½ cup olive oil
- salt and freshly ground black pepper
- 1 egg
- 1 tablespoon water
- 1 17¼-ounce package frozen puff pastry (2 sheets)
- 8 loin lamb chops (about 1½ inches thick), meat cut from bone and trimmed

This is an impressive make-ahead entree for an elegant dinner party. Pair with Greens With Anise Vinaigrette and Crostini, page 83, and a red Bordeaux.

In food processor, combine mint, garlic, and olive oil. Process until well blended. Season with salt and pepper to taste. Preheat oven to 425 degrees. In small bowl, combine egg and water and beat slightly.

On floured surface, roll each pastry sheet into a 14-inch square. Cut each into 4 squares. Place 1 piece of lamb in center and top with 2 teaspoons of the reserved mint mixture. Brush edges of pastry with egg mixture. Bring opposite corners of pastry together to enclose filling. Pinch seams together to seal. Place, seam side down, on baking sheet, 2 inches apart. (May be prepared to this point 4-6 hours in advance. Cover and chill. Bring to room temperature before proceeding.) Brush tops with egg mixture. Bake 15 minutes or until pastry is golden brown. Serve with remaining mint mixture.

Couscous Stuffed Lamb Chops

4 servings

- ¼ cup sugar
- ⅔ cup plus ¼ cup water, divided
- ½ pound fresh kumquats
- 1¼ cups chicken broth
- ⅓ cup chopped celery
- ¼ cup sliced green onions
- ¼ teaspoon freshly ground black pepper
- 1¼ cups uncooked couscous
- 2 tablespoons Grand Marnier or other orange flavored liqueur
- ¼ cup pine nuts, toasted (page 381)
- 4-8 lamb chops (about 1-inch thick), trimmed
- 2 tablespoons Worcestershire
- 1 tablespoon butter
- ½ teaspoon salt

Fresh kumquats are available from November to March.

In medium saucepan, combine sugar and ⅔ cup of the water and heat to boiling. Add kumquats, reduce heat to medium, and cook 10 minutes. Remove kumquats with slotted spoon, reserving syrup. Reserve 5 kumquats for garnish. Let remaining kumquats cool slightly. Chop, seed, and return to saucepan.

Add chicken broth, celery, green onions, and pepper. Heat to boiling. Cover, reduce heat, and simmer 5 minutes. Remove from heat, stir in couscous, cover, and let stand 5 minutes. Stir in Grand Marnier and toasted pine nuts.

Preheat broiler. Cut pocket in each lamb chop by cutting horizontally almost through to the bone. Spoon 1-2 tablespoons of the couscous mixture into each pocket and place on broiler pan, reserving remaining couscous mixture.

Brush tops with 1 tablespoon of the 1 tablespoon Worcestershire. Broil, 6 inches from heat, 4-6 minutes. Turn and brush with remaining Worcestershire. Continue broiling 4-6 minutes. Chops will be pink in center. Remove from oven and cover with foil to keep warm.

Combine remaining couscous mixture with butter, remaining ¼ cup water, and salt. Cover and microwave on high until thoroughly heated, 1-2 minutes, or heat in 350 degree oven, about 20 minutes. Arrange couscous on serving platter or individual serving plates. Place lamb chops on top, and garnish with reserved kumquats. Serve immediately.

Leg of Lamb with Jalapeño Chutney

8 servings

Jalapeño Chutney:

2 cups loosely packed, fresh mint leaves
1 cup loosely packed, fresh cilantro
1 small onion, quartered
2 medium cloves garlic, peeled and quartered
1 medium jalapeño pepper, seeded and quartered, or to taste
2 tablespoons fresh lemon juice
½ teaspoon salt
½ teaspoon dried dill weed
½ teaspoon paprika
½ teaspoon cayenne

Mint Marinade:

1 cup loosely packed, fresh mint leaves
1 cup loosely packed, fresh cilantro
12 large garlic cloves, peeled
3 tablespoons ground cumin
2 tablespoons ground coriander
1 tablespoon freshly ground black pepper
2 teaspoons salt
1 teaspoon cayenne
½ cup olive oil

Lamb:

1 6-7 pound leg of lamb, boned and butterflied

This incredible combination of flavors creates a sensational grilled summer entree. Leftover chutney is great as a dip with pita wedges.

In food processor combine 2 cups mint, 1 cup cilantro, onion, 2 cloves garlic, jalapeño, lemon juice, ½ teaspoon salt, dill, paprika, and ½ teaspoon cayenne. Process until well blended. Place in tightly covered jar and store in refrigerator up to 1 month.

In food processor, combine 1 cup mint, 1 cup cilantro, 12 cloves garlic, cumin, coriander, pepper, 2 teaspoons salt, and 1 teaspoon cayenne. Process, stopping occasionally to scrape sides of bowl, until well blended. With processor running, slowly pour olive oil through feed tube. Continue processing until mixture is smooth.

Place lamb in glass pan and spread evenly with marinade mixture. Cover with plastic wrap and chill overnight. Preheat grill to medium-high. Thread metal skewers through meat to make thickness more uniform and prevent thin areas from charring. Grill 15-20 minutes per side for medium-rare or until meat thermometer inserted into center registers 140-150 degrees. Remove skewers and slice thinly across grain. Serve with Jalapeño Chutney.

Marinated Leg of Lamb

8-10 servings

- 1 cup dry red wine
- ¾ cup beef broth
- 3 tablespoons orange marmalade
- 3 tablespoons red wine vinegar
- ¼ cup chopped onion
- 1 tablespoon dried marjoram
- 2 tablespoons dried rosemary
- 1 teaspoon seasoned salt
- 1 teaspoon crushed garlic
- 1 6-7 pound leg of lamb, boned and butterflied

Serve with Vegetable Pesto Pasta, page 178.

In medium saucepan, combine wine, beef broth, marmalade, vinegar, onion, marjoram, rosemary, salt, and garlic. Simmer 20 minutes. Place lamb in shallow baking pan and pour hot marinade mixture over lamb. Cover and marinate in refrigerator 8 hours, or up to overnight, turning occasionally. Preheat grill to medium. Grill lamb, fat side up, 30-45 minutes or until meat thermometer inserted into center registers 140-150 degrees, turning several times.

Lamb Pita Pockets

4 servings

Mint Salsa:

- 2 large ripe tomatoes, seeded and diced
- ¼ cup chopped green onions
- ⅓ cup chopped fresh mint
- 1 tablespoon fresh lime juice
- 1 fresh jalapeño pepper, cored, seeded, and minced
- ¼ teaspoon salt
- ¼ teaspoon freshly ground black pepper

Lamb Burgers:

- 1½ pounds lean ground lamb
- ¼ cup chopped fresh parsley
- 3 tablespoons chopped fresh mint
- 2 tablespoons fresh lemon juice
- 1 teaspoon minced garlic
- 1 teaspoon salt
- ½ teaspoon freshly ground black pepper
- 2 pita bread rounds, halved crosswise

Try substituting mango for the tomatoes for another great alternative to the summer burger. Pair with Lemon Couscous With Fresh Spinach, page 294.

In medium bowl, combine tomatoes, green onions, ⅓ cup mint, lime juice, jalapeño, ¼ teaspoon salt, and ¼ teaspoon pepper. Stir gently to blend and let stand at room temperature up to 2 hours.

Preheat grill to medium-high. In medium bowl, gently combine lamb, parsley, 3 tablespoons mint, lemon juice, garlic, 1 teaspoon salt, and ½ teaspoon pepper. Form into 4 patties, shaped to fit inside pita bread. Lightly oil grill and cook lamb until browned outside and slightly pink in center, 10-15 minutes, turning once or twice. Place in pita bread and top with reserved Mint Salsa.

Buffalo Bill Steaks

4 servings

- 1 tablespoon vegetable oil, divided
- 1 onion, halved lengthwise and thinly sliced
- ½ red bell pepper, cored, seeded, and cut into thin strips
- ½ yellow bell pepper, cored, seeded, and cut into thin strips
- 2 tablespoons coarse grain mustard
- ¼ cup water
- salt and freshly ground black pepper
- 4 4-ounce buffalo strip steaks (about 1-inch thick), trimmed

Keep in mind, buffalo contains less fat than beef, requires less cooking time, and will be dry if overcooked. Photo, page 228.

Preheat grill to medium. In large skillet, heat 2 teaspoons of the oil over medium heat. Add onion and cook, stirring frequently, 5 minutes. Add bell peppers and cook until onion is golden, about 10 minutes. If mixture becomes dry, add 1-2 tablespoons water. In small bowl, whisk mustard and water. Add to onion mixture and cook until most of the liquid has evaporated. Season with salt and pepper to taste. Remove from heat and cover. Brush steaks lightly with remaining 1 teaspoon oil and season generously with salt and pepper. Grill 3 minutes per side for medium-rare. Serve with onion mixture.

Ground Buffalo Steaks With Chile Verde Sauce

6 servings

Chile Verde Sauce:

- 1 tablespoon olive oil
- ½ cup chopped onion
- 1 cup chopped fresh Anaheim chiles
- 1 medium fresh jalapeño pepper, cored, seeded, and chopped
- ¾ cup loosely packed fresh cilantro leaves
- ½ cup chopped fresh tomatillos
- 1 clove garlic, peeled and quartered
- 2 teaspoons red currant jelly
- ½ teaspoon dried oregano
- 1 teaspoon Worcestershire
- 1 teaspoon chicken bouillon granules

Buffalo:

- 2 pounds ground buffalo
- 1½ tablespoons crushed black peppercorns
- 4 slices Monterey Jack cheese

Home on the range never tasted this good!

In medium skillet, heat olive oil over medium heat. Add onion and cook until soft, about 3 minutes. Transfer to food processor. Add chiles, jalapeño, cilantro, tomatillos, garlic, jelly, oregano, Worcestershire, and bouillon granules. Process until well blended. Return mixture to skillet and simmer, over medium heat, 15 minutes. Remove from heat. Preheat grill to medium. Shape buffalo into patties and press pepper into both sides. Grill patties 3-5 minutes per side for medium-rare. Top with cheese just before removing from grill. Place on platter and top with Chile Verde Sauce.

When the aspen leaves turn gold, the air turns crisp, and the days grow shorter, Coloradans are drawn outdoors. After a brisk hike, with fabulous views of shimmering gold, finish your autumn day with Chicken en Papillote and a wonderful Kiwi Sorbet.

Autumn in the Aspens

first course

Pears With Avocado and Lime 87

main dish

Chicken en Papillote 267

side dish

Carrot Basmati Rice Pilaf 306

bread

Armenian Cracker Bread 159

dessert

Kiwi Sorbet 358

wine

Vouvray

Clockwise from top:
Carrot Basmati Rice Pilaf
Chicken en Papillote

oultry

The humble hen is elevated to new heights in this collection of diverse recipes. You'll find delicious and memorable choices for an elegant dinner party or a casual family meal.

At left:
Pernod Chicken With Vegetables

Grilled Chicken With Couscous and Cherries

6 servings

- vegetable oil spray
- ¼ cup minced onion
- 1 cup chicken broth
- ½ cup water
- 1 cup uncooked couscous
- ¼ cup dried cherries
- ½ teaspoon chopped fresh sage
- ¼ teaspoon chopped fresh thyme leaves
- ¼ cup chopped tomato

Toasted Chili Sauce:

- 1 tablespoon chili powder
- 2 dried ancho chile peppers, crushed
- 1 teaspoon ground cumin
- 2 tablespoons vegetable oil
- ¼ cup chopped onion
- ½ teaspoon crushed garlic
- 2 tablespoons chopped fresh cilantro
- 1 cup fresh orange juice
- 2 tablespoons white vinegar
- 2 teaspoons honey
- salt

Chicken:

- 6 boneless, skinless chicken breast halves (about 1½ pounds total)

If dried ancho peppers are not available, substitute any other mild or medium dried pepper or a combination of mild and hot, such as chipotle.

Spray saucepan with vegetable oil spray. Add ¼ cup onion. Cook over low heat 5 minutes, stirring frequently, until soft, but not brown. Add chicken broth and water. Increase heat to high and heat to boiling. Add couscous and stir to combine. Cover and boil 30 seconds. Add cherries and remove from heat. Let stand, covered, 5 minutes. Pour off any remaining liquid and stir in sage, thyme, and tomato. Set aside to cool.

Place separate saucepan over medium heat until very hot. Quickly add chili powder, ancho peppers, and cumin. Toss or stir constantly until toasted, but not burned. Add oil and ¼ cup onion and cook about 5 minutes, stirring frequently. Stir in garlic, cilantro, orange juice, and vinegar. Reduce heat and simmer 15 minutes, or until onion is soft.

Transfer to food processor and puree. If sauce is very thin, return to heat and cook until reduced and slightly thickened. Stir in honey and season with salt to taste. Preheat grill to medium. Cut pocket in side of chicken breasts and stuff with cooled couscous mixture, securing with wooden picks. Reserve extra couscous mixture. Grill stuffed chicken breasts 5-10 minutes per side, or until chicken is no longer pink. Do not overcook. Transfer to serving platter and top with Toasted Chili Sauce. Serve remaining couscous mixture on the side.

Kiva Chicken With Red Chile Glaze

6 servings

- ⅓ cup flour
- ½ teaspoon salt
- ½ teaspoon freshly ground black pepper
- 6 boneless, skinless chicken breast halves (about 1½ pounds total)
- 2 tablespoons butter
- ¼ cup olive oil
- ½ cup finely chopped celery
- ¼ cup finely chopped onion
- 2 tablespoons chopped fresh parsley
- 2 tablespoons chicken broth
- 2 tablespoons dry vermouth
- ¾ cup red jalapeño pepper jelly
- ¾ cup crumbled goat cheese, such as Montrachet

Quick and easy with a festive look. Serve with Lemon Rice With Pine Nuts, page 307.

In shallow bowl, combine flour, salt, and pepper. Dredge chicken in flour mixture, shaking off excess. Set aside. In medium skillet, heat butter and olive oil over medium heat. Add celery, onion, and parsley and cook 3-5 minutes. Remove with slotted spoon. In same skillet, cook chicken breasts until lightly browned, 3-4 minutes per side. Sprinkle reserved celery mixture over each chicken breast. Add chicken broth and vermouth. Cover and simmer 5 minutes.

In small microwave-safe dish or saucepan, warm jelly until melted. Remove chicken breasts to serving platter and top with celery mixture. Drizzle with melted jelly and sprinkle with crumbled goat cheese.

Fresh Raspberry Chicken

6 servings

- 6 boneless, skinless chicken breast halves or thighs (about 1½ pounds total)
- ½ cup raspberry preserves, fruit-only type
- ½ cup frozen pineapple juice concentrate, thawed
- ½ cup soy sauce
- 2 tablespoons rice wine vinegar
- ½ teaspoon chili powder
- ½ teaspoon curry powder
- ½ teaspoon garlic powder
- ¼ cup fresh raspberries, mashed

Garnish:

- ¼ cup fresh raspberries

This healthful, boldly flavored dish is delicious over white or wild rice.

Place chicken in large baking pan. In small bowl, combine preserves, juice concentrate, soy sauce, vinegar, chili powder, curry powder, garlic powder and ¼ cup mashed raspberries. Pour over chicken and cover tightly with foil. Marinate in refrigerator, 2 hours or up to overnight.

Preheat oven to 350 degrees. Remove baking pan from refrigerator and place in oven. Bake, covered, 30-40 minutes. Remove from oven, transfer chicken to serving platter and top with pan juices. Garnish with fresh raspberries.

Kalamata Olive Chicken

6 servings

- ¾ teaspoon dried oregano
- ½ teaspoon cayenne
- ½ teaspoon freshly ground black pepper
- 6 boneless, skinless chicken breast halves (about 1½ pounds total)
- 1½ tablespoons olive oil
- 6½ tablespoons chilled butter, divided
- ½ cup chopped onion
- 2 teaspoons minced garlic
- 1¼ cups peeled, seeded, and chopped tomatoes
- ½ cup chicken broth
- 16–18 kalamata olives, pitted and sliced
- salt and freshly ground black pepper

Kalamata olives are dark, pungent, almond shaped olives from Greece. If not available, substitute other brine or oil-cured black olives.

In small bowl, combine oregano, cayenne, and ½ teaspoon pepper and rub into both sides of chicken breasts. Cover and let stand 30 minutes. In large, heavy skillet, heat olive oil and 1½ tablespoons of the butter over medium heat. Add chicken and cook until golden, about 5 minutes per side. Transfer to platter and cover with foil to keep warm.

In medium skillet, melt 2 tablespoons of the butter over medium heat. Add onion and cook 5 minutes. Add garlic and tomatoes and cook 2 minutes. Add chicken broth and olives and cook 5 minutes, stirring occasionally. Season with salt and pepper to taste. Stir in remaining 3 tablespoons butter, 1 tablespoon at a time. Spoon sauce over chicken and serve.

Pernod Chicken With Vegetables

4 servings

- 1 tablespoon butter
- 2 small carrots, peeled and cut into julienne strips
- 1 leek, cut into julienne strips and rinsed thoroughly
- 1 celery rib, cut into julienne strips
- 4 boneless, skinless chicken breast halves (about 1 pound total)
- salt and freshly ground black pepper
- 1 cup dry white wine
- ½ cup dry sherry
- ¼ cup Pernod or other anise flavored liquor
- ¼ cup mixed, chopped fresh herbs, such as basil, thyme, tarragon, or chives
- 1 cup whipping cream

Pernod and herbs combine to give this dish a distinctive and delectable flavor. Serve with noodles and a wine such as a Vouvray. Photo, page 260.

In large skillet, melt butter over medium heat. Add carrots, leek, and celery and cook 3-5 minutes. Remove to plate with slotted spoon, reserving butter. Preheat oven to 200 degrees. Season chicken with salt and pepper to taste. Place in same skillet over medium heat. Add wine, sherry, Pernod, and reserved carrot mixture. Reduce heat, cover, and cook until chicken is thoroughly cooked, about 8 minutes. Transfer chicken and vegetables to platter with slotted spoon, reserving poaching liquid. Tent with foil and keep warm in oven.

Return skillet to medium heat and add herbs. Cook until liquid is reduced by half, 5-10 minutes. Add cream and simmer until thickened and coats back of spoon, 10-15 minutes. Season with salt and pepper to taste. Place chicken on individual serving plates and top with vegetables and sauce.

Chicken Amaretto

6 servings

- ½ teaspoon salt
- ½ teaspoon freshly ground black pepper
- ½ teaspoon garlic powder
- ½ teaspoon curry powder
- 3 tablespoons flour
- 6 boneless, skinless chicken breast halves (about 1½ pounds total), cut into 1-inch cubes
- ¼ cup (½ stick) butter
- ½ pound fresh mushrooms, sliced
- ¼ cup Amaretto or other almond flavored liqueur
- 3 tablespoons fresh lemon juice
- 1 teaspoon finely grated lemon zest
- 1 tablespoon cornstarch
- 1½ cups chicken broth
- cooked rice or pasta

In bowl or plastic bag, combine salt, pepper, garlic powder, curry powder, and flour. Add chicken and toss to coat thoroughly. In large skillet, heat butter over medium-high heat. Add coated chicken pieces and brown on all sides. Add mushrooms, Amaretto, lemon juice, and lemon zest. Simmer 5 minutes. In small bowl, combine cornstarch and chicken broth and stir into chicken mixture. Cook over low heat, stirring constantly, until mixture bubbles and thickens. Serve over rice or pasta.

Chicken and Linguine With Grilled Vegetables

4 servings

- 4 boneless, skinless chicken breast halves (about 1 pound total)
- 1 zucchini, quartered lengthwise
- 1 medium red bell pepper, cored, seeded, and quartered
- 1 medium yellow bell pepper, cored, seeded, and quartered
- 1 cup Italian salad dressing, purchased or homemade, divided
- 6 ounces linguine, cooked al dente and drained
- ¼ cup freshly grated Parmesan cheese

Use red pepper linguine to add spice to this colorful, easy dish. Serve with Green Beans, Feta, and Pecans, page 89.

In glass dish, combine chicken, zucchini, and bell peppers. Add ½ cup of the salad dressing and toss to coat. Cover and marinate in refrigerator, up to 24 hours, turning once. Preheat grill to medium. Grill chicken and vegetables, reserving marinade, 15-20 minutes, turning once. Brush with reserved marinade occasionally. Remove to platter and cover with foil to keep warm.

Toss linguine with remaining ½ cup salad dressing. Slice grilled vegetables and toss with linguine mixture. Slice chicken breasts into ½-inch slices, without cutting all of the way through. Spread out to form a fan. Place on top of linguine and sprinkle with Parmesan.

Chicken en Papillote

4 servings

- parchment paper
- 48 inches butcher's twine
- 1 teaspoon olive oil, divided
- 4 boneless, skinless chicken breast halves (about 1 pound total)
- 1 teaspoon salt
- ½ teaspoon freshly ground black pepper
- 1 teaspoon minced fresh parsley
- 2 teaspoons fresh lemon juice
- 2 medium carrots, peeled and cut into 3x¼-inch strips
- 1 medium zucchini, cut into 3x¼-inch strips
- 4 green onions, cut into 3-inch lengths
- 1 red bell pepper, cored, seeded, and cut into ¼-inch strips
- 16 fresh snow peas, trimmed

This is a light and healthful way to showcase and enjoy your home garden produce. A variety of vegetables and herbs may be substituted. *Photo, page 258.*

Preheat oven to 375 degrees. Cut four 12x12-inch squares of parchment paper. Cut twine into four 12-inch lengths and set aside. Pour ¼ teaspoon olive oil in center of each parchment square. Place 1 chicken breast on top of oil. Sprinkle each with salt, pepper, parsley, and lemon juice. Top each chicken breast with carrots, zucchini, green onions, bell pepper, and snow peas.

Pull up all 4 corners of each parchment square and gather together. Tie with 1 length of butcher's twine, forming bows. (May be prepared to this point up to 2 hours in advance and chilled.) Place packages on non-stick baking sheet. Bake 30 minutes until paper is puffed and brown and chicken is tender. Allow guests to carefully unwrap their own package and enjoy the contents inside.

Grilled Chicken Breasts With Summer Salsa

4-8 servings

Summer Salsa:

¼ cup olive oil, divided
4 medium zucchini, diced
4 Italian plum tomatoes, chopped
¼ cup fresh lemon juice
½ teaspoon dried tarragon
2 teaspoons fresh mint
2 teaspoons fresh oregano
½ teaspoon minced garlic
1 teaspoon salt
½ teaspoon freshly ground black pepper
dash hot red pepper sauce

Chicken:

8 boneless, skinless chicken breast halves (about 2 pounds total)
salt and freshly ground black pepper

In large skillet, heat 2 tablespoons of the olive oil over medium heat. Add zucchini and cook until just tender, about 3 minutes. Stir in tomatoes and cook 3 minutes. In small bowl, combine remaining 2 tablespoons olive oil, lemon juice, tarragon, mint, oregano, garlic, salt, pepper, and hot red pepper sauce. Add to zucchini mixture and stir until well blended. Remove from heat.

Preheat grill to medium. Rub chicken breasts with salt and pepper to taste. Grill about 5 minutes per side. Transfer to platter and serve with Summer Salsa.

Honey Basil Chicken

4 servings

½ cup raspberry vinegar
1½ tablespoons Dijon mustard
2 tablespoons soy sauce
2 tablespoons honey
2 tablespoons minced fresh basil
½ teaspoon dried thyme
freshly ground black pepper
4 boneless, skinless chicken breast halves (about 1 pound total)

Serve with a green salad and Saffron Rice With Peppers, page 304, for a light and lively meal.

In shallow glass dish, combine vinegar, mustard, soy sauce, honey, basil, thyme, and pepper. Add chicken and turn to coat. Marinate at room temperature, 15 minutes. Preheat grill to medium. Grill chicken, reserving marinade, about 4 minutes per side, or until thoroughly cooked. Remove to platter and cover with foil to keep warm. Transfer reserved marinade to saucepan. Boil until reduced by half and pour over chicken.

Oaxacan Chicken With Avocado Lime Sauce

6–8 servings

- 1 bunch fresh cilantro, stemmed and chopped
- 6 tablespoons lime juice
- 2 teaspoons finely grated lime zest
- 1 cup fresh lemon juice
- 2 tablespoons vegetable oil
- 2 teaspoons minced garlic, divided
- salt
- 8 boneless, skinless chicken breast halves (about 2 pounds total)
- 2 large ripe avocados, peeled and seeded
- 2 green onions, finely chopped
- Tabasco
- 1 red bell pepper, cored, seeded, and quartered

Garnish:

fresh or purchased salsa

In the ancient Aztec diet, a sauce of avocado, lime, peppers, and tomato, rich in vitamin C, was a staple.

In medium bowl, combine cilantro, lime juice, lime zest, lemon juice, oil, 1 teaspoon of the garlic, and salt to taste. Remove and reserve ¼ cup for sauce. Combine remaining cilantro mixture and chicken and marinate in refrigerator, 2 hours, turning once.

In large bowl, mash avocados. Add reserved ¼ cup cilantro mixture, green onions, remaining 1 teaspoon garlic, and Tabasco to taste. Stir until well blended. Preheat grill to medium. Grill chicken, discarding marinade, about 7 minutes per side or until thoroughly cooked. During last 7 minutes of grilling time, add bell peppers to grill. Place chicken breasts on individual serving plates, spoon reserved avocado sauce on top. Slice bell peppers into strips and place on top of sauce. Garnish with salsa.

Bombay Chicken

10 servings

- ⅓ cup butter, divided
- 8 boneless, skinless chicken breasts (2 pounds total), cut into 2-inch pieces
- 1 cup chopped onion
- 1 teaspoon chopped garlic
- 2 teaspoons salt
- 2 tablespoons peeled, minced fresh ginger root
- ¼ teaspoon chili powder
- ¼ teaspoon cayenne
- 2 cups chopped ripe tomatoes
- ½ cup chicken broth
- ½ cup dry white wine
- ½ cup chopped cashews
- ½ cup flaked coconut
- 1 cup half and half
- 2 tablespoons cornstarch
- cooked rice or pasta

Garnish:

- ¼ cup thinly sliced green onions

This has a wonderful ginger flavor to please the most discriminating palate.

In heavy, deep skillet, melt half of the butter over medium heat. Brown chicken, adding remaining butter as necessary, about 3 minutes per side. Remove chicken to platter, reserving butter.

In same skillet, cook onion and garlic over medium heat, 5 minutes. Return chicken to skillet and add salt, ginger, chili powder, cayenne, tomatoes, chicken broth, and wine. Stir gently, cover, and cook 15 minutes. Add cashews and coconut. Cover, reduce heat to low, and cook until chicken is tender when pierced with fork, about 10 minutes.

In small bowl, combine half and half and cornstarch. Slowly stir into chicken mixture. Heat to boiling, stirring constantly. Reduce heat to low and simmer 5 minutes. Serve over cooked rice or pasta and garnish with green onions. (May be prepared up to 1 day in advance and chilled. Reheat over low heat.)

Kung Pao Chicken

4 servings

- 4 boneless, skinless chicken breast halves (about 1 pound total), cut into ½-inch pieces
- ¼ cup soy sauce, divided
- 2 tablespoons fresh lemon juice
- 2 tablespoons sugar
- 2 teaspoons cornstarch
- ¼ teaspoon crushed red pepper
- ¼ cup water
- 2 tablespoons canola oil
- 1 teaspoon minced garlic
- 1 small red bell pepper, cored, seeded, and cut into ½-inch pieces
- 1 onion, peeled and very coarsely chopped
- ¼ cup roasted peanuts
- cooked white rice

Try adding carrots and mushrooms to this classic, healthful Chinese entree.

Combine chicken and 2 tablespoons of the soy sauce. Chill 30 minutes. In small bowl, combine remaining 2 tablespoons soy sauce, lemon juice, sugar, cornstarch, crushed red pepper, and water. In wok or large skillet, heat canola oil over medium-high heat. Add reserved chicken mixture and garlic and stir-fry 3-4 minutes or until brown. Add bell pepper and onion and stir-fry 3 minutes. Add cornstarch mixture. Cook, stirring frequently, until slightly thickened. Add peanuts and toss. Serve over rice.

Indonesian Satay

4 servings

- 3 tablespoons fresh lime juice
- 3 tablespoons peanut oil
- 4 teaspoons soy sauce, divided
- 2 teaspoons crushed garlic, divided
- ¼ teaspoon cayenne, divided
- 4 boneless, skinless chicken breast halves (about 1 pound total), cut into ¾-inch strips
- ⅓ cup chunky peanut butter
- ⅓ cup hot water
- 1 tablespoon cider vinegar
- 1 cup coconut milk

Serve with rice, cucumbers, and fresh fruit.

In glass dish, combine lime juice, peanut oil, 2 teaspoons of the soy sauce, 1 teaspoon of the garlic, and ⅛ teaspoon of the cayenne. Add chicken and marinate in refrigerator, 4-24 hours. In small bowl, combine peanut butter, hot water, vinegar, remaining ⅛ teaspoon cayenne, remaining 1 teaspoon garlic, remaining 2 teaspoons soy sauce, and coconut milk. Stir until well blended and set aside. Preheat grill to medium. Thread chicken onto skewers and grill, discarding marinade, 3-4 minutes per side. Serve with reserved peanut sauce.

This may also be prepared as an appetizer. Marinate and grill chicken breasts whole and cut into bite size pieces. Place on platter with peanut sauce and spear with wooden picks.

Mu Shu Chicken

4-6 servings

- ½ cup dry sherry
- 2 tablespoons soy sauce
- 1 teaspoon sugar
- ½ teaspoon peeled, minced fresh ginger root
- ½ teaspoon minced garlic
- 6 boneless, skinless chicken breast halves (about 1½ pounds total)
- 8-10 8-inch flour tortillas
- 2 tablespoons vegetable oil
- 2 teaspoons sesame oil
- ½ pound fresh mushrooms, thinly sliced
- 1 medium onion, peeled and thinly sliced
- 1 cup bean sprouts
- ½ cup julienned carrots
- 2 cups shredded iceberg lettuce
- 2 large eggs, well beaten

Garnish:

hoisin sauce
sliced green onions
fresh cilantro leaves

In large bowl, combine sherry, soy sauce, sugar, ginger, and garlic and mix well. Add chicken, cover, and chill 30 minutes or up to 2 hours. Preheat oven to 300 degrees. Wrap tortillas in foil and warm in oven 15-20 minutes. Arrange chicken, reserving marinade, in single layer, in microwave-safe dish. Cover with plastic wrap. Place in microwave and cook, on high, 6-8 minutes or until meat is no longer pink. Rotate one quarter turn every 2 minutes. Remove chicken and cut into bite size pieces. Set aside.

In wok or large skillet, heat vegetable oil and sesame oil over high heat. Add mushrooms, onion, bean sprouts, and carrots. Cook, stirring frequently, until vegetables are lightly browned and liquid has evaporated, about 6 minutes. Add reserved marinade. Heat to boiling and cook, stirring occasionally, until reduced to one third, about 2 minutes. Add reserved chicken and lettuce and continue cooking, stirring frequently, until chicken is thoroughly heated, 2-3 minutes. Add eggs, stir until just set, and remove from heat. Spoon reserved chicken mixture into warmed tortillas. Roll up and garnish with hoisin sauce, green onions, and cilantro.

Sesame Chicken

4-6 servings

- ¾ cup sugar
- ¼ cup plus 2 teaspoons soy sauce, divided
- 2½ tablespoons white vinegar
- 6 teaspoons rice wine or dry sherry, divided
- 1 cup chicken broth
- 6 boneless, skinless chicken breast halves (about 1½ pounds total), cut into bite size pieces
- 2 egg whites, lightly beaten
- ¼ cup cornstarch
- ½ cup vegetable oil
- 1 teaspoon minced garlic
- 3-6 dried hot red pepper pods
- ¼ cup sesame seeds
- thinly sliced green onions
- cooked white rice

Here is another favorite Chinese dish that the family will love.

In medium bowl, combine sugar, ¼ cup of the soy sauce, vinegar, 4 teaspoons of the rice wine, and chicken broth. Whisk to blend and set aside. In separate bowl, combine chicken pieces, remaining 2 teaspoons soy sauce, and remaining 2 teaspoons rice wine. Marinate at room temperature, about 30 minutes. Add egg whites and cornstarch and stir until well blended.

In wok or large skillet, heat oil over medium-high heat. Cook chicken, in 3 batches, until golden on all sides, about 3 minutes. Remove with slotted spoon and drain on paper towels. Cover with foil to keep warm. Discard all but 2 tablespoons drippings from wok and reduce heat to medium. Add garlic and pepper pods and cook, stirring frequently, until peppers blacken, about 1 minute. Add reserved soy sauce mixture, increase heat to medium-high, and cook until sauce thickens, about 15 minutes. Add reserved chicken and sesame seeds and stir until coated. Top with green onions and serve with rice.

Chicken Zucchini Marinara

4 servings

4	boneless, skinless chicken breast halves (about 1 pound total)
¼	teaspoon salt
¼	teaspoon freshly ground black pepper
¼	cup flour
1	egg, lightly beaten
½	cup dry bread crumbs
2	tablespoons olive oil
1	cup sliced fresh mushrooms
1	cup Mountain Marinara (page 193) or purchased marinara sauce
1	tablespoon chopped fresh parsley
1	medium zucchini, cut lengthwise into eighths
1	tablespoon water
1	cup grated mozzarella cheese

Serve with Red Leaf Lettuce With Buttermilk Dressing, page 81.

Preheat oven to 375 degrees. Place chicken between 2 sheets of waxed paper. Pound to ½-inch thickness. Sprinkle with salt and pepper and set aside. Place flour, beaten egg, and bread crumbs into 3 separate, shallow dishes. Dredge chicken in flour, shaking off excess, then in egg and then in crumbs, pressing firmly to coat.

In large skillet, heat olive oil over medium-high heat. Add chicken and cook until golden, 3-4 minutes per side. Remove from skillet and transfer to large baking dish. Add mushrooms to same skillet and cook 30 seconds. Add marinara sauce and parsley. Cook 3 minutes, stirring frequently.

Place zucchini slices in shallow microwave-safe dish. Sprinkle with 1 tablespoon water. Cover and microwave on high, 2 minutes. Remove and drain. Place 2 of the zucchini slices on each chicken breast, forming an "x". Pour marinara mixture evenly over zucchini and sprinkle with mozzarella. Bake 10-15 minutes or until cheese is melted.

Pine Nut Chicken

6-8 servings

- 3½ slices white bread, torn into pieces
- ½ cup pine nuts, lightly toasted (page 381)
- 2 tablespoons yellow cornmeal
- 2 tablespoons fresh parsley
- 1½ teaspoons chopped garlic
- 1½ teaspoons finely chopped fresh sage or ½ teaspoon dried sage
- ½ teaspoon cayenne
- ¼ teaspoon salt
- 1 tablespoon egg white
- 3 tablespoons Dijon mustard
- 1½ teaspoons water
- 8 boneless, skinless chicken breast halves or thighs (about 2 pounds total)

Great hot or cold, this is a wonderful picnic dish.

Preheat oven to 375 degrees. Grease large baking pan. In food processor, combine bread, toasted pine nuts, cornmeal, parsley, garlic, sage, cayenne, and salt. Process to fine crumbs. Add egg white and pulse 3-4 times. Transfer to shallow dish. In small bowl, combine mustard and water. Spread evenly over chicken. Roll chicken in bread mixture and press to coat evenly. Arrange in prepared pan. Bake until coating is crisp and browned, about 30 minutes.

Ginger Chicken Kabobs

4 servings

- 1 bunch green onions, coarsely chopped
- 1 tablespoon sugar
- 2 tablespoons soy sauce
- 1 tablespoon Worcestershire
- 1 tablespoon vegetable oil
- 1 teaspoon salt
- 2 teaspoons peeled, grated fresh ginger root
- ¾ teaspoon ground allspice
- ¼ teaspoon crushed red pepper
- 4 boneless, skinless chicken breast halves (about 1 pound total), cut into 1½-inch pieces
- 16 medium fresh mushrooms, trimmed
- 16 cherry tomatoes
- 1 red onion, peeled and cut into 8 wedges
- 1 large yellow bell pepper, cored, seeded, and cut into 1½-inch pieces

Delicious served with Carrot Basmati Rice Pilaf, page 306 or brown rice.

In blender or food processor, combine green onions, sugar, soy sauce, Worcestershire, oil, salt, ginger, allspice, and crushed red pepper and puree. Pour over chicken and mushrooms. Cover and marinate in refrigerator, 2 hours. Place chicken, mushrooms, cherry tomatoes, red onion wedges, and bell peppers in alternating pattern on skewers. Preheat grill to medium or preheat broiler. Grill or broil about 10 minutes or until chicken is no longer pink, turning once.

Chicken Enchiladas Suizas

8 servings

6	boneless, skinless chicken breast halves (about 1½ pounds total)
1	tablespoon butter
1	cup chopped onion
1	green bell pepper, cored, seeded, and chopped
1	red bell pepper, cored, seeded, and chopped
8	ounces grated cheddar cheese
1	4-ounce can diced green chiles
1	cup purchased green chile salsa
½	cup chopped fresh cilantro
4	teaspoons ground cumin
2-3	canned chipotle chiles in adobo sauce (optional)
	salt and freshly ground black pepper
12-15	7-inch flour tortillas
10	ounces Monterey Jack cheese, grated
1	cup whipping cream
½	cup chicken broth
	Garnish:
	chopped avocado
	chopped tomato
	chopped fresh cilantro

A great casserole to serve after a day on the ski slopes. Serve with Fiesta Salad, page 85.

Place chicken in pan of rapidly boiling water to cover, and simmer 15-20 minutes. Remove from heat, drain, cool, and shred chicken. Preheat oven to 350 degrees. In medium skillet, melt butter over medium heat. Cook onion and bell peppers until just soft, 5-8 minutes. Transfer to large bowl. Add chicken, cheddar cheese, green chiles, salsa, cilantro, cumin, and chipotle chiles, if desired. Season with salt and pepper to taste and mix well.

Grease 10x15x2-inch baking pan or 2 smaller pans. Place 1 flour tortilla on flat surface and place about ⅓ cup chicken mixture along 1 edge. Roll up from filling side, and place, seam side down, in prepared pan. Repeat process with remaining chicken mixture. Sprinkle Monterey Jack over enchiladas. (May be prepared to this point up to 1 day in advance. Cover and chill.)

Combine cream and chicken broth and pour over enchiladas. Cover pan with foil and bake 30 minutes. Remove foil and continue baking 10 minutes or until thoroughly heated. Place 1 or 2 enchiladas on individual serving plates and garnish with avocado, tomato, and additional cilantro, if desired.

Feta Chicken in Phyllo

8 main dish servings
16 appetizer servings

2	tablespoons olive oil
1	medium onion, peeled and chopped
10	ounces fresh spinach, stemmed and chopped
1	ounce feta cheese, crumbled
2	tablespoons dry white wine
¼	teaspoon freshly ground black pepper
1	egg, lightly beaten
3	cups cubed cooked chicken
10	sheets phyllo pastry, thawed if frozen
½	cup (1 stick) butter, melted
⅔	cup dry bread crumbs
½	teaspoon paprika

This is an elegant meal and travels well for a buffet. Try with Greens With Pears, Asiago, and Cashews, page 85.

In large skillet, heat olive oil over medium heat. Add onion and cook until tender, stirring occasionally, about 5 minutes. Add spinach and cook until wilted, stirring frequently, about 3 minutes. Remove from heat and stir in feta, wine, pepper, egg, and chicken.

Preheat oven to 375 degrees. Place phyllo on flat surface. Trim to 16x12 inches. Working with 1 sheet at a time, keeping remaining covered with plastic wrap and damp towel, brush with melted butter and sprinkle with 1 tablespoon bread crumbs. Continue layering, brushing with butter, and sprinkling with bread crumbs, for a total of 5 layers.

Spread half of the chicken mixture, in a 2-inch strip, along short side of phyllo, leaving ½-inch border. Roll up, jelly roll style, starting with chicken mixture edge. Repeat process with remaining ingredients to form second roll.

Place, seam side down, 2-inches apart, on large baking sheet. Brush with butter. With sharp knife, cut diagonally, halfway through phyllo layers, in 1-inch increments. Sprinkle with paprika and bake 15-20 minutes, until golden brown. Remove from oven and let stand 10 minutes. Slice along cuts and serve.

Chicken With Fresh Tarragon and Tomatoes

4 servings

- 1 whole chicken (about 3½ pounds), cut up
- salt and freshly ground black pepper
- 5 tablespoons butter, divided
- 8 medium mushrooms, sliced
- 3 tablespoons finely chopped shallots
- ½ cup dry white wine
- 1 14-ounce can whole peeled tomatoes, drained, seeded, and coarsely chopped
- 1 tablespoon chopped fresh tarragon or 1 teaspoon dried tarragon
- ¼ teaspoon dried thyme
- ½ cup whipping cream (optional)
- 2 cups cooked white rice

Season chicken with salt and pepper to taste. In large skillet with tight fitting lid, melt 3 tablespoons of the butter over medium heat. Brown chicken pieces, in 1 layer, about 5 minutes per side. Cover, reduce heat to medium-low, and cook 25 minutes, reducing heat to low if necessary to prevent burning on bottom.

While chicken is cooking, melt remaining 2 tablespoons butter in small skillet. Add mushrooms, toss to coat, cover, and cook over medium heat, 3 minutes. Remove cover and cook until excess moisture has evaporated, about 3 minutes.

Transfer cooked chicken to heated serving platter and cover with foil to keep warm. Skim and discard grease from skillet, leaving only pan juices. Add shallots and cook, stirring constantly, over medium-high heat about 30 seconds. Add wine and cook about 2 minutes, stirring to scrape browned bits from bottom of skillet. Stir in tomatoes, reserved mushrooms, tarragon, and thyme. Cook over high heat 5 minutes. Reduce heat and stir in cream, if desired. Season with salt and pepper to taste and cook 2 minutes. Spoon sauce over chicken and serve with rice.

Jamaican Chicken

6-8 servings

- 4 whole chicken breasts (about 4 pounds total), split
- 1 cup purchased Jamaican hot sauce or Jamaican jerk marinade
- ½ cup fresh lime juice
- ¼ cup yellow, country-style mustard
- 1 cup mango or papaya juice
- 2 tablespoons white wine vinegar
- 3 tablespoons chopped shallots
- 2 tablespoons chopped fresh rosemary or 2 teaspoons dried rosemary
- 2 tablespoons chopped fresh basil or 2 teaspoons dried basil
- 1 tablespoon chopped fresh oregano or 1 teaspoon dried oregano
- 2 tablespoons mustard seed, crushed
- 1 teaspoon salt
- 1 teaspoon freshly ground pepper
- 1 bunch fresh mint, chopped
- 1 tablespoon peeled, finely chopped fresh ginger root
- 1 ripe mango, peeled, seeded, and diced

Garnish:

- 1 ripe mango, peeled, seeded, and thinly sliced

This is a very spicy dish. Serve with rice and a fruit salad, for a low-fat meal, high in vitamin C.

Place chicken in resealable plastic bag or glass pan. In large bowl, combine hot sauce, lime juice, mustard, mango juice, vinegar, shallots, rosemary, basil, oregano, mustard seed, salt, pepper, mint, ginger, and diced mango. Pour over chicken and marinate 2 hours, at room temperature.

Preheat grill to medium. Grill chicken, reserving marinade, 30-35 minutes, turning frequently and basting with marinade. Remove chicken to serving platter and garnish with mango slices. Pour remaining marinade into saucepan and boil 2-3 minutes. Transfer to serving bowl and pass with chicken.

Orange Chicken With Apricots and Currants

6-8 servings

- 4½ pounds chicken pieces
- salt and freshly ground black pepper
- 1 tablespoon peeled, minced fresh ginger root
- 1½ cups purchased orange marmalade, preferably Seville
- ⅓ cup apple juice
- ⅓ cup fresh orange juice
- 6 ounces dried apricots
- 4 ounces dried currants
- 3 tablespoons packed brown sugar

Apricots are a good source of vitamin A and compliment this healthful entree.

Preheat oven to 375 degrees. Place chicken pieces, skin side up, in shallow baking dish and season generously with salt and pepper. Sprinkle with ginger and spread with marmalade. Pour apple juice and orange juice into pan and bake 20 minutes.

Remove from oven and add apricots and currants, distributing evenly. Sprinkle with brown sugar and return to oven. Bake, basting frequently, until chicken is golden brown and shiny on top, 40-45 minutes. Remove chicken, apricots, and currants to warmed serving platter. Top with some of the pan juices and pour remaining juices into serving bowl to pass. Serve immediately.

Chutney Chicken

8-10 servings

- 3 tablespoons butter
- 2 tablespoons curry powder
- ¼ teaspoon ground cardamom
- ¼ cup dry white wine
- 6 pounds chicken pieces
- 1½ cups purchased mango chutney, chopped
- 2 tablespoons shredded coconut
- 1 tablespoon snipped fresh chives
- ½ cup golden raisins

Cardamom is one of the finest Indian flavorings. Pods can be used whole, or peeled and the seeds crushed.

Preheat oven to 350 degrees. In small saucepan, melt butter over low heat. Add curry powder and cardamom and cook 2-3 minutes. Add wine and stir until well blended. Remove from heat. Place chicken pieces in large baking pan. Pour butter mixture over chicken. Bake 30 minutes. Remove from oven and spread chopped chutney over chicken. Continue baking an additional 30 minutes, basting frequently.

Remove to serving platter. Pour pan juices into small saucepan and boil 3-4 minutes, until slightly reduced. Pour over chicken and sprinkle with coconut, chives, and raisins.

Almond Curry Chicken

6 servings

- ¾ cup blanched almonds
- ¼ cup vegetable oil
- 3½ pounds chicken pieces, skin removed
- 1 teaspoon minced garlic
- 1 1½-inch piece fresh ginger, peeled and minced
- ¾ cup finely chopped onion
- 1 teaspoon crushed red pepper
- ½ teaspoon turmeric
- 1 teaspoon salt
- 1 cup water
- 1 cup unsweetened coconut milk
- cooked rice
- purchased chutney

The technique of thickening savory dishes with almond paste was originated by the Persians in the tenth century.

In food processor, process almonds until they form a smooth paste, about 4 minutes. Set aside. In large skillet, heat oil over medium-high heat. Add chicken pieces in single layer and cook until lightly browned, about 3 minutes per side. Remove to platter. Discard all but 2 tablespoons drippings from skillet and add garlic, ginger, and onion. Cook, stirring frequently, 1 minute. Add crushed red pepper, turmeric, and salt and cook, stirring frequently, 5 minutes or until mixture turns reddish brown.

Stir in water and return reserved chicken to skillet. Cover and simmer until chicken is tender, about 25 minutes. Remove from heat. Skim and discard fat that has risen to surface. Add reserved almond paste and stir until well blended. Simmer uncovered, 5 minutes. Stir in coconut milk and heat to boiling. Cook 3 minutes, basting chicken occasionally. Serve with rice and chutney.

Roasted Chicken With Mushrooms

4-6 servings

- 1 whole chicken (about 5 pounds)
- salt and freshly ground black pepper
- garlic salt
- 1 orange, quartered
- 1 cup half and half, divided
- ½ pound small fresh mushrooms
- 3 tablespoons Grand Marnier

Garnish:

- fresh parsley sprigs

To vary this recipe, add 3 fresh rosemary sprigs to cavity before roasting and garnish with fresh rosemary sprigs. Try with an Alsacian Gewürztraminer.

Preheat oven to 425 degrees. Grease baking pan (just slightly larger than chicken). Rub chicken, inside and out with salt, pepper, and garlic salt. Place quartered orange in chicken cavity. Place chicken, breast side up, in prepared pan and roast 20 minutes. Remove from oven and reduce oven temperature to 350 degrees.

Pour half of the half and half over chicken. Return to oven and continue roasting 20 minutes. Pour remaining half and half over chicken and continue roasting for 1 hour, basting every 15 minutes. Place mushrooms around chicken, in cooking liquid. Pour Grand Marnier over chicken. Continue roasting 15 minutes longer. Transfer to serving platter. Garnish with parsley.

Green Mountain Pesto Chicken

4-6 servings

1 whole roasting chicken (6-7 pounds)

½ cup plus 1 tablespoon Basic Basil Pesto (page 193) or purchased basil pesto, divided

¼ cup dry white wine

chicken broth (about ¾ cup), divided

2 tablespoons flour

3 tablespoons half and half

salt and freshly ground black pepper

Garnish:

fresh basil sprigs

Classic roasted chicken updated with pesto. Serve with Savory Roasted New Potatoes, page 333, and Brussels Sprouts With Pecans, page 323, for a delicious Sunday dinner.

Separate skin and meat over breast and legs by sliding your fingers between them, to form pockets. Spread ½ cup of the pesto over breast and leg meat, under skin, inside cavity of chicken, and over outer skin. Truss and tuck wings under body. Place in large roasting pan. (May be prepared to this point up to 4 hours in advance. Cover and chill.)

Preheat oven to 450 degrees. Roast chicken 15 minutes. Reduce oven temperature to 375 degrees and roast about 1 hour and 15 minutes, basting occasionally with pan juices. Juices should be clear when chicken is pierced in thickest part of thigh. Transfer chicken to serving platter.

Pour pan juices into 1-cup or larger, glass measuring cup. Skim and discard grease from top. Add wine to roasting pan and heat to boiling, scraping up any browned bits. Pour into measuring cup with pan juices. Add any drippings from platter and enough of the chicken broth to measure 1 cup. Transfer to small, heavy saucepan.

In small bowl, combine about 2 tablespoons of the chicken broth and flour. Whisk to blend and add to dripping mixture. Heat to boiling, whisking constantly. Boil until thickened, stirring frequently, about 5 minutes. Stir in half and half and remaining 1 tablespoon pesto. Season with salt and pepper to taste. Transfer to serving bowl and pass with chicken. Garnish chicken with basil.

Chutney Glazed Roasted Hens With Stuffing

4 servings

Dried Fruit Stuffing:

¼ cup (½ stick) butter
1 tablespoon minced shallots
1 onion, peeled and minced
½ teaspoon minced garlic
¾ teaspoon dried sage, crumbled
⅛ teaspoon ground cloves
⅓ cup golden raisins
½ cup chopped dried apricots
salt and freshly ground black pepper
½ cup dry white wine
4 cups cubed, toasted, stale French bread
½ cup chopped celery

Hens:

4 Cornish hens, thawed if frozen
salt and freshly ground black pepper
¼ cup butter (½ stick), melted and cooled slightly
¼ cup fresh lemon juice
½ cup purchased mango chutney

In large skillet, melt butter over medium heat. Add shallots, onion, and garlic. Cook, stirring frequently, until golden, 8-10 minutes. Stir in sage, cloves, raisins, apricots, and season with salt and pepper to taste. Cook, stirring frequently, 1 minute. Stir in wine and boil until liquid has evaporated. Remove from heat and stir in bread cubes and celery. Season with salt and pepper to taste and cool to room temperature.

Preheat oven to 400 degrees. Divide cooled stuffing mixture between hens, packing cavities loosely. Place any remaining stuffing mixture in baking pan and set aside. Truss hens and sprinkle with salt and pepper to taste. Place on broiler pan, not allowing hens to touch. Brush with melted butter and roast 1 hour.

While hens are roasting, combine lemon juice and chutney in small saucepan. Season with salt and pepper to taste. Heat to boiling, stirring frequently and breaking up chunks with spoon. If mixture is still very chunky, transfer to food processor or blender, puree, and set aside.

Place reserved stuffing mixture in oven. Remove hens from oven and brush with chutney glaze. Return to oven and roast an additional 15-25 minutes, or until golden brown and thoroughly cooked. Remove hens and stuffing from oven. Place hens on individual serving plates and pass additional stuffing.

Fresh Herb Cornish Hens

6 servings

6 Cornish hens, thawed if frozen
salt and freshly ground black pepper
¾ cup (1½ sticks) butter, softened
1 cup chopped fresh parsley
½ cup snipped fresh chives
2 tablespoons chopped fresh rosemary
2 tablespoons chopped fresh thyme
6 tablespoons chopped fresh sage, divided
3 tablespoons olive oil

A great way to show off your herb garden. Serve with wild rice and a Sauvignon Blanc.

Preheat oven to 450 degrees. Season hens, inside and out, with salt and pepper to taste. In food processor or blender, combine butter, parsley, chives, rosemary, thyme, and 2 tablespoons of the sage. Process to form a paste and set aside. With your fingers, carefully separate skin from breast of each hen. Spread about 2 tablespoons of the butter mixture between skin and breast. Smooth skin back into place and truss.

Rub hens with olive oil and remaining 4 tablespoons sage. Place in roasting pan. Roast 20 minutes. Reduce heat to 350 degrees and roast until juices are clear when the thickest part of the thigh is pierced with fork, about 40 minutes. Baste frequently with pan juices. Remove to platter.

Hot Pepper Barbeque Sauce

6 cups

1 onion, peeled and quartered
2 cups water, divided
4 cups catsup
½ cup fresh lemon juice
½ cup cider vinegar
¼ cup packed brown sugar
1 tablespoon salt
1 tablespoon freshly ground black pepper
2 tablespoons dry mustard
2 tablespoons paprika
1 tablespoon crushed red pepper
1 teaspoon garlic powder
1 teaspoon chili powder
2 tablespoons Tabasco
2 tablespoons Worcestershire
2 tablespoons honey
¾ cup (1½ sticks) butter

A spicy sauce for the adventurous.

In food processor or blender, puree onion and ½ cup of the water and set aside. In large saucepan, combine remaining 1½ cups water, catsup, lemon juice, vinegar, brown sugar, salt, pepper, mustard, paprika, crushed red pepper, garlic powder, chili powder, Tabasco, Worcestershire, honey, and butter. Add reserved onion mixture and heat to boiling, cook 1-2 minutes. Remove from heat and cool slightly. Store in refrigerator. Best if made a few days in advance to allow flavors to blend. Serve warm with grilled chicken.

At left: Fresh Herb Cornish Hens, 285

Sicilian Barbeque Sauce

3 cups

- 2 tablespoons vegetable oil
- 2 medium onions, peeled and finely chopped
- ½ cup finely chopped fresh parsley
- 2 teaspoons minced garlic
- 1 cup packed brown sugar
- 2 cups water
- 2 8-ounce cans tomato sauce
- 3 tablespoons tomato paste
- 3 tablespoons fresh lemon juice
- ¼ cup fresh orange juice
- 2 teaspoons red wine vinegar
- 2 tablespoons paprika
- 2 teaspoons salt
- ½ teaspoon freshly ground black pepper
- ¼ teaspoon cayenne

In heavy saucepan, heat oil over medium heat. Add onions, parsley, and garlic and cook until onions are golden, about 15 minutes. Dissolve brown sugar in water and add to onion mixture. Add tomato sauce and tomato paste. Stir until well blended and simmer, uncovered, until thickened, about 30 minutes. Add lemon juice, orange juice, vinegar, paprika, salt, pepper, and cayenne. Simmer until thickened to the consistency of jam, about 30 minutes.

This slightly sweet sauce is great on baked or grilled chicken.

Duck in Ginger Mango Sauce

4 servings

2	ripe mangos (about 1¼ pounds), peeled and seeded
1½	cups chicken broth, divided
1	tablespoon peeled, chopped fresh ginger root
2	tablespoons minced shallots
⅓	cup dry red wine
2	tablespoons balsamic vinegar
4	duck breast halves, skinned
	salt and freshly ground black pepper
2	tablespoons vegetable oil
1	teaspoon chopped fresh rosemary
1-2	teaspoons sugar (optional)
	pinch cayenne
	Garnish:
1	ripe mango, peeled, seeded, and thinly sliced

Mango provides an attractive garnish for this wonderful sweet and sour sauce which is also delicious with chicken. Serve with your favorite Pinot Noir.

In food processor or blender, puree mangos. Add ¾ cup of the chicken broth and blend until smooth. In small saucepan, combine ginger, shallots, wine, and vinegar over medium heat. Simmer until mixture is reduced to about 3 tablespoons. Add ¼ cup of the chicken broth and heat to boiling. Strain, pressing to release moisture. Return liquid to saucepan, discarding pulp. Add pureed mango mixture and heat to boiling. Remove from heat.

Season duck with salt and pepper to taste. In heavy skillet, heat oil over medium-high heat. Add duck and cook about 3 minutes per side, or until medium-rare, still pink in center. Remove and cover with foil to keep warm.

Discard drippings from skillet and add remaining ½ cup chicken broth. Heat to boiling. Boil, stirring frequently, until reduced to ¼ cup. Add mango sauce and rosemary and simmer until thick enough to coat a spoon. Taste, add sugar if desired, and simmer briefly to dissolve sugar. Add cayenne and remove from heat. Cut duck in lengthwise slices. Spoon sauce onto plate and place duck slices on top, alternating with mango slices, if desired.

Duck With Fennel and Pears

6 servings

- 2 tablespoons butter, divided
- 6 duck breast halves, skinned
- 1 onion, peeled and chopped
- ½ teaspoon fennel seeds, crushed
- 1½ tablespoons flour
- 1½ cups chicken broth
- 5 tablespoons Pernod or other anise flavored liqueur
- 3 fennel bulbs, trimmed, quartered, and fronds reserved
- 3 firm ripe pears, peeled, cored, and cut into wedges

Boneless, skinless chicken breasts may be substituted for duck.

Preheat oven to 325 degrees. In large skillet, melt 1 tablespoon of the butter over medium heat. Add duck and brown, 3-5 minutes per side. Transfer to baking pan, reserving butter. To same skillet, add onion and cook until softened, about 5 minutes.

In small bowl, combine crushed fennel seeds and flour and sprinkle over onion. Add chicken broth and Pernod and heat to simmering, stirring frequently. Pour mixture over duck, cover, and bake 35 minutes or until tender. In large skillet, melt remaining 1 tablespoon butter over medium heat. Add fennel wedges and cook about 2 minutes. Add pears and continue cooking 3 minutes. Add duck mixture to skillet and heat to simmering. Transfer to serving platter and garnish with reserved fennel fronds.

Grilled Duck With Juniper Butter Sauce

6 servings

- 6 duck breast halves, skinned
- 2 tablespoons olive oil
- ½ cup (1 stick) plus 2 teaspoons butter, divided
- 20 juniper berries, finely crushed
- 3 teaspoons sugar, divided
- 1 tablespoon Grand Marnier or other orange flavored liquor
- ½ teaspoon freshly ground black pepper
- ½ teaspoon finely grated orange zest
- salt
- ⅓ cup fresh orange juice

Duck breasts and juniper berries may be purchased at fine butcher shops and specialty stores. This is great with Merlot.

Arrange duck breasts in baking dish, brush with olive oil, and let stand, at room temperature, 2 hours. In food processor, combine ½ cup of the butter, crushed juniper berries, 2 teaspoons of the sugar, Grand Marnier, pepper, and orange zest. Shape butter into cylinder, wrap in plastic wrap, and chill 1 hour.

Season duck with salt to taste. In heavy skillet, heat remaining 2 teaspoons butter over medium heat. Add duck and cook 2-3 minutes per side, pressing down firmly. Transfer to plate and cover with foil to keep warm. Add orange juice and remaining 1 teaspoon sugar to same skillet to deglaze. Slice duck and place on individual serving plates. Divide chilled butter mixture evenly among duck slices and top with reserved orange glaze.

Eastern Plains Pheasant

4 servings

- ½ cup dried apricot halves
- ½ cup bourbon
- 2 dressed pheasants (about 2 pounds each)
- 1 teaspoon salt
- 2 teaspoons dried thyme
- 2 small onions, peeled and quartered
- 1 teaspoon minced garlic
- ¼ cup honey
- ¼ cup frozen orange juice concentrate

An easy preparation for the hunter's reward.

In small bowl, marinate apricot halves in bourbon for 1 hour. Preheat oven to 350 degrees. Rinse birds and pat dry. Rub inside and out with salt and thyme. Remove all but 2 of the apricots from bourbon. Stuff each bird with 1 onion, half of the drained apricots, and half of the garlic.

Truss birds, tuck in wings, and place on baking sheet with sides, breast side up. Cover with foil. Roast, in middle of oven, about 45 minutes. Remove foil and continue roasting 15 minutes, to brown. While birds are roasting, remove remaining 2 apricots from bourbon and slice thinly. Set aside. Add honey and orange juice concentrate to reserved bourbon, whisk to blend, and use to baste birds during last 10 minutes of roasting. Remove birds from oven and split each. Place on serving platter and garnish with reserved sliced apricots.

Orange Salsa

2 cups

- 1½ cups sectioned oranges, seeded and chopped
- 3 tablespoons chopped green onions
- 4 teaspoons chopped fresh cilantro
- ½ fresh Anaheim chile, cored, seeded, and finely chopped
- 2 teaspoons balsamic vinegar
- ½ teaspoon sugar

Wonderful with grilled chicken breasts.

In medium bowl, combine oranges, green onions, cilantro, chile, vinegar, and sugar. Cover and chill 2 hours.

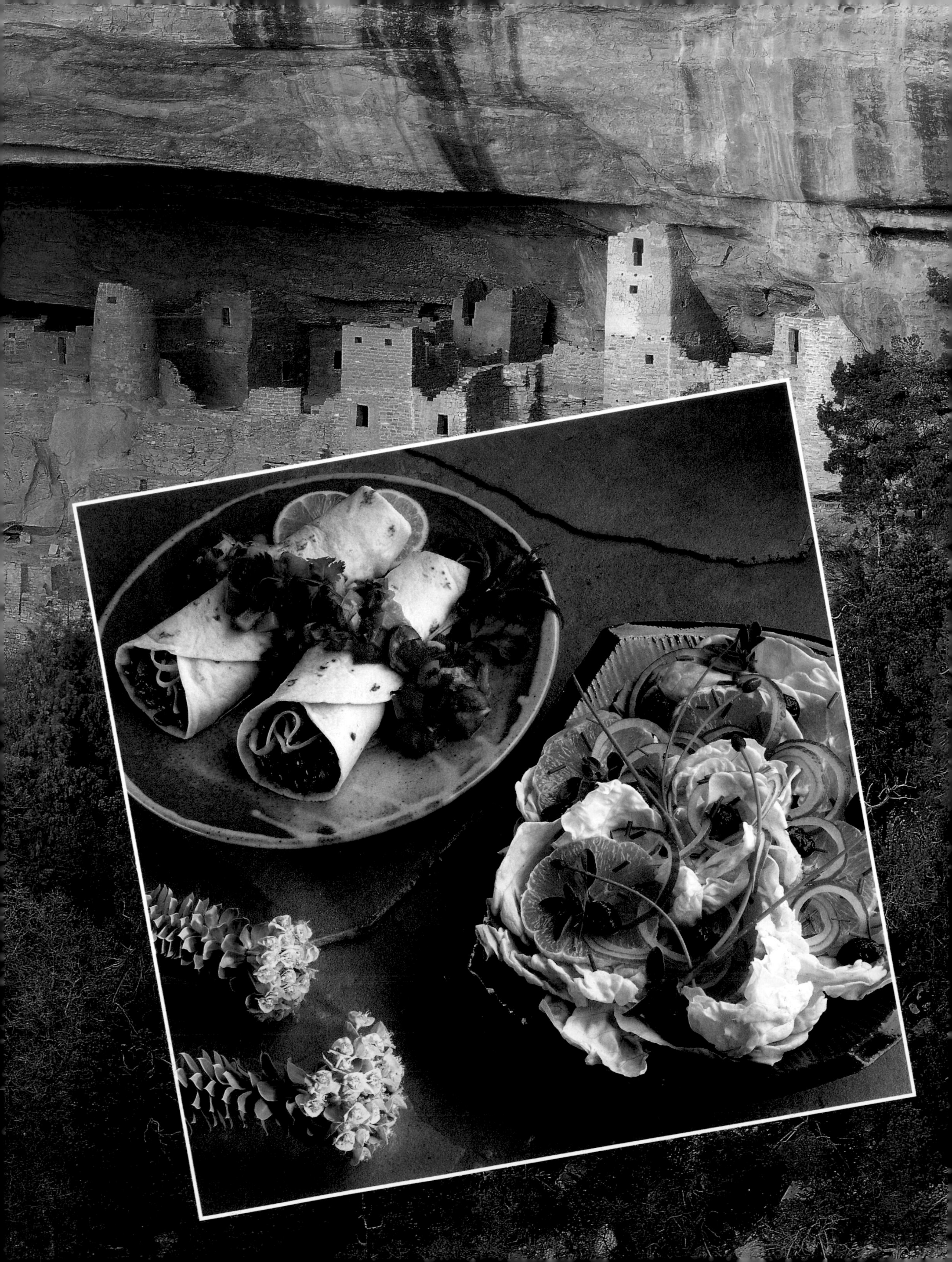

In Mesa Verde National Park, you can almost hear the ancient drums beating, and feel the harmony with nature that the people of long ago enjoyed. The mystique of those who once inhabited this land is carried on through the legacy of wonderful Southwestern cooking.

Casual Southwestern Supper

appetizer

Island Salsa 21

salad

Salad of Oranges and Onions 84

main dish

Easy Black Bean Burritos 313

dessert

Grand Marnier Flan 346

wine

Rioja, a light Spanish red

Clockwise from top:
Easy Black Bean Burritos
garnished with Island Salsa
Salad of Oranges and Onions

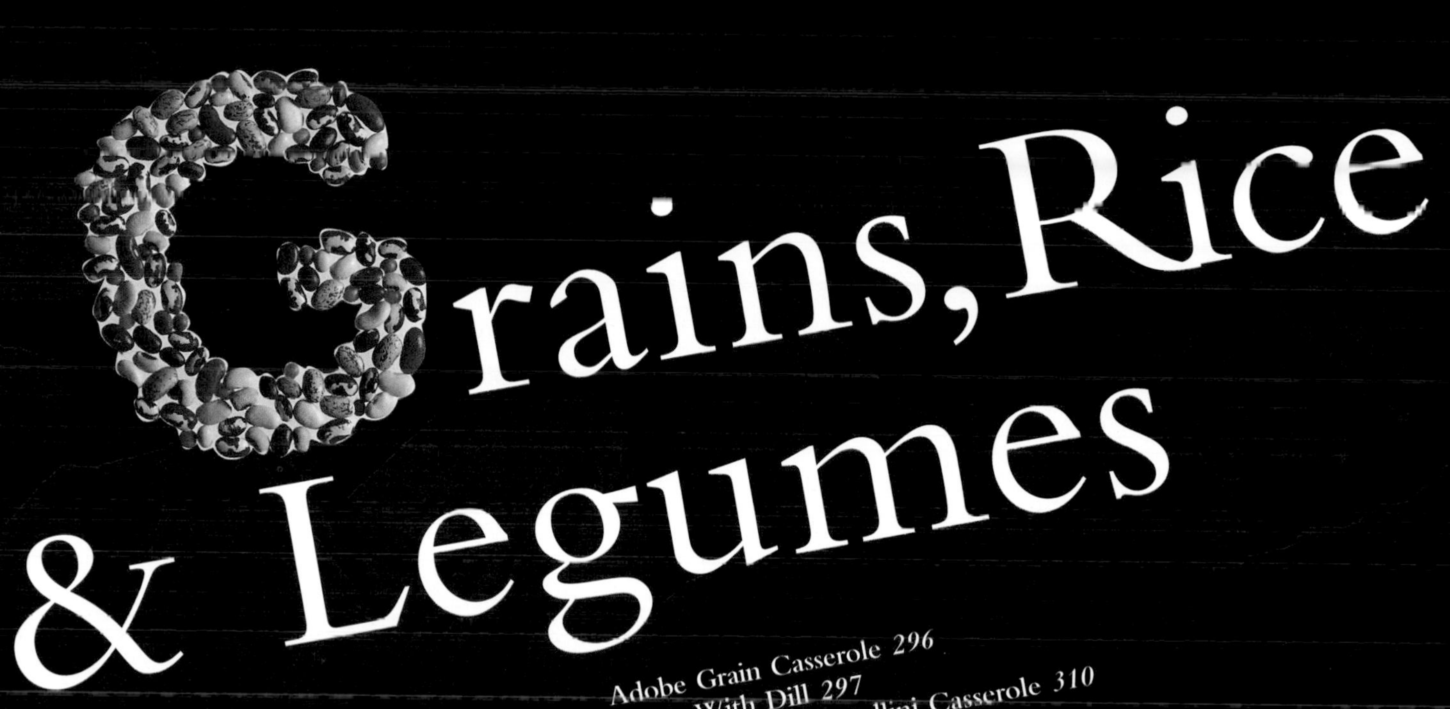

Grains, Rice & Legumes

With emphasis on more healthful fare, you'll enjoy perusing these ideas to add textural contrast and flavor to your meals. Grains like couscous, quinoa, and polenta are easy to prepare, nutritious, and fun!

Clockwise from top:
Confetti Beans With Jalapeño
Quinoa and Pepper Pilaf

Tabbouleh

8-10 servings

- 1 cup uncooked bulgur, soaked 30-40 minutes in hot water to cover and drained
- ¾ cup chopped fresh parsley
- ¼ cup chopped fresh mint
- ¼ cup chopped green onion
- 1 teaspoon dried oregano, crumbled
- ¼ cup fresh lemon juice
- 6 tablespoons olive oil
- ¼ teaspoon salt
- ⅛ teaspoon ground allspice
- ⅛ teaspoon ground nutmeg
- ⅛ teaspoon ground cloves
- 1 teaspoon ground cinnamon
- 10 drops Tabasco
- freshly ground black pepper
- ¾ cup peeled, chopped cucumber
- 1 large tomato, chopped

Garnish:

- romaine lettuce leaves
- plain yogurt

A healthful traditional vegetarian dish.

In large bowl, combine drained bulgur, parsley, mint, onion, and oregano. Toss to blend. Add lemon juice, olive oil, salt, allspice, nutmeg, cloves, cinnamon, and Tabasco. Season with pepper to taste. Stir until well blended. Chill 2 hours. Just before serving, stir in cucumber and tomato. Serve on romaine leaves and garnish with dollop of yogurt, if desired.

Lemon Couscous With Fresh Spinach

6-8 servings

- 2¼ cups chicken broth
- ¼ cup (½ stick) unsalted butter
- 1 10-ounce box uncooked couscous
- 3 tablespoons fresh lemon juice
- 3 large green onions, thinly sliced
- 1 small bunch spinach, washed, stemmed, and finely shredded
- 3 tablespoons chopped fresh chives (optional)

Quick and easy, this is the perfect side dish. Photo, page 302.

In medium saucepan, combine chicken broth and butter. Heat to boiling. Stir in couscous. Remove from heat, cover, and let stand 5 minutes. Fluff couscous with fork and stir in lemon juice, green onions, spinach, and chives, if desired. Serve hot or cold.

Mediterranean Couscous

6 main dish servings
8 side dish servings

- 1 tablespoon olive oil
- 2 teaspoons minced garlic
- 1 cup chopped onion
- 1½ cups boiling water
- 1 small fennel bulb, cut into thin strips
- 1 large red bell pepper, cored, seeded, and thinly sliced
- 1 large carrot, peeled and cut diagonally into ¼-inch slices
- 1 cup halved fresh mushrooms
- 2 medium zucchini, cut into 1-inch rounds
- 1½ cups Italian plum tomatoes, coarsely chopped
- ⅓ cup pitted kalamata olives or black olives
- 1½ teaspoons dried basil leaves
- 1½ teaspoons dried oregano leaves
- 1 teaspoon salt
- ¼ teaspoon ground cinnamon
- ¼ teaspoon freshly ground black pepper
- 2 tablespoons balsamic vinegar
- 1 cup uncooked couscous
- ¼ cup minced fresh basil leaves

A light Moroccan dish.

In large skillet, heat olive oil over medium heat. Add garlic and onion. Cook until just soft, about 2 minutes. Add water, fennel, bell pepper, carrots, mushrooms, zucchini, tomatoes, olives, basil, oregano, salt, cinnamon, and pepper. Increase heat to high and cook 10 minutes. Stir in vinegar and couscous. Cover and let stand 5 minutes. Remove from heat and stir in fresh basil.

Greek Couscous

4-6 main dish servings
6-8 side dish servings

- 2¼ cups chicken broth
- 1½ cups uncooked couscous
- 2 large tomatoes, seeded and chopped
- 6 ounces feta cheese, cut into ¼-inch pieces
- ½ cup minced watercress or arugula
- ¾ cup finely chopped green onions
- ⅔ cup olive oil
- 6 tablespoons fresh lemon juice
- salt and freshly ground black pepper
- 1 small head romaine lettuce, leaves left whole
- ½ cup Niçoise or Greek olives
- ¼ cup pine nuts, toasted (page 381)
- 10 cherry tomatoes, halved
- 1 medium cucumber, sliced

In small saucepan, heat chicken broth to boiling. Add couscous, cover, and remove from heat. Let stand 5 minutes. Fluff with fork. Place in medium bowl and cool to room temperature. Add tomatoes, feta, watercress, and green onions. In small bowl, combine olive oil, lemon juice, and salt and pepper to taste. Whisk to blend and add to couscous mixture. Toss to blend.

Line shallow bowl with romaine leaves and spoon couscous mixture into bowl. Top with olives and toasted pine nuts. Place tomatoes and cucumbers around outside edge.

Adobe Grain Casserole

4 main dish servings
6 side dish servings

- 2 medium carrots, peeled and thinly sliced
- 1 cup quartered fresh mushrooms
- 1 cup canned black beans, rinsed and drained
- 1 cup fresh or frozen corn kernels
- 1 cup vegetable or chicken broth
- ½ cup uncooked pearl barley
- ¼ cup snipped fresh parsley
- ¼ cup uncooked bulgur
- ¼ cup chopped onion
- 1 teaspoon finely minced garlic
- ¼ cup dry sherry
- ½ cup grated cheddar cheese

Mixing vegetables and grains results in a high quality protein and an excellent source of fiber.

Preheat oven to 350 degrees. In medium baking pan with cover, combine carrots, mushrooms, beans, corn, vegetable broth, barley, parsley, bulgur, onion, garlic, and sherry. Cover and bake 1 hour or until barley and bulgur are tender, stirring once, halfway through baking time. Remove from oven and sprinkle with cheese. Cover and let stand 5 minutes or until cheese is melted.

Creamy Polenta With Pepper Melange

3-4 main dish servings
6-8 side dish servings

Pepper Melange:

1 tablespoon unsalted butter
2 tablespoons extra virgin olive oil
2 medium onions, sliced into ¼-inch strips
2 large red bell peppers, cored, seeded, and cut into 1-inch triangles
2 large yellow bell peppers, cored, seeded, and cut into 1-inch triangles
1 teaspoon minced garlic
10 fresh basil leaves, thinly sliced or 1 tablespoon chopped fresh rosemary
3 ripe tomatoes, cored, seeded, and chopped
salt and freshly ground black pepper

Polenta:

6¼ cups water or chicken broth
1¾ cups yellow cornmeal
1 teaspoon salt

A colorful presentation of a Northern Italian staple. *Photo, page 302.*

In large skillet, heat butter and olive oil over medium heat. Add onions and bell peppers and cook until onions are golden brown, 10-12 minutes. Stir in garlic and basil and continue cooking 30 seconds. Add tomatoes, increase heat to high, and heat to boiling. Boil 3 minutes or until thickened. Remove from heat and season with salt and pepper to taste.

In top of double boiler, heat water or chicken broth to rolling boil, directly over high heat. Remove from heat. Slowly add cornmeal and 1 teaspoon salt, whisking to prevent lumps. Cover and place over rapidly simmering water. Cook 1½ hours, stirring occasionally with rubber spatula to prevent sticking. Spoon onto individual serving plates and top with Pepper Melange.

Barley With Dill

6-8 servings

¼ cup (½ stick) butter
1 medium onion, peeled and chopped
1¾ cups uncooked barley
1 teaspoon salt
1 teaspoon dried dill weed
½ teaspoon freshly ground pepper
4 cups chicken broth

Easy to prepare and high in fiber, this dish is great with chicken.

Preheat oven to 350 degrees. In medium saucepan, melt butter over medium heat. Add onion and cook until golden brown, about 10 minutes. Transfer to baking dish with lid. Add barley, salt, dill, pepper, and chicken broth. Mix thoroughly. Cover and bake 1½ hours.

Polenta With Gorgonzola

3-4 main dish servings
6-8 side dish servings

- 3 cups chicken broth
- ¼ cup dry white wine
- 1 cup polenta
- ¼ pound wild mushrooms, sliced
- 1½ tablespoons olive oil
- ¼ cup freshly grated Parmesan, divided
- ¼ cup Gorgonzola cheese, crumbled
- ⅛ cup drained and chopped oil-packed sun-dried tomatoes (optional)

Polenta should ideally be made with coarse textured cornmeal, but medium textured cornmeal, commonly found in supermarkets, may be used.

Grease 11x9-inch dish. In large saucepan, combine chicken broth and wine over medium heat. Heat to boiling. Gradually add polenta and stir until well blended. Reduce heat to low and cook 15 minutes, stirring constantly. Add mushrooms and continue cooking 10 minutes, until mixture is thick and pulling away from sides of pan. Stir in olive oil, half of the Parmesan, Gorgonzola, and sun-dried tomatoes, if desired.

Remove from heat and spread in prepared pan to ½-inch thickness. Sprinkle remaining Parmesan on top. Let stand 10 minutes. Cut into squares and serve.

Quinoa and Pepper Pilaf

3-4 main dish servings
6 side dish servings

- 1 cup uncooked quinoa, rinsed and drained
- 1¾ cups chicken broth
- 2 teaspoons olive oil
- ¼ cup diced red bell pepper
- ¼ cup diced yellow bell pepper
- 2 leeks, white part only, chopped, and thoroughly rinsed
- 2 medium carrots, peeled and diced
- 2 celery ribs, diced
- 1 teaspoon minced garlic
- 1 tablespoon freshly grated Parmesan cheese
- salt and freshly ground black pepper

Garnish:

- ¼ cup chopped fresh parsley

The Incas considered quinoa the "mother grain." It is an excellent source of protein. *Photo, page 292.*

In medium saucepan, combine quinoa and chicken broth over medium heat. Heat to boiling. Reduce heat to low, cover, and simmer until quinoa is very tender and liquid has been absorbed, about 15 minutes. Remove from heat.

In medium skillet, heat olive oil over medium heat. Add bell peppers, leeks, carrots, and celery. Cook, stirring occasionally, until just soft, about 6 minutes. Stir in garlic and continue cooking 1 minute. Stir into quinoa mixture. Stir in Parmesan and season with salt and pepper to taste. Garnish with chopped parsley. Serve hot.

Easy Tomato Risotto

4-6 servings

- 1½ tablespoons olive oil
- 1 cup uncooked Arborio rice
- 3 cups chicken broth, divided
- ½ cup water
- ⅓ cup dry white wine
- 6 small Italian plum tomatoes, cored and chopped
- 3 tablespoons chopped fresh basil
- ½ teaspoon freshly grated nutmeg
- ¼ cup freshly grated Romano cheese

A microwave version of a classic dish.

Place olive oil in 2½-quart microwave-safe dish. Heat, uncovered, on high 1 minute. Stir in rice and continue cooking 1 minute. Stir in 2 cups of the chicken broth, water, and wine and continue cooking 12 minutes. Stir in remaining 1 cup chicken broth, tomatoes, and basil and continue cooking 13 minutes. Stir in nutmeg and Romano. Serve immediately.

Risotto With Artichokes

2-4 main dish servings
4-6 side dish servings

- 1½ cups beef broth
- 1½ cups water
- 1½ tablespoons olive oil
- 2 tablespoons butter, divided
- ½ cup finely chopped onion
- 1 cup sliced artichoke hearts or 5 ounces water-packed artichoke hearts, drained and sliced
- 2 teaspoons minced garlic
- 1 cup uncooked Arborio rice
- ¼ cup dry white wine
- salt and freshly ground black pepper
- ¼ cup chopped fresh parsley
- ¼ cup freshly grated Parmesan cheese

Arborio is a short-grain, Italian rice with a rich and creamy texture.

Heat beef broth and water to simmering and keep warm over low heat. In large, heavy saucepan, heat olive oil and 1 tablespoon of the butter over low heat. Add onion and cook until it begins to soften, about 7 minutes. Add artichokes and garlic and cook until onion is soft, about 5 minutes. Add rice and cook until rice is opaque, 1-3 minutes.

Add wine and cook, stirring frequently, until liquid is completely absorbed, about 3 minutes. Add ½ cup of the heated broth mixture, and cook, stirring frequently until most of the liquid is absorbed, 3-5 minutes. Continue adding remaining 2½ cups broth, ½ cup at a time, letting liquid absorb after each addition. Cook, stirring constantly, until rice is tender and creamy. Cooking time after addition of rice should be 25-30 minutes. Halfway through cooking time, add salt and pepper to taste. When risotto is just tender, remove from heat. Add parsley, remaining 1 tablespoon butter, and Parmesan. Stir until well blended and serve immediately.

Risotto With Fennel and Peas

4 main dish servings
6-8 side dish servings

- 5-6 cups chicken broth
- 2 teaspoons olive oil
- 1 fennel bulb, trimmed and chopped
- 1 onion, peeled and chopped
- 1½ cups uncooked Arborio rice
- ½ cup dry white wine
- 1 cup frozen petite peas, thawed
- 1 cup freshly grated Romano cheese
- 2 tablespoons Pernod or other anise flavored liqueur

Heat chicken broth to simmering and keep warm over low heat. In large, heavy saucepan, heat olive oil over low heat. Add fennel and onion and cook until softened, 7-10 minutes. Add rice and stir 1 minute to coat grains. Add wine and cook, stirring frequently, until most of the liquid is absorbed, about 3 minutes.

Add ½ cup of the warmed chicken broth, and cook, stirring frequently, until most of the liquid is absorbed, 3-5 minutes. Continue adding remaining chicken broth, ½ cup at a time, letting liquid absorb after each addition. Cook, stirring constantly, until rice is tender and creamy. Add peas, Romano, and Pernod and stir until well blended. Serve immediately.

A comforting Italian specialty.

Wild West Pancakes

4 servings

- 1½ cups cooked wild rice
- 2 tablespoons butter, melted
- 1 teaspoon minced garlic
- 1 egg
- 2 tablespoons flour
- 6 tablespoons milk
- ¼ teaspoon salt
- ½ teaspoon baking powder
- 1 tablespoon butter

Garnish:

- sour cream
- snipped fresh chives

Great with lamb

Preheat oven to 200 degrees. In food processor, combine cooked wild rice, 2 tablespoons melted butter, garlic, egg, flour, milk, salt, and baking powder. Pulse about 10 times to form a coarse batter. In large, non-stick skillet, heat 1 tablespoon butter over medium heat.

Drop spoonfuls of batter to form silver-dollar size pancakes. Cook until batter begins to bubble. Turn and cook until golden brown. Remove to serving platter and place in oven to keep warm. Garnish with small dollop sour cream and chives.

Southwestern Wild Rice and Quinoa

6-8 main dish servings
12 side dish servings

- 6 cups water
- 1½ cups uncooked wild rice, rinsed thoroughly
- ¾ cup uncooked quinoa or ½ cup uncooked long-grain white rice, thoroughly rinsed
- 1 pound hot bulk pork sausage
- 1 pound mild bulk pork sausage
- ¼ cup white vinegar
- ¼ cup chili powder
- ½ cup packed, chopped fresh cilantro
- salt

Quinoa is the highest protein grain and grows well at Colorado's high altitude.

In large saucepan, heat water to boiling. Add wild rice, reduce heat to medium-low, cover, and simmer 45 minutes. Add quinoa, cover, and cook until grains are just tender, 15-20 minutes. Drain well and set aside.

Preheat oven to 350 degrees. Butter large shallow baking dish. In large skillet, brown hot and mild sausage over high heat, stirring frequently. Pour off drippings. Add vinegar, stirring to loosen browned bits. Add chili powder. In large bowl, combine sausage mixture, reserved cooked wild rice mixture, and cilantro. Mix lightly with fork and season with salt to taste.

Spoon mixture into prepared pan. (May be prepared to this point up to 2 days in advance. Cover and chill.) Bake uncovered, about 25 minutes, or until hot in center and lightly browned on top, 40 minutes, if chilled.

Curried Wild Rice

4-6 servings

- 6 slices bacon
- ½ cup chopped onion
- ½ cup grated carrots
- 2 cups cooked wild rice
- 2 egg yolks
- 1 cup half and half
- 1½ teaspoons curry powder
- ½ teaspoon salt
- 2 tablespoons butter

Wild rice is actually a long-grain grass, not a rice.

Preheat oven to 300 degrees. Butter soufflé dish or baking pan. In skillet, cook bacon until crisp over medium heat. Remove and place on paper towel to drain. Drain all but 1 tablespoon drippings and add onion and carrots. Cook until onion is soft, 3-5 minutes. Remove to bowl with slotted spoon. Crumble bacon and add to cooked onion mixture. Add cooked wild rice. Stir until well blended and place mixture in prepared dish.

In medium bowl, combine egg yolks, half and half, curry powder, and salt. Whisk to blend and pour over wild rice mixture. Dot top with butter. Place dish in larger baking pan and add boiling water to halfway up sides of dish. Bake until set, about 30 minutes.

Wild Rice With Peppers and Roasted Pecans

4-6 servings

- ½ cup coarsely chopped pecans
- 1 tablespoon unsalted butter, melted
- ⅛ teaspoon dried thyme, crumbled
- ⅛ teaspoon salt
- 2 tablespoons olive oil
- ½ cup sliced onion
- ½ red bell pepper, cut into julienne strips
- ½ yellow bell pepper, cut into julienne strips
- ¾ cup uncooked wild rice, wild rice blend, or other rice blend, thoroughly rinsed
- ½ cup long-grain rice
- 2¼ cups chicken broth
- salt and freshly ground black pepper

Fabulous with grilled or roasted meats.

Preheat oven to 375 degrees. In small baking dish, combine pecans, butter, thyme, and salt. Toss to coat. Bake 8 minutes or until crisp. Remove from oven and set aside. In large skillet, heat olive oil over medium heat. Add onion and bell peppers and cook until just soft, about 5 minutes. Remove from pan with slotted spoon and set aside.

Clockwise from top left: Lemon Couscous With Fresh Spinach, 294 Wild Rice With Peppers and Roasted Pecans, 303 Creamy Polenta With Pepper Melange, 297

Add rice to same skillet and cook 1 minute, stirring constantly. Stir in chicken broth and heat to boiling. Season with salt and pepper to taste. Transfer to large baking dish. Cover and bake 30 minutes. Stir in onion mixture and continue baking, covered, 15 minutes or until rice is tender and liquid is absorbed. Just before serving, stir in reserved toasted pecans.

Saffron Rice With Peppers

6-8 servings

- 2 cups fish or chicken broth
- 2 cups dry white wine
- 2 cups uncooked long-grain white rice
- ½ teaspoon powdered saffron
- ¼ cup olive oil
- 1 red bell pepper, cored, seeded, and chopped
- ½ cup chopped shallots
- 1 tablespoon minced garlic
- ¼ cup fresh chopped basil
- ½ teaspoon salt

Garnish:

thinly sliced red bell pepper

fresh basil leaves or fresh parsley sprigs

Add cooked shrimp and scallops for a delicious main course.

Preheat oven to 400 degrees. Lightly oil 6-cup ovenproof ring mold. In large saucepan, heat fish broth and wine to boiling over high heat. Add rice and saffron. Reduce heat to medium-low and cover. Simmer 15-20 minutes, until rice is tender and most of the liquid is absorbed, stirring occasionally.

In medium skillet, heat olive oil over medium heat. Cook bell pepper and shallots until shallots are translucent, about 5 minutes. Add garlic, chopped basil, and salt. Stir and remove from heat. Combine with rice mixture. Firmly press mixture into prepared mold. (May be prepared to this point up to 1 day in advance. Cover and chill. Bring to room temperature before proceeding.)

Bake 10 minutes. Release mold onto large serving platter by placing serving platter on top of mold and turning upside down. Garnish with bell pepper slices and basil leaves or parsley sprigs. This dish may also be prepared entirely in a saucepan, omitting the mold. After combining bell pepper mixture and rice, garnish and serve.

Rice With Fresh Vegetables

6 servings

- 1 tablespoon unsalted butter
- 1 cup chopped onion
- 1 pound zucchini, thinly sliced
- 3 cups cooked white or brown rice
- 1½ cups fresh corn kernels
- 1 medium tomato, chopped
- 1½ teaspoons salt
- ¼ teaspoon freshly ground black pepper
- ¼ teaspoon ground coriander
- ¼ teaspoon dried oregano

A light, colorful dish.

In medium saucepan, melt butter over medium heat. Add onion and zucchini and cook until tender. Add rice, corn, tomato, salt, pepper, coriander, and oregano. Cover and simmer 15 minutes.

Red Hot Rice

6-8 servings

- 2¼ cups chicken broth
- ¼ cup tomato sauce
- 2 tablespoons dry sherry
- 1 tablespoon oyster sauce
- 2 teaspoons sesame oil
- ½ teaspoon sugar
- 1 teaspoon Chinese chili sauce
- ½ teaspoon minced garlic
- 1 tablespoon peeled, finely minced fresh ginger root
- 2 tablespoons unsalted butter
- 1½ cups uncooked long-grain rice, washed and drained
- ½ cup raisins
- 5-6 dried Shiitake mushrooms, soaked in hot water for 20 minutes, stemmed, and minced
- ⅓ cup minced green onions
- ¼ cup pine nuts, toasted (page 381)

A low-fat Asian rice bursting with flavor.

In medium bowl, combine chicken broth, tomato sauce, sherry, oyster sauce, sesame oil, sugar, and chili sauce. In large saucepan, heat garlic, ginger, and butter over medium-high heat. Cook until butter sizzles, add rice, continue cooking 5 minutes, stirring constantly. Add raisins, mushrooms, and chicken broth mixture to rice mixture. Heat to boiling, stirring frequently. Reduce heat, cover, and simmer until all liquid is absorbed, 18-24 minutes. Remove cover and stir in green onions and toasted pine nuts. Serve immediately.

Indonesian Rice With Currants

4-6 servings

- 1 tablespoon unsalted butter
- ⅓ cup chopped onion
- 1 cup uncooked white rice
- 1½ cups chicken broth
- ½ cup dry white wine
- 1 teaspoon curry powder
- ⅓ cup currants

An easy, healthful, and aromatic side dish.

In medium saucepan, melt butter over medium heat. Add onion and cook 1 minute. Add rice, stir to coat, and cook about 45 seconds. Add chicken broth, wine, curry powder, and currants. Stir and heat to boiling. Reduce heat, cover, and simmer until rice is tender and liquid is absorbed, about 20 minutes. Serve immediately.

Carrot Basmati Rice Pilaf

2-3 main dish servings
4-6 side dish servings

- 1 tablespoon olive oil
- ¼ cup finely chopped shallots
- 2 tablespoons pine nuts
- 1 cup uncooked basmati rice
- 2-3 carrots, peeled and julienned, or grated
- 3 teaspoons finely grated orange zest
- ¼ teaspoon crushed or ground cardamom
- ⅛ teaspoon crushed red pepper (optional)
- 2¼ cups chicken broth, heated
- ½ teaspoon honey
- ⅛ teaspoon salt

Basmati rice is a fragrant, long-grain rice with a nut-like flavor. *Photo, page 258.*

In large saucepan, heat olive oil over medium heat. Add shallots and pine nuts. Cook 4-6 minutes. Add rice, carrots, orange zest, cardamom, and crushed red pepper, if desired. Cook 2 minutes, stirring frequently. Add warm chicken broth, honey, and salt. Cover pan tightly and simmer 12-15 minutes, until liquid is absorbed.

Fruit Curried Rice

6-8 servings

- 2¼ cups chicken broth
- 2 tablespoons soy sauce
- 2 tablespoons fresh lime juice
- 1 tablespoon curry powder
- ¾ teaspoon Chinese chili sauce
- ¼ teaspoon salt
- ½ teaspoon finely grated lime zest
- ⅓ cup unsweetened coconut milk
- 3 tablespoons unsalted butter
- 1 tablespoon peeled, minced fresh ginger root
- 1½ cups uncooked long-grain white rice, washed and drained
- ½ cup raisins
- ¼ cup slivered almonds, toasted (page 381)
- ⅓ cup minced red bell pepper
- ½ cup minced green onions
- 1½ cups diced fresh pineapple

A colorful collage of Far Eastern flavors.

In small bowl, combine chicken broth, soy sauce, lime juice, curry powder, chili sauce, salt, lime zest, and coconut milk. Stir until well blended.

In large saucepan, heat butter and ginger over medium-high heat. Cook until butter sizzles. Add rice, stir well, and cook 5 minutes. Add reserved chicken broth mixture. Heat to boiling, stirring constantly. Reduce heat to low, cover, and simmer until all liquid is absorbed, about 20 minutes. Remove cover and stir in toasted almonds, bell pepper, green onions, and pineapple. Serve immediately.

Lemon Rice With Pine Nuts

6-8 servings

- 3 cups chicken broth
- 1½ cups uncooked white rice
- 3 tablespoons butter
- 1 small onion, peeled and minced
- ¼ cup pine nuts, lightly toasted (page 381)
- ¼ cup fresh lemon juice
- 1 tablespoon fresh dill weed or 1 teaspoon dried dill weed
- 1½ teaspoons chopped fresh mint or ½ teaspoon dried mint
- salt and freshly ground black pepper

This is the perfect accompaniment to Kiva Chicken With Red Chile Glaze, page 263.

In large saucepan, heat chicken broth and rice to boiling. Reduce heat to low and cover. Simmer 15-18 minutes. Remove from heat and set aside.

In medium saucepan, melt butter over medium heat. Add onion and cook until translucent, about 5 minutes. Add reserved cooked rice, toasted pine nuts, lemon juice, dill, and mint. Season with salt and pepper to taste. Heat thoroughly. Serve immediately.

Confetti Beans With Jalapeño

10-12 servings

- 2 15-ounce cans black beans, drained and rinsed
- 1 15½-ounce can garbanzo beans, drained and rinsed
- 1 cup fresh or frozen corn kernels
- ½ large red bell pepper, cored, seeded, and finely chopped
- ½ large green bell pepper, cored, seeded, and finely chopped
- ½ large yellow bell pepper, cored, seeded, and finely chopped
- 3 ribs celery, finely chopped
- 3 green onions, finely chopped
- 2 fresh jalapeño peppers, cored, seeded, and thinly sliced
- 1 cup Italian salad dressing, homemade or purchased

Photo, page 292.

In large bowl, combine black beans, garbanzo beans, corn, bell peppers, celery, green onions, and jalapeños. Add salad dressing and toss well. Chill 6 hours. Serve as a side dish or as an appetizer with chips.

Piquant White Beans

6 servings

- 2 15-ounce cans Great Northern white beans, drained and rinsed
- ¼ cup chopped red onion
- 2 tablespoons olive oil
- ¼ cup raspberry vinegar
- freshly ground black pepper

Place beans in saucepan with water to cover. Heat to full rolling boil. Remove from heat and set aside. In small bowl, combine red onion, olive oil, and raspberry vinegar. Whisk to blend. Drain beans, toss with reserved oil mixture and season with black pepper to taste. Serve immediately.

Cinco Bean Bake

8-10 servings

- 5-6 strips bacon
- 2 medium onions, peeled and coarsely chopped
- ½ teaspoon minced garlic
- 1 15-ounce can white navy beans, drained
- 1 15-ounce can black beans, drained
- 1 15-ounce can pork and beans
- 1 15-ounce can red kidney beans, drained
- 1 15½-ounce can garbanzo beans, drained
- ¾ cup catsup
- ½ cup molasses
- ¼ cup packed brown sugar
- 1 tablespoon Worcestershire
- 1 tablespoon prepared mustard
- ¼ teaspoon freshly ground black pepper

You may substitute any variety of beans.

Preheat oven to 375 degrees. Lightly grease bean pot or large baking dish. In large skillet, cook bacon over medium heat until crisp. Remove, reserving drippings, and place on paper towel. To same skillet, add onion and garlic and cook until onion is translucent, 3-5 minutes. Remove with slotted spoon to paper towel. Crumble bacon.

In large bowl, combine bacon, onion mixture, navy beans, black beans, pork and beans, kidney beans, and garbanzo beans. Stir in catsup, molasses, brown sugar, Worcestershire, mustard, and pepper. Spoon into prepared pot. Cover and bake about 1 hour.

Cuban Black Beans

6 cups

- 1 pound dried black beans, rinsed, soaked overnight, drained, and rinsed again
- 4 ounces salt pork
- 1 small whole onion, peeled
- 2 tablespoons butter
- 1 large onion, peeled and diced
- 1 teaspoon minced garlic
- salt and freshly ground black pepper

This is a basic recipe for use with other recipes that call for black beans.

Place beans in large stockpot with enough water to cover. Add pork and whole onion and heat to boiling over high heat. Reduce heat to medium and simmer 2 hours or until beans are tender, adding more water if necessary, to keep covered. Remove from heat and discard whole onion.

In large saucepan, melt butter over medium heat. Add diced onion and garlic. Cook until translucent, about 5 minutes. Add 1 cup of the cooked beans and mash until well blended. Return mashed bean mixture to stockpot. Stir to blend and season with salt and pepper to taste.

Rum Baked Black Beans

8-10 servings

- 10 strips bacon
- 3 medium onions, finely chopped
- ½ teaspoon minced garlic
- 1¾ cups chicken broth
- 1½ cups red wine vinegar
- 1 tablespoon peeled, chopped fresh ginger root or 1 teaspoon ground ginger
- ½ teaspoon freshly ground black pepper
- 1 tablespoon dry mustard
- ½ cup honey
- ¼ cup packed brown sugar
- ¼ teaspoon ground cloves
- ½ teaspoon ground cinnamon
- 1 pound dried black beans, rinsed, soaked overnight, drained, and rinsed again
- 4 cups water
- ⅔ cup dark rum

A nice change from the traditional baked beans.

In large saucepan, cook bacon until crisp. Remove, reserving 2 tablespoons drippings. Place saucepan containing drippings over medium heat. Add onions and garlic and cook 5 minutes. Add chicken broth, vinegar, ginger, pepper, mustard, honey, brown sugar, cloves, and cinnamon. Heat to boiling, stirring frequently. Add beans and water and heat to boiling, stirring frequently. Reduce heat to low, cover, and simmer 1-2 hours, until beans are tender. Crumble bacon and chill.

Preheat oven to 325 degrees. Transfer to bean pot or baking dish with lid. Add bacon and rum and bake 2 hours. Reduce heat to 275 degrees and continue baking 4-5 hours. Remove cover and continue baking 30 minutes or until any remaining liquid evaporates and soft crust forms on top. Serve hot.

Four Corners Black Beans and Rice

4 main dish servings
6-8 side dish servings

- 2 tablespoons olive oil
- 1 medium onion, peeled and diced
- ¾ cup chopped green bell pepper
- 1 teaspoon crushed garlic
- 1½ cups peeled, seeded, and chopped tomatoes
- 2 cups Cuban Black Beans, page 309, or canned black beans, drained and rinsed
- 1 cup chicken broth
- 1 cup uncooked long-grain rice
- 1 cup water
- 1 cup dry white wine
- salt and freshly ground black pepper

Traditional pairing of rice and beans in a high-protein dish.

In large saucepan, heat olive oil over medium heat. Add onion, bell pepper, and garlic and cook about 5 minutes. Add tomatoes, beans, and chicken broth and simmer about 5 minutes, stirring frequently. Reduce heat to low, add rice, water, and wine. Cook, stirring occasionally, 15-20 minutes or until rice is tender. Season with salt and pepper to taste. Serve immediately.

Black Bean and Tortellini Casserole

6 servings

- 1 15-ounce can refried black beans with lime juice
- 8-10 ounces fresh spinach tortellini, stuffed with cheese
- ¾ cup chopped green onions
- 1 4-ounce can diced green chiles
- 1¼ cups sour cream
- ¼ cup fresh lime juice
- 2 ripe tomatoes, seeded and diced
- ½ cup chopped black olives
- 2 cups shredded Monterey Jack cheese

Garnish:

- ¼ cup chopped fresh cilantro

Serve with a green salad and tortilla chips.

Preheat oven to 350 degrees. Lightly grease 9x9-inch baking pan. Spread beans in bottom of prepared pan. Layer tortellini over beans. Sprinkle with green onions and green chiles. In small bowl, combine sour cream and lime juice and spread over green onions and green chiles. Top with tomatoes and olives. Sprinkle cheese over top, cover with foil, and bake 30 minutes. Uncover and continue baking 30 minutes, until cheese is bubbly and lightly browned. Remove from oven, cover with foil, and let stand 10 minutes. Garnish with cilantro.

Chilled Caribbean Black Beans With Shrimp

4 servings

2	15-ounce cans black beans, drained and rinsed
1	large green bell pepper, cored, seeded, and finely chopped
1	cup sliced celery
1	medium red onion, peeled, sliced, and separated into rings
¼	cup chopped fresh cilantro
1⅓	cups purchased picante sauce
½	cup fresh lime juice
¼	cup vegetable oil
¼	cup honey
¼	teaspoon salt
1	cup fresh or frozen corn kernels (optional)
3	cups water
1	pound medium shrimp in shells
	lettuce leaves
	cherry tomatoes, halved

Combine beans, bell pepper, celery, red onion, cilantro, picante sauce, lime juice, oil, honey, and salt. Add corn, if desired. Toss to blend. Cover and chill 8-10 hours. Heat water to boiling. Add shrimp and cook 3-5 minutes or until shrimp are pink. Drain and rinse with cold water. Chill 1 hour. Peel and devein. Line individual serving plates with lettuce leaves and spoon black bean mixture in center. Arrange shrimp and cherry tomatoes on top.

A creative and colorful combination.

Provençal Beans With Lamb

6-8 servings

- 2 cups dried Great Northern white beans, rinsed, soaked overnight, drained, and rinsed again
- 1 cup chopped celery
- 1 cup chopped onion
- 1 fennel bulb, cored and chopped
- ½ teaspoon dry mustard
- 1 tablespoon fresh thyme or rosemary
- 2 teaspoons salt
- ¼ cup packed brown sugar
- 1½ cups dry white wine, divided
- 2 tablespoons olive oil
- 2 teaspoons minced garlic
- 2 pounds lean lamb meat, cubed

Shoulder chop meat works well in this recipe.

In Dutch oven, combine beans, celery, onion, fennel, mustard, thyme, salt, brown sugar, and 1 cup of the wine. Add enough water to cover. Heat to boiling, cover partially, and simmer until beans are tender, about 2 hours.

Preheat oven to 325 degrees. In large skillet, heat olive oil over medium heat. Add garlic and lamb. Brown lamb on all sides and add to bean mixture. Add remaining ½ cup wine to same skillet and deglaze pan, scraping up any brown bits, and add to bean mixture. Bake 2 hours, stirring occasionally, adding more wine or water, if necessary to keep moist.

Easy Black Bean Burritos

4-8 servings

- ½ teaspoon dried minced onion
- 1 teaspoon minced garlic
- 1 15-ounce can black beans, drained and rinsed
- 1 teaspoon ground coriander
- ½ cup sour cream
- ¼ cup purchased salsa
- 8 flour tortillas
- 1 cup grated Monterey Jack cheese

Photo, page 290.

In large saucepan, combine onion, garlic, beans, coriander, sour cream, and salsa. Cook over medium heat, mashing beans with back of spoon, about 5 minutes or until thoroughly heated. Layer tortillas between paper towels and heat on high in microwave 30 seconds or until just warmed. Divide bean mixture among tortillas, sprinkle with cheese, roll up, and serve.

Pinto Bean and Chicken Burritos

4 servings

- 2 boneless, skinless chicken breast halves (about 8 ounces total), cut into ½-inch strips
- 1 tablespoon olive oil, divided
- 1 teaspoon minced garlic, divided
- freshly ground black pepper
- ½ cup chopped onion
- 1 15-ounce can pinto beans, rinsed and drained
- Tabasco
- 4 10-inch flour tortillas
- ½ cup purchased salsa, divided
- 1 cup shredded Monterey Jack cheese

Garnish:

- sour cream
- purchased salsa

In medium bowl, combine chicken strips, 2 teaspoons of the olive oil, and ½ teaspoon of the garlic. Season with pepper to taste. Chill at least 15 minutes or up to 1 hour. In medium non-stick skillet, cook chicken mixture over medium heat until thoroughly cooked, about 10 minutes. Remove and set aside.

In same skillet, heat remaining 1 teaspoon olive oil over medium-low heat. Add onion and cook until soft, stirring occasionally. Stir in remaining ½ teaspoon garlic and cook 1 minute. Stir in beans and heat thoroughly. Remove from heat and season with Tabasco to taste. Stir in reserved cooked chicken. (May be prepared to this point up to 24 hours in advance. Cover and chill.)

Preheat oven to 350 degrees. Spoon chicken mixture down center of each tortilla. Top with salsa. Roll up and place, seam side down, in baking pan. Sprinkle with cheese. Cover with foil and bake until thoroughly heated, about 15 minutes, or 30 minutes if chilled. Garnish with sour cream and salsa.

There is nothing better than gathering around a harvest fresh from the earth, with a view of the Rocky Mountains on the horizon. Our farmlands give us a bounty of fresh vegetables to serve cool and crisp or sautéed, perfect for a hay ride or a carefree country picnic.

Carefree Country Picnic

soup

Delicious Apple Soup 48

main dish

Smoked Turkey Sandwich With Apricot Mayonnaise 71

side dish

Coyote Corn 329

dessert

Mocha Brownies 368

wine

Mosel Riesling

Clockwise from top left:
Mocha Brownies
Smoked Turkey Sandwich
With Apricot Mayonnaise
Coyote Corn

Vegetables

With vegetables, we've focused on sensational taste and vibrant colors. Understanding that these dishes should complete and compliment a terrific meal, we've also made sure that they are quick and easy for the cook.

Clockwise from top:
Colorful Colorado Broccoli
Asparagus Wrapped in Prosciutto

Asparagus Wrapped in Prosciutto

4-8 servings

- 24 fresh asparagus spears, trimmed
- 4 ounces provolone cheese, cut into 8 equal pieces
- 4 paper thin slices prosciutto, halved lengthwise

Garnish:

red bell pepper, roasted (page 381) and cut into sixteen ⅛-inch strips

If using very thin asparagus spears, allow more per bundle. Photo, page 316.

Blanch asparagus in rapidly boiling water until just tender, about 1 minute. Drain, immerse in ice water to stop cooking process, and drain again. Place 1 piece of the cheese in middle of 3 asparagus spears. Wrap 1 slice of the prosciutto around asparagus and cheese bundle. Repeat process with remaining ingredients. Place bundles in microwave-safe dish and cover with plastic wrap. (May be prepared up to 4 hours in advance and chilled.)

Immediately before serving, place covered dish in microwave. Cook on high 3 minutes, or until heated thoroughly and cheese is slightly melted. Remove from microwave and carefully remove plastic wrap. Garnish each bundle with crossed roasted pepper strips and serve immediately.

Asparagus Stir-Fry

4-6 servings

- 1 pound fresh asparagus, trimmed and cut diagonally into 1-inch pieces
- 2 teaspoons vegetable oil
- ½ pound fresh mushrooms, stemmed and quartered
- 2 tablespoons dry sherry
- 5 ounces snow peas, trimmed
- ½ cup thinly sliced onion
- 2 teaspoons soy sauce
- 1 tablespoon oyster sauce
- 1 tablespoon sugar
- salt and freshly ground black pepper
- 1½ teaspoons cornstarch
- 1 tablespoon cold water

A variety of wild mushrooms may be used in this recipe. Tree oyster mushrooms are especially good.

Blanch asparagus in rapidly boiling salted water, 2 minutes. Drain, immerse in ice water, drain again, and set aside. In medium skillet, heat oil over medium heat. Add mushrooms and sherry and cook 3 minutes. Add reserved asparagus, snow peas, onion, soy sauce, oyster sauce, and sugar. Season with salt and pepper to taste and stir to combine.

Cook, stirring frequently, until vegetables are tender and heated thoroughly, about 3 minutes. In small bowl, combine cornstarch and water and add to asparagus mixture. Continue cooking until vegetables are glazed.

Cold Sesame Asparagus

6-8 servings

- 2 pounds fresh asparagus, trimmed and cut into 2-inch pieces
- 1½ tablespoons soy sauce
- 1 teaspoon sugar
- 1 tablespoon rice vinegar
- ½ teaspoon salt
- 1 tablespoon sesame oil

Excellent summer side dish.

Blanch asparagus in rapidly boiling water, until just tender, about 1 minute. Drain and immerse in ice water. Drain again, pat dry, and set aside. In large bowl, combine soy sauce, sugar, vinegar, salt, and sesame oil. No more than 1 hour before serving, add asparagus to soy sauce mixture and toss. Chill until ready to serve, at least 30 minutes.

Green Bean Sauté

4-6 servings

- 1 pound fresh green beans, trimmed and cut into 2-inch pieces
- 2 tablespoons butter
- 1 medium onion, peeled and thinly sliced
- ½ teaspoon salt
- freshly ground black pepper
- 1 tablespoon finely chopped fresh parsley
- 1 tablespoon balsamic vinegar

Cook green beans in rapidly boiling salted water until just tender, about 10 minutes. Drain, immerse in ice water, drain again, and set aside. In large skillet, melt butter over medium heat. Add onion and cook until light golden brown, about 10 minutes. Add reserved beans, salt, and pepper. Cook until thoroughly heated. Sprinkle with parsley and vinegar and toss to combine.

Cashew Green Beans

4-6 servings

- 1½ pounds fresh green beans, trimmed and cut into 1½-inch pieces
- 3 tablespoons butter
- ½ teaspoon freshly ground black pepper
- ¼ cup finely chopped fresh parsley
- 1 cup dry roasted cashews

Photo, page 226.

Cook green beans in rapidly boiling salted water until just tender, about 10 minutes. Drain, immerse in ice water, drain again, and set aside. In medium saucepan, melt butter over medium-low heat. Add pepper and parsley and stir to blend. Add reserved beans and cook until thoroughly heated. Transfer to warm serving bowl and top with cashews.

Green Bean Pepper Parmesan

4-6 servings

1 tablespoon canola oil
2 tablespoons water
1 medium yellow bell pepper, cored, seeded, and diced
¼ cup chopped onion
½ teaspoon minced garlic
1 pound fresh green beans, trimmed and cut into 1-inch pieces
1 teaspoon dried basil
¼ teaspoon salt
½ cup freshly grated Parmesan cheese, divided

In large, heavy skillet, heat canola oil over medium heat. Add water, bell pepper, onion, and garlic. Cook until onion is soft, about 3 minutes. Add beans, basil, and salt. Cover and steam until beans are just tender, about 7 minutes. Remove from heat and stir in ¼ cup of the Parmesan. Transfer to serving dish and sprinkle with remaining ¼ cup Parmesan. Serve immediately.

Colorful Colorado Broccoli

4-6 servings

1½ pounds broccoli, stemmed and broken into flowerets
1 tablespoon olive oil
1 small onion, peeled and thinly sliced
½ teaspoon minced garlic
½ cup chicken broth, divided
1 teaspoon dried basil
⅛ teaspoon cayenne
8 ounces jícama, peeled and cut into thin strips
3 Italian plum tomatoes, cut into 4-6 wedges
2 tablespoons freshly grated Parmesan cheese

Photo, page 316.

Cook broccoli in boiling salted water until just tender, 5 minutes. Drain, immerse in ice water, drain, and set aside. In heavy skillet, heat olive oil over medium heat. Add onion, garlic, and about 2 tablespoons of the chicken broth. Cook until onion is soft, about 2 minutes. Add basil, cayenne, and remaining chicken broth and cook about 2 minutes. Add reserved broccoli and jícama and cook until heated thoroughly, stirring frequently. Add tomatoes and Parmesan and toss gently to combine. Serve immediately.

Clockwise from top: Green Bean Pepper Parmesan, 321 Raspberry Carrots, 326

Easy Broccoli Soufflé

6-8 servings

- 3 tablespoons butter
- 3 tablespoons flour
- 1 cup milk
- ¾ pound broccoli, cooked and chopped
- 3 eggs
- ½ cup mayonnaise
- 4 green onions, coarsely chopped, including tops
- salt and freshly ground black pepper

Other cooked vegetables may be substituted for broccoli. Have fun experimenting.

Preheat oven to 350 degrees. In large saucepan, melt butter over medium-low heat. Cook until foamy. Sprinkle with flour and cook, stirring constantly, 3 minutes. Gradually add milk and cook, stirring constantly, until thickened.

In food processor or blender, puree cooked broccoli, eggs, mayonnaise, green onions, and reserved flour mixture. Season with salt and pepper to taste. Pour into ungreased 1-quart soufflé dish and bake 1 hour. Soufflé will puff up and brown on top. It will fall slightly when removed from oven.

Pecan Broccoli With Goat Cheese

6-8 servings

- 2 pounds broccoli, stems removed, broken into flowerets
- 1 red bell pepper, roasted (page 381), peeled, and thinly sliced
- 3 tablespoons finely chopped fresh basil
- 2 tablespoons balsamic vinegar
- 2 tablespoons olive oil
- ¼ teaspoon salt
- ¼ teaspoon freshly ground black pepper
- ¼ cup chopped pecans, toasted (page 381)
- 2 ounces goat cheese, crumbled

Pair with Chilled Tenderloin With Two Sauces, page 232, for a summer party.

Place broccoli in microwave-safe bowl and add 1 inch of water. Cover with plastic wrap. Poke several holes in plastic wrap and microwave on high 4 minutes. Carefully remove plastic wrap. Immerse broccoli in ice water and drain thoroughly. Return to bowl, add roasted peppers and basil, and toss to combine.

In small bowl, whisk vinegar, olive oil, salt, and pepper. (May be prepared to this point several hours before serving, cover and refrigerate.) Just before serving, pour vinegar mixture over the broccoli mixture and toss. Top with toasted pecans and goat cheese. Serve cold or at room temperature.

Brussels Sprouts With Pecans

4-6 servings

- ¼ teaspoon salt
- 1 pound Brussels sprouts, trimmed
- 3 tablespoons butter
- ¼ cup chopped pecans
- freshly ground black pepper

Serve with roasted chicken or turkey.

To large saucepan of boiling water, add salt and Brussels sprouts. Cover and cook until tender, about 10 minutes. Drain and place in shallow serving dish and cover to keep warm. In small saucepan, melt butter over medium heat. Cook until brown. Add pecans and toss until lightly browned. Pour over Brussels sprouts and sprinkle with pepper to taste.

Warm Caraway Cabbage

6 servings

- 1 tablespoon canola oil
- 1 16-ounce bag fresh cole slaw, or 8 cups mixed green and red shredded cabbage and carrots
- 1¼ teaspoons caraway seeds
- ⅓ cup golden raisins
- 3 tablespoons balsamic vinegar
- 2 teaspoons sugar
- ¾ cup unsweetened apple juice
- salt and freshly ground black pepper

Try with bratwurst.

In large, shallow skillet, heat canola oil over high heat. Add cabbage mixture and stir-fry until just wilted, 2-3 minutes. Add caraway seeds, raisins, vinegar, and sugar. Stir-fry 1 minute. Add apple juice and continue cooking over high heat, stirring occasionally, until most of the juice is absorbed and cabbage is cooked, about 8 minutes. Season with salt and pepper to taste. Serve immediately.

Red Cabbage With Apples

8 servings

- ½ cup water
- ½ cup red wine
- 1 head red cabbage, shredded
- 1 small bay leaf
- 1 medium onion, peeled, and studded with 4 whole cloves
- 3 tart apples, peeled, cored, and shredded
- 3 tablespoons butter
- 1 tablespoon flour
- ¼ cup packed brown sugar
- ⅓ cup apple cider vinegar
- ½ teaspoon salt
- ¼ teaspoon freshly ground black pepper
- ½ teaspoon ground allspice
- ¼ cup chopped fresh parsley

In large, heavy stockpot with tight fitting lid, heat water and wine to boiling. Add cabbage, bay leaf, and onion. Cover and cook over medium heat 10 minutes. Add apples, stir to combine, and continue cooking 10 minutes.

In small saucepan, melt butter over low heat. Sprinkle with flour and whisk until smooth. Add brown sugar, vinegar, salt, pepper, and allspice. Cook until slightly thickened. Add to cabbage mixture and toss to coat. Cook over medium heat 10 minutes. (May be prepared to this point up to 1 day in advance. Cover and chill. Reheat over low heat.) Remove bay leaf and onion. Place in serving dish and sprinkle with parsley.

Elegant Carrot Purée

4-6 servings

- 1 quart water
- ½ cup sliced onion
- ¼ cup chopped leeks, thoroughly rinsed
- 2 tablespoons diced celery
- 1 bouquet garni (1 bay leaf and 2 whole cloves tied in cheesecloth)
- 1 pound carrots, peeled and sliced into ½-inch pieces
- 2 green onions, very finely minced
- 2 tablespoons butter
- ½ cup whipping cream
- ¼ teaspoon freshly ground nutmeg
- salt and freshly ground black pepper

Serve with Crusted Pork Roast With Dijon Cider Gravy, page 242.

In large saucepan, combine water, onion, leeks, celery, and bouquet garni. Heat to boiling. Reduce heat and simmer 10-15 minutes, until vegetables are tender. Add carrots and simmer about 15 minutes, or until thickest part of carrot can be easily pierced with a fork.

Remove ½ cup of the cooking liquid and set aside. Drain carrot mixture, discarding bouquet garni. Transfer to food processor. Process, leaving some small chunks. Return processed mixture to saucepan and add green onions, butter, cream, and nutmeg. Season with salt and pepper to taste. (May be prepared to this point up to 1 day in advance. Cover and chill.) Heat thoroughly over low heat. Thin with reserved broth, if desired. Serve hot.

Raspberry Carrots

4 servings

5 carrots, peeled and cut into ¼-inch slices
2 tablespoons butter
2 tablespoons water
⅛ teaspoon salt
2 teaspoons raspberry vinegar
1 teaspoon packed brown sugar
1 tablespoon snipped fresh dill weed or tarragon

Photo, page 320.

In heavy saucepan, combine carrots, butter, water, and salt. Simmer until tender, 15-20 minutes. Add vinegar and brown sugar. Toss gently and cook over medium heat, 1-2 minutes. Place in serving dish and sprinkle with dill.

Vegetable Ribbons With Pesto

4-6 servings

3 large carrots, peeled
2 medium zucchini
2 medium yellow squash
¼ cup Basic Basil Pesto, (page 193) or purchased basil pesto
salt and freshly ground black pepper

Garnish:

fresh basil leaves

Using vegetable peeler, cut ribbon-like slices from carrots, zucchini, and yellow squash, using as much of the vegetable as possible. (Draw the peeler in lengthwise motions, as if peeling vegetables.)

To medium saucepan, add ½ inch of water. Heat to boiling. Add carrots, cover, and cook over medium heat 2-3 minutes. Add zucchini and yellow squash and continue cooking 1-2 minutes. Drain well and place in serving bowl. Add pesto and season with salt and pepper to taste. Toss to coat, garnish with basil leaves, and serve immediately.

A colorful, quick, and easy dish.

Anasazi Corn Cakes With Red Pepper Sauce

10-12 cakes

Red Pepper Sauce:

1 tablespoon butter
2 teaspoons finely chopped garlic
⅓ cup finely chopped roasted red bell pepper (page 381)
1 tablespoon flour
¼ cup vegetable or chicken broth
dash Tabasco

Anasazi Corn Cakes:

¼ cup yellow cornmeal
½ cup boiling water
2-3 cups fresh or frozen corn kernels
1-2 fresh jalapeño peppers, stemmed, seeded, and finely minced
2 green onions, finely chopped, including tops
2 eggs
¼ cup plain yogurt
½ cup flour
2 tablespoons butter, melted
¼ teaspoon salt
1 teaspoon sugar
½ teaspoon baking powder
½ teaspoon baking soda
vegetable oil spray

Garnish:

¼ cup finely chopped fresh cilantro

Try with grilled pork tenderloin or pair with Cucina Bean Salad, page 88, for a vegetarian meal.

In small saucepan, melt 1 tablespoon butter over medium heat. Add garlic and cook until soft, but not brown, about 2 minutes. Add roasted bell pepper and cook 1 minute. Sprinkle with flour and stir until well blended. Add vegetable broth and Tabasco and simmer until thickened, 3-5 minutes. (May be prepared several hours in advance and reheated over low heat.)

Preheat oven to 200 degrees. Place cornmeal in small bowl. Pour boiling water over cornmeal and set aside. In large bowl, combine corn, jalapeño, and green onions. In food processor, combine eggs, yogurt, flour, melted butter, salt, sugar, baking powder, baking soda, and reserved cornmeal mixture. Process until smooth. Pour over reserved corn mixture and stir to blend.

Spray non-stick skillet or griddle with vegetable oil spray and preheat over medium heat. Using ¼ cup batter, cook small batches, about 3 minutes per side. Remove to serving platter and place in oven to keep warm. Serve with Red Pepper Sauce and garnish with cilantro.

Vegetarian Moussaka

6 main dish servings

- 2 pounds eggplant, sliced crosswise into ½-inch slices
- ½ teaspoon salt plus additional for eggplant
- ¼ cup plus 2 tablespoons olive oil, divided
- 1 cup minced onion
- ½ teaspoon minced garlic
- 1 16-ounce can tomatoes, drained and chopped
- 2 teaspoons tomato paste
- ½ teaspoon ground cinnamon
- ¼ teaspoon dried oregano
- ¼ teaspoon ground allspice
- 2 tablespoons butter
- 2 tablespoons all purpose flour
- ¾ cup milk
- ground nutmeg
- ground white pepper
- 2 eggs, lightly beaten
- 1 cup ricotta cheese
- ⅓ cup freshly grated Parmesan cheese, divided

Serve with Spinach and Kiwi Salad, page 86.

Arrange eggplant slices in single layer on paper towels and salt generously. Let stand 30 minutes, pat dry, and set aside. In large saucepan, heat 2 tablespoons of the olive oil over medium heat. Add onion and cook until soft, 5-10 minutes. Add garlic, tomatoes, tomato paste, ½ teaspoon salt, cinnamon, oregano, and allspice. Reduce heat to low and simmer, stirring occasionally, 25 minutes.

In large saucepan, melt butter over low heat. Whisk in flour and cook, whisking constantly, 2-3 minutes. Remove from heat and gradually add milk, whisking constantly. Season with nutmeg, salt, and white pepper to taste. Return to low heat and simmer, stirring constantly, until thickened, about 3 minutes. Set aside to cool. In medium bowl, combine eggs and ricotta cheese. Gradually add to cooled milk mixture and stir until well blended.

Preheat broiler. Grease 2 baking sheets. Arrange reserved eggplant slices in single layer on prepared baking sheets. Using half of the remaining ¼ cup olive oil, brush tops of slices and broil 5-6 minutes until golden brown. Turn, brush with olive oil, and broil 5-6 minutes. Place on paper towels and set aside. Reduce oven temperature to 325 degrees. Grease 13x9x2-inch baking pan.

Spread half of the tomato mixture in prepared baking pan. Top with half of the eggplant slices and sprinkle with half of the Parmesan cheese. Cover with remaining tomato mixture and remaining eggplant slices. Spoon ricotta mixture over eggplant and sprinkle with remaining Parmesan cheese. Bake 45-50 minutes or until top is set. Let stand 30 minutes before serving.

Coyote Corn

4 servings

- 2 tablespoons butter
- 2½ cups fresh or frozen corn kernels
- 3-4 sun-dried tomatoes, soaked in hot water 15 minutes, drained, and chopped
- 3 tablespoons finely chopped fresh basil
- ⅓ cup chopped green onions, including tops
- salt and freshly ground black pepper

Photo, page 314.

In medium skillet, heat butter over medium-high heat until foam subsides. Add corn and sun-dried tomatoes and cook, stirring frequently, about 4 minutes. Place in serving bowl and add basil and green onions. Season with salt and pepper to taste. Toss to combine. Serve warm or at room temperature.

Fabulous Fennel

4-6 servings

- 3 medium fennel bulbs (about 2 pounds)
- 2 tablespoons butter
- 1 medium onion, peeled and finely chopped
- 2 medium tomatoes, seeded and chopped
- ¼ teaspoon dried thyme
- ¼ cup beef broth
- 2 teaspoons Sambuca or other anise flavored liqueur
- salt and freshly ground black pepper

This is a delectable and different side dish to serve with roasted meats.

Trim stems from fennel bulb and trim bottoms. Chop fronds from stems and reserve 2 tablespoons, discarding stems. Chop bulb and cook in boiling salted water 2-3 minutes. Drain and set aside. In medium saucepan, melt butter over medium-low heat. Add onion and cook until just browned, 5-10 minutes. Add tomatoes, thyme, beef broth, and cooked fennel. Cover and cook over low heat until tender, about 25 minutes.

Remove cover and cook until liquid evaporates, 3-5 minutes. Add Sambuca, increase heat to medium, and cook 2 minutes. Season with salt and pepper to taste. Place in serving dish and garnish with reserved chopped fennel fronds. Serve immediately.

Classic Creamed Mushrooms

6 servings

- 3 tablespoons butter, divided
- 1¼ pounds fresh mushrooms, stems trimmed, and thinly sliced
- 1 tablespoon flour
- ⅔ cup whipping cream
- 1 tablespoon sherry
- ½ teaspoon freshly ground black pepper
- ½ cup beef broth
- ¼ cup dry bread crumbs
- ¼ teaspoon dried sage, crumbled
- ¼ cup freshly grated Parmesan cheese

A rich, traditional side dish.

Preheat oven to 350 degrees. Lightly grease 6 individual ramekins or small oven-proof dishes. In medium skillet, melt 1 tablespoon of the butter over medium-low heat. Add mushrooms and cook 10 minutes, stirring frequently. Drain and set aside.

In medium saucepan, melt remaining 2 tablespoons butter over medium-low heat. Whisk in flour, cream, sherry, and pepper. Whisk until smooth. Add beef broth and whisk until well blended and smooth. Gently stir in mushrooms and remove from heat. Spoon into prepared dishes. In small bowl, combine bread crumbs, sage, and Parmesan. Sprinkle over mushroom mixture. Bake 20 minutes or until hot and bubbly.

Baked Sweet Onions

4-8 servings

- 4 large sweet onions, peeled
- 4 12-inch square pieces of foil
- ¼ cup butter (½ stick), cut into 4 equal pieces
- salt and freshly ground black pepper
- ½ cup freshly grated Parmesan cheese, divided

Walla Walla or Vidalia onions work well in this dish.

Preheat oven to 400 degrees. With sharp knife, cut onions into quarters, without cutting completely through bottoms. Place 1 onion on 1 foil square. Press 1 tablespoon of butter into cut onion, sprinkle with salt and pepper to taste, and top with 2 tablespoons of the Parmesan cheese. Crush foil around onion but do not cover top. Place in baking pan. Repeat with remaining 3 onions and bake 1 hour.

High Plains Onion Pie

4 main dish servings
6-8 side dish servings

- ¼ cup plus 2 tablespoons butter, divided
- 1 cup finely crushed crackers, such as Ritz
- 3 cups peeled, very thinly sliced yellow onion
- 2 eggs, lightly beaten
- ¾ cup milk
- 1 teaspoon salt
- freshly ground black pepper
- ½ cup shredded sharp cheddar cheese

Preheat oven to 350 degrees. Place ¼ cup of the butter in 9-inch pie plate. Place in oven to melt. Remove from oven and add cracker crumbs, mixing well with fork. With spoon, press crumbs into bottom and sides of pan to form crust. Set aside.

In large skillet, melt remaining 2 tablespoons butter over medium heat. Add onion and cook until tender, but not brown, about 10 minutes. Spread evenly in prepared crust. In medium saucepan, combine eggs, milk, salt, and pepper to taste. Cook, stirring frequently, over medium heat, until hot, but not boiling. Pour over onions and sprinkle with cheese. Bake 30-35 minutes, until cheese is lightly browned. Cut into wedges and serve immediately.

Bistro Peas With Lettuce

6-8 servings

- 3 cups shredded iceberg lettuce, divided
- 2 pounds fresh peas, shelled or two 10-ounce packages frozen peas, thawed
- ⅓ cup chopped green onions, including tops
- 1 teaspoon sugar
- ¼ teaspoon salt
- ¼ teaspoon dried ground summer savory
- ground white pepper
- 2 tablespoons butter

A French classic.

Place 1½ cups of the lettuce in large saucepan with tight fitting lid. Top with peas and green onions. Sprinkle with sugar, salt, summer savory, and white pepper to taste. Dot with butter and top with remaining 1½ cups lettuce. Cover tightly and cook over medium-low heat 5-10 minutes, until peas are tender. (Moisture to cook peas is provided by the lettuce, do not add extra liquid.) Serve immediately.

Peas With Pine Nuts

6-8 servings

- ½ cup chicken broth
- 2 green onions, thinly sliced, including tops
- 2 pounds fresh peas, shelled or two 10-ounce packages frozen peas, thawed
- 2 tablespoons butter
- ⅓ cup pine nuts
- 1 tablespoon minced fresh rosemary
- salt and freshly ground black pepper

Photo, page 194.

In medium skillet, combine chicken broth and green onions. Heat to boiling, add peas, reduce heat, and simmer 2 minutes. Remove from heat, drain, and set aside. In same skillet, melt butter over medium heat. Add pine nuts and cook, stirring frequently, 2-3 minutes, or until lightly browned. Add rosemary and cook 1 minute. Add reserved pea mixture and heat thoroughly. Season with salt and pepper to taste. Serve immediately.

Glazed Peppers With Almonds

6-8 servings

- 3 tablespoons olive oil
- ⅓ cup slivered almonds
- ⅓ cup golden raisins, soaked in warm water 20 minutes and drained
- 2 medium red bell peppers, cored, seeded, and cut into ¼-inch strips
- 1 medium yellow bell pepper, cored, seeded, and cut into ¼-inch strips
- 2 medium green bell peppers, cored, seeded, and cut into ¼-inch strips
- 2 tablespoons sugar
- 3 tablespoons red wine vinegar
- 1½ teaspoons salt

A colorful addition to plain grilled meats.

In large saucepan, heat olive oil over medium heat. Add almonds and cook, stirring occasionally, about 3 minutes or until lightly browned. Add raisins and cook 1 minute. Stir in bell peppers, sugar, vinegar, and salt. Cover and cook 20 minutes. Remove cover and cook until peppers are very tender and slightly glazed, 10-15 minutes, occasionally stirring gently. If peppers begin to stick to pan, add 1-2 tablespoons warm water. Remove from heat, and serve warm or at room temperature.

Potato and Yam Gratin

6-8 servings

- 1 tablespoon butter
- ¾ cup whipping cream
- ¾ teaspoon salt
- ¾ teaspoon ground white pepper
- dash freshly ground nutmeg
- 1 pound russet potatoes
- 1 pound yams
- ⅓ cup snipped fresh chives
- ½ cup freshly grated Parmesan cheese

Outstanding with lamb or pork.

Preheat oven to 350 degrees. Butter 8x8x2-inch baking pan. In small bowl, combine cream, salt, white pepper, and nutmeg. Set aside. Peel potatoes and yams and slice very thinly. (A mandoline or food processor works well. Place potatoes in ice water to prevent discoloration. Drain and pat dry before assembling.)

Cover bottom of prepared pan with single layer of potatoes, slightly overlapping slices. Drizzle lightly with cream mixture. Cover with single layer of yams, slightly overlapping slices. Drizzle lightly with cream mixture. Sprinkle with chives and Parmesan. Repeat layering with remaining ingredients, ending with Parmesan. Cover pan with foil, dull side out. Bake 30 minutes. Remove foil and continue baking 30-45 minutes, until cheese is browned and potatoes are tender when pierced with fork.

Savory Roasted New Potatoes

6-8 servings

- 16 small red new potatoes, cut into large bite size pieces
- 1 teaspoon minced fresh garlic
- ½ teaspoon paprika (hot variety, if available)
- 2 tablespoons minced fresh rosemary
- ½ teaspoon salt
- ¼ teaspoon freshly ground black pepper
- 1 tablespoon Worcestershire
- ¼ cup olive oil

Photo, page 194.

Preheat oven to 375 degrees. Place potatoes in large baking pan and sprinkle with garlic, paprika, rosemary, salt, and pepper. Toss to combine.

In small bowl, combine Worcestershire and olive oil and drizzle over potatoes. Toss to coat. Bake in lower half of oven, stirring occasionally, 45-55 minutes or until browned and tender.

Heavenly Potatoes

6-8 servings

- 3 pounds russet potatoes, pricked with fork
- ¼ cup (½ stick) butter, softened
- ½ cup milk
- ¾ cup whipping cream
- 3 ounces Gruyère cheese, grated
- 3 tablespoons freshly grated Parmesan cheese

Garnish:

chopped fresh parsley

Photo, page 226.

Preheat oven to 400 degrees. Place potatoes directly on oven rack and bake 45-60 minutes, or until easily pierced with fork. Remove from oven, cool slightly, and halve lengthwise. Grease 13x9x2-inch or 3-quart baking pan. Scrape out potato flesh. Discard peels or reserve for another use. Mash potato flesh with electric mixer or hand masher until smooth. Add butter and milk and stir until blended. Spread in prepared pan.

Increase oven temperature to 500 degrees. With electric mixer, whip cream to soft peaks and fold in Gruyère by hand. Spread evenly over potatoes and sprinkle with Parmesan. Bake until heated thoroughly and topping is golden brown, about 10 minutes. Garnish with parsley and serve warm.

Herb Roasted Vegetables

8 servings

- 1 butternut squash, peeled and cut into 2-inch pieces
- 1 pound fresh green beans, trimmed and halved
- 1 pound fresh mushrooms, quartered
- 2 medium leeks, cut into 2-inch pieces and rinsed thoroughly
- 1 medium red bell pepper, cored, seeded, and cut into eighths
- 1 large onion, peeled and coarsely chopped, or 2 cups pearl onions, peeled
- 1 pound new potatoes, quartered
- ⅓ cup canola oil
- ¼ cup chopped fresh rosemary
- ¼ cup chopped fresh sage
- salt and freshly ground black pepper

Excellent served with roasts, steak, game, or salmon.

Preheat oven to 425 degrees. In large, heavy roasting pan combine squash, green beans, mushrooms, leeks, bell peppers, onion, and potatoes. (Any combination of vegetables may be substituted.) Add canola oil, rosemary, and sage. Season with salt and pepper to taste and toss to coat. Roast 1-1½ hours, stirring every 20 minutes.

Mashed Potatoes With Carrots and Chiles

8-10 servings

- 20 cloves garlic, unpeeled
- 2 pounds russet potatoes, peeled, if desired, and quartered
- 1½ pounds red potatoes, peeled, if desired, and quartered
- 3 large carrots, peeled and cut into ¾-inch pieces
- 1 3-ounce package cream cheese, softened
- ½ cup sour cream
- ⅓ cup milk
- 1 4-ounce can chopped green chiles, drained or 1 fresh Anaheim chile, cored, seeded, and diced
- 1 teaspoon salt
- 2-3 tablespoons butter, divided
- dash Tabasco

Garlic becomes smooth and mellow when cooked. Serve with Grilled Onion Flank Steak, page 235.

In medium saucepan, simmer garlic cloves, in water to cover, 30 minutes. Drain, cool slightly, and press garlic out of peels, discarding peels. Set aside. Grease 13x9x2-inch or 3-quart baking pan, if desired.

In large stockpot, steam potatoes and carrots over boiling water 20-25 minutes, or until potatoes and carrots are tender when pierced with fork. Drain, and beat with electric mixer or hand masher until well mashed. Add cooked, peeled garlic, cream cheese, sour cream, milk, green chiles, salt, 2 tablespoons of the butter, and Tabasco sauce. Beat until smooth and fluffy (there will be chunks of carrot in the mixture).

Serve immediately or transfer to prepared pan and dot with the remaining 1 tablespoon butter. Cover with foil. (May be prepared to this point several hours in advance and chilled.) Preheat oven to 350 degrees and bake 30 minutes. Remove foil and continue baking 25 minutes or until heated thoroughly.

Oriental Spinach

4 servings

- 1 tablespoon olive oil
- 1 tablespoon butter
- 1 teaspoon minced garlic
- 1 teaspoon peeled, grated fresh ginger root
- 4 cups (about ¾ pound) fresh spinach, stemmed
- 1 tablespoon soy sauce
- 1 tablespoon dry sherry
- 1 teaspoon sugar

A simple, last minute preparation.

In large skillet, heat olive oil and butter over medium heat. Add garlic and ginger and cook 30 seconds. Increase heat to high and add spinach. Stir and turn spinach quickly until coated and begins to wilt, about 2 minutes. Sprinkle with soy sauce, sherry, and sugar. Cook, stirring constantly, 1 minute. Serve immediately.

Winter Squash With Sausage

4 servings

- 2 large acorn squash, halved and seeded
- 2 tablespoons canola oil
- ½ medium onion, peeled and chopped
- 1 cup sliced fresh mushrooms
- ¼ cup chopped red bell pepper
- 1 teaspoon minced garlic
- 1 pound turkey Italian sausage
- 1 slice Italian bread, cubed (about 1 ounce)
- freshly ground black pepper
- 2 tablespoons freshly grated Parmesan cheese, divided

Serve with a green salad for a complete family meal.

Place squash halves, cut side down, in microwave-safe dish and add ¼ inch of water. Cover with plastic wrap and cook on high, 15-20 minutes or until tender when pierced with fork. (May also be baked in 350 degree oven, 50-60 minutes.)

In large skillet, heat canola oil over medium heat. Add onion and mushrooms and cook 5 minutes. Add bell pepper and garlic and cook 1 minute. Remove from skillet with slotted spoon and drain on paper towels. Discard drippings.

In same skillet, brown and crumble sausage over medium-high heat. Drain, add onion mixture and bread cubes, and season with pepper to taste. Reduce heat to medium and cook 3 minutes, stirring occasionally. Remove squash from microwave, carefully remove plastic wrap, and turn squash cut sides up. Spoon one quarter of the sausage mixture into each squash half, and top with Parmesan. Serve immediately.

Autumn Acorn Squash

4 servings

- 2 medium acorn squash, halved and seeded
- salt and freshly ground black pepper
- 1 cup unsweetened applesauce, divided
- ¼ cup raisins, divided
- 4 teaspoons butter, divided
- 4 teaspoons packed dark brown sugar, divided
- ground cinnamon

A simple, old-fashioned favorite.

Preheat oven to 350 degrees. Season squash with salt and pepper to taste. Place, cut side down, in baking pan. Bake 50-60 minutes or until tender when pierced with fork. Remove from oven and turn squash halves right side up.

In center of each squash, place one quarter each of the applesauce, raisins, butter, and brown sugar. Stir to blend slightly. Return to oven and bake 10-12 minutes to heat filling ingredients. Remove from oven, sprinkle with cinnamon to taste, and serve immediately.

Spectacular Spaghetti Squash

3-4 main dish servings
6-8 side dish servings

- 1 spaghetti squash (3-4 pounds)
- 2 tablespoons olive oil
- 1 tablespoon butter
- 8 ounces fresh mushrooms, sliced
- 2 medium ripe tomatoes, chopped
- 1 medium zucchini, cut into ¼-inch slices
- 5-6 green onions, chopped, including tops
- 1 teaspoon minced garlic
- 1 medium red bell pepper, cored, seeded, and cut into ⅛-inch strips
- ¼ pound fresh snow peas, trimmed
- ¾ cup freshly grated Parmesan cheese

Preheat oven to 350 degrees. Bake whole squash 1 hour or until tender when pierced with fork. Remove from oven and allow to cool 5-10 minutes. Halve lengthwise and remove seeds. With a fork, pull out spaghetti-like strands and place in large serving bowl. Set aside.

In large skillet, heat olive oil and butter over medium heat. Add mushrooms, tomatoes, zucchini, green onions, garlic, bell pepper, and snow peas. Cook until soft, 4-5 minutes. Pour over squash and toss to combine. Sprinkle with Parmesan and serve immediately.

Spaghetti Squash Curry

6-8 servings

- 1 spaghetti squash (3-4 pounds)
- 1 teaspoon cumin seed
- 1 teaspoon curry powder
- 1 cup plain yogurt
- ½ cup sour cream
- 2 tablespoons packed dark brown sugar
- 2 tablespoons chopped fresh mint
- 2 tablespoons chopped fresh basil
- 1 teaspoon salt
- ½ cup chopped pecans, toasted (page 381)
- freshly ground black pepper

Unique and delicious.

Preheat oven to 350 degrees. Bake whole squash 1 hour or until tender when pierced with fork. Remove from oven and allow to cool 5-10 minutes. Halve lengthwise and remove seeds. With fork, pull out the spaghetti-like strands. Divide in half and place in 2 bowls. Set aside. Reduce oven temperature to 325 degrees.

In small skillet, heat cumin seed over medium heat, stirring constantly, 2 minutes. Add curry powder and heat 1 minute. Pour over half of the squash. Add yogurt, sour cream, brown sugar, mint, basil, and salt. Toss to combine. Mound mixture in center of oven-proof serving platter. Surround with remaining half of the squash and garnish with toasted pecans. Sprinkle with pepper to taste. Bake until thoroughly heated, 10-12 minutes. Serve immediately.

Sautéed Swiss Chard With Cream

6 servings

- 2 tablespoons butter
- 3 green onions, minced, including tops
- 2 pounds Swiss chard, stemmed, and cut crosswise into 1-inch strips
- ½ cup whipping cream
- salt and freshly ground black pepper
- freshly ground nutmeg
- ½ cup freshly grated Parmesan cheese

A member of the beet family which is available in two varieties, green and red.

In large skillet, melt butter over medium heat. Add green onions and cook until soft, about 3 minutes. Add Swiss chard and cook until wilted, about 1 minute. Add cream, increase heat to medium-high and cook, stirring frequently, until cream reduces and thickens. Season with salt, pepper, and nutmeg to taste. Stir in Parmesan and serve immediately.

Tabernash Baked Tomatoes

6 servings

3 medium firm ripe tomatoes, halved
6 teaspoons dry sherry, divided
salt and freshly ground black pepper
2 ounces cream cheese, softened
¼ cup mayonnaise
¼ cup freshly grated Parmesan cheese
2 tablespoons chopped fresh dill weed

Preheat oven to 350 degrees. Place tomatoes, cut side up, in baking pan. Using a fork, pierce top surfaces. Pour 1 teaspoon of the sherry over each tomato half and sprinkle with salt and pepper to taste. Bake15 minutes. In bowl, combine cream cheese, mayonnaise, and Parmesan and stir until well blended. Remove tomatoes from oven. Just before serving, place 1-2 tablespoons of the cheese mixture on top of each tomato half. Sprinkle with dill and serve warm.

Tossed Cherry Tomatoes

4-6 servings

1 tablespoon butter
1 teaspoon crushed garlic
⅓ cup slivered almonds
1 pint fresh cherry tomatoes, any variety
2 tablespoons chopped fresh basil

In medium skillet with lid, melt butter over medium heat. Add garlic and almonds and cook until golden brown, about 3 minutes. Remove from heat and allow to cool 15-20 minutes. Add cherry tomatoes, cover, and set aside. Just before serving, remove cover and place over high heat. Shake skillet vigorously, about 30 seconds or until heated thoroughly, but not mushy. Do not overcook. Add basil and serve immediately.

Simple and delicious.

In the summer, our ski slopes are transformed into meadows of cascading wildflowers, and become hosts for Colorado's renowned music festivals. Lie back, bask in the sun, listen to a classical prelude and have a grand finale of Bittersweet Chocolate Torte.

Grand Finale

desserts

wine

Cremant Sparkling Wine

Clockwise from top left:
Raspberry Hazelnut Torte
White Chocolate Mousse in Cookie Cups
Bittersweet Chocolate Torte

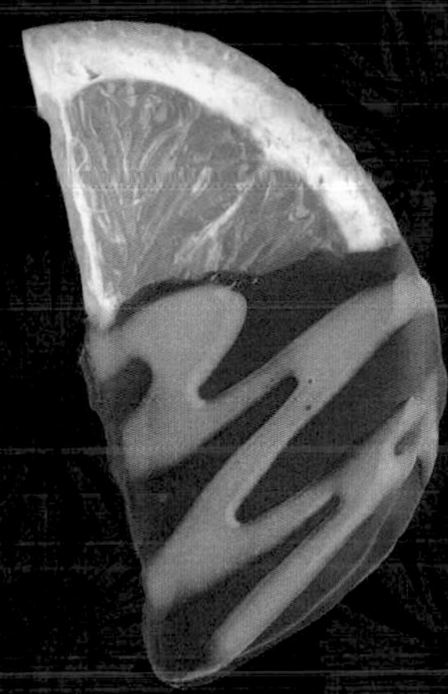

Desserts

This sampler of irresistible desserts will delight both the palate and the eye. You'll find elegant show-stoppers, new twists on old-fashioned favorites, plus some special coffees to finish your evening.

Clockwise from top:
Chocolate Raspberry Tart
Plum Almond Tartlets

Bittersweet Chocolate Torte

10-12 servings

- 8 ounces bittersweet or semisweet chocolate, chopped
- ¾ cup (1½ sticks) unsalted butter, softened
- ¾ cup sugar
- 7 eggs, separated, at room temperature
- 1½ cups ground nuts, such as almonds, walnuts, toasted hazelnuts, or pecans
- 2 cups Chocolate Ganache (recipe below), warmed

Garnish:

- 1 cup finely chopped nuts (optional)
- 1½ cups powdered sugar
- 1 egg yolk
- 3-4 drops lemon juice

The ultimate classic. Photo, page 340.

Preheat oven to 350 degrees. Grease 10-inch springform pan (with 3-inch sides). Line bottom of pan with parchment or waxed paper. Butter paper and dust with flour, tapping to cover. Discard excess flour.

In top of double boiler, over simmering water, melt chocolate until smooth. Remove from heat and let cool slightly. In large bowl, cream butter and sugar until light and fluffy. Add egg yolks, 1 at a time, blending well after each addition. Beat in cooled chocolate and 1½ cups ground nuts.

In separate large bowl, beat egg whites until stiff and glossy but not dry. Using rubber spatula, gently, but thoroughly, fold egg whites into chocolate mixture. Pour into prepared pan and smooth top.

Bake until the top puffs and crust forms, 40-50 minutes. Do not overbake. Cool in pan 15 minutes. Turn out onto wire rack and cool thoroughly. Peel off paper. Transfer to serving plate and spread warmed Chocolate Ganache over top and sides.

Garnish with 1 cup finely chopped nuts, if desired, pressing into sides. In small bowl, combine powdered sugar, egg yolk, and lemon juice. Stir until smooth and transfer to pastry bag, fitted with very narrow tip. Pipe a spiral pattern on top of torte. Using a thin-bladed knife, drag 8 equidistant lines from center to outside edge. Repeat between each line, dragging the opposite direction.

Chocolate Ganache

2 cups

- 1 cup whipping cream
- 10 ounces semisweet or bittersweet chocolate, chopped
- 1-2 tablespoons Grand Marnier or other orange flavored liqueur

May be served warm as a sauce over many desserts.

In saucepan, scald cream by heating to just below boiling (indicated by small bubbles forming around edges). Remove from heat and gently stir in chocolate. Stir until smooth and chocolate is thoroughly melted. Stir in Grand Marnier. Cool to room temperature.

Raspberry Hazelnut Torte

12 servings

Meringue Layers:

8 egg whites, at room temperature
¼ teaspoon cream of tartar
¼ teaspoon salt
2 teaspoons white vinegar
2 cups sugar
2 cups finely ground hazelnuts or almonds
2 teaspoons Frangelico or other hazelnut flavored liqueur

Filling:

2 cups whipping cream
2 tablespoons powdered sugar
1 teaspoon Frangelico or other hazelnut flavored liqueur
1 pint fresh raspberries (about 1½ cups)

Garnish:

fresh raspberries
powdered sugar

Prepare this show-stopping dessert for a special occasion. Photo, page 340.

Preheat oven to 325 degrees. Grease two 9-inch springform pans. Line bottoms with parchment paper. Grease and flour parchment paper and sides of pans. In large bowl, beat egg whites, cream of tartar, and salt until soft peaks form. Add vinegar. Gradually add sugar and continue beating 5-6 minutes until mixture holds stiff peaks and is glossy. Fold in nuts and 2 teaspoons Frangelico. Spread half of the mixture evenly into each of the prepared pans.

Bake 1½ hours, until lightly browned and pulls away slightly from edge of pan. Remove from oven and cool thoroughly on rack. (Meringue will fall in center as it cools. Sides may be slightly crumbly.) Run wet knife around edge to loosen meringues. Remove from pans and carefully remove parchment paper.

In small bowl, whip cream to soft peaks. Add powdered sugar and 1 teaspoon Frangelico. Beat to blend. Place 1 of the meringue shells, right side up, on serving plate. Remove ½ cup of the whipped cream mixture and reserve for garnish. Fill meringue with half of the remaining whipped cream mixture and top with raspberries. Spoon remaining half of the whipped cream mixture over raspberries. Place remaining meringue, upside down, on top of whipped cream mixture. Garnish top with fresh raspberries and reserved whipped cream. Sift powdered sugar over torte and plate. Chill 4-6 hours to allow meringue to soften. Cut with a serrated knife.

Crème Brûlée With Chocolate

4 servings

- 5 egg yolks
- ½ cup plus 2 tablespoons sugar, divided
- 2 cups whipping cream
- 1 tablespoon pure vanilla extract
- 2 ounces semisweet chocolate, chopped, divided

A delicious and easy make ahead dessert!

Preheat oven to 300 degrees. In large bowl, whisk egg yolks and ½ cup of the sugar. In small, heavy saucepan, heat cream to simmering over low heat. Add to yolk mixture, whisking constantly. Add vanilla, whisk to blend, and set aside.

Divide chocolate among four ¾-cup custard dishes or ramekins. Ladle cream mixture over chocolate. Place cups in baking pan and add enough hot water to pan to come halfway up sides of cups. Bake until just set in center, about 55 minutes. Remove cups from water and cool. Cover and chill overnight.

Preheat broiler. Sprinkle ½ tablespoon sugar over top of each chilled mixture. Broil, watching carefully, until sugar melts and browns slightly, about 2 minutes. Cool 5 minutes before serving.

Grand Marnier Flan

6 servings

- ¾ cup sugar
- 3 tablespoons Grand Marnier or other orange flavored liqueur
- 3 eggs
- 3 egg yolks
- 2 teaspoons pure vanilla extract
- 1 14-ounce can sweetened condensed milk
- 1¾ cups milk
- 2 ounces cream cheese, softened

The silky texture of this flan is out of this world.

Preheat oven to 350 degrees. Please refer to page 381 for special information about making caramel before proceeding with recipe. In medium saucepan, combine sugar and Grand Marnier over medium heat. Cook, stirring constantly, until sugar dissolves. Continue cooking, swirling occasionally, until light golden brown. Pour into 9-inch flan pan or 1-quart mold. Quickly tip pan to spread caramel evenly over bottom.

In blender or food processor, combine eggs, egg yolks, vanilla, condensed milk, milk, and cream cheese. Pour over caramel mixture. Place flan pan in large baking pan. Add enough boiling water to come halfway up sides of flan pan.

Bake, in center of oven, 45-50 minutes or until knife inserted in center comes out clean. Cool, upright on rack, to room temperature. Cover with plastic wrap and chill 4 hours or up to 2 days. Run knife along inside edge of pan. Place serving plate face down over pan and invert to release flan.

Chocolate Caramel Walnut Tart

10 servings

Pastry:

- 1⅓ cups flour
- 1 tablespoon plus 1 teaspoon sugar
- ¼ teaspoon salt
- ¾ cup (1½ sticks) unsalted butter, chilled and cut into ½-inch pieces
- ¼ cup very cold water (or more)

Filling:

- 1 cup whipping cream
- 1⅓ cups sugar
- ⅓ cup water
- 1 egg
- 1 egg yolk
- 1½ teaspoons pure vanilla extract
- ¼ cup (½ stick) unsalted butter, melted
- 1⅔ cups chopped walnuts, lightly toasted (page 381)
- 1 cup semisweet chocolate chips

A rich and impressive finale. Photo, page 374.

Sift flour, sugar, and salt into large bowl. Cut in ¾ cup butter with pastry cutter or 2 knives until mixture resembles coarse meal. Sprinkle with cold water and mix quickly with fork until dough just holds together, adding more water if necessary. (May be prepared in food processor.) Form into disk, sprinkle with flour, and wrap tightly with plastic wrap. Chill 30 minutes.

Preheat oven to 375 degrees. Grease 11-inch tart pan with removable bottom. Roll out chilled pastry on lightly floured surface to ⅛-inch thickness. Gently press dough into bottom and sides of prepared pan and trim excess dough from edges. Line pastry with foil and fill with pie weights or dried beans. Bake 7-8 minutes, remove weights and foil, and continue baking until browned, 15-20 minutes. Remove from oven and cool on rack. Increase oven temperature to 400 degrees.

Please refer to page 381 for special information about making caramel before proceeding with recipe. In small saucepan, scald cream by heating to almost boiling. Remove from heat and cover to keep warm. In large, heavy saucepan, combine sugar and water and cook over low heat until sugar dissolves, swirling pan occasionally. Increase heat to medium-high, and heat to boiling. Continue cooking until mixture is light golden brown, stirring occasionally. Remove from heat. Carefully and gradually whisk in hot cream. Mixture will bubble. Return to medium-low heat and cook 3 minutes. Remove from heat and cool 15 minutes.

In small bowl, whisk egg and egg yolk to blend, add to cooled caramel mixture, whisking to blend. Stir in vanilla, ¼ cup melted butter, and walnuts. In top of double boiler, melt chocolate over simmering water, stirring frequently to prevent burning. Pour about half of the melted chocolate into prepared pastry, forming a thin coating on bottom. Let stand 5 minutes to set. Pour reserved walnut mixture evenly over chocolate. Place tart on large baking sheet and bake 15 minutes. Reduce oven temperature to 375 degrees and continue baking 15 minutes. Remove from oven and cool on rack about 30 minutes.

Warm any remaining chocolate and spoon into pastry bag fitted with small writing tip or paper cone. Pipe over surface of tart, forming lacy pattern. Serve at room temperature.

Almond Tart

8-10 servings

Pastry:

1 cup flour
1 tablespoon sugar
pinch salt
½ cup (1 stick) unsalted butter, softened
1 tablespoon pure vanilla extract
1½ teaspoons water

Filling:

¾ cup sugar
¾ cup whipping cream
1 tablespoon Grand Marnier or other orange flavored liqueur
½ teaspoon pure almond extract
pinch salt
1 cup sliced almonds

A delicious tart, ideal for the novice baker.

Preheat oven to 400 degrees. Lightly grease 9-inch tart pan with removable bottom. In food processor, combine flour, sugar, salt, and butter. Pulse until mixture resembles coarse meal. In small bowl, combine vanilla and water. With processor running, gradually add vanilla mixture to flour mixture. Process until dough just comes together. Press into prepared tart pan. Bake until set and lightly browned, about 10 minutes. Remove from oven and reduce oven temperature to 350 degrees.

In small bowl, combine sugar, cream, Grand Marnier, almond extract, and salt. Beat with fork until slightly thickened. Stir in almonds and mix well. Turn into prepared crust. Bake until the top forms a crust similar to pecan pie, 45-55 minutes. Remove from oven and cool thoroughly before serving.

Purple Plum Tart

8 servings

Pastry:

1 cup flour
¼ cup powdered sugar
6 tablespoons (¾ stick) unsalted butter, chilled and cut into pieces
2-3 tablespoons whipping cream, chilled

Almond Filling:

½ cup plus 1-2 tablespoons sugar
¼ cup (½ stick) unsalted butter, softened
¾ cup blanched slivered almonds, toasted (page 381), and ground
2 tablespoons flour
1 egg
1½ teaspoons brandy
4-5 medium purple or red plums (about 1 pound), pitted and thinly sliced

An easy and impressive summertime dessert.

In food processor, combine 1 cup flour and powdered sugar. Add 6 tablespoons butter and pulse until mixture resembles coarse meal. Gradually add cream and process until moist clumps form. Gather dough and press to form a flat disk. Wrap tightly in plastic wrap and chill 30 minutes.

Preheat oven to 350 degrees. Roll out chilled dough on lightly floured surface to 11-inch circle. Transfer to 9-inch tart pan with removable bottom. Press gently into bottom and sides, allowing dough to extend above edge of pan. Fold edges over to form double thick sides. (May be prepared to this point up to 1 day in advance. Cover tightly with plastic wrap and chill.)

Line pastry with foil and fill with pie weights or dried beans. Bake until edges are slightly browned, 10-15 minutes. Remove pie weights and foil and continue baking 5 minutes, until golden brown. Remove from oven and cool on rack, leaving oven on.

In medium bowl, beat ½ cup of the sugar and ¼ cup butter until smooth. Blend in ground nuts and 2 tablespoons flour. Add egg and brandy and blend well. Spread evenly over cooled crust. Place plum slices, slightly overlapping edges, in concentric circles over filling, covering thoroughly. Sprinkle with the remaining 1-2 tablespoons sugar. Bake about 50 minutes, until filling is set and top is lightly browned. Plums should be tender. Remove from oven and cool on rack. Serve warm or at room temperature.

Chocolate Raspberry Tart

8 servings

Crust:

- 1¼ cups flour
- 1½ tablespoons sugar
- pinch salt (optional)
- ½ cup (1 stick) unsalted butter, well chilled or frozen 30 minutes
- 1 egg yolk, lightly beaten
- 2 tablespoons very cold water

Chocolate Filling:

- ½ cup (1 stick) unsalted butter
- 4 ounces semisweet chocolate, coarsely chopped
- ¾ cup sugar
- 2 eggs
- 1 egg yolk
- ½ teaspoon pure vanilla extract
- ¼ cup half and half

Topping:

- ¼ cup seedless raspberry jam , melted
- 1 pint fresh raspberries, rinsed and drained

Photo, page 342.

Preheat oven to 375 degrees. Grease 9-inch tart pan with removable bottom. In food processor, combine flour, 1½ tablespoons sugar, and salt, if desired. Add ½ cup butter and process until mixture resembles coarse meal. Combine egg yolk and water. Gradually add to flour mixture and process until dough just holds together.

Press dough into flat disk and wrap tightly in plastic wrap. Chill 30 minutes. Using floured rolling pin, roll out on floured surface. Press into bottom and sides of prepared pan. Line crust with foil and fill with pie weights or dried beans. Bake until edges are slightly browned, 10-15 minutes. Remove pie weights and foil, and continue baking 5 minutes, until golden brown. Remove from oven and cool on rack. Reduce oven temperature to 350 degrees.

In heavy saucepan, melt ½ cup butter and chocolate over low heat. Add ¾ cup sugar, eggs, egg yolk, and vanilla and stir until smooth. Remove from heat. Stir in half and half and pour into prepared pastry. Bake 25-30 minutes or until center is nearly set when shaken. Remove from oven and cool on rack, to room temperature. Remove from pan. Using small brush, spread half of the melted jam over top of tart. Carefully arrange fresh raspberries over jam and drizzle with remaining melted jam. Serve at room temperature or chilled.

Strawberry Dream Tart

8-10 servings

Crust:

1¼ cups flour
1½ tablespoons sugar
pinch salt (optional)
½ cup (1 stick) unsalted butter, well chilled or frozen 30 minutes
1 egg yolk, lightly beaten
2 tablespoons very cold water

Lemon Cream Cheese Filling:

1 3-ounce package cream cheese, softened
1 tablespoon fresh lemon juice
1 teaspoon grated lemon zest
¾ cup sugar
1 cup whipping cream
½ pound fresh strawberries, sliced
1 pound whole fresh strawberries, stemmed
¼ cup currant jelly
1 tablespoon triple sec or Grand Marnier

This is even better than strawberry shortcake.

Preheat oven to 375 degrees. Grease 9-inch tart pan with removable bottom. In food processor, combine flour, 1½ tablespoons sugar, and salt, if desired. Add butter and process until mixture resembles coarse meal. Combine egg yolk and water. Gradually add to flour mixture and process until dough just holds together.

Press dough into flat disk and wrap tightly in plastic wrap. Chill 30 minutes. Using floured rolling pin, roll out on floured surface. Press into bottom and sides of prepared pan. Line crust with foil and fill with pie weights or dried beans. Bake until edges are slightly browned, 15-18 minutes. Remove pie weights and foil and continue baking 5-8 minutes, until golden brown. Remove from oven and cool on rack.

In food processor, process cream cheese until fluffy. Add lemon juice, lemon zest, and ¾ cup sugar. Process until smooth, scraping down sides of bowl as necessary. In medium bowl, whip cream to soft peaks. Fold cream cheese mixture into whipped cream. Place half into prepared pastry. Layer sliced strawberries over cream mixture and cover with remaining half of the cream mixture. Arrange whole strawberries, pointed ends up, over entire tart.

In small saucepan, melt jelly over low heat and stir in triple sec. Remove from heat and let cool about 5 minutes, stirring occasionally to prevent film from forming. Spoon or brush jelly mixture over strawberries and chill 3-5 hours.

Frozen Pumpkin Praline Torte

12 servings

- 1 quart praline ice cream, slightly softened
- 1 16-ounce can cooked pumpkin
- 2 cups sugar
- 2½ teaspoons ground cinnamon
- 2 teaspoons ground nutmeg
- ½ teaspoon salt
- 2 cups whipping cream, divided
- ¼ cup packed light brown sugar
- 2 tablespoons unsalted butter
- 1 tablespoon water
- 10 pecan halves
- ½ cup chopped pecans

A terrific alternative to pumpkin pie.

Place 8-inch springform pan in freezer at least 30 minutes. Quickly spoon ice cream into chilled pan, pressing into bottom and sides. Place 2 large pieces of plastic wrap, in a criss-cross pattern, over ice-cream. Press plastic wrap gently against ice cream to form ½-inch thick shell. Freeze about 2 hours, until firm.

In medium saucepan, combine pumpkin, sugar, cinnamon, nutmeg, and salt over medium-high heat. Heat to boiling, stirring constantly. Remove from heat and transfer to large bowl. Chill 1 hour until thoroughly cool.

In bowl, whip 1½ cups of the cream to soft peaks. Fold into cooled pumpkin mixture. Remove ice cream shell from freezer and remove plastic wrap. Spread pumpkin mixture evenly over crust. Cover with plastic wrap and freeze 3 hours or up to overnight.

Just before serving, combine brown sugar, butter, and water in small saucepan. Heat to boiling over medium-high heat, stirring constantly. Cook 2-3 minutes or until thickened and golden brown. Remove from heat and stir in pecan halves. Set aside to cool. Whip remaining ½ cup cream to soft peaks.

Remove torte from freezer. Place on round serving platter, and remove sides of pan. Using pastry bag, pipe whipped cream around bottom edge of torte. Garnish top with dollops of whipped cream and sprinkle with chopped pecans. Arrange glazed pecan halves around the top edge. Keep frozen until ready to serve. (May be prepared 1-2 days in advance.)

Frozen Berry and White Chocolate Terrine

6-8 servings

- 16 ounces frozen raspberries, thawed
- 1 cup sugar, divided
- 1 tablespoon crème de cassis or other berry flavored liqueur
- ½ teaspoon fresh lemon juice
- ¼ cup water
- 6 egg yolks
- 4 ounces imported white chocolate
- 2 teaspoons pure vanilla extract
- 1⅔ cups whipping cream, chilled

Sauce:

- 8 ounces frozen raspberries, thawed
- 2 tablespoons sugar
- 1 tablespoon crème de cassis or other berry flavored liqueur

Garnish:

- white chocolate curls
- fresh raspberries or blackberries
- fresh mint leaves

This is also gorgeous made with frozen blackberries. *Photo, page 374.*

Line 9x5-inch loaf pan with 2 pieces of plastic wrap, criss-crossed. In food processor or blender, combine 16 ounces raspberries and ¼ cup of the sugar. Puree and strain. Measure 1⅓ cups strained puree and place in small, heavy saucepan, reserving any remaining puree for sauce. Cook over medium heat, stirring occasionally, until reduced to about 1 cup, about 8 minutes. Transfer to bowl and chill 30 minutes. Stir in 1 tablespoon crème de cassis and lemon juice and chill.

In medium metal bowl, combine remaining ¾ cup sugar, water, and egg yolks. Set bowl over saucepan of simmering water. Cook until mixture reaches 140 degrees on candy thermometer, whisking constantly. Continue cooking 3 minutes, scraping down sides of bowl occasionally and whisking constantly. Remove bowl from saucepan. Melt white chocolate in microwave, watching carefully as it scorches easily. Add to egg yolk mixture, add vanilla, and beat until cool.

In large bowl, whip cream to stiff peaks. Gently mix a quarter of the whipped cream into cooled white chocolate mixture and fold in remaining whipped cream. Remove raspberry puree from refrigerator. Transfer 1½ cups of the reserved white chocolate mixture to medium bowl and fold in puree. Pour a third of the remaining white chocolate mixture into prepared loaf pan. Cover with raspberry mixture. Top with remaining white chocolate mixture, spreading evenly. Fold plastic wrap over to cover and freeze overnight or up to 2 days.

In food processor or blender, puree 8 ounces raspberries, 2 tablespoons sugar, and 1 tablespoon crème de cassis. Strain to remove as many seeds as possible. Add any reserved raspberry puree.

Remove terrine from pan. Remove plastic wrap and slice into 1-inch thick slices. Place on individual serving plates and drizzle with small amount of sauce. Garnish with white chocolate curls, raspberries and mint. (Prepare at least 1 day in advance. Terrine and sauce may be frozen up to 1 week.)

Citrus Cheesecake

10-12 servings

Crust:

- 1½ cups graham cracker crumbs
- 6 tablespoons (¾ stick) unsalted butter, melted
- ½ cup packed light brown sugar
- ¾ teaspoon ground cinnamon

Filling:

- 6 eggs, separated, at room temperature
- 1¾ cups sugar
- 3 tablespoons flour
- 3 tablespoons unsalted butter
- 1 tablespoon finely grated orange zest
- 1-2 teaspoons finely grated lemon zest
- 1 tablespoon Curaçao or other orange flavored liqueur
- ½ teaspoon salt
- 4 8-ounce packages cream cheese, softened
- 1 cup whipping cream

Garnish:

fresh fruit

Preheat oven to 500 degrees. In medium bowl, combine graham cracker crumbs, 6 tablespoons melted butter, brown sugar, and cinnamon. Reserve ¼ cup for topping. Press remaining crumb mixture into bottom and partially up sides of 10-inch springform pan.

In large bowl, beat egg yolks about 10 minutes. In separate bowl, combine sugar and flour and gradually add to egg yolk mixture. Beat until well blended. In small saucepan, melt 3 tablespoons butter over low heat. Add orange zest and lemon zest. Cook 5 minutes, stirring frequently. Cool slightly and beat into egg yolk mixture. Blend in Curaçao and salt. Gradually add cream cheese and beat until thoroughly blended.

Beat egg whites until stiff. In separate bowl, whip cream to soft peaks. Gently fold egg whites and whipped cream into cream cheese mixture. Pour into prepared crust and top with reserved crumb mixture. Bake 10 minutes. Reduce oven temperature to 225 degrees and continue baking 1 hour and 15 minutes. Turn oven off and allow cheesecake to cool in oven with door slightly ajar. Chill 8 hours or up to overnight. Center will sink slightly, fill with fresh fruit.

Icy Espresso Mousse

8 servings

- 8 ounces bittersweet or semisweet chocolate, chopped
- ½ cup brewed espresso, or 1½ teaspoons instant espresso dissolved in ½ cup boiling water
- 3 tablespoons crème de cacao
- 2½ cups heavy whipping cream, chilled, divided
- ½ cup sugar
- 1 tablespoon powdered sugar

Garnish:

white chocolate curls

An easy, elegant finish to a Mexican meal.

In top of double boiler, over simmering water, combine chocolate and espresso. Cook over low heat, stirring constantly, until chocolate is melted and smooth. Remove from heat and cool to lukewarm. Stir in crème de cacao.

Using chilled beaters and chilled bowl, whip 2 cups of the cream and sugar until stiff peaks form. Using rubber spatula, gently fold whipped cream mixture into cooled chocolate mixture. Spoon into 2-quart serving dish or soufflé dish. Cover with foil and freeze at least 4 hours or preferably, overnight.

Whip remaining ½ cup cream and powdered sugar until soft peaks form. Remove mousse from freezer. Spoon into individual serving dishes and top with a dollop of the whipped cream mixture. Garnish with white chocolate curls, if desired.

Chocolate Mocha Delight

10-12 servings

- 12 ounces (2 cups) semisweet chocolate chips
- 2 tablespoons powdered instant coffee
- 1½ tablespoons sugar
- 2 tablespoons water
- 7 eggs, separated
- 1 teaspoon pure vanilla extract
- ½ 9-ounce package chocolate wafer cookies, finely crushed

Garnish:

whipped cream

fresh strawberries or raspberries

Our mocha version of chocolate mousse.

In top of double boiler, over simmering water, combine chocolate chips, coffee, sugar, and water. Heat, stirring frequently, until chocolate is melted and mixture is smooth. Remove from heat and cool to room temperature. Add egg yolks and vanilla and stir until smooth. Beat egg whites until stiff and gently fold into chocolate mixture.

Sprinkle thin layer of cookie crumbs in individual dessert glasses or bowls. Spoon chocolate mixture over crumbs. Sprinkle with additional crumbs. Chill 2 hours or up to overnight. Garnish with dollop of whipped cream and strawberries or raspberries.

White Chocolate Mousse in Cookie Cups

12 servings

Pecan Cookie Cups:

- ¼ cup (½ stick) unsalted butter
- ¼ cup packed light brown sugar
- ¼ cup light corn syrup
- 3½ tablespoons flour
- ½ cup finely chopped pecans
- 1 teaspoon pure vanilla extract

White Chocolate Mousse:

- ½ cup powdered sugar
- 3 eggs, separated
- 1 fresh vanilla bean
- 6 ounces imported white chocolate, divided
- 1¼ teaspoons unflavored gelatin
- 3 tablespoons very cold water
- 1 cup whipping cream

Garnish:

- dark chocolate curls
- fresh strawberries

Fresh vanilla beans are available at gourmet specialty stores. If fresh, they will be moist and flexible.

Preheat oven to 325 degrees. Grease and flour several large baking sheets. In medium saucepan, melt butter over low heat. Add brown sugar and corn syrup. Heat to boiling, stirring constantly. Remove from heat and stir in flour and chopped pecans. Stir in vanilla.

Place 2-3 teaspoons of the batter on baking sheet and smooth slightly. Repeat with remaining batter, spacing about 6 inches apart. About 3 cookies will fit onto a large baking sheet. Bake 10-12 minutes until golden brown.

Remove from oven and cool on baking sheet 1 minute. Invert a muffin tin and place on flat surface. Lift each cookie carefully with spatula and place over ungreased backs of muffin cups. Press down gently to form cups. Cool 3-5 minutes and gently remove to rack and cool thoroughly. The cookies will be fragile. (May be prepared 1 day in advance and stored, at room temperature, in air-tight container.)

In large bowl, combine powdered sugar and egg yolks. Split vanilla bean lengthwise and scrape seeds into sugar mixture. Beat with electric mixer until thickened. In top of double boiler, over simmering water, melt white chocolate, stirring constantly. Remove from heat and allow to cool 5-10 minutes. Fold cooled white chocolate mixture into sugar mixture.

In small glass bowl, combine gelatin and cold water and allow to stand 5 minutes. Place bowl in saucepan partially filled with hot water and stir occasionally until gelatin is dissolved. Stir into white chocolate mixture.

Whip egg whites until stiff and fold into white chocolate mixture. Whip cream to soft peaks and fold into white chocolate mixture. Cover with plastic wrap and chill 8 hours or up to overnight. Just before serving, spoon into Pecan Cookie Cups. Garnish with dark chocolate curls and strawberries.

Lemon Snow Balls

10 servings

5 large lemons
2 teaspoons finely grated lemon zest
¾ cup fresh lemon juice
1 cup milk
1 cup whipping cream
1 cup sugar
Garnish:
fresh raspberries
mint leaves

For easier preparation, omit lemon shells and spoon into individual serving bowls.

Cut lemons in half lengthwise to resemble boats. Cut small sliver of peel from bottom of lemons to stabilize base. Remove pulp from lemons to form a shell using a spoon or melon-baller. Cover with plastic wrap and freeze.

In large freezer-safe bowl, combine lemon zest, lemon juice, milk, and cream. Add sugar and stir until dissolved. Cover with plastic wrap and freeze 8 hours or up to overnight.

Remove from freezer. If necessary to break up ice crystals, process in food processor or beat with electric mixer until smooth. Do not over process, mixture should hold very firm peaks. Spoon into lemon shells, cover, and freeze until firm, 2 hours or up to 3 days. Garnish with fresh raspberries and mint.

A delicious make ahead treat.

Orange Banana Ice Cream

2 quarts

- ¾ cup fresh lemon juice
- 1¼ cups fresh orange juice
- 3 bananas, peeled and mashed
- 1½ cups sugar
- 3 cups milk
- 3 cups half and half

Garnish:
freshly grated orange zest
fresh mint leaves

Beautiful served in Pecan Cookie Cups, page 356.

In large bowl, combine lemon juice, orange juice, and mashed bananas. Stir until well blended. Add sugar, milk, and half and half and stir until well blended. Pour into ice cream freezer and freeze according to manufacturer's directions. Garnish with orange zest and mint.

Kiwi Sorbet

1 quart

- 4 kiwi fruit (½ pound), peeled and cubed
- ¾ cup sugar
- ⅔ cup fresh lemon juice
- ½ cup Midori liqueur
- 2 tablespoons light corn syrup
- ½ cup cold water

Garnish:
fresh raspberries

In food processor bowl, combine kiwi, sugar, and lemon juice. Chill 1 hour. Puree and add Midori, corn syrup, and water. Mix well. Place in ice cream freezer and freeze according to manufacturer's directions. The alcohol extends freezing time. Garnish with fresh raspberries.

Strawberry Ice

1 quart

- ¾ cup sugar
- 1⅓ cups water
- 4 pints fresh strawberries, washed, stemmed, and pureed (about 3 cups)
- 2 tablespoons finely grated lime zest
- 2 tablespoons fresh lime juice
- 1 tablespoon fresh orange juice

Garnish:
fresh mint leaves

For an elegant presentation, layer with kiwi fruit slices in parfait glasses.

In small saucepan, combine sugar and water and cook over low heat until sugar dissolves. Remove from heat and cool 15-20 minutes. In large bowl, combine strawberry puree, lime zest, lime juice, orange juice, and cooled sugar mixture. Stir until well blended. Pour into 1-quart freezer-safe container and freeze overnight. Remove from freezer, and allow to stand at room temperature 20-30 minutes or until soft enough to serve. Garnish with mint leaves.

Tiramisu

6-8 servings

- ¾ cup strong espresso
- 5 tablespoons dark rum, divided
- 20-22 Italian ladyfingers, divided
- 8 ounces mascarpone cheese
- 3 eggs, separated
- 3 tablespoons sugar, divided
- 1 cup whipping cream
- ¼ teaspoon pure vanilla extract
- pinch salt
- 3 ounces bittersweet or semisweet chocolate, grated

Italian ladyfingers are hard and crisp unlike common sponge-type ladyfingers. Tiramisu means "pick-me-up" in Italian.

In small, shallow dish, combine espresso and 3 tablespoons of the rum. Working with 11 of the ladyfingers, 1 at a time, quickly dip into espresso mixture, turning twice. They should be moistened but not falling apart. Line 8x8x2½-inch dish with moistened ladyfingers. Place close together to form solid layer, cutting to fit when necessary.

In large bowl, beat mascarpone and remaining 2 tablespoons rum and set aside. In top of double boiler, over barely simmering water, whisk egg yolks and 1½ tablespoons of the sugar until light and foamy, about 2 minutes. Remove from heat and beat into reserved mascarpone mixture. In small bowl, whip cream and vanilla until firm. Fold into mascarpone mixture. In separate bowl, beat egg whites and salt to soft peaks. Gradually add remaining 1½ tablespoons sugar and beat until stiff, but not dry. Fold into mascarpone mixture.

Pour half of the mascarpone mixture over ladyfinger layer in dish, smoothing top. Sprinkle with half of the chocolate. Dip remaining 11 ladyfingers as before and layer over chocolate. Top with remaining half of the mascarpone mixture, smoothing top and sprinkle with remaining chocolate. Dish will be very full. Cover with foil and chill 4 hours or up to overnight. Just before serving, spoon onto individual serving plates.

Bread Pudding With White Chocolate

6-8 servings

- 3 ounces French baguette, torn into bite size pieces
- 1½ cups half and half
- ½ cup whipping cream
- 4 ounces white chocolate
- 1 egg
- 4 egg yolks
- ¼ cup sugar
- ½ teaspoon pure vanilla extract

White Chocolate Sauce:

- ¾ cup whipping cream
- 4 ounces white chocolate, finely chopped

Garnish:

- semisweet chocolate curls
- fresh mint leaves
- fresh raspberries

This is a fabulous update to a classic favorite.

Preheat oven to 350 degrees. Grease 8-inch round cake or pie pan. Place bread pieces in prepared pan and set aside. In large saucepan, heat half and half and ½ cup cream until hot, but not boiling.

Melt 4 ounces white chocolate in double boiler or in microwave. Watch carefully, white chocolate scorches easily. In medium bowl, beat egg, egg yolks, and sugar, until well blended. Whisk in several tablespoons of the hot cream mixture to temper egg mixture. Whisk tempered egg mixture into remaining hot cream mixture and stir in vanilla. Add melted white chocolate and whisk until blended. Pour over bread pieces and bake 35-40 minutes. Remove from oven and set aside to cool.

In small saucepan, heat ¾ cup cream until hot, but not boiling. Add 4 ounces finely chopped white chocolate, whisking until melted and thoroughly blended. Cut bread pudding into wedges and top with White Chocolate Sauce. Garnish with chocolate curls, mint leaves, and raspberries. Bread pudding may be served warm or at room temperature. Sauce should be warm.

Cranberry Pudding Cups

12 servings

- 3 tablespoons unsalted butter, softened
- 1 cup sugar
- ½ cup water
- ½ cup evaporated milk
- 2 cups flour
- 1 teaspoon salt
- 2 teaspoons baking soda
- 2 cups fresh or frozen cranberries, rinsed and drained

Butter Sauce:

- ½ cup (1 stick) unsalted butter
- 1¾ cups sugar
- 1 cup evaporated milk
- 2 teaspoons pure vanilla extract

A traditional holiday dessert sure to become a family favorite.

Preheat oven to 350 degrees. Grease 12-cup muffin tin. In large bowl, cream 3 tablespoons butter and 1 cup sugar until well blended. In small bowl, combine water and ½ cup evaporated milk. Sift flour, salt, and baking soda into separate bowl. Alternately add milk mixture and flour mixture to butter mixture, beating well after each addition. Stir in cranberries. (Batter will be stiff.)

Fill prepared muffin cups three quarters full. Bake 20-30 minutes or until wooden pick inserted into center comes out clean. Cool and remove from muffin tin. (May be prepared up to 1 day in advance. Cool thoroughly, cover and store at room temperature.)

In heavy saucepan, combine ½ cup butter, 1¾ cups sugar, 1 cup evaporated milk, and vanilla over medium-high heat. Heat to boiling, stirring frequently. Remove from heat and set aside. (Sauce may be prepared up to 3 weeks in advance. Cover and chill.) Place pudding cups on individual serving plates and top with warmed Butter Sauce.

Pecan Apple Pear Pie

8-10 servings

Pastry:

- 2½ cups flour
- ½ teaspoon salt
- 1 teaspoon sugar (optional)
- 1 cup (2 sticks) unsalted butter, chilled and cut into small pieces
- ¼ cup or more very cold water

Filling:

- ¼ cup (½ stick) unsalted butter, very soft, divided
- ¾ cup pecan halves
- ⅓ cup packed brown sugar
- 3 Granny Smith apples, peeled, cored, and thinly sliced
- 3 tablespoons flour
- 1 teaspoon cinnamon
- ¾ cup sugar
- 3 medium, firm ripe pears, peeled, cored, and thinly sliced
- 2 tablespoons lemon juice

Butter Rum Sauce:

- ½ cup firmly packed brown sugar
- 1 tablespoon cornstarch
- 1 cup water
- ½ teaspoon rum extract
- 2½ tablespoons unsalted butter

In food processor, combine 2½ cups flour, salt, and 1 teaspoon sugar, if desired. Add 1 cup butter pieces and process or until mixture resembles coarse meal. Gradually add ¼ cup cold water and process just until dough holds together. Divide dough in half. Press dough into flat disks, and wrap tightly in plastic wrap. Chill at least 30 minutes.

Preheat oven to 450 degrees. Line 9-inch pie pan with foil, allowing a 1-inch overhang. Spread 2 tablespoons of the butter on foil. Press pecans, round side down, in butter. Pat ⅓ cup brown sugar into butter. Using floured rolling pin, roll out 1 disk of dough on floured surface. Press into bottom and sides of pan but do not trim. Arrange apple slices over crust.

In small bowl, combine 3 tablespoons flour, cinnamon, and ¾ cup sugar. Sprinkle half over apples. Top with pears, arranging evenly so top crust will lay flat. Sprinkle with remaining half of the flour mixture. Melt remaining 2 tablespoons butter and add lemon juice. Pour over pears. Roll out remaining crust and place on top of pears. Trim edges closely and seal crusts together. Gently push crust edges toward center of pie. Bake 10 minutes, reduce oven temperature to 375 degrees, and continue baking 40 minutes.

In small saucepan, combine ½ cup brown sugar, cornstarch, and 1 cup water. Cook, over medium heat, stirring occasionally, until thickened and clear. Stir in rum extract and 2½ tablespoons butter. Remove pie from oven, cool 5 minutes, and invert onto large serving plate. Serve with hot Butter Rum Sauce and vanilla ice cream, if desired.

TRIPLE BERRY PIE

8 servings

Pastry:

- 2½ cups flour
- ½ teaspoon salt
- 1 teaspoon sugar (optional)
- 1 cup (2 sticks) unsalted butter, well chilled and cut into small pieces
- ¼ cup or more very cold water

Filling:

- 1 pint fresh blueberries (2 cups), rinsed, stemmed, and drained
- 2 pints fresh strawberries (4 cups), stemmed and halved
- ½ pint fresh raspberries (1 cup), rinsed and drained
- 2 tablespoons cornstarch
- ¼ cup water
- ¾ cup plus 1 tablespoon sugar, divided
- 1 large egg, lightly beaten

Garnish:

vanilla ice cream

For a decorative look, cut top pastry into ½-inch strips and weave on top of filling in a lattice pattern.

In food processor, combine flour, salt, and 1 teaspoon sugar, if desired. Add butter and process until mixture resembles coarse meal. Gradually add ¼ cup cold water, and process just until dough holds together. Divide dough in half. Press dough into flat disks, and wrap tightly in plastic wrap. Chill at least 30 minutes.

Preheat oven to 375 degrees. Lightly grease 9-inch pie pan. In large bowl, combine blueberries, strawberries, and raspberries. In small bowl, combine cornstarch and ¼ cup water and stir until smooth. Add ¾ cup of the sugar. Pour over berries and toss. Let stand 20 minutes, stirring occasionally.

Using floured rolling pin, roll out 1 disk of dough on floured surface. Press into bottom and sides of prepared pan. Pour berry mixture into crust. Roll out remaining pastry. Place over berry mixture, pressing edges together. Crimp or decorate edges. Brush pastry with beaten egg and sprinkle top with remaining 1 tablespoon sugar. Cut 3-5 slits in top to vent.

Bake 40-50 minutes or until crust is lightly browned. If edges brown too quickly, tent with foil. Serve warm or at room temperature. Garnish with vanilla ice cream.

Apple Parchment Pie

8 servings

- 12 sheets phyllo pastry, thawed if frozen
- 1 cup sugar
- 1 tablespoon cinnamon
- 1 teaspoon finely grated orange zest
- ¾ cup (1½ sticks) unsalted butter, melted
- 6-8 tablespoons Grand Marnier
- 8 medium Granny Smith apples, peeled, cored, and thinly sliced

A sophisticated version of the all-American apple pie.

Preheat oven to 400 degrees. Grease 9-inch deep-dish pie pan. Cover phyllo with plastic wrap and damp towel and let stand 10 minutes. In small bowl, combine sugar, cinnamon, and orange zest. Place 1 phyllo sheet in prepared pan. Brush with enough melted butter to lightly moisten phyllo. Sprinkle with 1 tablespoon of the reserved sugar mixture and 1 teaspoon Grand Marnier. Repeat process with 5 more phyllo sheets.

Arrange apples in circular pattern over prepared phyllo crust. Brush apples with melted butter and sprinkle with 5-6 tablespoons of the sugar mixture and 2-3 tablespoons of the Grand Marnier. Repeat phyllo layering process with remaining 6 phyllo sheets (omitting sugar and Grand Marnier from top sheet). Trim corners from phyllo sheets, turn edges up, and pinch lightly to seal. Bake 40-50 minutes or until golden brown. If phyllo browns too quickly, tent with foil. Remove from oven and cool on rack. Cut with serrated knife.

Baked Pears With Rum and Cream

4-8 servings

- 4 firm ripe pears, peeled, halved, and cored
- ¼ cup (½ stick) unsalted butter
- ¼ cup packed brown sugar
- ¼ cup dark rum
- ½ cup whipping cream

Garnish:

vanilla ice cream or frozen yogurt

This is rich with great old-fashioned taste.

Preheat oven to 350 degrees. Arrange pears, cut side down, in 10-inch baking dish. In small saucepan, melt butter and stir in brown sugar and rum. Pour over pears, moving pears around to coat. Bake 40 minutes, basting frequently. Remove from oven and pour cream over pears. Continue baking 15-20 minutes. Place in individual serving bowls, and spoon hot sauce over pears. May be served over vanilla ice cream or frozen yogurt, if desired.

Plum Almond Tartlets

6 servings

- ¼ cup sliced almonds, lightly toasted (page 381)
- ¼ cup plus 1 teaspoon sugar, divided
- ½ teaspoon ground cinnamon, divided
- ¼ cup (½ stick) unsalted butter
- 3 sheets phyllo pastry, thawed if frozen, cut into eighteen 6-inch squares
- ½ teaspoon powdered sugar
- 4 firm ripe plums (about 1 pound), pitted and quartered
- 2 teaspoons fresh lemon juice
- 1 tablespoon peach schnapps or rum
- vanilla ice cream

Offer these elegant individual desserts at a summer dinner party. Photo, page 342.

Preheat oven to 375 degrees. In food processor, combine toasted almonds, 1 teaspoon of the sugar, and ¼ teaspoon of the cinnamon. Process to fine powder, about 10 seconds. In saucepan, melt butter over medium-high heat, and clarify by skimming and discarding the white solids from surface.

Prepare twelve ½-cup muffin tin by lightly brushing 6 of the cups with clarified butter, leaving an unbuttered cup between each buttered one. Line each buttered cup with 1 phyllo square, allowing points to extend above edges of cups. Brush inside of phyllo with clarified butter and sprinkle lightly with reserved almond mixture. Top with 6 additional phyllo squares, butter, and almond mixture. Repeat again with remaining 6 phyllo squares and butter but omit almond mixture. Reserve remaining clarified butter for plum mixture, and almond mixture for garnish.

Cover muffin tin loosely with foil and bake 5-6 minutes. Remove from oven and carefully remove foil. Remove baked phyllo shells and cool on rack. Sift powdered sugar over cooled shells. (May be prepared up to 2 days in advance and stored, covered loosely, at room temperature.)

In large skillet, combine plums, remaining ¼ cup sugar, remaining ¼ teaspoon cinnamon, lemon juice, and any remaining clarified butter. Cook over medium-high heat, stirring frequently, until tender and juicy, 5-8 minutes. Remove plums with slotted spoon and set aside. Add schnapps to skillet and cook over medium heat, stirring to deglaze skillet. Remove from heat and reserve juices.

Just before serving, divide plums evenly among baked shells with slotted spoon. Top with small scoop of ice cream and drizzle with reserved juices. Garnish with any remaining almond mixture.

Plum Creek Peach Crisp

10-12 servings

- 1¼ cups flour
- ½ cup packed dark brown sugar
- ½ cup (1 stick) unsalted butter, chilled and cut into pieces
- 2 teaspoons finely grated orange zest
- ¼ teaspoon plus pinch salt, divided
- 12-14 plums, pitted and cut into ½-inch wedges (about 6 cups)
- 4 medium peaches, peeled, pitted, and cut into ½ inch-wedges (about 2 ½ cups)
- ½ cup sugar
- 2 tablespoons quick-cooking tapioca
- 1 teaspoon fresh lemon juice
- vanilla ice cream

A fantastic way to showcase summer ripened plums and peaches.

In food processor, combine flour, brown sugar, butter pieces, orange zest, and ¼ teaspoon salt. Pulse until mixture forms small clumps. (May be prepared, to this point, 1 day in advance. Cover and chill.)

In large bowl, combine plums, peaches, sugar, tapioca, lemon juice, and pinch salt. Let stand at least 30 minutes and up to 2 hours, stirring occasionally. Preheat oven to 350 degrees. Grease 11x7x2-inch pan or 2-quart baking pan. Spoon plum mixture into prepared dish and top with flour mixture. Bake until fruit is tender and topping is brown and crisp, 45-60 minutes. Cool slightly and spoon into deep serving bowls. Serve with vanilla ice cream or frozen yogurt, if desired.

Apple Cranberry Crumble

6-8 servings

- 1 12-ounce package fresh cranberries, rinsed and drained
- 4 Granny Smith apples, peeled, cored, and coarsely chopped
- 1½ cups sugar, divided
- 10 tablespoons (1¼ sticks) unsalted butter, chilled and cut into small pieces
- 1 cup flour
- 1¼ cups sliced almonds, divided

An easy and flavorful casual dessert.

Preheat oven to 375 degrees. Grease 2½-3-quart baking pan. In prepared baking pan, combine cranberries, apples, and ¾ cup of the sugar. Toss to combine and spread evenly.

In food processor, combine butter, flour, remaining ¾ cup sugar, and ¼ cup of the almonds. Process until small clumps form. Transfer to large bowl and gently mix in remaining 1 cup almonds, keeping dough in small clumps. Cover cranberry mixture with dough. Bake about 50 minutes or until browned. Serve warm with vanilla ice cream or frozen yogurt, if desired.

Blueberry Picnic Cake

12-15 servings

- 4 eggs, separated
- 2 cups plus 2 tablespoons sugar, divided
- 1 cup (2 sticks) unsalted butter, softened
- ½ teaspoon salt
- 2 teaspoons pure vanilla extract
- 3 cups flour, divided
- 2 teaspoons baking powder
- ⅔ cup milk
- 2 pints fresh blueberries, washed, stemmed, and dried

A simple, melt-in-your-mouth cake.

Preheat oven to 350 degrees. Grease 13x9x2-inch baking pan. In medium bowl, beat egg whites until stiff. Gradually add ½ cup of the sugar and beat until well blended. In large bowl, cream butter until fluffy. Add salt and vanilla. Gradually add 1½ cups of the remaining sugar and beat until blended. Add egg yolks and beat until light and creamy. Add 2½ cups of the flour, baking powder, and milk and mix thoroughly. Fold in reserved beaten egg whites.

Gently shake dry blueberries with remaining ½ cup flour to prevent settling during baking, and fold into batter. Spread evenly in prepared pan. Sprinkle with remaining 2 tablespoons sugar. Bake 50-60 minutes or until cake begins to pull away from sides of pan and wooden pick inserted into center comes out clean. (May be halved and baked in an 8x8x2-inch pan.)

Lemon Pound Cake

10-12 servings

- 1¼ cups (2½ sticks) unsalted butter, softened, divided
- 1¾ cups sugar
- 3 eggs
- 3 cups flour
- ½ teaspoon baking soda
- ½ teaspoon salt
- 1 cup buttermilk
- 4 tablespoons finely grated lemon zest, divided
- ½ cup fresh lemon juice, divided
- 2 cups powdered sugar

Decorate top of cake with fresh pansies for a beautiful summer brunch.

Preheat oven to 325 degrees. Grease and flour 10-inch bundt pan. In large bowl, cream 1 cup of the butter and sugar until fluffy. Beat in eggs, 1 at a time. Combine flour, baking soda, and salt. Add to butter mixture, a little at a time, alternating with buttermilk, beating after each addition. Add 3 tablespoons of the lemon zest and ¼ cup of the lemon juice. Beat until well blended. Pour into prepared pan. Bake about 1 hour and 15 minutes or until wooden pick inserted into center comes out clean. Cool in pan, about 10 minutes. Invert onto serving platter.

In medium bowl, cream remaining ¼ cup butter and powdered sugar. Stir in remaining 1 tablespoon lemon zest and remaining ¼ cup lemon juice and mix until well blended. Spread on slightly warm cake.

Mocha Brownies

20 brownies

- 2¼ cups packed brown sugar
- ¾ cup (1½ sticks) unsalted butter
- 2 tablespoons instant espresso or coffee powder
- 1 tablespoon hot water
- 2 eggs
- 2 tablespoons pure vanilla extract
- 2 cups flour
- 2 teaspoons baking powder
- ½ teaspoon salt
- 1 cup chopped pecans
- 1 cup semisweet chocolate chips

A delectable chewy brownie for coffee lovers. *Photo, page 314.*

Preheat oven to 350 degrees. In medium saucepan, combine brown sugar and butter over medium-low heat. Cook until butter is melted. Dissolve espresso powder in hot water and stir into butter mixture. Cool to room temperature. Beat eggs and vanilla into cooled butter mixture. Sift together flour, baking powder, and salt. Stir into butter mixture. Stir in pecans and chocolate chips. Grease 11x7x2-inch baking pan. Spread evenly into prepared pan. Bake until lightly browned, about 30 minutes. Do not overbake. Cool. Cut into 2-inch squares.

Chocolate Peanut Butter Brownies

24 brownies

- 1 cup plus 1 tablespoon flour, divided
- ¼ teaspoon baking powder
- ½ teaspoon salt
- ¾ cup (1½ sticks) unsalted butter
- 3 ounces unsweetened chocolate, finely chopped
- 3 eggs
- 1⅓ cups packed dark brown sugar
- 1½ teaspoons pure vanilla extract
- ¾ cup creamy peanut butter
- ¼ cup sugar
- ¼ teaspoon cinnamon
- 6 tablespoons half and half

Don't count on any leftovers!

Preheat oven to 350 degrees. Grease 9x13x2-inch baking pan. In small bowl, sift 1 cup of the flour, baking powder, and salt. Set aside. In medium saucepan, melt butter and chocolate over very low heat, stirring until smooth. Set aside to cool slightly. In large bowl, combine eggs, brown sugar, and vanilla. Whisk to blend. Stir in melted chocolate mixture. Gradually add flour mixture and stir until blended. Pour into prepared pan.

In medium bowl, with electric mixer, combine peanut butter, sugar, cinnamon, half and half, and remaining 1 tablespoon flour. Mixture will be stiff. Drop mixture randomly, by spoonfuls, on top of brownie mixture. Drag knife through peanut butter mixture all over surface, almost touching bottom of pan, to marbleize brownies. Bake about 25 minutes, until firm when touched lightly. Cool thoroughly before cutting.

Raspberry Buttons

4-5 dozen

- 1 cup (2 sticks) unsalted butter
- ⅔ cup sugar
- 2 eggs, separated
- 2 cups flour
- 1 teaspoon salt
- 1 teaspoon pure vanilla extract
- 8 ounces walnuts, finely ground
- 1 10-ounce jar raspberry preserves
- powdered sugar

A wonderful holiday or tea cookie.

In large bowl, cream butter and sugar. Add egg yolks, flour, salt, and vanilla and mix thoroughly. Shape into 1-inch balls and chill 1 hour. Preheat oven to 375 degrees. Dip cookies, 1 at a time, into unbeaten egg whites and roll in ground walnuts. Place 2-inches apart on ungreased baking sheet.

Bake 5 minutes, remove from oven, and make a dent in center of each cookie with your thumb. Fill dents with ½ teaspoon raspberry preserves. Return to oven and continue baking 10-15 minutes. Do not overbake. Cool thoroughly. Just before serving, dust with powdered sugar.

Chocolate Hazelnut Crescents

3-4 dozen cookies

- ¾ cup (1½ sticks) unsalted butter, softened
- ½ cup sugar
- 1 egg yolk
- 1¼ cups flour
- 1¼ cups toasted, peeled, (page 381) and ground hazelnuts
- 6 ounces bittersweet or semisweet chocolate, chopped
- ¼ cup half and half
- 2 tablespoons finely chopped hazelnuts

A lovely addition to any cookie tray.

Preheat oven to 350 degrees. In large bowl, cream butter and sugar until fluffy. Add egg yolk, flour, and ground hazelnuts. Mix until well blended and dough is smooth. Pinch off 2 teaspoons of dough and roll into 2½-inch long roll. Place on ungreased baking sheet, bending ends in to form crescent shape. Repeat with remaining dough. Bake 12-15 minutes, until golden. Cool on baking sheets 10 minutes. Transfer to rack and cool thoroughly.

Line baking sheets with waxed paper. In top of double boiler, melt chocolate over simmering water. Gradually add half and half, stirring constantly to blend. Dip 1 cookie, diagonally, halfway into chocolate mixture, letting excess chocolate run back into pan. Place on prepared baking sheets and quickly sprinkle dipped portion with chopped hazelnuts. Repeat with remaining cookies. Let stand, at room temperature, until chocolate sets, about 30 minutes.

Pecan Tea Cookies

6-7 dozen

- 1 cup (2 sticks) unsalted butter, softened
- ½ cup sugar
- 1 egg yolk
- 3 tablespoons pure maple syrup
- ½ teaspoon pure vanilla extract
- 1¾ cups flour
- 1¼ cups pecan halves, lightly toasted (page 381)

The elegant slice and bake cookie.

In large bowl, beat butter with electric mixer until it whitens and holds soft peaks, 5-8 minutes. Add sugar and beat until well blended. In small bowl, combine egg yolk, maple syrup, and vanilla. Whisk until well blended. Add to reserved butter mixture and beat well. Add flour and mix until just combined. Gently fold in toasted pecans. Wrap dough in plastic wrap and chill 30 minutes, or until firm.

Divide dough into 4 equal pieces and work with 1 at a time, keeping remaining pieces chilled. Turn out onto lightly floured surface, using only enough flour to prevent dough from sticking. With your hands, pack dough into a solid patty. It is important that there are no holes in patty. Roll patty, with your palms, into log, about 1½-inches in diameter. Wrap in plastic wrap and freeze 30 minutes, or until firm enough to slice. Repeat with remaining dough. (Dough may be stored, well wrapped, in the freezer for up to 3 months.)

Preheat oven to 325 degrees. Using sharp knife, slice logs into ⅜-inch rounds. Place 1-inch apart on non-stick baking sheet. Bake 12-15 minutes, until firm and lightly browned.

Mocha Chocolate Cookies

3 dozen

- 2 ounces unsweetened chocolate
- 6 ounces semisweet chocolate
- 2 tablespoons unsalted butter
- 2 eggs
- ¾ cup sugar
- 2 teaspoons instant coffee powder
- ½ teaspoon pure vanilla extract
- ¼ cup flour
- ¼ teaspoon baking powder
- ⅛ teaspoon salt
- 1 cup semisweet chocolate chips
- 2 cups chopped walnuts or pecans

A chocoholic's bliss.

Preheat oven to 350 degrees. Line large baking sheets with foil. In top of double boiler, over simmering water, melt unsweetened chocolate, semisweet chocolate, and butter. Stir until smooth and remove from heat. Combine eggs, sugar, coffee, and vanilla and beat with electric mixer, 2 minutes. Add cooled chocolate mixture and beat to blend. Add flour, baking powder, and salt and beat until well blended. Stir in chocolate chips and walnuts.

Drop by heaping teaspoons, 1-inch apart, onto prepared baking sheets and bake 10-12 minutes. Tops will be dry and crisp, and centers soft and chewy. Do not overbake. Let cool slightly before serving.

Chocolate Almond Shortbread Cookies

6 dozen

- 1 cup (2 sticks) unsalted butter, softened
- ⅔ cup sugar
- 1 egg yolk
- 1 teaspoon pure vanilla extract
- 2 cups sifted flour
- ¼ teaspoon salt
- 1⅓ cups finely chopped blanched almonds

Dipping Chocolate:

- 6 ounces semisweet chocolate
- 3 tablespoons unsalted butter
- 1 tablespoon hot water
- ½ cup chopped blanched almonds

In large bowl, cream 1 cup butter and sugar until light and fluffy. Add egg yolk and vanilla and stir to blend. Add flour, salt, and 1⅓ cups almonds and stir until well blended. Divide dough into 2 pieces and shape each into a 1½-2-inch roll. Wrap in plastic wrap and chill until firm, about 2 hours.

Preheat oven to 350 degrees. Line baking sheets with parchment paper. With sharp knife, cut dough into ¼-inch thick slices. Place 1-2 inches apart on prepared baking sheets and bake 8-10 minutes, until lightly browned. Remove from oven and cool on rack.

In top of double boiler, melt chocolate and 3 tablespoons butter over simmering water. Add hot water and stir until smooth. Dip edge of each cookie into chocolate and quickly sprinkle with chopped almonds. Cool on rack until chocolate hardens.

Nut Shortbread Triangles

35-40 bars

- 1 cup (2 sticks) unsalted butter, softened
- 1 cup sugar
- 2 cups flour
- 1 egg, separated
- 1 teaspoon pure vanilla extract
- ¾ cup chopped pecans

Super easy and incredibly good.

Preheat oven to 300 degrees. Grease 14x11-inch baking pan. In large bowl, combine butter, sugar, flour, egg yolk, and vanilla. Blend thoroughly, using electric mixer. Spread evenly into prepared pan. Beat egg white until foamy and spread over dough. Sprinkle with pecans and bake 30-35 minutes. Remove from oven and immediately cut into triangles. Allow to cool slightly before removing from pan.

Scottish Delights

5 dozen

- ¾ cup (1½ sticks) unsalted butter, softened
- 1 cup sugar
- 1 cup packed brown sugar
- 2 eggs
- 1 teaspoon pure vanilla extract
- 1½ cups flour
- 2 teaspoons baking powder
- 1 teaspoon baking soda
- 1 teaspoon salt
- 1 cup shredded coconut
- 3 cups quick-cooking oatmeal

Preheat oven to 375 degrees. In large bowl, cream butter, sugar, and brown sugar. Add eggs and vanilla and beat until well blended. In separate bowl, combine flour, baking powder, baking soda, salt, coconut, and oatmeal. Add to butter mixture and stir until well blended. Drop by rounded teaspoons onto ungreased baking sheet. Bake 10 to 12 minutes.

Almond Espresso Biscotti

3 dozen

- 2 cups flour
- 1 cup sugar
- ½ teaspoon baking soda
- ½ teaspoon baking powder
- ½ teaspoon salt
- ½ teaspoon cinnamon
- ½ teaspoon ground cloves
- 1 egg yolk
- ⅓ cup strong coffee or espresso, cooled
- 1 tablespoon milk
- 1 teaspoon pure vanilla extract
- ¾ cup toasted (page 381), coarsely chopped almonds
- ½ cup semisweet chocolate chips

Biscotti are delicious Italian dipping cookies. They are hard and should be served with hot beverages like cappuccino or coffee.

Preheat oven to 350 degrees. Grease and flour large baking sheet. In large bowl, with electric mixer, gently combine flour, sugar, baking soda, baking powder, salt, cinnamon, and cloves. In small bowl, whisk egg yolk, espresso, milk, and vanilla. Add to flour mixture. Beat until dough is formed and stir in toasted almonds and chocolate chips.

Place dough on floured surface and knead several times, adding flour if needed to prevent sticking. Divide dough in half. With floured hands, form each piece of dough into a flat 2x12-inch log. Arrange logs at least 3 inches apart on prepared baking sheet. Bake 35 minutes. Cool on baking sheet 10 minutes.

Reduce oven temperature to 300 degrees. Place logs on cutting board and slice crosswise and diagonally, into ¾-inch thick slices. Arrange slices on baking sheet and bake 8-10 minutes per side, or until pale golden brown. Transfer to rack, cool, and store in airtight container up to 1 month.

Macadamia Coconut Biscotti

3 dozen

- ½ cup (1 stick) butter, softened
- ½ cup sugar
- 2 eggs
- ¼ teaspoon almond extract
- 2 cups flour
- 1½ teaspoons baking powder
- ¼ teaspoon ground nutmeg
- ¼ teaspoon salt
- ⅔ cup macadamia nuts
- ½ cup flaked coconut

The addition of butter in this biscotti results in a finer texture than the others.

Preheat oven to 325 degrees. Grease and flour large baking sheet. In large bowl, cream butter and sugar until fluffy. Beat in eggs and almond extract. In separate bowl, combine flour, baking powder, nutmeg, and salt. Add to butter mixture and beat until dough is formed. Stir in nuts and coconut.

Divide dough in half. Form each piece into a flat 2x12-inch log. Arrange logs at least 3 inches apart on prepared baking sheet. Bake 25 minutes. Cool on baking sheet 10 minutes. Place logs on cutting board and slice, crosswise and diagonally, into ¾-inch thick slices. Arrange slices on baking sheet and continue baking, about 5 minutes per side. Cool on rack. Store up to 1 week.

Ginger Cocoa Biscotti

3 dozen

- 2½ cups flour
- 1 cup sugar
- ¼ teaspoon cinnamon
- ¼ teaspoon ground cloves
- 1 teaspoon baking soda
- ½ teaspoon salt
- 2 tablespoons unsweetened cocoa powder
- 2 eggs
- 2 tablespoons peeled, grated fresh ginger root
- ¼ cup milk
- ½ teaspoon almond extract
- 1¼ cups blanched whole almonds, lightly toasted (page 381), and coarsely chopped

Dip one half of the biscotti in melted semisweet chocolate. Photo, page 374.

Preheat oven to 350 degrees. Grease and flour large baking sheet. In large bowl, with electric mixer, gently combine flour, sugar, cinnamon, cloves, baking soda, salt, and cocoa. In small bowl, whisk eggs, ginger, milk, and almond extract. Add to flour mixture. Beat until dough is formed and stir in toasted almonds.

Place dough on floured surface and knead several times, adding flour if needed to prevent sticking. Divide dough in half. With floured hands, form each piece into a flat 2x12-inch log. Arrange logs at least 3 inches apart on prepared baking sheet. Bake 35 minutes. Cool on baking sheet 10 minutes.

Reduce oven temperature to 300 degrees. Place logs on cutting board and slice crosswise and diagonally, into ¾-inch thick slices. Arrange slices on baking sheet and bake 8-10 minutes per side, or until light golden brown. Transfer to rack, cool, and store in airtight container up to 1 month.

Considering Coffee

Coffee's Constant Allure

From its exotic beginnings in Africa and Arabia, coffee's popularity swept through Europe and The Americas in the Seventeenth Century. The distinctive aroma of freshly roasted beans and coffee's dark, robust taste charm the senses. Its modern day renaissance in coffee bars and home kitchens across the country inspires sociability and conversation. Few drinks are as heartwarming and pleasurable as coffee. Its possibilities are infinite, offering the perfect compliment to a delicious assortments of foods. The following tips and recipes will enable you to savor delicious, gourmet coffee drinks to accompany any meal you may create.

Brewing the Perfect Cup of Coffee

When brewing coffee, always use fresh, cold water, and a clean coffee decanter. In general use 1½-2 tablespoons of coffee for each 6 ounce cup. For optimal flavor, purchase beans whole and grind them at home as needed. Stored in airtight containers, beans will last for 2-3 weeks at room temperature, if unopened. If necessary, you may store the beans in the freezer for 1 month or longer. Serve coffee within 1 hour of brewing and never reheat. Coffee should be kept hot but never allowed to boil. When steaming milk for coffee drinks, be sure to use cold whole or low fat milk.

Coffee Drinks

Café au Lait: Equal parts of steamed milk and freshly brewed, strong coffee, usually 6 ounces of each.

Café Mocha: Freshly brewed hot coffee (6 ounces) blended with ⅓ cup heated chocolate milk, topped with whipped cream.

Iced Coffee: Use coffee brewed 1½ to double strength. Blend ⅔ cup cooled coffee and ⅓ cup cold milk, pour over ice.

Espresso: Made from espresso coffee beans in an electric machine or stove-top maker. Traditionally served in a warmed demitasse, filling the cup half way (about 1½ ounces). Usually garnished with a small piece of lemon or orange peel which is twisted into the coffee for flavor.

Cappuccino: Equal parts of freshly brewed espresso and steamed milk, topped with an equal amount of foam from the steamed milk.

Café Latte: Freshly brewed espresso (1½ ounces) placed in a large mug and filled the rest of the way with steamed milk (7-8 ounces), topped with a thin layer of foam from the steamed milk.

Iced Latte: Cooled freshly brewed espresso (3 ounces) and 6-8 ounces cold milk in a tall glass, over ice cubes.

Clockwise from top: Ginger Cocoa Biscotti, 373 Chocolate Caramel Walnut Torte, 347 Frozen Berry and White Chocolate Terrine, 333

Coffee Garnish

3 tablespoons

1 tablespoon packed light brown sugar
1 tablespoon very finely ground coffee
1 tablespoon ground cinnamon

Variation

Chocolate Coffee Garnish:

1 tablespoon finely grated chocolate

Combine brown sugar, ground coffee, and cinnamon. Mix well and store in a tightly covered container. Add chocolate, if desired. Sprinkle over coffee drinks.

Vanilla Cinnamon Coffee

2 servings

½ vanilla bean, sliced lengthwise
2 cinnamon sticks, each broken in half
coffee
¾ cup whipping cream

Garnish:

Coffee Garnish (recipe above)

Place sliced vanilla bean and broken cinnamon sticks in coffee maker carafe. Brew 12 ounces coffee. While coffee is brewing, whip cream until soft peaks form. Strain coffee into 2 mugs, top with whipped cream, and sprinkle with Coffee Garnish, if desired.

Viennese Coffee

2 servings

2 ounces semisweet chocolate
2 tablespoons heavy cream
2 8-ounce cups freshly brewed coffee

Garnish:

whipped cream
ground cocoa or Chocolate Coffee Garnish (recipe above)

In top of small double boiler, over simmering water, melt chocolate. Add cream and stir until well blended. Remove from heat, whisk in coffee and beat until frothy. Pour into 2 cups, top with whipped cream, and dust with cocoa or Chocolate Coffee Garnish, if desired.

Spiced Espresso

2 servings

- 6 ounces freshly brewed espresso
- dash allspice
- ¼ teaspoon ground cinnamon
- 3 teaspoons sugar
- 3 ounces half and half
- 2 teaspoons chocolate syrup, divided

Garnish:

whipped cream

In frothing pitcher, combine espresso, allspice, cinnamon, sugar, and half and half. Steam until hot and frothy. Pour into 2 mugs and stir 1 teaspoon chocolate syrup into each. Garnish with whipped cream, if desired.

Cinnamon Espresso Shake

2 servings

- 2 cinnamon sticks, broken into 2-3 pieces
- 6 ounces freshly brewed espresso
- 1 cup cold milk
- 1½ cups vanilla ice cream, slightly softened
- 2 tablespoons packed brown sugar

Garnish:

- 1 tablespoon Coffee Garnish (page 376)

Instant espresso may be substituted for freshly brewed espresso.

Place cinnamon stick pieces in hot espresso. Cool thoroughly and chill 1 hour. In blender, combine milk and ice cream. Blend until smooth. Add brown sugar and blend. Remove cinnamon sticks from espresso. Add espresso to ice cream mixture. Blend well. Pour into 2 tall glasses and sprinkle with Coffee Garnish.

Pantry

The following categories list the *Colorado Collage* cook's ideal pantry items. A well-chosen pantry is key to efficient menu planning and grocery shopping. A home kitchen, stocked with these various items, would be well-equipped to cook the majority of our recipes, by shopping only for the necessary fresh ingredients. Compare your pantry inventory to these suggestions, and begin expanding where needed. Soon, you will have the perfect *Collage* pantry, a time-saver in itself.

Oils and Vinegars: Oils: canola, chili, chili sesame, hot chili, olive, peanut, safflower, sesame, and vegetable; vinegars: balsamic, champagne, cider, raspberry, red wine, rice wine, seasoned rice, sherry, tarragon, and white wine.

Baking Needs: Baking powder; baking soda; brown sugar; cheesecloth; chocolate: bittersweet, semisweet chips, unsweetened, and white; cocoa powder; coconut; cornmeal; cornstarch; cream of tartar; dry yeast; extracts: almond, maple, and vanilla; flour: unbleached and whole wheat; oatmeal: quick and regular; parchment paper; powdered sugar; powdered instant espresso; salt: table and coarse; sugar; unflavored gelatin; and wheat germ.

Bottled Sauces and Juices: Apple cider; barbecue sauce; catsup; Chinese chili paste (such as Sambal Oelek); Chinese chili sauce; clam juice; hoisin sauce; honey; hot black bean sauce; hot red pepper sauce; Italian salad dressing; light corn syrup; maple syrup; molasses; oyster sauce; plum sauce; Tabasco; and Worcestershire.

Dry Herbs and Spices: Allspice; anise seed; basil; bay leaves; caraway seeds; cardamom; chervil; chili powder; cinnamon: ground and sticks; cloves: ground and whole; coriander; cumin; curry paste; curry powder; dill weed; fennel seeds; garlic powder; ginger: ground and crystallized; Greek seasoning; Italian seasoning; marjoram; mint; mustard seed; dry mustard; nutmeg; oregano; paprika; pepper: black, cayenne, crushed red, and white; peppercorns: black and green; rosemary; saffron: threads and powder; sage; savory; tarragon; thyme; and turmeric.

Dried Goods: Ancho chiles; Asian rice noodles; assorted pasta shapes; beans: black and pinto; bulgur; Chinese egg noodles; couscous; orzo; peanut butter: plain and chunky; pearl barley; polenta; quinoa; rice: arborio, basmati, long-grain, white, and wild; and sun-dried tomatoes.

Canned Goods and Condiments: Anchovy fillets; anchovy paste; artichoke hearts; beans: black, cannelini, garbanzo, kidney, pinto, refried, and white navy; broth: beef, chicken, and vegetable; capers; chipotle peppers in adobo sauce; green chiles; horseradish; jellies: apple, apricot, currant, and jalapeño; mandarin oranges; mango chutney; mayonnaise; milk: coconut, sweetened condensed, and evaporated; mustard: dijon and honey; pineapple; salsa; tomatoes: paste, plum, puree, juice, stewed, oil-packed sun-dried, and whole; and water chestnuts.

Nuts, Seeds, and Berries: Almonds: blanched, slivered, and whole; cashews; currants; dried cherries; hazelnuts; macadamia nuts; peanuts; pecans; pine nuts; pistachios; poppy seeds; raisins; sesame seeds; sunflower seeds; and walnuts.

Freezer: Blueberries; chopped spinach; corn kernels; orange juice concentrate; peas; phyllo pastry; puff pastry; unsalted butter; and wonton skins.

Wines and Liquors: Amaretto; applejack or Calvados; bourbon; brandy; crème de cacao; crème de cassis; dark rum; Frangelico; Grand Marnier; Kahlúa; kirsch; Midori; Pernod or Sambuca; sherry; sweet vermouth; tequila; vodka; and wine: red and white.

Ingredient Definitions

Chiles:
Anaheim - mildest and most commonly used of the fresh green chiles, it is pale green, about 6 inches long.
Ancho - also referred to as a dried poblano chile, usually deep red in color and 4-6 inches long. Also sold as pasilla chile.
Chipotle - from the Aztec words for "smoked" and "chile," these are smoked jalapeño chiles, found in dried form or canned in adobo sauce. Since they are very hot, 1-3 chiles are adequate to give a unique, smoked capsicum flavor to a dish. Canned chipotle chiles keep for several months, in refrigerator, after opening, if stored in a glass jar.
Jalapeño - small, bright green, plump chile usually about 2 inches long. It is the most commonly used hot chile.
Serrano - slender, green chile, about 2 inches long, and the hottest chile commonly available.
Fennel: Often mislabeled "sweet anise," fennel has a sweet, delicate flavor, more subtle than anise. Fresh fennel has a broad, bulbous celery-like base, with green stalks, and feathery leaves which resemble fresh dill. The base can be eaten raw, chopped or julienned, in salads. Fennel also gives excellent flavor to soups, stews, and fish. When cooked, the flavor becomes even lighter, more elusive than when raw. Use leaves as a garnish.
Ginger Root: Fresh ginger root is found year round in the produce section of most supermarkets, and has a tough, tan-colored skin which is usually removed. It should be minced for use in recipes. Crystallized, candied, or preserved stem ginger in syrup may be substituted.
Jícama: A large, bulbous root vegetable with a sweet, nutty flavor, white crunchy flesh, and thin brown skin which should be peeled before using. Jícama can be used raw or cooked, and is often used in southwestern cooking.
Mascarpone Cheese: A rich, delicate Italian cream cheese, commonly used for Tiramisu and Coeur à la crème desserts.
Olives:
Kalamata - dark, almond-shaped pungent olive from Greece, preserved in vinegar and olive oil.
Oil-cured black - smaller than kalamata, with wrinkled skin, cured in olive oil.
Niçoise - small, brown-green-black olive which is salt brine cured, with a high pit to meat ratio.
Olive Oil:
Extra virgin - most aromatic and flavorful olive oil, made from very ripe fruits, which are "cold pressed" in traditional stone presses, without use of heat or chemicals. Usually green in color. This high quality oil should be used for dipping and in salads. Excessive heat destroys its delicate aroma and flavor.
Virgin - second pressing of fruits, still using traditional methods, less flavorful.
Olive oil - oil is extracted from olive pulp, using heat and chemical solvents.

Polenta: Cornmeal comes in 3 textures, fine, medium, and coarse. The coarse texture is called polenta, and best for use in this northern Italian dish. Medium texture cornmeal, which is most commonly found in the supermarket, may also be used to make polenta and cornbread.
Prosciutto: This is the Italian word for ham. Also called Parma ham, for the town where pigs are specially bred for this ham. It is seasoned, salt-cured, air-dried, and pressed so that the flesh is very firm. Serve very thinly sliced with melon or other fruits for first course, or add thicker slices (diced) to soups, pastas, and other dishes.
Quinoa: Originally cultivated by the Incas in the high Andean plains. This grain has the highest protein quality of any grain. It grows well in high altitudes and has been recently cultivated in Colorado. It is sweet in flavor and soft textured. The grains are pale yellow or black seeds, just larger than mustard seeds.
Rice:
Basmati - from the word meaning "queen of fragrance," basmati rice is a long-grained, delicate, aromatic rice with nutty taste. Requires shorter cooking time than other rices (15-20 minutes).
Arborio - a medium-grain, shiny rice from Italy, used to make risotto. It develops a sticky, creamy texture when cooked. It should not be rinsed before cooking, to retain starch.
Saffron: A fragrant spice, which is the yellow-orange stigmas from small purple crocus flowers. Available either ground or in threads, which are better quality. Used in paella, pasta, risotto, and soup. Known as the world's most expensive spice. Flavor is released by heat.
Tomatillo: A plum-sized, bright green fruit covered with a light green papery husk. Cultivated by the Aztecs, it has a tart flavor, which is enhanced by cooking. Good in salsas and green Mexican sauces, also good paired with chiles, cilantro and garlic. Husk should be removed before cooking.
Vanilla Bean: Fruit pod of an orchid native to Mexico. The beans contain seeds which greatly enhance recipes. Beans should be moist and plump, never dry and shriveled. The beans are usually cut in half and split lengthwise to allow infusion in liquid.
Vinegar: (from the French word "vinaigre" which means soured wine)
Balsamic - intense, sweet-tart vinegar, made from the white Trebbiano grape, whose juice is first reduced, then aged at least 6 years. Essential pantry item!
Rice vinegar - made from fermented rice, in both China and Japan, this vinegar has a mild, slightly sweet flavor, and is good in salads and Asian dishes.
Wine vinegar - made from fermented red and white wines, sherry, or Champagne. Mild and versatile.

Culinary Herbs

Fresh herbs enhance flavor and add a new dimension to favorite recipes. Joyfully, they are now readily available in most supermarkets, but many can be grown easily at home for seasonal or year round enjoyment. These are some of our favorites:

Basil: There are many varieties of this herb, the most common being sweet basil, bush basil, dark opal, and lemon basil. Basil is essential for Italian cooking, with its overtones of mint and clove. It is the basis for classic pesto, and pairs with tomatoes, in green salads. Basil is an annual plant, which should be placed in a sunny, sheltered location, or can be planted indoors in pots.

Chives: Chives are an excellent garnish or addition to salads, soups, vegetables, fish, or poultry. They lose their flavor when cooked, so are best fresh from the garden. This hardy perennial plant with mild onion flavor grows well in most soils, but best in light rich soil, in a sunny location. Flowerheads are small, round, pale mauve, and edible, but should be cut off to keep flavor in the leaves.

Cilantro/Coriander: The fresh leaves are called cilantro, and the nutty tasting seeds are called coriander. Fresh cilantro leaves are essential in Mexican, and Asian cooking, and have a piquant, spicy, citrus flavor. Use in salsas, as garnish, and in stir-fry. It is an annual plant which should be grown in full sun.

Dill: Fresh dill leaves have a delicate caraway taste, and finely cut, feathery shape. Use with salads, cucumbers, fish, seafood, chicken, and yogurt. It is a hardy annual which should be grown in full sun.

Mint: Peppermint and Spearmint are the most popular varieties of mint. Peppermint is used in teas, and has dark purple stems and green leaves. Spearmint's flavor is traditionally paired with lamb, and its mild, sweet taste accents vegetables, fruits, and salsas. It is one of the oldest culinary herbs used in Mediterranean cooking. This perennial grows easily in full sun or light shade, and frequent cuttings encourage branching. Plant in containers to avoid spreading and cut new growth for best flavor.

Parsley: The two most familiar varieties of parsley are curly leaf and Italian flat leaf. Curly leaf is used primarily for garnishing. Italian flat leaf has a much stronger flavor and is used as a flavoring. This versatile herb is great in salads, as well as in slow cooking dishes. Parsley is a hardy biennial plant.

Rosemary: Rosemary is an evergreen shrub, with needle-like leaves and strong piney scent and flavor. One of the most popular culinary herbs, especially in the Mediterranean, it is delicious with roast or grilled lamb, chicken, potatoes, and vegetables. Rosemary is a perennial which thrives in hot sun. Best planted in a container which can be brought indoors during winter, and kept in a sunny window. Start with a healthy, rooted plant, as it does not grow well from seed.

Sage: This herb is best known for use in poultry stuffing, and is a natural partner for pork, sausage, and cheese. Fresh sage is a perennial, and has a more balanced, richer flavor than dried sage. Its leaves are narrow, pale, and grey-green with a rough texture. A good decorative garden plant, sage is sun-loving, and grows to 2½ feet in height.

Tarragon: French tarragon, with its distinctive peppery-anise flavor, is one of the best culinary herbs for savory cooking, essential to French cuisine. Use with chicken and fish, cooked vegetables, and in sauces and salad dressings. It is a half-hardy perennial which needs a sunny location in good garden soil. Russian tarragon should not be used, its flavor is very inferior.

Thyme: Used in bouquet garni, thyme has tiny leaves and a minty, tea-like flavor. It is excellent with fish, poultry, and in soups and sauces. Thyme is a perennial. It can be grown in a pot and brought indoors during winter.

Hints, Techniques & Definitions

Baking Techniques:

Beating Egg Whites - bowl and beater(s) should be completely dry and clean. Egg whites should not contain any yolk. Beat egg whites a few minutes on low, until foamy. Increase speed to medium and beat until soft peaks form. Increase speed to high and gradually add sugar, if required. Beat until stiff, glossy peaks form. Use immediately, as they should not be allowed to stand. A round bottom, copper bowl is ideal for beating egg whites.

Folding Egg Whites - to incorporate into batter, begin with ⅓ egg whites to lighten batter, then fold in the rest, folding from top to bottom of the bowl.

Caramel Technique for Baking - when making caramel for a dessert recipe, combine sugar and water in a small bowl and stir until sugar almost dissolves. Pour into saucepan. Heat to boiling, brushing sides of pan with pastry brush dipped in cold water to prevent sugar crystals from forming on sides of pan. Cover pan with tight fitting lid and boil 1 minute. Uncover and continue boiling, swirling pan occasionally, until sugar turns golden brown, 10-15 minutes. Do not stir.

Cooking with Yogurt - yogurt may be used in place of mayonnaise or sour cream in salad dressings or cold sauces, or you may try a 50-50 blend. Yogurt may also be used in warm sauces, in place of cream. Stir in at the last minute, being careful not to boil, or it will curdle. Or combine almost boiling sauce with yogurt in blender and purée. Serve immediately. In place of cream for baking, mix 1 cup yogurt with 2 tablespoons cornstarch, to prevent separation.

Preparing Pastry - when preparing pastry, all ingredients should be as cold as possible. Roll out pastry on lightly floured surface.

Unsalted Butter - this is preferable for baking and most uses. It is generally fresher, and should be stored in freezer. Salted butter has more moisture which can adversely affect baking.

Blanch: Plunge vegetables or fruit into boiling water for a brief time, to bring out the color, loosen the skins, or mellow flavor. After blanching, plunge into ice cold water to set color and stop cooking.

Caramelizing Onions: In large skillet, melt 2 tablespoons butter over medium heat. Add 1 thinly sliced onion and cook until transparent, about 5 minutes. Add 2 teaspoons brown sugar, reduce heat to low, and cook, stirring occasionally, until golden brown, about 20 minutes.

Julienne: To cut fresh vegetables or other foods into matchstick size strips.

Melting Chocolate: Chocolate is traditionally melted in a double boiler over barely simmering water. It may also be melted, carefully, over direct low heat in saucepan, or in microwave. Chocolate scorches easily, so watch constantly. In microwave, for 6 ounces of chocolate, cook on high for 2-2½ minutes, stirring every 30 seconds.

Peeling Hazelnuts: Toast hazelnuts in 1 layer, in baking pan, in preheated 350 degree oven, 10-15 minutes, or until lightly colored and skins blister. Wrap nuts in clean towel and let steam 1 minute. Rub nuts with towel to remove as much of the skins as possible.

Roasting Bell Peppers: Preheat broiler or preheat grill. Cut peppers in half lengthwise and remove stem and seeds. If using broiler, place cut side down, on baking sheet, and broil in oven, about 3 inches from the heat, until skin blisters and turns black, 3-5 minutes. If using open grill, place skin side down and roast until skin is evenly charred. Remove and place in plastic bag. Seal and let steam for 10-15 minutes. Remove from bag and peel away skin.

Roasting Garlic: Whole garlic cloves, unpeeled, can be roasted in a 325-425 degree oven until skin begins to brown, about 1 hour. Cool, cut off the top, and squeeze out clove. Roasted garlic has a sweeter, more subtle taste than fresh garlic.

Roux: A roux is a mixture of oil or melted butter and flour cooked over low heat, at least 2 minutes. It is used as a base for thickening sauces and soups.

Toasting Nuts: The flavor of nuts is enhanced by toasting. Preheat oven to 350 degrees. Place nuts in baking pan and toast for 10-15 minutes, stirring occasionally, until golden brown. Note: some nuts, such as pine nuts, will toast in less time, so watch carefully. Nuts may also be toasted in the microwave. They will not change color though they will taste toasted. Place nuts on plate and microwave on high 3-4 minutes, turning plate one half turn midway through cooking time.

Scald: To heat a liquid, usually milk, just to boiling point.

Zesting: Removing the outermost, fragrant, colored peel of citrus fruits. The inner white pith is bitter and should not be used.

Acknowledgements

Sponsors

The Peppercorn

Adplex

Gill Foundation

Recipe Testers

The Junior League of Denver gratefully acknowledges the enormous commitment and contribution of the women who tested recipes for this cookbook. They generously gave their time and talents in order to select and perfect the recipes we've included. We salute their perseverance and their cooking skills.

★ = Section Heads

Corinne Lamb Ablin★
Faith Albrecht
Cindy Hansen Alexander★
Crista Barwin Bailey
Suzi Beavers
Joanne Belitz
Lindsay Bell
Margo M. Boyle
Rosemary Anderson Buehler
Jean Dawson Burkhart★
JoAnn Callas
Joy Carlson
Mary Allen Carson
Lee Clayton
Sara Busche Cobb★
Cami Cooper★
Susan de Geus-Batt
Susan DeVita Deagle
Barbara Deline
Gretchen Hickisch Dewey
Cindy Dohse
Cynthia Graff Ellis
Priscilla C. Englert
Renee L. Erickson
Laura Ewald
Karen B. Fisher
Jan Johnson Fiske
Katherine Upton Fulford
Sharon McHugh Funk
Nancy Hall Gargan
Angie Young Gatton
Susan M.H. Gills
Carrie M. Gilmore
Judith Lamme Green
Anne Kuzell Hackstock
Anne Levorsen Hammer
Gail Good Hartley
Sharon Hartman
Marianne Hayes
Helen Swinney Heele
Debra Fagan Heikens
Karen Zain Henry★
Holly Penwell Hess
Mary Lou Hibben★
Catherine Cockerham Hilker
Deborah Lupo Hoellen
Maureen Malone Hoffman
Cathy Carlos Hollis
Carolyn McFarland Hunter
Leeann Iacino★
Stephanie Ismert★
Lisa B. Jensen
Mary S. Johnson
Laura Karr
Suzanne Kelly
Wendy Woerner Kent
Barbara Knight
Toni Brescian Kochevar
Rebecca Nelson Lawrence
Martha Olney Lee
Laura Lindley
Marilyn List
Lisa Harber Maher
Ann C. McFarlane
Leslie Melzer
Claire DeMeo Mindock
Marcia Wright Mix
Sylvia Neville
Diane Marcuson Newcom
CiCi Nock
Victoria McHale Norris
Lynn Mueller Parham
Carolyn Callan Peterson
Margot Carleen Planchard
Judy Pardue Polidori
Kimberlee Piper Powelson★
Debbie Raeder
Sarah Condit Rawley★
Suzanne Reece
Judi Lattin Richardson
Sharon Meisler Ripps
Suzanne J. Robinson
Andrea Noren Rogers
Kathryn Records Ryan
Linda Schenkein
Nancy Fraze Schotters
Stacey Davis Schuham
Lisa Gamel Scott
Linda Bowen Scott
Sharon Early Severance
Elyse Shofner
Lynne Moore Siegel
Jane Siekmeier
Trish Sillars-Craver
Amy Jo Smith★
Tracy Glaves Spalding
Elizabeth Barton Spurr
Maggie Taylor
Page Thompson Tredennick
Katie Lucht Van Schaack
Glenda Varnell
Jane A. Vonderahe
Jodi Waggoner
Toti Walker
Karen Walker
Barbara Ward
Katie Hite Wilkins
Laura Fox Williamson
Marcia Sirios Wolff
Martine Ernst Wollenweber
Lisen Woods
Sherrie Tobin Zeppelin

Acknowledgements

Recipe Contributors

The Junior League of Denver extends a sincere thank you to the hundreds of members, families, and friends who submitted their favorite recipes. Their generosity in sharing recipes, helpful hints, and wonderful cooking tips is most appreciated. We sincerely hope we have not inadvertently omitted any contributor.

Mary Oliveros Accord
Corinne Lamb Ablin
Karen Albin
Faith Albrecht
Cindy Hansen Alexander
Patricia Alexander
Ann Allison
Mary Ellen Anderson
Laura M. Andrews
Christine R. Armstrong
Susan Arrigan
Dana Atchison
Jill Athenour
Tom Athenour
Michele Austin-Miller
Crista Barwin Bailey
Cynthia Ballantyne
Neena Wells Ballard
Maureen K. Barker
Jan Barreth
Patricia Gorman Barry
Margaret Bathgate
Virginia Bayless
Shirley Beaudoin
Suzi Beavers
Ann Beck
Nancy Beck
Joanne Belitz
Lindsay Bell
Marbie Bradford Bell
Jacqueline C. Bennett
Marsha P. Berger
Teresa L. Bergman
Jen E. Biernbaum
Jill L. Blackett
Christopher A. Blakeslee
Suzanne N. Blakeslee
Bev Born
Jane Borozan
Julie Bottom
Vicki Bourret
Shirley Bowen
Margo M. Boyle
Lisle Loosli Bradley
Marjorie Brescian
Carolyn Brock
Jane Holsteen Brown
Marilyn Brown
Amy S. Brownlee
Linda Brune
Judi Bruce
Rosemary Anderson Buehler
Jean Dawson Burkhart
Joann Morgan Burstein
Patricia Bardwell Callan
JoAnn Callas
Janey Campbell
Rebecca Cockerham Campbell
Kirsten Carlisle
Joy Carlson
Kris Carr
Mary Allen Carson
Reena Carter
Shara Castle
Margaret Chapman
Susan W. Chenier
Mary A. Clar
Lee Clayton
Sara E. Clayton
Sara Busche Cobb
Mary Eleanor Cockerham
Cami Cooper
Betty Coppock
Jina B. Craft
Marilyn Craver
Dorinda Davis Cudney
Jill Darrah
Barbara Dash
Lynn Davidson
Sally H. Davidson-Marovich
Margaret S. Davis
Sally Davis
Lois Dawson
Susan de Geus-Batt
Susan DeVita Deagle
Pat Deitemeyer
Barbara Deline
Judi Desnoyers
Gretchen Hickisch Dewey
Robert L. Dewey
Barbara Dewire
Tina Dill
Sara Bell DiManna
Laura M. Dirks
Judith B. Divito
Cindy Dohse
Stephanie Doss
Cathy Doty
Corry Doty
Louise J. Douglass
Fay Dreher
Lori J. Dunnan
Joyce Duncan
Jeanne Eckelberg
Karen Edwards
Lois Edwards
Eve M. Ehrenberg
Jean Larson Ehrenberg
Amanda Cockerham Elliott
Cynthia Graff Ellis
Molly Elvig
Priscilla C. Englert
Betty Engstrom
Renée L. Erickson
Laura Ewald
Martha Ewald
Linda L. Fankboner
Barbara H. Ferguson
Julie Lynch Fernandez
Sharon S. Fightmaster
Ellen K. Fisher
Karen B. Fisher
Nanette Fishman
Jan Johnson Fiske
Karen Fiske
Joann Fleischman
Christina Foster
Inge Fox-Jones
Layna R. Frodine
Katherine Upton Fulford
Valerie Fuller
Sharon McHugh Funk
JoAnn Gadkowski
Lois Brink Gaffigan
Nancy Hall Gargan
Angie Young Gatton
Mrs. Mary Gerber
Bridget Gerhardy
Carrie M. Gilmore
Theresa Gilpatrick
Marybeth Goddard
Diana A. Goldy
Marilyn Taylor Gordon
Nikki Gordon
Lori Goryl
Marilyn Gottesfeld
Lisa Groebe
Susan Graves
Judy Wong Greco
Debbie Green
Judith Lamme Green
Linda Green
Theresa Griffith

Acknowledgements

Recipe Contributors

Norma Jean Grow
Arlene Gustafson
Joan M. Guyn
Anne Kuzell Hackstock
Martha Louise Hagerty
Cynthia G. Halaby
Connie Chernosek Hambrook
Lisa Hamburg
Anne Levorsen Hammer
Marilyn Harrison
Gail Good Hartley
Sharon Hartman
Roberta Teodonno Harty
Carol Keppler Hawkins
Keller Hayes
Marianne Hayes
Colleen Healey
Helen Swinney Heele
Debra Fagan Heikens
Kurt Heisler
Jane Ann Hejmanowski
Niki Esmay Heller
Susan A. Heller
Dawn N. Henry
Karen Zain Henry
Helen Herley
Holly Penwell Hess
Mary Lou Hibben
Torchy M. Hickish
Carey Nivens Hicks
Janey Hildestad
Catherine Cockerham Hilker
Arlene Hirschfeld
Deborah Lupo Hoellen
Josephine Hoffman
Maureen Hoffman
Cathy Carlos Hollis
Jane Hollis
Phyllis Hollis
Louise W. Holst
Connie L. Holtz
Eleanor Downey Horlacher
Diane Hornbecker
Cynthia A. Horrigan
Sharla E. Hotchkiss
Jane Houston
Sharon Hulse
Pam Hummel
Carolyn McFarland Hunter
Lilly Huppert
Joyce Hutchins
Leeann Iacino
Hal Ingebretsen
Karen Isaak
Stephanie Ismert
Julie Jacobsen
Connie Jacoway
Lisa S. Jensen
Terri Johnson
Marla J. Johnson
Mary S. Johnson
Patti Talbot Johnson
Jean Evans Jones
Rickie Jones
Stewart H. Jones
Kelly Jorgenson
Kathye A. Julander
David Karmona
Laura Karr
Maureen Keefner
Debra Keesling
Audrey A. Keller
Bob Kellogg
Susan Kelly
Suzanne Kelly
Katherine Kennedy
Wendy Woerner Kent
Diane Kepner
Jon Kidder
Katherine M. Kinch
Lucy Kishbaugh
Nancy M. Klumb
Barbara Knight
Andrea V. Knoll
Toni Brescian Kochevar
Carmel S. Koeltzow
Helen W. Koernig
Denise Kolb
Abbie Kozik
Myrna Krohn
Gayle Kubista
Ravelle R. Kundinger
Judith Sibley Laine
Judith A. Lambert
Lillian Lattin
Rebecca Nelson Lawrence
Martha Olney Lee
Marc Lefkovics
Anne Lehigh
Veda Leopold
Emily C. Levorsen
Laura Bevier Levorsen
Colleen Lewer
Laura Lindley
Camilla Lindsay
Marilyn List
Karen S. Lozow
Mary Lucken
Nancy Lukken
Lee Lundberg
Pamela G. Lush
Karen Helling MacCarter
Tricia MacHendrie
Laura Maddock
Lorilyn Simmons Magazine
Lisa Harber Maher
Shirley Malone
Janet Manning
Bonnie Mascatelli
Sean B. Massad
Ceil Matson
Renie Max
Louann May
Susan Warner McCann
Mary Frances McCarthy
Karen Lewis McClure
Maureen McDonald
Virginia McDonald
Ann C. McFarlane
Phoebe McFarlane
Blair Lindberg McGroarty
Elizabeth Peck McGuire
Sue McMillan
Adrienne O. McNamara
Kathi Mecklenburg
Leslie Melzer
Flora Mercer
Joy Mercer
Geraldine Merlander
Jeri Michener
Margaret Millard
Melissa J. Miller
Pattie Miller
Claire DeMeo Mindock
Marcia Wright Mix
Dorothy Mock
Kathy Mohn
Barbara S. Moore
Louise Moore
Michelle Moore
Beverly Morrato
Preston Motes
Helen Ruth Mozer

Acknowledgements

Recipe Contributors

Mrs. John F. Mueller
Paul Mueller
Shellie R. Munn
Patricia Myers
Karen Myers-Hackem
Peggy Nance
Betty Nayoski
Joan Nelson
Sylvia Neville
Diane Marcuson Newcom
Cici Nock
Suzann Noll
Peggy Norris
Victoria McHale Norris
Ann B. O'Donnell
Carolyn Koskinen O'Donnell
Ellen A. O'Donnell
Nancy O'Donnell
Sally Obregon
Ellen Oliveros
Neva Olson
Kathy Oman
Shirley S. Owens
Steven Paluck
Victoria Paluck
Lynn Mueller Parham
Marge Pepon
Deanna H. Person
Camille Lagrave Peterson
Carolyn Callan Peterson
Marilyn G. Pickering
Carol Pierce
Ann D. Pierson
Traycee Pinkard
Charlotte L. Piper
John R. Piper
Sally M. Pistilli
Sarah Pittock
Margot Carleen Planchard
Judy Pardue Polidori
Bill Powelson
Kimberlee Piper Powelson
Nancy M. Progar
Lynne Quoy
Debbie Raeder
Marguerite Rankin
Ellie Raeder
Sarah Condit Rawley
Dru Ray
Joyce Ray
Lisa Ray
Ruth Anne Raymond
Gay Lynn Rediger
Suzanne Reece
Jessica Reed
Marcia Reid
Henni Restall
Cecilia Rice-Peterson
Beth V. Richards
Judi Lattin Richardson
Jill Richman
Brenda D. Rickert
Sharon Meisler Ripps
Allison C. Rittner
Suzanne J. Robinson
Andrea Noren Rogers
Hindi Roseman
Marcia Rothenberg
Caroline Royer
Cindy Runkel
Kathryn Records Ryan
Aline S. Sandomire
Linda Sandoval
Kathleen M. Sauer
Tina Scavo
Sue Schafer
Patricia Russo Schassburger
Linda Schenkein
Linda Schierburg
Karen Schmidt
Kathy Schmidt
Patricia Holst Schneider
Deborah Scholbe
Nancy Fraze Schotters
Bronwyn Schuetze
Robert A. Schuetze
Stacey Davis Schuham
Karen J. Schuster
Kathy Scott
Linda Bowen Scott
Lisa Gamel Scott
Russell Scott III
Mindy Scovell
Debbie Secrest
Margaret M. Seep
Vicki Segro
Sharon Early Severance
Stacy Sheeley
Gina Sheridan
Elyse Shofner
Cappy Shopneck
Lynne Moore Siegel
Jane Siekmeier
Trish Sillars-Craver
Marjorie A. Skalet
Jan Smedley
Amy Jo Smith
Anne Smith
Catherine Smith
Douglas Smith
K. David Smith
Ronda Barlow Smith
Sarah B. Snyder
Jill M. Sokol
Margaret Sommers
Tracy Glaves Spalding
A. Christy Speirn-Smith
Carol S. Spensley
Sandra Sprinkle
Elizabeth Barton Spurr
Martha Starick
Nancy Constan Stathopulos
Amy Stevens
Lenore T. Stoddart
Kathy R. Strandberg
Sonia M. Strickland
Ibbie Stroh
Debi Suitor
Ann Swanson
Rindy Swenson
Joan Swinehart
Sonnie Talley
Jenny Tallmadge
Betsy Tapp
Nichole Tautz
Maggie Taylor
Marilyn Shields Taylor
Kathryn Sullivan Terry
Karen D. Thomas
Debbie Tilton
Carolyn Touchette
Susan Tracy
Page Thompson Tredennick
Lucile B. Trueblood
Debbi Tryon
Patricia A. Turcheck
Mimi Turrill
Joan C. Underwood
Katie Lucht Van Schaack
Cynthia VanCise
Glenda Varnell
Diane Metz Veio
Jane Curtin Vertuca

Acknowledgements

Recipe Contributors

Tina Vessels
Kerry Vickers
Buzz Victor
Gayle Vincent
Jane A. Vonderahe
Susan Voyvodic
Jodi Waggoner
Karen Walker
Toti Walker
Barbara Ward
Mary Jan Waters
Mark L. Watson
Barbara J. Webb
Jacquelin B. Weber
Lauri Bannister Weber
Debby Weigandt
Nancy Wellnitz
Marcella Wells
Mrs. Joan Wells
Darlene R. Wesbrook
Christine Wester
Julie Wham
Jeanne Wilde
Sarah Farris Wilensky
Katie Hite Wilkins
Laura Fox Williamson
Kenny Wilson
Mary Wilson
Shannon Winckel
Marcia Sirios Wolff
Martine Ernst Wollenweber
Marianne Wood
Lisen Woods
Lorraine Woods-Bowinski
Linda Young
Deloris K. Zain
Jane Zeeb
Sherrie Tobin Zeppelin
Joanne M. Zoellner

Photography Credits

John Fielder, Photographer

For information about John Fielder's other books, calendars, cards, and fine art prints, please contact Westcliffe Publishers at 303-935-0900.

Page 2: Mt. Sneffels, San Juan Mountains, near Ridgway.

Page 4: Ski tracks through the trees, White River National Forest, near Vail.

Page 6: Old cabin along the Cimarron River, Uncompahgre National Forest, San Juan Mountains.

Page 8: Alpine lake below Isolation Peak, Rocky Mountain National Park.

Page 10: Spring wildflowers below the Pawnee Buttes, Pawnee National Grasslands, northeastern Colorado.

Page 16: Dunes and shadows, Great Sand Dunes National Monument, San Luis Valley.

Page 44: Morning light in the Beckwith Mountains, Gunnison National Forest.

Page 134: Thunderheads growing high above the plains of southeastern Colorado.

Page 194: Indian paintbrush wildflowers beside Willow Creek, Maroon Bells–Snowmass Wilderness.

Page 226: Fence of aspen boles snakes its way toward the peaks of the Sneffels Range, San Juan Mountains.

Page 258: Indian summer blue skies, along the Yampa River, near Steamboat Springs.

Page 290: Cliff Palace, an eight-hundred-year-old Anasazi cliff dwelling, Mesa Verde National Park.

Page 340: Indian paintbrush wildflowers, Maroon Bells–Snowmass Wilderness.

Bob Castellino Photographer, R. L. Castellino Designs, Boulder, Colorado.

Page 76: Summer Boulder Flatirons.

Page 314: Farm in Boulder County.

Acknowledgements

Professional Contributors

The Junior League of Denver would like to express its gratitude to those who have supported this project with their professional expertise and in-kind donations. We appreciate their hard work, dedication, and contributions which made this book possible.

Sam Arnold, Arnold and Company
Yumiko Baron, Le Central French Restaurant
Michael Bortz, Palmetto Grille
Odran Campbell
Patricio Casias, Cafe Brazil
Mary A. Clark, Blue Point Restaurant
Colorado State University Cooperative Extension
Cook's Mart
Michail Deyenhart, Tante Louise
Kevin Dowling, Northeast Seafood Products
Epicurean Catering
Paul Ferzacca, Two Elk Lodge, Vail
Mark Fischer, Caribou Club, Aspen
Kristi Fisher, Copy Writer
Hyatt Regency, Beaver Creek
Donald E. Jankura, Lodging And Hospitality Consultant
John Kessler, The Denver Post
David LaGant, Denver Buffalo Company
Steven Langer, Panache Catering
Lori Lathrop, Index
Sarah Leffen, The Seasoned Chef
Daniel Lokens, Las Brisas
Jim Lorio, The Boulder Arts & Crafts Co-op
Tim Luksa
Tom McNeill
Mark Monette, Flagstaff House
Luc Meyer, The Left Bank, Vail
Molly Ng, Molly's Oriental Shop and Cooking School
James O'Connor, Le Petit Gourmet
Ed Orr, The Tyrolean Inn, Vail
The Perfect Setting
Karl Rinehart, Le Central French Restaurant
Thomas Salamunovich, Sweet Basil, Vail
Jim Schlarbaum
Tim Schlarbaum
Jimmy Schmidt, Rattlesnake Grill
Will Schneider, Chambers Wines and Liquors
Cindy Schulz
Sheryl Stafford
Westin Hotel-Tabor Center

A

B

C

D

E

F

G

N

O

P

Q

R

T

U

V

W

Y

Z

C & C
Publications

Colorado Cache • Crème de Colorado • Colorado Collage

The Junior League of Denver, Inc.
6300 East Yale Avenue
Denver, Colorado 80222
(303) 782-9244

Name ______
Address ______
City/State/Zip ______
Telephone ______

C & C
Publications

Mailing Label — Please print and fill out completely

Colorado Cache • Crème de Colorado • Colorado Collage

The Junior League of Denver, Inc.
6300 East Yale Avenue
Denver, Colorado 80222
(303) 782-9244

SHIP TO: ______

Please send me the best-selling classic cookbooks indicated below:

Title	Quantity	Price	Tax (Colorado residents only)	Total
COLORADO CACHE	______	$15.95	$.48 per book	$
CRÈME DE COLORADO	______	$19.95	$.60 per book	$
COLORADO COLLAGE	______	$24.95	$.79 per book	$
Total number of books ordered	______			

plus $3.00 each for shipping and handling
(Canadian orders: $6.00 each for shipping and handling.)

TOTAL ENCLOSED $ ______

Please charge my VISA ______ or Mastercard ______
Expiration date ______

Card number ______
Cardholder's Signature ______

Please make checks payable to:
JUNIOR LEAGUE OF DENVER, INC.
Please do not send cash. Sorry, no C.O.D.'s

Send to: C & C Publications
The Junior League of Denver, Inc.
6300 East Yale Avenue, Suite 110
Denver, Colorado 80222 • (303) 782-9244

Profits from the sale of these cookbooks are used to support the purpose and programs of The Junior League of Denver, Inc.
Prices subject to change without notice.

C & C
Publications

Colorado Cache • Crème de Colorado • Colorado Collage

The Junior League of Denver, Inc.
6300 East Yale Avenue
Denver, Colorado 80222
(303) 782-9244

Name ______
Address ______
City/State/Zip ______
Telephone ______

C & C
Publications

Mailing Label — Please print and fill out completely

Colorado Cache • Crème de Colorado • Colorado Collage

The Junior League of Denver, Inc.
6300 East Yale Avenue
Denver, Colorado 80222
(303) 782-9244

SHIP TO: ______

Please send me the best-selling classic cookbooks indicated below:

Title	Quantity	Price	Tax (Colorado residents only)	Total
COLORADO CACHE		$15.95	$.48 per book	$
CRÈME DE COLORADO	______	$19.95	$.60 per book	$
COLORADO COLLAGE	______	$24.95	$.79 per book	$
Total number of books ordered	______			

plus $3.00 each for shipping and handling
(Canadian orders: $6.00 each for shipping and handling.)

TOTAL ENCLOSED $ ______

Please charge my VISA ______ or Mastercard ______
Expiration date ______

Card number ______
Cardholder's Signature ______

Please make checks payable to:
JUNIOR LEAGUE OF DENVER, INC.
Please do not send cash. Sorry, no C.O.D.'s

Send to: C & C Publications
The Junior League of Denver, Inc.
6300 East Yale Avenue, Suite 110
Denver, Colorado 80222 • (303) 782-9244

Profits from the sale of these cookbooks are used to support the purpose and programs of The Junior League of Denver, Inc.
Prices subject to change without notice.